# MARX, THE YOUNG HEGELIANS, AND THE ORIGINS OF RADICAL SOCIAL THEORY
## Dethroning the Self

This is the first major study of Marx and the Young Hegelians in twenty years. The book offers a new interpretation of Marx's early development, the political dimension of Young Hegelianism, and that movement's relationship to political and intellectual currents in early-nineteenth-century Germany and France.

Warren Breckman challenges the orthodox distinction drawn between the exclusively religious concerns of Hegelians in the 1830s and the sociopolitical preoccupations of the 1840s. He shows that there are inextricable connections between the theological, political, and social discourses of the Hegelians in the 1830s; and he demonstrates that a proper understanding of these connections recasts our understanding of the development of radical social theory in the 1840s.

The book draws together an account of major figures such as Feuerbach and Marx, with discussions of lesser-known but significant figures such as Eduard Gans, August Cieszkowski, Moses Hess, and F.W.J. Schelling, as well as of such movements as French Saint-Simonianism and German "Positive Philosophy."

Wide-ranging in scope and synthetic in approach, this is an important book for historians of philosophy, theology, political theory, and nineteenth-century ideas.

Warren Breckman is an associate professor of Modern European Intellectual History at the University of Pennsylvania.

MODERN EUROPEAN PHILOSOPHY

*General Editor*
Robert B. Pippin, University of Chicago
*Advisory Board*
Gary Gutting, University of Notre Dame
Rolf-Peter Horstmann, Humboldt University, Berlin
Mark Sacks, University of Essex

This series contains a range of high-quality books on philosophers, topics, and schools of thought prominent in the Kantian and post-Kantian
European tradition. It is nonsectarian in approach and methodology
and includes both introductory and more specialized treatments of these
thinkers and topics. Authors are encouraged to interpret the boundaries
of the modern European tradition in a broad way and in primarily philosophical rather than historical terms.

*Some Recent Titles:*
Frederick A. Olafson: *What Is a Human Being?*
Stanley Rosen: *The Mask of Enlightenment: Nietzsche's Zarathustra*
Robert C. Scharff: *Comte After Positivism*
F.C.T. Moore: *Bergson: Thinking Backwards*
Charles Larmore: *The Morals of Modernity*
Robert B. Pippin: *Idealism as Modernism*
Daniel W. Conway: *Nietzsche's Dangerous Game*
John P. McCormick: *Carl Schmitt's Critique of Liberalism*
Günter Zöller: *Fichte's Transcendental Philosophy*
Frederick A. Olafson: *Heidegger and the Ground of Ethics*
Charles L. Griswold: *Adam Smith and the Virtues of Enlightenment*

# MARX, THE YOUNG HEGELIANS, AND THE ORIGINS OF RADICAL SOCIAL THEORY

## Dethroning the Self

WARREN BRECKMAN

**CAMBRIDGE**
UNIVERSITY PRESS

CAMBRIDGE UNIVERSITY PRESS
Cambridge, New York, Melbourne, Madrid, Cape Town, Singapore, São Paulo

Cambridge University Press
The Edinburgh Building, Cambridge CB2 8RU, UK

Published in the United States of America by Cambridge University Press, New York

www.cambridge.org
Information on this title: www.cambridge.org/9780521624404

First published 1999
First paperback edition 2001

*A catalogue record for this publication is available from the British Library*

*Library of Congress Cataloguing in Publication data*
Breckman, Warren (date)
Marx, the young Hegelians, and the origins of radical social
theory / Warren Breckman.
p.   cm. – (Modern European philosophy)
Revision of thesis (doctoral) – University of California, Berkeley.
Includes bibliographical references and index.
1. Marx, Karl, 1818–1883.  2. Hegel, Georg Wilhelm Friedrich,
1770–1831 – Influence.  3. Philosophy, German – 19th century.
4. Political science – Philosophy – History – 19th century.  5. Social
sciences – Philosophy – History – 19th century.   I. Title.
II. Series.
B3305.M74B717   1999
193 – dc21                                              98-15205
                                                        CIP

ISBN 978-0-521-62440-4 hardback
ISBN 978-0-521-00380-3 paperback

Transferred to digital printing 2008

*to my parents, Kris and Ruth*

# CONTENTS

# ACKNOWLEDGMENTS

In the course of writing this study, I have incurred many debts of gratitude, and it is a pleasure to be able to recognize them at last. This book evolved from a doctoral thesis written at the University of California at Berkeley between 1989 and 1993. I could not have begun graduate studies at Berkeley without the support of a Mellon fellowship in the humanities, and I could not have finished without the assistance of a Social Sciences and Humanities Research Council of Canada doctoral fellowship that generously funded my research in Berlin during 1989 and 1990. During my years at Berkeley, I benefited immensely from the unstinting encouragement of my doctoral advisers, Martin Jay and Martin Malia. I hope that something of their insight, knowledge, and exemplary scholarship is reflected in this book. I am also grateful to Paul Thomas and Jose Crisostomo de Souza, who made up two-thirds of a floating seminar on the Left Hegelians which wended its way through Berkeley's taverns. A Social Sciences and Humanities Research Council of Canada postdoctoral fellowship allowed me to return to Berlin in 1994 and to expand the project well beyond its original scope. In its various incarnations, my study has been improved by the generous comments of Laurence Dickey, John Toews, Hermann Klenner, and Walter Jaeschke, as well as by several of my new colleagues at the University of Pennsylvania, including Jeff Fear, Lynn Hunt, Margaret Jacob, Alan Kors, and Bruce Kuklick. I am also glad to thank Terry Pinkard, whose identity was revealed to me after his anonymous review of my manuscript for Cambridge University

Press proved so constructive. Of course, even at the end of a study to which many people have contributed their expertise, responsibility for any mistakes or errors in judgment lies with me.

This project has accompanied me on an itinerant path through Berkeley, Toronto, Berlin, Winnipeg, Philadelphia, and Paris, and along the way, many friends have enlivened my labors with intellectual camaraderie and good humor. Special thanks to Lars Trägardh, Elliot Neaman, Heath Pearson, Don Forgay, Susan Hunt, Michael McLean, Vince Rutherford, Margaret Mack, David Shapard, Sylke Schwertfeger-Otto, Duncan Fisher, Lucretia Grindle, David Ames Curtis, Randy Kaufman, and Paul Rosenberg. My deepest debt remains to my family and especially to my parents, Kris and Ruth. In acknowledgment of their unfailing encouragement, their example of commitment, and their love, I dedicate this book to them.

# INTRODUCTION

It is now a question, so to speak, of founding a Kingdom, the Kingdom of the Idea, of thought which contemplates itself in all that exists and is conscious of itself. The founder of *this* Kingdom will naturally bear no name, will not be an individual, or will be this individual which alone *is*, the World Spirit. Further, it is a question of overthrowing from its throne the ego, the *self* in general, which, especially since the beginning of Christianity, has dominated the world, which has conceived itself as the only spirit to exist. (Ludwig Feuerbach to Hegel, 1828)

When the communist regimes of the European East Bloc recently toppled in an inverted version of the domino theory, a feature of political thought that had largely escaped notice among western political theorists in the 1970s and 1980s abruptly moved into the foreground. That is, the dissidents of central and eastern Europe contributed greatly to the recovery of "civil society" as a descriptive and normative political concept. An idea rooted in the high age of bourgeois political self-assertion against absolutist and feudalist ideals of social order, civil society had all but fallen from use in the twentieth century. Revived by dissidents like Vaclav Havel and Adam Michnik as a weapon against the oppressive regimes of the Soviet Bloc, the ideal of civil society pitted society against the state, association against sovereignty, plurality against unity, civility against force, persuasion against coercion. A parallel "return to civil society" among political theorists in the West was motivated partly by eastern European examples, but it was also prompted by a

desire to revitalize the civic life of the western liberal democracies in the face
of the perceived dilemmas of bureaucratization and statism.[1] Although the
traumas of democratization and liberalization in central and eastern Europe
during the 1990s have undoubtedly revealed ambiguities and difficulties in
the concept of civil society, this social and political ideal has proven remarkably appealing across the political spectrum in the West.

In thus resurrecting civil society as a normative ideal and, frequently, as a
polemical weapon, eastern European dissidents and western political theorists have had recourse to a rich discursive tradition embracing a range of
figures from John Locke to Tom Paine, Montesquieu to Tocqueville, Kant to
Hegel. Not surprisingly, given the breadth of this lineage, the notion of a "revival of civil society" can and has meant almost anything to its present advocates, depending on the orientation of the speaker. One finds neo-liberals
who associate civil society narrowly with a free market economy, communitarians who regard civil society as a sphere for the construction and expansion of social solidarity, or social democrats who regard civil society as the
strategic site of a democratizing process that should encompass the political state, the economy, the workplace, and the formal and informal institutions of society.

Within this extraordinarily heterogeneous discourse, the one major
area of agreement is that Karl Marx's total rejection of the concept of civil
society is inadequate to the project of expanding democratic life within
complex societies. Here, it is the consensus that is new, not the insight itself. For the shortcomings of Marx's critique of civil society are now openly
acknowledged even by those who remain sympathetic to some conception
of socialism, retain elements of a Marxian critique of capitalism, or, mini-
mally, as in the case of Jacques Derrida, "take inspiration from a certain spirit
of Marxism."[2] One of the crucial problems lies in Marx's critical stance not

---

1   The most thorough discussion of this issue is found in Andrew Arato and Jean L. Cohen,
    *Civil Society and Political Theory* (Cambridge, Mass., 1992). See in addition the discussions in
    John Keane, *Democracy and Civil Society*, (London, 1988), John Keane, ed., *Civil Society and
    the State. New European Perspectives* (London, 1988), and the essays in *Eastern Europe . . . Cen-
    tral Europe . . . Europe*, a special issue of *Daedalus* (Winter 1990). Hegel's categories of civil
    society and the state also gained importance in the 1980s in Anglo-American reevaluations
    of Marxism. See, for example, Jean L. Cohen, *Class and Civil Society: The Limits of Marxian
    Critical Theory* (Amherst, 1982); Z. A. Pelczynski, ed., *The State and Civil Society: Studies in
    Hegel's Political Philosophy* (Cambridge, 1984); and Richard Dien Winfield, *The Just Economy*
    (New York, 1988). A good example of the American liberal appropriation of the theme of
    civil society is found in Michael Walzer, "The Idea of Civil Society: A Path to Social Recon-
    struction," *Dissent* (Spring 1991), pp. 293–304.
2   Jacques Derrida, *Specters of Marx. The State of Debt, the Work of Mourning & the New Interna-
    tional*, trans. Peggy Kamuf (New York, 1994), p. 88.

only toward capitalist economies, but toward the "civil" dimension of civil society, the conceptual and legal recognition of the spheres of voluntary association, personal autonomy, and the institutional expression and protection of individual rights. With good reason, Jean Cohen and Andrew Arato characterize the current debate about civil society as "post-Marxist" because it proceeds from a chastened skepticism toward Marx's totalizing critique of the modern forms of state and society.[3] Nonetheless, if the present debate takes for granted the need to go beyond Marxism, one of its characteristic moves has been to look behind Marx for inspiration and theoretical guidance.

This post-Marxist interest in pre-Marxist social theory has significantly enhanced the fortunes and relevance of Hegel, the master thinker whom the young Marx triumphantly claimed to have overcome. The contemporary discussion has posed anew questions about the gains and losses incurred by Marx's radical rejection of the categories of Hegelian political philosophy. It has renewed interest in Hegel's account of the historical emergence of modern selfhood and his complex analyses of the dynamics of modern civil society, not only its economic interactions but also the formal and informal institutions that struggle to secure society's ends: personal liberty as well as social welfare. Whereas Hegel exploited the dual meaning of the German term *bürgerliche Gesellschaft* in order thus to describe civil society as *both* the "bourgeois" sphere of market relations and the "civic" sphere of institutionalized individual and communal rights, Marx identified "civil society" narrowly with "bourgeois society" – that is, with the capitalist economy. Of course, Marx did not thereby renounce the struggle for individual freedom or fulfillment, but he fundamentally redefined the terms of that struggle. For, in his reconceptualization of political philosophy and economic science, individualism became "bourgeois individualism," while the "civic" dimension of civil society, particularly western liberalism's commitment to individual civil rights, became an ideological appendage or veil of economic relations. The current discussion of civil society reminds us of what was at stake in the conflict between Hegel and his radical follower, and it invites us to revisit and rethink this earlier debate about civil society, the seminal moment in the 1840s when Hegel's political philosophy yielded to Marx's thoroughgoing critique.

Marx's critical reworking of Hegel's political philosophy has been the subject of many studies, yet for all the attention paid to this crucial dimension of Marx's intellectual development, explanations for both his departure

---

3  Arato and Cohen, *Civil Society and Political Theory*, p. 70.

from Hegel and his deep ambivalence toward individualism remain unsatisfying. Accounts of Marx's defection from Hegel remain inadequate so long as they treat Marx's critical engagement with Hegel's *Rechtsphilosophie* in relative isolation. Of course, many studies have linked Marx to the Young Hegelians' repudiation of Hegel's theological and metaphysical aspirations. However, insofar as scholars have assumed a more or less strong contrast between the theological and philosophical preoccupations of Young Hegelians like David Friedrich Strauss and Ludwig Feuerbach and the political concerns of Marx, much of the literature on Marx and early German socialist theory has shed little light on the broader reception and transformation of Hegelian political philosophy in the 1830s and early 1840s. A central contention of the present work is that a longer view of the radical Hegelian engagement with Hegel's political philosophy will greatly illuminate not only Marx's theoretical break from Hegel but also the political dimension of Young Hegelianism as a whole and its relationship to the political currents of *vormärz* Germany.

Our understanding of Marx's critique of individualism has likewise been hampered by a tendency to treat this vital aspect of his thought in isolation from the context within which it was articulated. It is another of my basic contentions that historians and theorists alike have been too quick in assuming that an adequate source for Marx's attitude lies in his opposition to the private property regime of capitalism and the doctrine that underpins classical political economy and liberal bourgeois society, namely what C. B. Macpherson once called "possessive individualism." Evident as Marx's problematic views on the individual in society and the nature of civil rights may be, the sources of these views and the process whereby Marx arrived at them remain obscure unless we recognize the extent to which his thought was influenced by contemporaneous German debates about civil society and politics. Attending to those debates about the conditions of civil society will restore Marx's early theoretical peregrinations, as well as the target of his critique, to their appropriate intellectual context, which was not, in the first instance, a context of cosmopolitan discourse about modern liberalism.

## Selfhood in Politics and Religion

In resolving to follow these debates of the 1830s and early 1840s, the historian immediately encounters a challenging complication. For the discussion of civil society in the early nineteenth century cannot be disengaged from the theologico-philosophical discussion of the period. Or, to put it simply, the constellation of concerns involved in the question of civil society – the relationship between society and the state, individual and community, economics and politics, the private person and the public citizen, self-interest and altruism – were intimately tied to religious questions. This is true not only because Hegel himself explicitly linked his description of civil society to his account of the rise of *Christian* or, more specifically, *Protestant* personhood. Nor is it true merely because the Protestant and Catholic polities of early-nineteenth-century Germany insisted on an intimate relationship between the church and state. It is true because the question of civil society was, as it still is today, essentially related to the question of the nature of sovereignty; and this question in turn devolved upon a more basic question about the nature of the self in its manifold roles as "sovereign," "citizen," and "subject." In the context of Christian Germany in the early nineteenth century, this most basic *political* question was posed in the theologico-philosophical disputes of the day.

A proper recognition of the overlapping domains of theology, philosophy, and politics in the discourse of civil society in the 1830s and early 1840s will enable us better to understand Marx's critique of individualism and liberalism. It also promises to bring the political dimension of Young Hegelianism into bolder relief. Marx himself has been partly responsible for associating the Young Hegelians with an essentially *apolitical* critique of theology and metaphysics. Take, for example, Marx's comments on Ludwig Feuerbach, the most significant philosopher among the Young Hegelians. Even at the height of his admiration for Feuerbach, Marx complained that he "referred too much to nature and too little to politics."[4] However radical Feuerbach may have been in certain spheres, Marx contended that his political intentions were exhausted in vague evocations of "Love" as the bond of humanity. Throughout the 1840s, Marx repeatedly criticized Feuerbach for his neglect of politics and continuing fascination with religion and theology, a complaint that Engels canonized in his 1886 work on Feuerbach.[5] By posing his judgment of Feuerbach in dualistic terms – "nature" *or* "politics," "theology" *or* "politics" – Marx implied that these discourses are dichotomous. He was surely aware of their overlapping significance, as shown in his famous remark that "criticism of religion is the premise of all criticism." Yet the point is too easily forgotten that in the 1840s, Marx's efforts to shift critical attention decisively from metaphysics and theology to society, politics

---

4   Marx to Arnold Ruge, 13 March 1843, in Marx and Engels, *Collected Works,* vol. 1 (New York, 1975), p. 400.
5   Friedrich Engels, *Ludwig Feuerbach and the End of Classical German Philosophy* (Moscow, 1976).

and economics, as well as his desire to distance himself from his Hegelian predecessors, virtually demanded that he speak in terms of sharply opposed discourses. Hence, presenting his own socioeconomic critique as the real supercession of the preoccupations of the anti-theological Hegelians, he could pronounce the criticism of religion "completed."[6] Time to move on to politics and society.

Followers and students of Marx and Engels have widely accepted this self-representation of their formative early years, and so in the scholarly literature it has become standard to argue that in the major works of Marx's early years he translated Feuerbach's methodology and outlook from "theology" into "politics." More generally, it remains a commonplace among scholars that a shift occurred within the radical Hegelianism of the early 1840s from the critique of religion and philosophy to the critique of politics. This narrative has a long lineage, traceable not only to Marx and Engels but also to the influential nineteenth-century historian of philosophy J. E. Erdmann.[7] Erdmann treated the disintegration of Hegelianism as a reversal of the process whereby Hegel had integrated the diverse philosophical sciences: As Hegel had progressed from logic and metaphysics, to the philosophy of religion, to the philosophy of the state, so his critical disciples moved from a critique of logic and philosophy of religion to criticism of the other branches of the Hegelian synthesis. Influential as Erdmann's account has been, one searches in vain for these three stages in Hegel's own development or that of his followers. In arriving at this rather schematic narrative, it seems, Erdmann imposed his own assumptions about the foundational status of logic and ontology on both Hegel and his critics, instead of remaining open to the complexities of Hegelianism's breakdown and radicalization.

The historical account of the Hegelian School has, of course, grown more complex and nuanced in the many decades since Erdmann, as has sensitivity to the political aspects of early Hegelianism. John Toews's important work has studied in detail the *political* Hegelians of the 1820s and 1830s, an inquiry that has been extended in the more recent study by Wolfgang Eßbach.[8] Despite this salutary attention to Hegelian political writings, however, more must be done to demonstrate the interpenetration of the differ-

6  Marx, "Contribution to the Critique of Hegel's Philosophy of Right. Introduction," *Collected Works*, vol. 3, p. 175.
7  J. E. Erdmann, *Die deutsche Philosophie seit Hegels Tode* (Stuttgart-Bad Cannstatt, 1964; originally published 1866).
8  John Toews, *Hegelianism. The Path Toward Dialectical Humanism, 1805–1841* (Cambridge, 1980), and Wolfgang Eßbach, *Die Junghegelianer. Soziologie einer Intellektuellengruppe* (München, 1988).

ent aspects of Hegelian debate. Moreover, despite welcome exceptions such as those of Toews, Eßbach, Walter Jaeschke, and Marilyn Chapin Massey, the tendency persists to view the history of Hegelianism in terms of a progression from the religious concerns of radical Hegelians in the 1830s to the political and social preoccupations of Left Hegelianism in the 1840s.[9] Scholars have varied over precisely when the Hegelian School turned from "religion" to "politics," or when Hegelians turned from Hegel's *Phenomenology of Spirit* and his *Lectures on the Philosophy of Religion* to his *Philosophy of Right* as the locus of their orientation, but the attempt to identify such a "moment" has figured in much of the scholarship on the Hegelian movement.[10] Even the astute question that Shlomo Avineri directed toward students of Feuerbach still assumes a progression from one discourse to another: "Was it an immanent consequence in Feuerbach's critique of religion to pass over to a critique of politics and the existing state?"[11] The terms often used to distinguish the radical Hegelianism of the 1830s from that of the 1840s further entrench the assumption of a sharp break. Hence, Hegelian critics of religion like David Friedrich Strauss and Feuerbach in the 1830s are routinely designated as "Young Hegelians," while radical critics of society and politics in the 1840s like Moses Hess, Arnold Ruge, or the young Marx are called "Left Hegelians," as if the radicalism of the 1830s has no right to a political epithet. This is curious, because it was Strauss who coined the phrase "Left Hegelian" to describe himself in 1837. Although he clearly meant to refer to theological divisions within the Hegelian School, his choice of terms placed him metaphorically within the political topography of postrevolutionary Europe.[12]

Against this scholarly pattern, we have Feuerbach declaring in 1843 that

9  The works of Jaeschke and Chapin Massey have been particularly important to the approach adopted in the present study. See Jaeschke, "Urmenschheit und Christologie. Eine politische Christologie der Hegelschen rechten," *Hegel-Studien*, 14(1979), pp. 73–107, and Chapin Massey, *Christ Unmasked. The Meaning of the "Life of Jesus" in German Politics* (Chapel Hill, 1983).

10  See Karl Löwith, *From Hegel to Nietzsche. The Revolution in Nineteenth-Century Thought*, trans. David E. Green (New York, 1964), esp. p. 333. More recently, see Harold Mah, *The End of Philosophy, The Origin of "Ideology." Karl Marx and the Crisis of the Young Hegelians* (Berkeley, 1987). For other examples, see André Liebich, *Between Ideology and Utopia. The Politics and Philosophy of August Cieszkowski* (Boston, 1979), p. 20; and William Brazill, *The Young Hegelians* (New Haven, 1970), p. 8.

11  Avineri in "Diskussion zu Feuerbach und die Theologie," *Atheismus in der Diskussion. Kontroversen um Ludwig Feuerbach*, ed. Hermann Lübbe and Hans-Martin Sass (Grünewald, 1975), p. 67.

12  On the contemporary reception of Strauss's use of political epithets, see Eßbach, *Die Junghegelianer*, pp. 138–40.

"theology is for Germany the single practical and effective vehicle of politics, at least at present."[13] How are we to assess this remark? Certainly, Feuerbach too foresaw a secular future when political discussion would be just that. Does that mean that the discussion of theology in 1843 was just a way of scoring indirect political points against a regime that used religion to legitimize its rule? By 1843, Feuerbach may have been willing to distinguish between the critique of religion and its indirect political consequences. But with growing stridency throughout the 1830s and early 1840s, he had insisted on the *practical* importance of his philosophical work. Nor was Feuerbach alone in making such an assertion during the 1830s. Indeed, it was a claim common to numerous Hegelians who challenged the religious and political *status quo* in the 1830s. How should we understand such claims to practical significance?

The difficulty in answering this question lies in the persistent tendency of scholars to posit a more or less abrupt transition from theologico-philosophical to political argument within the Hegelian Left. Scholars have essentially projected the categories of the self-consciously politicized 1840s back into the 1830s and found them absent. From this standpoint, the political meanings of Hegelian radicalism in the 1830s are easily missed or not fully understood. I believe that in the 1830s, religious, political, and social themes constituted a unity, or a thematic constellation, even if at different moments one or another issue took prominence over others. Little can be gained by imposing upon the 1830s the definitions of the 1840s, when this unity had already begun to break into what we readily recognize as relatively autonomous discourses of politics, society, theology, and philosophy. Instead of proposing a break between the "theological" 1830s and the "political" 1840s, then, I hope to shed light on the development of Hegelian radicalism by taking seriously the unity of religious, social, and political issues in the thought of critical Hegelians during the 1830s. In fact, this unity itself was a major *political* issue for early left-wing Hegelians like Feuerbach, and its breakup into more discrete discourses must, therefore, become a problem for the historian. From this perspective, the concerns of the nascent Hegelian Left during the 1830s emerge as deeply political, though in a manner that is appropriate to the overlapping theological and political concerns of the time.

To underscore something already said, for intellectuals operating in the Christian culture of early-nineteenth-century Germany, fundamental issues

13   Feuerbach to Arnold Ruge, 10 March 1843, *Feuerbach. Briefwechsel, vol. 2 (1840–1844)*, ed. Werner Schuffenhauer and E. Voigt (Berlin, 1988).

of politics and religion were intimately tied to basic questions about the nature of selfhood. Major Hegelians like Feuerbach and Eduard Gans, or Hegelian "fellow travelers" like Heinrich Heine, August Cieszkowski, and Moses Hess, were centrally concerned with the problem of the self, and this preoccupation was not strictly limited to theological or philosophical inquiry. They also explored the status of the self in contemporary society and politics, as well as the social and political conditions within which the qualities of the person might be most fully actualized. In this way, their thought intersected with the wider contemporary discussion of sovereignty, the state, and civil society, insofar as that discussion centered on the self in its role as sovereign, citizen, and subject.

## The Controversy over Personality

For German intellectuals in the 1830s and 1840s, these questions about selfhood crystallized in a wide-ranging debate over the nature of *Persönlichkeit* or personality. Even at the time this was an esoteric debate, and it has remained a relatively obscure theme in the intellectual history of early-nineteenth-century Germany. Such neglect is surprising, however, because it directly contradicts the importance of the question of personality for the theologians and philosophers of the age. I aim in this book to recapture the force of that original debate about personality and to demonstrate its significance for the development of radical political and social theory in the nineteenth century. My approach is motivated by the conviction that moving the theme of personality from the periphery to the center of our awareness illuminates the political and social concerns of Hegelians from Feuerbach to Marx, thereby recasting our understanding of the theoretical conflicts and the transformation of German philosophical and political discourse in the crucial years from 1830 to 1848.

The controversy over personality warrants our serious attention because it marked the most important point of intersection for the discussion of theological, social, and political issues in the 1830s. As the moderate Hegelian Carl Ludwig Michelet noted in 1841, the discussion of "the personality of God has dominated the history of philosophy in the last ten years."[14] The idea of personality was also a central issue among political theorists. Karl Schubarth, who gained considerable notoriety in the 1830s for his broadside attacks on Hegel, called personality nothing less than the highest principle

---

14 Michelet, *Vorlesungen über die Persönlichkeit Gottes und Unsterblichkeit der Seele* (Berlin, 1841), p. 7.

of the Prussian state, an opinion that the Prussian crown prince was happy
to second.[15] By 1841, another moderate Hegelian could declare personality to be a life-and-death issue for Prussian politics.[16] Indeed, for Hegelians
and non-Hegelians alike, the theological idea of personality was inseparable
from its political and social meanings.

In the context of a society attempting to reestablish political, social, and
religious order after decades of revolutionary turmoil, conservatives readily
moved from theology to political theology, discovering in the idea of the personal God an exemplar of the monarch's personal sovereignty over the state.
Even further, the notion of personality underpinned the discussion of civil
society, because personhood stood at the center of contemporary conceptions of property. German political theology in the era of Restoration represented a particularly forceful articulation of the tripartite homology recently
described by Jean Bethke Elshtain as "sovereign God, sovereign state, sovereign self."[17] Whatever unity the Hegelian School had enjoyed in the 1820s
was to shatter on this pyramidal rock in the course of the 1830s. Conservative Hegelians reaffirmed the links between God, monarch, and property
owner, while radical Hegelians came gradually to embrace the full consequences of the dissolution of the Christian idea of personality. The Young
Hegelians' rejection of Christian personalism thus furnishes us with a key to
understanding their revolt against religion, monarchy, and bourgeois civil
society.

In the chapters that follow, much more will be said about the meaning of
personality within the context of debate in the 1820s, '30s, and '40s. However, because the modern familiarity with the term immediately poses risks
of misunderstanding, some clarifications are in order. First, it must be said
that the concept of personality remained somewhat vague even for its champions. Far from reducing the usefulness of the concept, however, this lack
of clarity actually enhances its utility for our purposes. Our interest, after all,
is not really in establishing a valid or workable notion of personhood but
rather in tracing the vagaries of an idea and its impact upon a specific historical moment. What Lovejoy once called the "metaphysical pathos" of the

15  Schubarth, "Über die Unvereinbarkeit der Hegelschen Staatslehre mit dem obersten
    Lebens- und Entwicklungsprinzip des Preußischen Staats" (1839), *Materialien zu Hegels
    Rechtsphilosophie, vol. 1*, ed. Manfred Riedel (Frankfurt, 1975), pp. 249–66.
16  [F. W. Carové], "*Hegel, Schubarth und die Idee der Persönlichkeit in ihrem Verhältniss zur preußis-
    chen Monarchie*, von Dr. Immanuel Ogienski," *Hallische Jahrbücher*, nos. 68–73 (März, 1841),
    p. 269.
17  Jean Bethke Elshtain, "Sovereign God, Sovereign State, Sovereign Self," *Notre Dame Law
    Review*, vol. 66, no. 5 (1991), pp. 1355–84.

obscure still serves as a useful reminder that clarity of conceptualization often stands in inverse proportion to the historical effect of a specific idea.[18] This does indeed seem to have been the case in the controversies that will concern us, since the concept of personality acquired immediate force because it was a term that gathered together a range of meanings within the concrete political, social and ideological context of the 1830s. Precisely because personalism became shorthand for a constellation of ideas, it could produce a ferment that a more clearly defined term might not have.

In the context of early-nineteenth-century Germany, personality, or personhood, did not have the *psychological* meaning familiar to us; it did not refer to the psychological makeup of the individual or to individual temperament or character. Perhaps the best way to get a sense of what Christian personalists meant by these terms is to distinguish between the related concepts of the "person" and the "subject." The distinction is subtle, and it was not clearly articulated by early-nineteenth-century German philosophers and theologians, conditioned as they were by two centuries of philosophic discourse that had treated "subject" and "person" as virtual synonyms. The identification of the two terms began as early as the seventeenth century, when the person was defined epistemologically as a being with consciousness, where, as Charles Taylor puts it, "consciousness is seen as a power to frame representations of things."[19] This was, of course, also basic to Kant's concept of the subject, but he went even further by linking his epistemological argument to a modern idea of individual autonomy. Moreover, in defining the subjective conditions of knowledge as well as the ethical conditions of personal autonomy, Kant tied his concept of the person to universal categories of the "human" as such. In Kant's strict philosophical usage, the "subject" is that conscious apperceptive unity which recognizes itself as the active agent of knowledge. A tension between the concepts of "subject" and "person" began to appear once it was recognized that even if Kant himself conceived the subject as a conscious and autonomous human individual, in truth the concept of the subject *per se* says nothing about the *particular* identity of the subject. That is, one could accept in the main Kant's idea of subjectivity without being committed to his description of who or what that subject is. Hence the ease with which post-Kantian philosophers

---

18   A. O. Lovejoy, *The Great Chain of Being* (Cambridge, 1936), p. 11.

19   Charles Taylor, *Human Agency and Language* (Cambridge, 1985), p. 98. A similar chronology in the history of the "subject" as well as emphasis on the role of consciousness in framing representations is found in Martin Heidegger, "The Age of the World Picture," *The Question Concerning Technology and Other Essays*, trans. William Lovitt (New York, 1977), esp. p. 133.

could extend Kant's epistemological argument about the subject from the conscious human "I" to "God" or "Absolute Spirit." One contemporary of Kant, G. C. Lichtenberg, even claimed that insofar as the subject thinks "ideas," knowledge does not actually require a *personal* subject. To replace the expression "I think," Lichtenberg proposed "it [the idea] is thinking."[20] More recently, the potential depersonalization of the notion of subjectivity received a radical formulation in Roland Barthes' claim that "language knows a 'subject,' not a 'person,' and this subject [is] empty outside of the very speech-act which defines it."[21]

Like the subject, the person suggests an idea of autonomy, self-containment, and self-identity. Indeed, scholars have speculated that one etymological root of person is the Latin *per se una*, "that which is one by itself." A person is always also a subject. Nonetheless, the idea of human personhood suggests the *total* life of an individual, defined not only by a universally shared human essence but also by the contingent attributes of that particular individual. The person is thus conceived as an irreducibly unique locus of consciousness, rationality, and will. As Emile Durkheim wrote, "to be a person is to be an autonomous source of action. Man acquires this quality only insofar as there is something in him which is his alone and which individualizes him, as he is something more than a simple incarnation of the generic type of his race and his group."[22] The association of personhood with particularity is further underlined if we consider that Ludwig Feuerbach once judged the principle of personality to be inimical to philosophy, precisely because "personality *in concreto*" cannot be incorporated into philosophy's vocational impulse toward abstraction and generalization.[23]

This emphasis on empirical particularity derives from both the classical and Christian sources of the modern concept of personhood. One distant etymological root of "person" was the Greek word *prosopon*, the mask that actors donned in a drama. This theatrical sense survived in the Roman usage, where *persona* first designated the particular role played by an individual within human relations. Hence, the Roman "law of persons" was at first a description of the different rights and duties accorded to individuals bear-

20  Quoted in Adolf Trendelenburg, "A Contribution to the History of the Word Person," *Monist* (1910), p. 387.
21  Quoted in Jerrold Seigel, "The Human Subject as a Language-Effect," *History of European Ideas*, vol. 18, no. 4(1994), p. 481.
22  Durkheim, *On Morality and Society. Selected Writings*, ed. Robert Bellah (Chicago, 1973), pp. 140–1. See also Wolfhart Pannenberg, "Person und Subjekt," in *Identität*, ed. Odo Marquard and Karlheinz Stierle (München, 1979), pp. 407–22.
23  Feuerbach, "Zur Kritik der positiven Philosophie" (1838), *Ludwig Feuerbach. Gesammelte Werke*, vol. 8, ed. Werner Schuffenhauer (Berlin, 1973), p. 189.

ing different status or *personae* within Roman society. The law of persons
gradually lost this particularist focus and evolved toward a general description of the rights and duties of citizens. Nonetheless, it remained tied to differences among humans, between citizens and slaves, men and women. It
was primarily under the stimulus of Christianity that *persona* came to be associated with the human individual *per se*. The Old Testament idea of man
created in God's image and likeness and the Christian tenets of the Incarnation, the divine love accorded to each individual, and the resurrection of
the body combined to impart infinite worth to the single person. Significantly, this belief in the endless value of the individual person was predicated
upon a relationship of analogy between the human person and the divine
personality of God, traditionally conceived as complete in Himself, neither
conditioned by nor dependent on anything external to Himself. Unlike the
concept of the "subject," therefore, the *Christian* concept of "person" remains incomplete without relation to the archetypal divine person, a relationship expressed doctrinally in the symbolism of the Trinity.[24]

Although Kant treated the "self," the "person," and the "subject" as essential cognates, in early-nineteenth-century Germany the universality of Kant's
new theory of the subject came into conflict with the older emphasis on the
empirical particularity of the individual. We will defer discussion of the passage from Enlightenment universalism to a revival of particularistic notions
of selfhood until Chapter 1 and at this point simply note that although the
lines of this passage were obscure, they may be detected in the neo-humanist
ideal of *Bildung*, or self-cultivation, articulated by Wilhelm von Humboldt,
the Romantic insistence on individuality, and the vigorous reassertion of
the Christian idea of personhood itself. With his usual insight, Georg Simmel recognized this shift when he distinguished between eighteenth- and
nineteenth-century notions of individualism. The creed of the eighteenth
century, Simmel contended, emphasized the realization of universal capacities in each individual, while that of the nineteenth underscored the task
of each individual to realize his or her irreplaceable and unique capacities.
Where the earlier century associated individualism with the doctrine of free
competition, the later century associated it with the division of labor among
differently endowed individuals. The earlier was an individualism of equality, the later an individualism of inequality.[25] Theodor Adorno perceived the

24  See Dieter Henrich, "Die Trinität Gottes und der Begriff der Person," *Identität*, pp. 612–20.
25  See the discussion of Simmel in Nicholas Abercrombie, *Sovereign Individuals of Capitalism*
    (London, 1986), pp. 20–2. More recently, Louis Dumont has treated these two forms of
    individualism as typical expressions of national character in *German Ideology: From France to
    Germany and Back* (Chicago, 1994).

shift similarly when he traced the decline of the concept of "personality" from Kant's abstract principle to an identification of personhood with the "sensuous" qualities of empirical individuals.[26]

Here, it is also worth distinguishing the Christian personalism of early-nineteenth-century Germany from the "personalism" associated with the French Catholic thinker Emmanuel Mounier and the journal *Esprit*, which he founded in 1932 and edited until his death in 1950. Although Mounier drew on Christian tenets in describing his idea of personality, he was equally dependent upon the existentialist belief that human beings have no essence but define themselves through choice and action. Like the personalists of the preceding century, Mounier never did offer a clear definition of personalism, but in his case this was a deliberate expression of his basic commitment to an existentialist critique of essentialism. Moreover, despite Mounier's emphasis upon the uniqueness of each and every person, a real difference from the earlier Christian personalists emerges in his insistence that personality is ultimately fulfilled through generosity, human solidarity, and collective action.[27] Personalism, from Mounier's pen, is essentially synonymous with egalitarianism and socialism. His conclusions could hardly be more different from those of early-nineteenth-century thinkers who tied personalism to hierarchy, inequality, and private property.

Committed to the primacy of the person as a separate, discrete spiritual being, the Christian personalism of the early nineteenth century rejected all attempts to reduce the human being to an immanent order of society, politics, or history. Likewise, adhering to a belief that God and Christ are the archetypes of human personhood, Christian personalists rejected all efforts to reconceptualize the divine as an immanent presence in the world. On both counts, the reassertion of Christian and Romantic ideas of individuality and personhood in the early nineteenth century put Hegelians on the defensive, because Hegel's philosophy of religion and history appeared to his many critics as an extreme expression of the abstract universalism inaugurated by the enlightened language of Kant's critical philosophy. However, whereas Hegel himself maintained an ambiguous stance *vis à vis* the charges of pantheism or panlogism leveled against him, the radical Hegelians of the 1830s willingly embraced what their contemporaries saw as the pantheistic implications of Hegel's philosophy. This was as true of Feuerbach's evolving

26  Theodor Adorno, "Glosse über Persönlichkeit," *Stichwörte. Kritische Modelle 2* (Frankfurt, 1969), p. 640.

27  Michel Barlow, *Le socialisme d'Emmanuel Mounier* (Toulouse, 1971), pp. 71–89; and Joseph Amato, *Mounier and Maritain: A French Catholic Understanding of the World* (University, Alabama, 1975).

critique of religious belief in the 1830s as it was of progressive Hegelian opposition to conservative political theory.

Left-wing Hegelians were as willing as conservatives to make direct connections between the idea of the personal God, society, and politics. Consequently, integral to their critique of the personal God and of Christ the God-Man, they attacked the idea of personality as it was used to support a restorationist political theology that they identified with authoritarian monarchy, asocial egoism, political apathy, and atomistic individualism. It should be perfectly clear that I am not suggesting that leftist Hegelians attacked all notions of personhood; like Hegel himself, the Young Hegelians embraced the beliefs that self-consciousness is the distinctive feature of human life and that individual autonomy is the goal of both theory and practice. Their critique of Christian personalism in the 1830s and early 1840s entailed a rejection of certain ideas of the self and their implications for society and politics, not a rejection of selfhood *per se*. Indeed, the leftist Hegelians' running battle against Christian personalism is significant largely because their negative destruction of Christian notions of the person was accompanied by their increasingly strident efforts to resituate the human person in the immanent order of society, politics, and history.

## Context and Meaning

The works of the Young Hegelians unified theological, political, and social themes in large measure because they were written within a context in which this unity was taken for granted. This was true not only for the specific Hegelian philosophical subculture to which many young German intellectuals were exposed but for the larger Protestant and Catholic cultures of Germany as well. Left-wing Hegelians addressed this larger Christian culture either directly or through critical engagements with its self-appointed spokesmen. It would be misleading to assume that they or their intended audience was oblivious to the intertwining of religion and politics in their writings. If we are to appreciate the political and social dimensions of progressive Hegelian thought in the years from 1830 to 1843, the year in which Marx articulated his fundamental critique of Hegel and his ethical commitment to socialism, we must reconstruct the rhetorical and ideological context within which their concepts regain their range of contemporary meanings and their nuanced resonance.[28]

28  In offering a fuller description of the rhetorical and ideological context that structured debate among Hegelians of the 1830s and 1840s, this study aims to correct tendencies

I emphasize the plural "meanings" because I do not want to suggest that the writings of these figures can be reduced to one meaning through reference to an omnipresent and all-explaining context that overwhelms the nuances of text and individual motive.[29] Nor is it my aim to declare, through the license of contextual explanation, that the theological and metaphysical works of a thinker like Ludwig Feuerbach are really *about* politics. While Eduard Gans, Arnold Ruge, and Moses Hess were primarily political thinkers, the same cannot be said of Feuerbach. His great contributions were in the areas of philosophy of religion and what might broadly be called philosophical anthropology. Even in the case of Feuerbach, however, we encounter theological and philosophical tracts with political meanings that it is our task to understand. We will not arrive at these meanings primarily through biography or isolated close readings of individual texts but through a contextual approach that will restore a range of meanings to the writings of Feuerbach and the other critical Hegelians. As this remark suggests, my intention is to disclose meaningful relationships – a nexus of relations between different discourses, as well as their relations to an intellectual, cultural, and political setting, rather than a reduction of these relations to a hierarchy of

either toward an excessive focus on the internal dynamics of Hegelianism or toward sociopolitical reductionism. The former tendency is well illustrated in Karl Löwith's *From Hegel to Nietzsche* and Peter Cornehl's *Die Zukunft der Versöhnung. Eschatologie und Emanzipation in der Aufklärung, bei Hegel und in der Hegelschen Schule*. The underlying assumption of these distinguished books is that the emergence of divisions within the Hegelian School is explained by tracing these divisions to the contradictory impulses in Hegel's thought itself. In this view, the master's construction was doomed to shatter in the clumsier hands of the epigones. By contrast, Harold Mah's recent work *The End of Philosophy, The Origin of "Ideology"* explains the transformation of Hegelianism through the action of "external" social and political forces. Mah depicts a statically homogeneous Hegelianism in the 1830s, which was shattered around 1840 by the combined pressure of mounting political reaction and the growing social problem. These contextual factors have been carefully studied not only by Mah but also by Gustave Mayer in the 1910s and 1920s, and in the 1980s by Toews and Eßbach. But Mah is particularly insistent on portraying the radicalization of Hegelianism as a kind of reflex to an apparently more primary sociopolitical reality. To be sure, the importance of these factors is beyond question. Intensifying political reaction, particularly in Prussia in the late 1830s, contributed significantly to the self-conscious politicization of Left Hegelianism as well as to its disillusionment with Hegel's "statism." Further, the problem of pauperism and the first stirrings of industrial transformation in Germany highlighted the urgency of social problems and the possible inadequacy of strictly political responses to them. Nonetheless, the vital point is that the Hegelian response to worsening political and social conditions in Germany was not unmediated. Hence, we return to the need to understand more clearly the ideological context that shaped the conceptualization of sociopolitical problems.

29   The possible pitfalls of a contextual approach to intellectual history are perceptively discussed in Dominick LaCapra, "Reading Exemplars: *Wittgenstein's Vienna* and Wittgenstein's *Tractatus*," in *Rethinking Intellectual History: Texts, Contexts, Language* (Cornell, 1983).

cause and effect.[30] This context is at once chosen from a range of more or less pertinent contexts so as to illustrate neglected aspects of radical Hegelianism in the 1830s; but it was also a context in which these radical thinkers participated. This intellectual setting presented certain problems and interrelations, and it framed the manner in which these problems were conceptualized. As engaged participants, these German intellectuals were influenced by this context even as their interventions helped shape it.

My argument about the course of radical Hegelian thought depends upon a careful reconstruction of the ideological milieu wherein Hegelianism came under fire during the 1830s. Continually intensifying debate between Hegelians and anti-Hegelians exerted a powerful influence upon the course of Hegelianism in the 1830s. Hegelianism never enjoyed unchallenged dominion in German intellectual life, not even in Prussia, where for a time it was favored by the minister for Religious and Educational Affairs, Karl von Altenstein. In fact, Hegelians had constantly to defend their philosophical and political positions against a wide array of critics. Yet this was not simply a case of entrenched camps' lobbing charges at each other across a sharp divide. Rather, in the fluid atmosphere of German intellectual life in the 1820s and 1830s, the interactions were often more subtle. Debates about the meaning of Hegel's philosophy external to the Hegelian School helped to clarify not only the School's relationship to competing philosophical views. External debate also clarified choices within the School, thereby contributing to the dissolution of Hegelianism as anything like a unified world view. One of the goals of the present study is to broaden our understanding of these interactions between Hegelians and non-Hegelians in the 1830s as an important dimension of the overall transformation of philosophical discourse in this period. Too often treated as if it were closed to outside influence, the Hegelian School was in fact fully subject to the "ideological cacophony" of the 1830s.[31] This openness to a range of influences even extended to a significant reception of new French social thought by the nascent Hegelian Left in the 1830s.

The chief task of the opening chapters of this book is to describe the emergence of Christian personalism as the most significant theological,

---

30 The distinction between "meaningful" and "causal" relations, derived from Max Weber's pursuit of "the subjective-meaningful complex of action," is discussed in Laurence Dickey, *Hegel: Religion, Economics, and the Politics of Spirit 1770–1807* (Cambridge, 1987), p. 299 n18. On "nexuses," see Carl Dahlhaus, *Between Romanticism and Modernism: Four Studies in the Music of the Later Nineteenth Century*, trans. Mary Whittall (Berkeley, 1980), p. 80.
31 The phrase is from Jacques d'Hondt, quoted in Thomas Petermann, *Der Saint-Simonismus in Deutschland. Bemerkungen zur Wirkungsgeschichte* (Frankfurt, 1983), p. 48.

philosophical, and political rebuttal of Hegel's alleged pantheistic philosophy. Numerous Protestant, Pietistic, and Catholic theologians and philosophers polemicized against Hegelian pantheism, but Chapter 1 will argue that the so-called "Positive Philosophy" of the elderly F.W.J. Schelling most profoundly influenced the personality controversy by giving philosophic respectability to Christian personalism. In Chapter 2, Schelling reappears as one of the forces shaping the personalist political theology of Friedrich Julius Stahl, who was widely regarded as Hegelianism's most formidable opponent in political philosophy during the 1830s. Chapter 3 explores the work of Ludwig Feuerbach in the 1830s from the vantage point of his response to the personalist currents of German theology and philosophy. Concentrating on an examination of his first published book, *Thoughts on Death and Immortality,* and his 1835 essay on Friedrich Julius Stahl, the chapter argues not only that Feuerbach's long engagement with Christian personalism exerted a crucial influence upon the evolution of his critique of Christianity and his eventual turn against Hegel himself but also that his opposition to personalism lay at the heart of an emerging political and social radicalism in Feuerbach's work in the 1830s that scholars have too frequently neglected. Chapter 4 shifts to a more general discussion of two politicized paths that the Hegelian critique of personalism followed in the 1830s. On the one hand, personalist political theology mushroomed into a significant theme of the controversies sparked by the publication of David Friedrich Strauss's *Life of Jesus* in 1835. The dispute about the political meanings of Strauss's rejection of the Christian Incarnation deepened the antipathy between Hegelians and their critics, and it came to divide Hegelians along political lines. On the other hand, the chapter argues that the German discussion of personalism was influenced by the incursion of new social ideas coming from France. Specifically, the blend of social criticism and pantheism found in the so-called "New Christianity" of the Saint-Simonians gave German critics of personalism new resources for conceptualizing the relationship between religion and social order. Chapter 5 will explore this contention through a discussion of August Cieszkowski, Heinrich Heine, Moses Hess, and, finally, Feuerbach, whose major writings of the early 1840s will be reconsidered as important examples of this confluence of German and French currents of radicalism.

My depiction of Feuerbach as a religio-political critic of what I will call "Christian civil society" is likely to be one of the most controversial dimensions of this book.[32] However, the payoff comes in the form of a deepened

32  Much more will be said about the notion of "Christian civil society" in the following

understanding of the impact of 1830s philosophic radicalism, of which Feuerbach's work was the outstanding exemplar, upon the course of Left Hegelian political and social thought in the 1840s. Once again, I am aiming to disclose not firm causal relations but rather meaningful relations within a constellation of themes. The chapters devoted to the interrelationship of political, social, and theological critique in the thought of Feuerbach, Gans, Heine, Hess, and Cieszkowski establish the ideological, philosophical, and rhetorical conditions for understanding the emergence of the more explicitly political and social radicalism of 1840s Left Hegelianism. The final two chapters offer detailed analyses of Arnold Ruge and Karl Marx, the major Hegelians of the early 1840s whose works most decisively shifted to the explicit ground of social and political critique. Marx, as we will see, went much further than any other radical Hegelian in loosening the thematic unities that had bound together theological and sociopolitical radicalism in the 1830s. Nonetheless, we will be in a position to recognize just how much Marx was shaped by the themes bound up in the philosophical, political, and social critique of Christianity.

Thus, the radical Hegelians' campaign against Christian ideas of the person – their attempt to "dethrone" the self, as the young Feuerbach put it in an audacious letter to Hegel in 1828 – leads us to the heart of their opposition to the conditions of their present. Hostility toward Christian personalism set Young Hegelian radicals against what was both the sovereign discourse of their day and a particular discourse of sovereignty. The controversy over sovereign personhood became a crucial vehicle for the discussion of state and civil society among the nascent intellectual Left in the Germany of the 1830s and 1840s. It crystallized the deeper assumptions of Hegelians and non-Hegelians alike about the human person and the social and political conditions that best actualize personhood. Finally and most important, it provides us with a crucial context within which to understand and assess Marx's critique of individualism and his conversion to socialism, arguably the most significant event in the history of political theory in the early nineteenth century.

chapters. I borrow the phrase from Karl Löwith, *From Hegel to Nietzche: The Revolution in Nineteenth-Century Thought,* trans. D. E. Green (New York, 1964); and Lucio Colletti, "The Idea of 'Bourgeois-Christian' Society," *From Rousseau to Lenin: Studies in Ideology and Society* (London, 1972), pp. 249–83.

# 1

## AT THE END OF IDEALISM: FROM "NIHILISM" TO "POSITIVE PHILOSOPHY"

In a classic article, Gustav Mayer once suggested that the religious and philosophical battles of the 1820s and 1830s were the most intense that Germany had witnessed since the Reformation.[1] Whatever truth there is in Mayer's claim is due in large measure to the enormously controversial effects of Hegel's philosophy. The 1820s are often presented as years of ascendancy for Hegelianism among German intellectuals, but much would be lost to our understanding of the intellectual history of the early nineteenth century if we neglected the fact that outside the circle of Hegel's supporters, Hegelianism faced opposition from a wide variety of camps. The fact that Hegelianism was beleaguered in the 1820s and 1830s is hardly surprising. After all, fame tends to draw opponents into the open, whether out of petty resentment or a genuine sense that public recognition of one's enemy has raised the stakes of debate. More important, however, the controversy over Hegelianism also reflected the general situation of German and particularly Prussian intellectual life.

This dispute may be regarded as the last and climactic episode in the intense debate about the course of German philosophy that had begun with Kant's revolutionary redefinition of the tasks of philosophy in the 1780s. Kant had a powerful impact on German intellectual life in the late eighteenth

---

1 Gustav Mayer, "Die Junghegelianer und der preussische Staat," *Historische Zeitschrift*, 121 (1920), p. 416.

century, particularly through the dissemination of Kantian ideas in popular organs such as the *Allgemeine Literatur-Zeitung* and the *Allgemeine deutsche Bibliothek,* as well as through Kant's exchanges with his many critics, including the *Popularphilosophen* who opposed Kant even as they championed enlightenment values.[2] Debate about Kant was quickly overshadowed by attempts to surpass him. In little over a decade and against the backdrop of the French Revolution and warfare that engulfed Europe, Karl Leonhard Reinhold attempted to ground Kantian critical Idealism in a more adequate theory of mental representation, J. J. Fries advanced an anthropological restatement of Kant, J. G. Fichte reformulated Kantianism as a radical philosophy of subjective freedom, Schelling made an audacious attempt to radicalize Fichte's program in a new philosophy of nature, and numerous Romantic poets found in Kant the inspiration for a new and unbounded role for imagination in art and social life. Besetting this vertiginous expansion of the claims of Idealism was F. H. Jacobi's reaction against philosophical rationalism, which condemned the whole pantheon of modern philosophy, from Descartes and Spinoza to Lessing, Kant, and Fichte. Public interest in these developments was intense from the 1790s to the 1830s, decades encompassing revolution, warfare, and the restoration of monarchy throughout Europe.

As Hegel gained prominence, his relationship to post-Kantian philosophy increasingly became the central issue in these publicly waged philosophic battles. Hegel invited this scrutiny, especially once his readers began to understand his claim to be the summation and supercession of modern philosophy. Furthermore, Hegel's assertion that there was no ultimate distinction between the conceptual scheme of his philosophy and "reality" itself made it very easy for his contemporaries to regard a debate about Hegel as a crucial part of a broader debate about the spiritual and political condition of that modern reality. By the 1820s, after his move to Berlin, an appreciable number of students and supporters were willing to identify Hegel as the definitive philosopher of modernity, as the thinker of the "Absolute." Ironically enough, however, his tremendous appeal among certain young German intellectuals may be partially explained by the fact that the general climate had become so unreceptive to the kind of message of cultural and spiritual rebirth that some discovered in Hegel.

This was, after all, the era known in Germany as the Biedermeier Age, remembered nostalgically or derisively for its preoccupation with privacy and

---

2  On the *Popularphilosophen* and Kant, as well as the general philosophical situation in Germany during the 1780s and 1790s, the fundamental work is Frederick Beiser, *The Fate of Reason. German Philosophy from Kant to Fichte* (Cambridge, Mass., 1987).

domesticity. After the intense mobilization of energies and sentiments during the revolutionary decades and the upsurge of patriotism during the wars
against Napoleon, after the defeat of republicanism and the continent-wide
restoration of monarchy in 1815, many people were content to regard hearth
and home as the ideal sites of individual self-realization.[3] Max Wundt's attempt in 1935 to identify a specific "Biedermeier" style of thought led him
to a claim that applied equally to the political and social life, philosophy, and
theology of the period: "One can describe the *Weltanschauung* of the period
as personalism." "Everything is personal," claimed an 1832 essay by Immanuel
Hermann Fichte, son of the more famous thinker whose subjective Idealism
had been so important to the vision of the post-Kantians and Romantics.[4]
In such a climate, a philosophy associated, whether rightly or wrongly, with
the Promethean ideals of Romanticism, with the divinization of humanity,
with freedom and individual self-determination, provoked reactions from
across the spectrum of opinion. Theological opponents of Hegel's philosophy of religion ranged from the neo-orthodox Protestant circle of the *Evangelische Kirchenzeitung,* edited by Ernst Wilhelm Hengstenberg, to Pietists like
Friedrich Tholuck and Julius Müller, to the theological rationalists Heinrich
Paulus, Julius Röhr, Karl Gottlieb Bretschneider, and the circle of the *Allgemeine Kirchenzeitung.* Catholic theologians also expressed opposition, particularly the Catholic Tübingen School led by Franz Anton Staudenmaier
and Johann Evangelist Kuhn.[5] Among philosophers, Friedrich Schelling,
renowned in his youth as the prince of Romantics, and the so-called "Speculative Theists," Christian Weisse and Immanuel Hermann Fichte, led a
sophisticated campaign against Hegel that was carried into the pages of
Fichte's *Zeitschrift für Philosophie und spekulative Theologie,* described by Erdmann as the "audience chamber of all anti-Hegelians."[6]

It is not my intention to canvass the full range of this critical opposition
to the Hegelian School, which would be an enormous task that would likely
yield disproportionately small results. Instead, this and the next chapter
will focus on the development of "personalist" thought as the core theme
of anti-Hegelianism and as the putative alternative to the entire legacy of
German Idealism. We must trace a double trajectory through both chapters:
on one side, the evolving discourse of Idealism in the years between Kant

---

3  For an overview of this mood in western Europe, see Catherine Hall, "The Sweet Delights
   of Home," *A History of Private Life. Vol. IV. From the Fires of Revolution to the Great War,* ed.
   Michelle Perrot (Cambridge, Mass., 1990), pp. 47–93.
4  Max Wundt, "Die Philosophie in der Zeit des Biedermeiers," *Deutsche Vierteljahrsschrift,* I,
   XIII(1935), p. 136.
5  Walter Jaeschke, *Reason in Religion,* p. 353.
6  J. E. Erdmann, *A History of Philosophy,* vol. 3, trans. W. S. Hough (London, 1890–2), p. 20.

and Hegel; on the other, the development of a counter-discourse stretching from F. H. Jacobi to the elderly Schelling, the Speculative Theists, and
Stahl, a counter-discourse that was simultaneously opposed to, and implicated in, Idealism. The controversy over Hegel intertwined religious and
political issues, and any separation of the two risks distorting their unity.
Nonetheless, for analytical purposes, this chapter will focus on the religious
and speculative philosophical discussion. The "religious" dimension was
the unifying element and the *sine qua non* of German philosophy in the early
nineteenth century. "The possibility of knowing and understanding God,"
Hegel wrote in his *Philosophy of History*, is "a question which is of prime importance in our time."[7] In the eyes of Hegel and his contemporaries, the
epistemological, political, social, and ethical concerns of the age all depended
on the successful answer to that question.

## The Pantheism Controversy

In 1832, Heinrich Heine declared that pantheism is "the religion of [Ger-
many's] greatest thinkers, of our best artists. . . . Pantheism is the open secret of Germany."[8] Others were also pronouncing the open secret, though
more often to denounce than to celebrate it.[9] Nowhere was this tension so
prominent as in the contemporary debate about Hegel's religious and political philosophy. Although we shall see that the terms of that debate went
well beyond the perennial antithesis of immanent and transcendent conceptions of divinity, at the simplest level, Hegel had been accused of pantheism since the publication of *Phenomenology of Spirit*, which some critics
read as a continuation of Schelling's philosophy of nature. Charges of pantheism leveled against a major German thinker were hardly new, however.
They had in fact become something of a permanent theme in German intellectual life since the late eighteenth century, when the *Pantheismusstreit*
had exercised the best minds of the era. The Pantheism Controversy commands our attention not only because it helped to shape the language that
was later applied to Hegel but also because it acted as a catalyst for Hegel
and the other post-Kantian Idealists' attempts to correct and surpass Kant.
    The *Pantheismusstreit* brought to a climax a century of attacks on the

---

7   Hegel, *Werke*, vol. 12, ed. Eva Moldenhauer and Karl M. Michel (Frankfurt, 1970), p. 26.
8   Heinrich Heine, *Religion and Philosophy in Germany*, trans. John Snodgrass (Albany, 1986),
    p. 79.
9   See, for example, Gottlob Benjamin Jaesche's voluminous work, *Der Pantheismus nach seinem
    verschiedenen Hauptformen, seinem Ursprung und Fortgange, seinem speculativen und praktischen
    Werth und Gehalt. Ein Beitrag zur Geschichte und Kritik dieser Lehre in alter und neuer Philosophie*,
    3 vols. (Berlin, 1826).

teachings of Spinoza by Germany's academic and ecclesiastical establishment. According to Frederick Beiser, Spinoza's rationalism and his plea for freedom of conscience had made him "the patron saint" of the "vanguard of the *Aufklärung* in the late seventeenth and early eighteenth centuries in Germany."[10] These attributes also made the "accursed Jew of Amsterdam" a target of wrath for generations of conservative Germans. Although few of Spinoza's texts were widely available and little was actually known of him, a swipe at Spinoza became a common rite of passage for young men entering the ecclesiastical or academic establishment. The polarized response to Spinoza focused above all on his attempt to replace the anthropomorphic conception of God with a strictly rational notion of God as a universal substance consisting of infinite attributes. Thus identifying God with the nature of the universe and its laws, Spinoza went on to apply the same rationalistic spirit to biblical criticism in the *Tractatus theologico-politicus*. Boldly claiming that the Scripture was not the product of divine revelation but of history and culture, Spinoza declared that "the Bible leaves reason absolutely free, that it has nothing in common with philosophy, in fact, that Revelation and Philosophy stand on totally different footings."[11] Philosophy had now to derive the nature of the divine or the infinite strictly by reason alone.

The course of the philosophy of religion in eighteenth-century Germany was essentially contained in the various alternatives posed by the epochal task set by Spinoza. He bequeathed to his eighteenth-century successors the liberating and frequently agonizing awareness of the gap between the historical faith and the demands of reason. Some *Aufklärer*, like Hermann Reimarus, argued that the supernatural elements of revealed religion could be discarded to leave a religious essence in accordance with reason and nature. Conversely, Kant drew a critical line between what we can know and what we cannot. Without denying the existence of God or his importance in human life, Kant removed the possibility of any philosophical knowledge of his attributes or his existence. Both J. G. Fichte and Hegel took Spinoza at his word and, while differing from him and from each other in their conceptions of divinity, held that autonomous reason can achieve a clear and sufficient idea of God. Beyond the ken of philosophy, wrote Fichte in 1798, "We know no other God, but also need no other."[12] For Lessing, by contrast, the gap between reason and the historical faith had become by 1777 an

10   Beiser, *Fate of Reason*, p. 51. Margaret Jacob makes a similar point in *The Radical Enlightenment: Pantheists, Freemasons and Republicans* (London, 1981).

11   Spinoza, *A Theologico-Political Treatise*, trans. R.H.M. Elwes (New York, 1951), p. 9.

12   J. G. Fichte, "On the Foundation of Our Belief in a Divine Government of the Universe," in *Nineteenth Century Philosophy*, ed. Patrick L. Gardiner (New York, 1969), pp. 24–5.

"ugly, broad ditch which I cannot get across, however often and however earnestly I have tried to make the leap."[13]

It is appropriate that Lessing, who sounded a note of despair absent from these other major figures, should have become the object of a heated dispute over the nihilistic potential of rational philosophy. The *Pantheismusstreit* began in the mid-1780s when Moses Mendelssohn undertook to defend his deceased friend against Friedrich Heinrich Jacobi's charge that Lessing had become a Spinozist pantheist. We can leave aside the details of Mendelssohn's tepid defense of Lessing or the contributions to the debate by Herder, Kant, and other lesser figures and concentrate on Jacobi's position.[14] At issue for Jacobi was not simply whether Lessing had come to accept unorthodox views but rather the authority of reason itself, particularly in matters of religion and morality.[15] If Lessing, the most celebrated figure of the German Enlightenment, was led by the spirit of rational inquiry to embrace the deterministic and atheistic doctrine of Spinoza, Jacobi argued, then fatal doubt must be cast on the cherished belief of such Berlin *Aufklärer* as Mendelssohn that the tenets of orthodox faith could be defended by reason. Indeed, in a stinging rebuke to the *Aufklärung* spirit, he charged that all speculative philosophy ends in determinism, fatalism, and atheism. "Nihilism," the term coined by Jacobi to indicate the direction in which he thought Enlightenment philosophy was headed, became in his view the central problem of all philosophy.[16]

Jacobi did not actually reach this sweeping conclusion solely from his encounters with Lessing but rather from the problem of knowledge of God as posed by his readings of Spinoza, Hume, and, most important, Kant. Kant's restriction of critical reason to the sphere of experience drew a veil over the divine, thus limiting reason to the more modest task of examining religious *experience*, which is not at all the same as seeking to know God. Although both natural and supernatural theology thereby suffered a serious blow, Jacobi could endorse Kant's claim that God cannot be an object of cognition; but he emphatically rejected Kant's attempt to reconceive the God of faith as a postulate of practical reason.[17] Instead, Jacobi removed the question of God,

13  G. E. Lessing, "On the Proof of the Spirit and of Power," *Lessing's Theological Writings*, trans. Henry Chadwick (Stanford, 1956), p. 55.
14  The key texts of the dispute are collected in H. Scholz, ed., *Die Hauptschriften zum Pantheismus Streit zwischen Jacobi und Mendelssohn* (Berlin, 1916).
15  Beiser, *Fate of Reason*, pp. 77–81.
16  Ibid., p. 81.
17  This redefinition of God as a postulate of practical or ethical reason was introduced in the *Critique of Pure Reason* and refined in works from *Critique of Practical Reason* to "Religion

the highest object of human spiritual and intellectual yearning, from the domain of philosophy altogether. In Jacobi's account, reason depends for its ground on something radically other, an unconditioned Being that itself cannot be known, because to be known would imply that this Being is an object for a knower rather than the absolute grounding for the possibility of knowing.[18] What is demanded is a *salto mortale,* a leap from the "elastic point" of faith that reveals the living God as the creator and possibility of the world. Even reason itself must conclude that "I am not, and I do not wish to be, if He is not! – Indeed, I myself cannot be the highest essence for me. Thus my reason teaches me instinctively: God. With irresistible force the highest in me points to a highest being above and outside of me."[19] Intuitive certitude and emotional need convinced Jacobi that such a God could not be merely a first cause or an infinite substance but must be a transcendent personal intelligence who is unconstrained by the conditioned world of created objects.

Jacobi drew a significant and novel ontological consequence from his emotional argument for a personal God. Where Spinozism negates the autonomous existence of things by subsuming them all as attributes of the infinite substance, faith in a God who is "above and outside" affirms the real existence of finite temporal objects. Jacobi used the word "Realismus" to describe this perception of the created world as really existing in its finitude, and he championed this sort of realism as the only antidote to Spinozist nihilism.[20] He extended this realist argument to the question of human subjectivity. While Kant and his followers struggled to derive a suitable theory of the subject from the doctrine of transcendental apperception, Jacobi traced certitude of self to the immediate experience of being and the intuition of the underivable foundation, the unconditioned ground of our own conditioned existence.[21] In a paradoxical move, however, Jacobi proceeded from this argument about our dependence to an assertion of the

within the Limits of Pure Reason Alone." Walter Jaeschke has shown that Kant's "ethicotheology" satisfied few of his contemporaries. It elicited among philosophers of the 1780s and 1790s a range of responses from moral atheism to various overextensions of practical theology, none of which upheld Kant's desire to ground ethical action upon the autonomy of moral reason. See Jaeschke, *Reason in Religion,* pp. 11–122.

18   Beiser, *Fate of Reason,* p. 67.
19   F. H. Jacobi, "Open Letter to Fichte," (1799) *Philosophy of German Idealism,* ed. Ernst Behler (New York, 1987), p. 132.
20   See especially N. Wilde, *F. H. Jacobi: A Study in the Origin of German Realism* (New York, 1966).
21   See Jacobi, "Open Letter," p. 132. On K. L. Reinhold's attempt to reinforce the Kantian theory of the subject by developing a theory of the "faculty of representation" – that is, of consciousness as such – see Dieter Henrich, "The Origins of the Theory of the Subject," *Philosophical Investigations in the Unfinished Project of Enlightenment,* ed. Axel Honneth, et al. (Cambridge, Mass., 1992), pp. 55–70 and Beiser, *Fate of Reason,* pp. 226–65. On Fichte and

autonomy of the human person as part of the created world. Once again, Jacobi meant to rescue free and autonomous individuals and the domain of human values from the nihilistic monism of universal rationality. Interestingly, in sharp contrast to the political inclinations of early-nineteenth-century Christian personalists, Jacobi combined this theistic argument for human freedom with a moderate liberal political outlook; indeed, some have argued that his concern to limit reason in the domain of theology was motivated in the first instance by his anxieties about the potentially despotic thrust of Enlightenment rationalism in politics.[22] Jacobi's example is a salutary reminder that Christian personalism could be put to diverse political uses depending on context and individual character.

Jacobi's responses to Spinoza, Lessing, Kant, and Mendelssohn and, in 1799, to Fichte's denial of a personal God all reached one conclusion. Unless rationalism accepts its limits, philosophy must arrive at a doctrine of necessity and uniformity that negates the idea of the personal God and suppresses the freedom and autonomous reality of human beings and values. He thereby set before his readers a stark either/or choice between "nihilism" and "realism." Jacobi's rejection of speculative philosophy's inquiries into the Absolute came virtually at the beginning of the Idealist period in Germany. But this irruption of fideism and theism within the domain of philosophy anticipated in striking ways the period of Idealism's breakdown. In the early-nineteenth-century debates about Hegel's alleged panlogism and pantheism, variants of Jacobi's theistic realism were to experience a second birth, as was his theologically oriented concern for individual freedom. Heinrich Heine may have contemptuously dismissed Jacobi in 1832 as "a gossiping old woman, disguised in the mantle of philosophy."[23] Yet, in the sharpness of Heine's words, one can gauge the persistence of the challenge posed by Jacobi's choice.

## Religion and Self-Knowledge in Idealism

Jacobi opened the theistic counter-movement to rationalist philosophy. His ideas were to find fertile soil in the 1820s and 1830s when orthodox theistic

Hegel, see Robert Pippin, *Hegel's Idealism. The Satisfactions of Self-Consciousness* (Cambridge, 1989); Frederick Neuhouser, *Fichte's Theory of Subjectivity* (Cambridge, 1990); and below.

22  Fania Oz-Schwarzenberger, *Translating the Enlightenment: Scottish Civic Discourse in Eighteenth-Century Germany* (Oxford, 1995), pp. 257–79; Frederick Beiser, *Enlightenment, Revolution, and Romanticism. The Genesis of Modern German Political Thought, 1790–1800* (Cambridge, Mass., 1992), pp. 138–53.

23  Heine, *Religion and Philosophy in Germany*, p. 79.

philosophers confronted Hegel; but in more immediate terms, the *Panthe-ismusstreit* had paradoxical effects. For one thing, Jacobi's *Briefe über die Lehre des Spinoza* (1785), intended to be damning, inadvertently stimulated inter-est in Spinozism by identifying it as the creed of Lessing, the most respected figure of the German Enlightenment, and by providing a reasonably good synopsis of Spinoza's views. More profoundly, although the likes of Hegel and Schelling tended to revile Jacobi, he helped to crystallize the concerns of the post-Kantian Idealists as they confronted Kant's legacy. First, Jacobi's critique of reason drew a sharp line between faith and knowledge, a divide that challenged the holistic impulses of the post-Kantians. Second, Jacobi's separation of faith and knowledge underscored the more general problem of skepticism introduced by Kant's separation of phenomena from things-in-themselves. The skepticism problem intersected with a third concern. Ja-cobi's theistic realism focused attention on the need for an adequate theory of subjectivity, particularly a theory that would resolve the ambiguous onto-logical status of the Kantian subject and provide a firmer basis for human autonomy than that provided by Kantian practical philosophy. Jacobi's at-tempt to establish self-certitude and autonomy upon our intuitive belief in the unconditioned ground of all being, the personal God, proved highly consequential for the course of post-Kantian Idealism. As Dieter Henrich writes, "the connection between self-certitude and certitude of the uncon-ditioned" means that "if self-certitude should be explained theoretically, the form of knowledge pertaining to the unconditioned would have to be pressed into service."[24] Jacobi thereby helped focus misgivings about Kantian phi-losophy upon the problem of the unconditioned – in other words, the prob-lem of God.

The Kantian dualism was deeply troubling for Schleiermacher, Schelling, Hölderlin, and Hegel, the precocious young thinkers of the 1790s, and for each of them, the recovery of self-knowledge depended upon the possibil-ity of access to the unconditioned Absolute. In this search for knowledge of the Absolute, Schelling's youthful philosophy of nature was pathbreaking. Although Schelling accepted Kant's and Fichte's claims about the con-structive role of the human subject in the formation of experience, he was eager to avoid a one-sided subjectivism that would negate the objective re-ality of nature, a danger that he detected in Fichte.[25] In response, Schelling shifted from the "man-centered" philosophy of Kant and Fichte to a "Spirit-

24  Henrich, "Origins," pp. 81–2.
25  See especially F.W.J. Schelling, "Introduction," *Ideas for a Philosophy of Nature as Introduction to the Study of This Science*, trans. E. E. Harris (Cambridge, 1988).

centered" philosophy in which both nature and man are participants in a universal spiritual activity, the self-realization of God.[26] The world-positing activity of absolute subjectivity, an idea combining Spinozism and Kantianism, became one of the central themes of post-Kantian Idealism, as expressed in Schelling's vitally important identity thesis: "Nature should be Mind made visible, Mind the invisible Nature." Hence, Schelling articulated a crucial claim for the existence of an "absolute identity of Mind *in us* and Nature *outside us.*"[27] Schelling's premise suggests that the shift to Spirit actually remained man-centered, because it rested on the ultimate identity of divine and human subjectivity, established either through intuition, as in Schleiermacher, Schelling, or the Romantic poets, or through the unfolding of absolute subjectivity in the history of human consciousness, as in Hegel.[28] Kant's critical restriction of knowledge to the domain of experience could thereby be honored in the breach, for the new Idealists made God *identical* with the human experience of Him.

This claim for the identity of experience and reality, of the concept and the object, had a revolutionary effect upon the understanding of religion. As Emil Fackenheim has aptly written, "Religion is no longer understood as the attempt of man to relate himself to a God outside himself. It is a self-transformation of finite into infinite spirit; and in the true religious experience this self-transformation becomes total identification. The true religious experience and the true God are identical."[29] Each of the major post-Kantian Idealists advanced a version of this fundamental claim. Hence, for example, Schleiermacher's enormously influential concept of piety centered upon the individual believer's conscious "feeling" that she or he is "utterly dependent or, which is to say the same thing, [is] in relation to God." Religious feeling, in Schleiermacher, is thus essentially an intuition of the whole which is God and the unity of the self with God. Schelling transferred feeling from religion to aesthetics, claiming that artistic genius intuitively expresses the absolute identity of conscious and unconscious, subject and object, self and cosmos.[30] Schelling's virtual apotheosis of artistic genius accorded well with

26  I extend Charles Taylor's formulation in *Hegel* (Cambridge, 1975), p. 72, from Hegel to the other major post-Kantians.
27  Schelling, *Ideas*, p. 42.
28  Here, I agree with Dickey's observation on Hegel in *Hegel*, pp. 153–5.
29  Emil Fackenheim, "Schelling's Philosophy of Religion," *University of Toronto Quarterly*, XXII, no. 1 (Oct. 1952), pp. 3–4.
30  F.W.J. Schelling, "Deduction of a Universal Organ of Philosophy, or Main Propositions of the Philosophy of Art According to Principles of Transcendental Idealism," *Philosophy of German Idealism*, esp. p. 213.

the general view of his Romantic contemporaries, the Schlegel brothers, Hölderlin, and Novalis, all of whom believed that intuition enables the artist to unite subjectivity with the totality of humanity and nature.[31]

In their emphasis upon the intuitive ground of this union, the Romantic poets, as well as Schelling and Schleiermacher, were not terribly distant from Jacobi, though of course they intuited a very different form of divinity. However, while the poets recognized in Jacobi a kindred sensibility, Schelling and Schleiermacher both refused to take his leap of faith, preferring instead to traverse what they considered the hard ground of knowledge. Schelling and Schleiermacher would settle for nothing less than the identity of faith and knowledge, or, more precisely, they would rest only with a knowledge that sublates faith into the higher certainty afforded by the recognition of universal subjectivity. It was on the basis of their assertion about the nature of subjectivity that both could claim the identity of man and God as the conclusion of philosophic "science."

There is now considerable controversy over the extent to which Hegel's philosophy should be categorized, alongside Schelling's, as a metaphysics based on the notion of an absolute "substance-Subject, a Divine Mind, or a Spirit Monad."[32] Perhaps the most significant recent challenge to this long-standing view has come from Robert Pippin. In *Hegel's Idealism*, Pippin maintains that the key to comprehending Hegel's undertaking lies in clarifying his relationship to Kant: "Is there a way of understanding the 'subject-object identity' formulations of Hegel's absolute Idealism as what he says they are, *extensions* of Kant's project, rather than a complete rejection, or a transformation so radical that Kant is no longer recognizable in it?"[33] Answering in the affirmative, Pippin argues that Hegel considered his own work to be a completion of Kant's doctrine of transcendental apperception. In the first critique, Kant had maintained that experience depends on two faculties of knowledge: the subject's intuition, or reception, of the sensible manifold and the spontaneous activity of the subject, which involves both the exercise of categories of understanding and the inward self-constitution of the "I," that is, the apperceptive unity of the self-consciousness that allows the subject to know itself as the subject of experience. However, in the second edi-

31  Friedrich Schlegel wrote, for example, "Through the artist mankind becomes a single individual, since he unites the men of the past and of posterity in the present. He is the higher organ of the soul, where the living spirits of all outer humanity meet and in whom the inner man acts immediately." Quoted in Bernard M.G. Reardon, *Religion in the Age of Romanticism. Studies in Early Nineteenth Century Thought* (Cambridge, 1985), p. 19.
32  Pippin, *Hegel's Idealism*, p. 168.
33  Ibid., p. 92.

tion of the *Critique of Pure Reason*, Kant attempted to unite these two faculties of knowledge by regarding the forms of intuition as determinations of
the understanding. On this view, there is no "given" sensible content to which
the categories of understanding then impart form; rather, even sensible intuition is subject to a "minimal conceptualization."[34]

Kant did not pursue this line, but Pippin claims that for Hegel, building
on his critical reading of Fichte, the implications of this revision were clear.
If two faculties are at work, subjectivity is dependent upon natural sensibility; the subject encounters a restriction on its free self-determination. Moreover, a dualistic structure introduces skepticism about the extent of human
knowledge, because it divides our conceptual scheme – the forms by which
we know – from things in themselves. However, if the distinction between
intuition and understanding, content and form of knowledge, receptivity
and intelligibility is collapsed, then the way is cleared to overcome both
Kantian limits. First, the autonomy of the subject would be ensured by fully
recognizing the role of the self-positing, self-reflexive, self-determining subject in determining both the form and content of knowledge. Fichte was
particularly preoccupied with the issue of autonomy as he attempted to
come to terms with the epistemological and practical implications of this revised Kantian doctrine of transcendental apperception.[35] Hegel was equally
concerned with the problem of autonomy and accepted the idea of self-
positing subjectivity, but like Schelling, he believed that Fichte's highly subjective Idealism had not resolved the skepticism problem. Hence, Hegel also
tried to demonstrate the "objectivity" of our subjective capacities. As Pippin
describes it, Hegel's task was to understand the way in which Reason projects "itself as the order and stucture of what there is, all in a way not empir-
ically determined or metaphysically grounded; and . . . this problem, which
constitutes the content of speculative philosophy, is *some* sort of special re-
flexivity, a self-relation the results of which will not simply fix the limits of a
subjective faculty but will determine, 'absolutely,' *what there is*."[36] This special self-relation develops not as the apperceptive unity of an isolated, private, inner ego but as the faculty of an historical, social, collective subjectivity, which Pippin identifies with Hegel's notion of "Spirit." Hegel may have
gone beyond Kant in his theory of subjectivity, Pippin maintains, but he remained a critical Idealist preoccupied by the transcendental conditions of

34  Ibid., p. 30.
35  In addition to Pippin, see Neuhouser, *Fichte's Theory of Subjectivity*, especially chapters three
     and four.
36  Pippin, *Hegel's Idealism*, p. 69.

human knowledge and their adequacy to the world. Hence, Hegel's was a lifelong search for an "absolute or final account of what it is to know, and not a knowledge of a divine Absolute."[37]

Pippin's densely argued work deepens our understanding of Hegel's relationship to Kant and Fichte; moreover, by shearing Hegel's theory of subjectivity of all Platonic, Spinozist, and Christian trappings, Pippin has made him considerably more relevant, and palatable, to contemporary philosophers. However, as he himself acknowledges, Hegel was "the last philosopher in our tradition to have offered a positive account of the 'whole.' That is, he tried to understand the unity of such different domains as science, ethics, art, religion, politics, and philosophy."[38] In contrast to a study intent on delineating a "philosophically defensible" Hegel, a historical account must take seriously the holistic ambition that belongs integrally to any consideration of the historical Hegel and his impact on his contemporaries. This holds particularly for the domains of religion and metaphysics. The young Hegel studied theology at the Tübingen seminary, the mature Hegel produced a voluminous series of lectures in the philosophy of religion, and he always considered himself to be a Protestant philosopher. He was a full participant in his generation's preoccupation with the relationships between faith and knowledge, religion and philosophy, human and divine, although he arrived at a remarkably original position on every issue he addressed.

## Hegel's Speculative Recovery of Theology

Even Hegel's earliest works struck an original stance toward the central philosophical questions of his generation. The strong Kantian tenor of his 1795–6 essay "The Positivity of the Christian Religion," written while Hegel worked as a private tutor in Berne, yielded to a more critical stance toward the Kantian conception of Christianity as a religion of moral imperatives in his next major essay. "The Spirit of Christianity and Its Fate," probably written in 1798–9 in Frankfurt, pitted the abstract universality of Kant's ethics of duty against a conception of ethics that situates virtue within a communal context.[39] Hegel reconceived Christianity not as a religion of duty but as one of love, whose message of brotherhood he sought to make the basis of a new community bound by solidarity. Freely adapting Rousseau's notion

37   Ibid., p. 247.      38   Ibid., p. 260.
39   See "The Spirit of Christianity and Its Fate," *Early Theological Writings*, trans. T. M. Knox (Philadelphia, 1948), esp. pp. 214f and the pointed comment on the "self-coercion of Kantian virtue," p. 244.

of civic religion, Hegel could present Christianity as a *Volksreligion* capable of reconciling individual inclination and communal standards and overcoming the fragmentation and alienation of modern economic and political life.

Two observations are particularly relevant to our discussion. First, the young Hegel's new emphasis upon the actualization of ethics in specific, concrete, determinate social contexts signaled his emergence as a philosopher of "ethical life," or *Sittlichkeit*.[40] This remained his central sociopolitical concept for the rest of his life, even if his later work was to offer a much more elaborate formulation of the notion of *Sittlichkeit*. Second, his identification of Christianity as the unifying agent for ethical life anticipated his mature conception of the Christian principle of freedom. Even in the 1797–8 essay, Hegel's interest was less in the soteriological dimension of Christianity than in its capacity to provide a base for the actualization of ethical life in this world. To this end, Hegel challenged the Christian fixation on the unique status of Christ, the God-man, stressing instead the shared essence of man and Jesus Christ.[41] Consequently, Hegel believed that Christ had declared "himself against personality, against the view that his essence possessed an individuality opposed to that of those who had attained the culmination of friendship with him (against the thought of the personal God). . . ."[42] As this passage clearly shows, Hegel articulated a vision, not of pantheism or the deification of the human being, but of the potential of the human to become godlike through rising to the shared essence of divinity.[43] From very early in his career, Hegel made the denial of orthodox Christian personalism central to his intersecting conceptions of the divine itself, humanity's relation to the divine, and the actualization of "Christian" ethical life or *Sittlichkeit*. His mature philosophical system leaves no room for an omniscient and omnipotent personal God. Nonetheless, as he reconceptualized the philosophy of religion as part of his theory of absolute subjectivity, he strove more vigorously than the other Idealists to recover the idea of the personality of God.[44]

---

40  On this subject, see Dickey, *Hegel*, esp. pp. 181f.

41  "Spirit of Christianity," p. 239.

42  Ibid., pp. 269–70.

43  See the distinction between "becoming God-like" and "becoming God" used by Dickey, "Hegel on Religion and Philosophy," *The Cambridge Companion to Hegel*, ed. F. Beiser (Cambridge, 1993), p. 326. Hegel's comment in "Spirit of Christianity" (p. 239) illuminates the properly conceived relationship between human and divine: "Difference in might of spirit, in degree of force, is not unlikeness, but the weaker hangs on the superior like a child, or can be drawn up to him."

44  Claude Welch, *Protestant Thought in the Nineteenth Century, Volume 1, 1799–1870* (New Haven, 1972), p. 100, n26. See also the comment of Reardon, *Religion*, p. 18: "On the

Already in the *Phenomenology of Spirit* (1807), the great work that announced his departure from predecessors and contemporaries alike, Hegel
embedded his account of the development of human subjectivity within a
larger spiritual drama. The *Phenomenology* takes the form of a historical account of the movement of self-consciousness, each mode of thought yielding to another that transcends its contradictions yet preserves its partial
truths within a higher, more embracing comprehension of reality. Hegel
traced a complicated spiritual advancement, wherein human consciousness
moves through various forms of sense-certainty, empiricism, metaphysical
dogmatism, mysticism, and analytical rationalism (*Verstand*)[45] to arrive at
a higher form of reason (*Vernunft*) that penetrates the manifold of being,
recognizes the deeper unity underlying division – the so-called "identity of
identity and non-identity" – and incorporates into itself the movement of
contradiction and conflict that is the movement of the world itself. This is
the development of "Spirit" as Pippin describes it, an evolving social com-
petence that allows both objective knowledge and self-conscious awareness
of the subject's role in constituting knowledge. It is a historical development
not only toward "absolute knowledge" but also, significantly, toward absolute
freedom, because the progress of Reason promises to overcome all alienating externality. As Hegel wrote in the *Philosophy of Right*, "Since it is in
thought that I am first by myself, I do not penetrate an object until I understand it; it then ceases to stand over against me and I have taken from it
the character of its own which it had in opposition to me. . . . I am at home
in the world when I know it, still more so when I have understood it."[46]

The capacity of Reason to recognize itself in the world, to recognize its
own spontaneous activity in determining "what there is," may be plausibly
understood in the strictly transcendental terms that Pippin presents; however, Hegel's own ambitions seemed to extend beyond critical Idealism's
orientation toward questions of epistemology. Hence, Hegel identified the
development of human subjectivity with the emergence of finite spirit's consciousness of its participation in the self-realization of Absolute Spirit, or God,
in and through the world. The coming–to–self-consciousness that Hegel
traces in the history of human consciousness is nothing less than the coming–

whole, the Idealists had difficulty in reconciling infinity with both transcendence and personality: a transcendent infinite seemed a *contradictio in adiecto*, while a personal deity was
simply an anthropomorphism."

45   For Hegel's critique of Enlightenment "Understanding" (*Verstand*), see *Phenomenology of
Spirit*, trans. A. V. Miller (Oxford, 1977), pp. 329–55.

46   Hegel, *Philosophy of Right*, trans. T. M. Knox (New York, 1967), Addition to Paragraph 4,
p. 226.

to–self-consciousness of God, Absolute Spirit's self-conscious recognition of itself as "being all truth and [containing] all reality within that truth."[47] Every aspect of the Hegelian thesis of the identity of God and human knowledge has been subject to widely varying interpretations, as we will see when we turn to Hegel's opponents and followers alike. However, it seems likely that Hegel intended to suggest neither that God becomes man, nor that man becomes God; rather, their unity produces a new identity in self-conscious spirit: "The divine nature is the same as the human, and it is this unity that is beheld."[48] From this self-conscious unity, Hegel claimed, emerged absolute subjectivity as the principle and reality of the world. He considered this to be a crucial "correction" of Spinoza, whose description of God as universal substance lacks the element of subjectivity,[49] and of the young Schelling, whose conception of God as a vitalistic creative force of nature also left little room for the subjective. Even more important for our purposes, the claim that absolute subjectivity entails the identity in difference of human and divine laid the foundation for Hegel's attempt to recover the idea of personality for an absolute Idealist philosophy of religion.

Hegel's effort to preserve the idea of personality hinged on the contrast between "abstract" and "concrete" personality. Hegel criticized enlightened Understanding – which analyzes by dissection and division without revealing the unity beneath the surface disparity of objects – for its belief that each person has a "rigid, reserved, independent, self-centred existence." Significantly, Hegel anticipated the concerns of his disciples when he attributed the same abstract conception of personhood to the Protestant sects of his age.[50] Abstract personhood, Hegel argued, must be superseded by a more concrete form once it is recognized that the self develops through processes of mutual recognition. In the structure of recognition, so important to the dialectical moves of the *Phenomenology*, the self comes to realize that its own identity is formed by a subtle play of independence from and dependence on others, because self-consciousness requires recognition of its existence from others, just as it must acknowledge both the affinity and the otherness of the other if that recognition is to have meaning. Hegel's lectures on the

47  *Phenomenology*, p. 415.    48  Ibid., p. 460.
49  See Jaeschke, *Reason in Religion*, p. 253; and G.H.R. Parkinson, "Hegel, Pantheism, and Spinoza," *Journal of the History of Ideas*, 3, 38(1977), pp. 449–59. Interestingly, Parkinson argues that Hegel's criticism of Spinoza is wrong, in part because he was too quick to assimilate Spinoza to an "oriental intuition" of universal substance, but also because his reading of Spinoza was distorted by his disagreement with Schelling, whose nature philosophy Hegel was inclined to project onto Spinoza.
50  Andrew Shanks, *Hegel's Political Theology* (Cambridge, 1991), pp. 66–7.

philosophy of religion in the 1820s describe "concrete personality" as the product of the process of recognition in relationships of love. Such a relationship alienates the abstract, isolated person in another, but it thereby extends personality toward universality: "It is just this winning back of personality by the act of absorption, by the being absorbed into the other, which constitutes the true nature of personality."[51] We shall see in subsequent chapters that Hegel's contrast between "abstract" and "concrete" personality became a volatile and ambiguous issue in the controversies between Hegelians and their opponents. Although Hegel himself was surely aware of the controversial nature of his conception of concrete personality, he could hardly have anticipated the volatility of an idea that held vital importance for every aspect of his mature philosophy.

In the philosophy of religion, Hegel applied the model of concrete personality to the fundamental Christian doctrine of the Trinity. According to Hegel, enlightened understanding founders on the notion of a personal God because it can conceive only abstract personality and so cannot go beyond orthodoxy's "childlike" conception of the three distinct persons of the Father, the Son, and the Holy Spirit. Conversely, Hegel argued that the notion of the Trinity expresses the truth of divine personhood, understood *concretely* as the self-relation of personality in the other:

> We say that God eternally begets His Son, that God distinguishes Himself from Himself, and thus we begin to say of God that He does this, and that in being in the Other whom He has brought into definite existence, or posited, He is simply with Himself, has not gone outside of Himself, and this is the form of love; but, at the same time, we ought to know that God is Himself just this entire act. God is the beginning; He does this definite thing; but He is equally the end only, the totality, and it is as totality that God is Spirit. God thought of simply as the Father is not yet the True.[52]

Despite the importance of this idea of personality for Hegel and, incidentally, for later nineteenth-century interpretations of the Trinity, his orthodox contemporaries found it to be pretty weak fare. Indeed, it is not at all surprising that conservative theologians had more than a little trouble recognizing the loving personal God of Christian dogma in Hegel's philosophical formulation.

Hegel's idea of the Absolute presupposes that "the object of religion as well as philosophy is eternal truth in its objectivity, God and nothing but

---

51 Hegel, *Lectures on the Philosophy of Religion*, vol. 3, trans. E. B. Speirs and J. Burdon Sanderson (London, 1962), pp. 24–5.
52 Ibid., p. 12.

God, and the explication of God."[53] It is well known, however, that although Hegel believed that religious faith and philosophical knowledge share an identical object, he nonetheless distinguished between the form in which religion and philosophy express that content. Religion apprehends the Absolute "naïvely" because it does not recognize its absolute content "thinkingly" but rather represents this content "pictorially," symbolically, as a divinely revealed narrative of events. Consequently, religious consciousness knows the truth of religion in an unfree way, receiving that truth from authority instead of as a free determination of the self. Philosophy, in Hegel's view, appropriates the content of religion by demonstrating the rational necessity of the core of truth in religion. For Hegel, this did not mean the point-by-point rationalization of religious dogma as theological rationalists and even some of Hegel's own disciples attempted but rather the transfiguration and supersession of religious representation in philosophical truth. In typical Hegelian fashion, this was to be an *Aufhebung*, a supersession that preserves what it overcomes. Hence, Hegel seemed to believe that philosophy comes to the rescue of a religious content that cannot defend itself against the withering critique of Enlightenment.

Hegel sounded a pessimistic note about the meaning of the strategic retreat of Christianity into philosophy in his 1821 lectures when he envisioned philosophy as a "sanctuary" for religion, with the new priesthood of philosophers pledged to shepherd the Truth from a hostile or indifferent world.[54] In fact, however, the general thrust of Hegel's thinking on this subject in the 1820s was much less resigned. Far from depicting Christianity as homeless in the world, most of Hegel's work in the 1820s demonstrated his belief that his philosophical appropriation broadened and enriched Christianity, rather than displacing or effacing traditional cultic practice. Moreover, his entire metaphysics hinged on his conviction that the world was becoming more and more "Christian," albeit in a refigured philosophical form. That is, religion's taking refuge in the Concept meant the actualization of Christianity's innermost truths in the world, because the Concept was nothing more nor less than the comprehension of actuality.[55] Not only the four lecture series on the philosophy of religion given during the 1820s, but also the lectures on the philosophy of history express this conviction. Hegel's

53  Hegel, *Lectures on the Philosophy of Religion*, vol. 1, p. 19. See also his opening remarks in *The Science of Logic*, trans. A. V. Miller (New York, 1976), p. 3.
54  *Lectures on the Philosophy of Religion*, vol. 3, p. 151.
55  See Jaeschke, *Reason in Religion*, pp. 350–1; Jaeschke, "Christianity and Secularity in Hegel's Concept of the State," *The Journal of Religion*, 61, 1981, pp. 127–45; and Dickey, "Hegel on Religion and Philosophy," pp. 309–11.

38        DETHRONING THE SELF

intentions here seem clear enough, but the results of the transmigration of religion into philosophy were anything but clear. A philosophical recovery of religion that appoints thought as the "absolute judge before which the content must verify and attest its claims" has, after all, sworn its first loyalty to rational critique.[56] As the subsequent history of the Hegelian School showed, religion in any recognizable form is unlikely to survive such a trial despite the initial good will of the judge.

According to Hegel, the rational appropriation of religion's truth required philosophical comprehension of the role of historical religion in the development of human consciousness of the Absolute. His writings in the mid-1790s had criticized positive religions because, in the Kantian view he then held, they were external restrictions on the moral autonomy of the rational self, but in his mature thought, he came to regard positive religions as legitimate, though subordinate, aspects of genuine religion.[57] However, unlike Schleiermacher, who had viewed all the historical faiths as variants on the eternal truth of the one true religion,[58] Hegel placed the history of specific religions within the larger historical process of the evolution of consciousness. This understanding of the history of religion was already present in the *Phenomenology*, as was the essential idea of the metaphysics of religion that Hegel held until his death in 1831.[59] In lectures of 1821, 1824, 1827, and 1831, the philosophy of religion gained still greater systematic exposition, and the *history* of religion won greater influence on the system-

---

56  *Lectures on the Philosophy of Religion*, vol. 3, p. 148.
57  See Fackenheim, *Religious Dimension*, p. 53.
58  Jaeschke in *Reason in Religion*, pp. 113–16, observes that Schleiermacher's stress on the "intuition of the universe" as the true content of all faiths radically depreciates the historical features of religion. His charge that this led Schleiermacher into "total subjectivism," however, does not take adequate account of controversies between those who see Schleiermacher as the father of modern religious individualism and those who emphasize the social dimension in his thought. For the former position, which equates religious individualism with liberal individualism, see esp. Yorick Spiegel, *Theologie der bürgerliche Gesellschaft: Sozialphilosophie und Glaubenslehre bei Friedrich Schleiermacher* (Munich, 1968), and Richard Crouter's response, "Schleiermacher and the Theology of Bourgeois Society: A Critique of the Critics," *Journal of Religion*, 66(1986). Claude Welch, *Protestant Thought*, pp. 66–8, counters the subjectivist charge by emphasizing that the individual's relation is always to something *other* than himself. The tensions between radical individuality and the community of faith in Schleiermacher's thought are explored in Gerald N. Izenberg's *Impossible Individuality. Romanticism, Revolution, and the Origins of Modern Selfhood, 1787–1802* (Princeton, 1992), pp. 18–27; and Günther Wenz, "Neuzeitliches Christentum als Religion der Individualität? Einige Bemerkungen zur Geschichte protestantischer Theologie im 19. Jahrhundert," *Individualität*, ed. Manfred Frank and Anselm Haverkamp (Munich, 1988), esp. pp. 127–9.
59  Jaeschke, *Reason in Religion*, p. 184.

atic form of the philosophy of religion.[60] On this view, all historical religions prior to Christianity contain "some truth" as the different moments of the gradual yet determinate self-revelation and self-realization of spirit, but they are fragmentary, representing a bifurcation in spirit between consciousness and self-consciousness.[61] That is, the religious consciousness does not recognize its connection to the object of religion. So the moment of freedom is displaced in Greek religion from the life of the polis into the Olympian gods, in Old Testament Judaism from the believer to the omnipotent God and His law, and in Roman religion from the individual person to the divinized Emperor. Christianity consummates the history of religion, Hegel maintained, for it alone among the world's faiths attributes freedom to human beings as such, in their full worth as persons.

Hegel's thoughts on the emergence of Christianity from the legacy of the anthropomorphic Greek divinities and Judaic monotheism, the religion of "sublimity" that he came to regard as the representation of the pure spirit of mankind, cannot detain us here. For the present discussion, it is enough to consider Walter Jaeschke's observation that from the publication of the *Phenomenology* to his death, Hegel believed that the "immediate presupposition of Christianity was not the religion of the Old Testament, but the Roman world."[62] For in the emergence of Christianity, Hegel detected the dialectical supersession of the Roman political and legal principle of personality. It was Roman jurisprudence that first defined personhood, but it did so in inadequate terms, Hegel believed. In Hegel's interpretation of that history, the Roman self had retreated from all concrete embodiments in reaction to the collapse of the classical *polis*, where the substantial community had proven itself incompatible with subjective selfhood.[63] Roman law reflected this withdrawal into interiority, for it assigned to the self a universal and abstract "legal status" as "person," rather than as a uniquely endowed particular self or as a member of a particular *polis*. The dignity of the person was thus recognized in Roman law's guarantee of personal "rights," but these rights and this person were strictly abstract, the Romans having exchanged a richly

60  Ibid., p. 208.
61  See Hegel, *Werke*, vol. 12, p. 242.
62  Walter Jaeschke, "Christianity and Secularity," p. 134. See esp. Hegel, *Werke*, vol. 12, p. 386.
63  See in particular *Phenomenology*, pp. 279–89. It should be observed that selfhood is not simply pitted against community in the *polis* but develops out of the tension between the *polis*'s dependence upon individual ethical action and its need to cancel that individual action in order to preserve its substantial unity as an ethical order. This was the conflict that Hegel identified in the myth of Antigone. In a sense, then, the "person" of Roman law is the graduate of the *polis*.

shared common life for a *universal* community that is "soulless and dead, and is alive only in the *single* individual, *qua* single."

Atomized and "empty," the person seeks his or her content in a "manifold existence in the form of 'possession' and . . . stamps it with the same abstract universality, whereby it is called 'property.'"[64] The right of personality in Roman law is thus reduced to the right of property and exchange, because subjectivity can be understood only as the assertion of the self's mastery over external reality. True to Hegel's system, in which nothing is ever lost, he did not believe that the right of personality was ever abandoned once it had entered the world. Indeed, as we shall see in Chapter 2, his understanding of the modern rational freedom of the person unified the juristic and religio-philosophical dimensions of the history of "personhood." Nonetheless, the Roman legal definition of personality was inadequate because its abstract formalism separated the person from a substantial community, thereby denying the self a concrete life while subjecting him to an ethical order that nevertheless continued to exist but came to be vested in the one person of the emperor.[65] Moreover, by making personal right depend on the ability to own property, Roman law denied personhood to the propertyless.

According to Hegel, Christianity replaced this imperfect concept with a truly universal *and* concrete concept of personhood. "The positive moment in the conception of the personality and freedom of the human," writes Walter Jaeschke, "lies in the religious knowledge that the absolute Being is a specific self-consciousness, and man has infinite value as man, not just in other respects. Expressed theologically: the human is the object of God's infinite love."[66] Expressed philosophically, it is only in Christianity that the "cardinal distinction" between consciousness and self-consciousness is overcome, that God is "*thought of* as self-consciousness." For the divine ceases to be something "alien to the self's knowledge only when the self has produced it and therefore beholds the determination of the object as its *own*, consequently beholds *itself* in the object."[67] Christianity is thus the "Absolute Religion" because God and man come to self-consciousness in the mutually interpenetrating self-relation of the self in the other – that is, in the relational formation of concrete personality. This is *represented* in religious consciousness as the incarnation of God in his Son and *comprehended* by philosophy as the

---

64   Ibid., pp. 289–91.
65   The nullification of private persons by the one person of the emperor is discussed with particular clarity in *The Philosophy of History*. See *Werke*, vol. 12, p. 387.
66   Jaeschke, "Christianity and Secularity," pp. 134–5.
67   *Phenomenology*, p. 417.

unity in difference of human and divine, of finite and infinite, in free subjectivity and selfhood. Christianity is thus not a religion of a specific people or tribe, for it makes a universal claim on the human as such. Nor is it merely "positive" like the other determinate religions; its tenets are revealed, but they are also the very movement of consciousness and inwardly appropriable as such. Consciousness knows no limitation in Christianity, Hegel believed, for it has recognized itself in the divine. Unity of man and God is thereby reconciled to the post-Kantian demand for the rational autonomy of the subject.

## Pietism and Orthodoxy against Hegel

Some of Hegel's pupils saw clearly the deep ambiguities in Hegel's philosophical appropriation of Christianity, as when the young Marx asked, "What kind of clients are those whom the defending lawyer can only save from conviction by killing them himself?"[68] However, the majority of Hegel's followers in the 1820s and 1830s chose to interpret his philosophy of religion conservatively. So, the leading figures of the Hegelian School that began to form in Berlin after Hegel accepted Fichte's former chair in philosophy at the University of Berlin in 1818 believed that far from challenging orthodoxy, the philosophical appropriation of religious content would reinvigorate traditional belief because it appeared to rescue Christian dogma from skepticism without compromising its essential message. John Toews writes that Christian Hegelians like Philipp Marheinecke, Karl Daub, Karl Friedrich Göschel, Kasimir Conradi, and Isaak Rust all placed an "overwhelming emphasis on the identity of content rather than the difference of form between Christian religion and Hegelian philosophy, and thus [stripped] Hegel's philosophy of religion of most of its critical, dynamic, historical qualities."[69] A smaller number of Hegelians were more acutely aware of the tension between religion and philosophy, and they recognized the significant difference between religious and philosophical cognition of the Absolute. Hence, after a long intellectual and personal struggle with the implications of Hegelianism, Karl Rosenkranz formulated an influential "new accommodation" between faith and reason that emphasized the transfiguring power of philosophy, rather than the mere preservation of dogma. A still smaller group of Hegelians rejected even this tepid accommodation. As early as 1823, Hermann Hinrichs and Christian Kapp both claimed that philosophy,

68   Karl Marx, *Collected Works*, vol. 1 (New York, 1976), p. 103.
69   Toews, *Hegelianism*, p. 151.

not theology, was the only path to knowledge of God. For Kapp, the more radical of the two, the transition from religious to philosophical consciousness was so fundamental that he regarded it as nothing less than a change in epoch.

Very few non-Hegelian Christians entertained seriously the notion that Hegel was anything but poisonous to religious faith. Opposition to Hegel's philosophy of religion united otherwise disparate groups, ranging from biblical fundamentalists to more sophisticated philosophers of religion and politics. However, although their approaches to Hegel varied widely, they ultimately shared a similar goal. Against what they perceived as Hegel's pan-logical system and its apparent negation of the personal God, Hegel's opponents all sought to recover the "living," "free," "actual," "personal" God.[70] The effort to salvage the God of orthodox theism, whether through orthodox or "speculative" means, was linked to a parallel effort to preserve the personality of the individual, made in God's image, against the corrosive effect of Hegel's allegedly anti-individualist system.

This anti-Hegelian discourse grew very strong in the 1830s and prompted a range of responses from Hegelians; but by 1830, debate about Hegel's philosophy of religion had already directed attention to the central question of the personality of God. Hegel's association with the youthful Schelling's philosophy of nature during their years together at the University of Jena in the early 1800s had established his reputation as a pantheist, and despite his increasingly explicit criticism of Schelling, many considered him a Schellingian even in the 1820s.[71] Prior to around 1816, Hegel had been overshadowed by the persistence of Romanticism, which had found a congenial atmosphere in the religious and nationalist fervor aroused by the wars against Napoleon, but just as his following grew modestly from the small but fervent circle that had gathered in his last two years at Jena, so too did critical scrutiny of his work. His arrival in Berlin in 1818 brought the philosopher a fame unmatched in his early career, and with this new prominence came public debate about the meaning of his work. Controversy about his politics was sparked by his lectures on political philosophy in 1818–19 and the publication of the *Philosophy of Right* in 1821, in which he polemicized against the Historical School of Law, the reactionary Carl Ludwig von Haller, and the Romantic nationalist J. J. Fries; and his lectures on the philosophy of re-

70 Jaeschke, *Reason in Religion*, p. 400.
71 F. W. Graf, "Der Untergang des Individuums. Ein Vorschlag zur historisch-systematischen Rekonstruktion der theologischen Hegel-Kritik," *Die Flucht in den Begriff. Materialien zu Hegels Religionsphilosophie*, ed. F. W. Graf and F. Wagner (Stuttgart, 1982), p. 280.

ligion, first given in 1821, provoked even more reaction. At the same time, Hegel decisively alienated the other "philosophical" school of theology, the Schleiermacheans. In a preface to a book by Hermann Hinrichs in 1822, Hegel delivered the strongest thrust in a public duel with Schleiermacher that had begun with Hegel's support of the dismissal of Christian de Wette, a friend of Schleiermacher's, from the University of Berlin and quickly escalated into a conflict between Schleiermacher's theology of feeling and Hegel's speculative philosophy of religion.[72]

Schleiermacher was not immune to the suspicions of orthodox theologians and Pietists,[73] but Hegel's endorsement of Hinrichs' strong claims for the superiority of philosophical over theological knowledge and his support of Karl Daub and Philipp Marheinecke in their polemics against Schleiermacher confirmed the orthodox in their belief that Hegel was a pantheist, a Spinozist, or a panlogist, all descriptions that in the orthodox parlance of the day amounted to a charge of atheism.[74] The Pietistic theologian August von Tholuck advanced this charge aggressively in an anonymous 1823 work,[75] and the accusation that Hegel's system negated the personal God became the stock in trade of conservative Protestants such as Ernst Hengstenberg, editor of the *Evangelische Kirchenzeitung*, the major organ of theological and political reaction founded in 1827 by the Pietists Ludwig von Gerlach and Adolf Le Coq. These attacks on Hegel came as part of a mounting conservative attempt to police religious discourse, an intensely politicized campaign against heterodoxy that must be understood as a response to the evolution of Prussian Protestantism in the first decades of the nineteenth century.

The convergence of two phenomena decisively shaped Prussian Protestantism in the years after 1815. First of all, the union of Calvinist Reformed

---

72  See H.F.W. Hinrichs, *Die Religion im inneren Verhältnisse zur Wissenschaft: Nebst Darstellung und Beurtheilung der von Jacobi, Kant, Fichte und Schelling gemachten Versuche dieselbe wissenschaftlich zu erfassen, und nach ihrem Hauptinhalte zu entwickeln, mit einem Vorworte von G.W.F. Hegel* (Heidelberg, 1822; reprint, Brussels, 1970). The conflict between Schleiermacher and Hegel is well documented. See Toews, *Hegelianism*, pp. 49–67; and Richard Crouter, "Hegel and Schleiermacher at Berlin: A Many-Sided Debate," *Journal of the American Academy of Religion*, 48(March, 1980), pp. 19–43. More recently, Jeffrey Hoover has argued that the conflict originated in Schleiermacher's concern that Hegel's appointment to Berlin would augment the rightward shift in Prussian politics. See "The Origin of the Conflict Between Hegel and Schleiermacher at Berlin," *Owl of Minerva*, 20, 1 (Fall 1988), pp. 69–79.

73  On the strained relationship between Schleiermacher and the leaders of the Awakening, see Robert M. Bigler, *The Politics of German Protestantism. The Rise of the Protestant Church Elite in Prussia, 1815–1848* (Berkeley, 1972), pp. 131–2.

74  See Graf and Wagner, "Einleitung," pp. 28–9.

75  Jaeschke, *Reason in Religion*, p. 362.

and Lutheran churches in 1822 greatly augmented the existing alliance between Protestant orthodoxy and political authority. At the end of the War of
Liberation, numerous German sovereigns had moved to reunite the Protestant faiths within their territorial churches. This policy was pursued vigorously by the Prussian king, Friedrich Wilhelm III, a pious Calvinist who
wished to reconcile the Lutheran majority to his own beliefs. In 1822,
Friedrich Wilhelm III's ecclesiastical and liturgical reforms climaxed in the
creation of the Prussian Union (*Preussische Landeskirche*), a unified state
church with a common liturgy and a rigid ecclesiastical structure with the
Prussian king designated *summus episcopus*. The Union met initial resistance
from both Calvinists and Lutherans, but by 1830 the new ecclesiastical organization had gained wide acceptance.[76] Of course, an extremely close relationship between ruler and religion had always existed in Lutheran lands,
and the supervision of all religious denominations had been a prerogative
of the Prussian absolutist state throughout the eighteenth century.[77] But
whereas in the time of the irreligious Friedrich II the regulation of religion
had become little more than a political expedient in the name of domestic
harmony,[78] the appearance of the devout Friedrich Wilhelm III, intensely
interested in liturgical reform, and the union of faiths under his control
were bound to tighten the interweaving of politics and religion in Prussia.
Especially after the revolutionary tumults from 1789 to 1815, Friedrich Wilhelm clearly regarded the assertion of neo-orthodoxy in the church as an
inseparable part of the task of restoring political authority to the monarchical state.

The second factor shaping Prussian Protestantism was the revival and
transformation of Pietism in the 1810s and 1820s. Religious revivalism was

---

76  I draw this description largely from W. O. Shanahan, *German Protestants Face the Social
    Question. Volume 1. The Conservative Phase, 1815–1871* (Notre Dame, 1954), pp. 94f and
    Bigler, *Politics of German Protestantism*, pp. 3–75. See also Robert M. Berdahl, *The Politics of
    the Prussian Nobility. The Development of a Conservative Ideology, 1770–1848* (Princeton,
    1988), p. 251. Hegel maintained a studied silence on this issue, although his *Philosophy of
    Right* makes clear his opposition to the unity of church and state.

77  The nature of the relationship between the ruler and the church varied more widely
    among the Calvinist German states. Heinz Schilling distinguishes usefully between the
    "civic Calvinism" of northwest Germany, where the defense of communal autonomy in po-
    litical and religious matters was paramount, and the "court Calvinism" of those areas
    where the ruler and the state forged a close alliance with the Calvinist church. See
    Schilling, *Civic Calvinism in Northwestern Germany and the Netherlands: Sixteenth to Nineteenth
    Centuries* (Kirksville, Mo., 1992).

78  Günther Birtsch, "The Christian as Subject. The Worldly Mind of Prussian Protestant The-
    ologians in the Late Enlightenment Period," *The Transformation of Political Culture. England
    and Germany in the Late Eighteenth Century*, ed. Eckhart Hellmuth (Oxford, 1990), pp. 310–11.

part of a general western European reaction against the rationalism of the Enlightenment and the excesses of the revolutionary epoch, but in Prussia, the "Awakening"of the 1820s also tapped into the powerful currents of Pietism that had exerted great influence over German culture in the eighteenth century. However, quite unlike the spontaneous formation of lay devotional societies among commoners that had characterized Pietism at the end of the 1700s, the Awakening was preeminently a movement organized by aristocratic and intellectual elites. In Toews's apt phrase, this was a "revival from above."[79] The revival thrived among the Pomeranian nobility, led by the von Below brothers, Adolf von Thadden, and the von Gerlach brothers. Their dominance gave the movement a profoundly conservative cast, strengthened by the web of relationships that formed among Pietist nobles and bourgeois intellectuals in Berlin, notably the orthodox theologians Ernst Hengstenberg, August Tholuck, and Johannes Wichern. Even Friedrich von Savigny, the great legal scholar, opened his home to regular devotional meetings.[80]

In the initial stages of the Awakening, many of the Junker Pietists embraced the original emphasis of seventeenth- and eighteenth-century Pietism upon intense inward religious experience, a personal relation to God, and the literal acceptance of the Lutheran idea of the priesthood of all believers. The mixed legacy of these Pietist beliefs led Prussian officials initially to view the Awakening with some suspicion.[81] On one side, the profoundly private and individualistic nature of Pietism could produce a spiritual retreat from political and social engagement. On the other side, Pietism challenged existing religious and political institutions by the very nature of the Pietists' desire for authentic relations among men and between men and God. In the seventeenth and eighteenth centuries, this frequently translated into practical reform impulses aimed at actualizing Pietism's millennarian hopes for godly relations on earth.[82] Government misgivings soon faded, however, not only because the Awakening grew increasingly conservative in its doctrine but also because Crown Prince Friedrich Wilhelm declared his sympathies for religious revivalism. Conforming to the pressures of its aristocratic provenance, the revival itself began to regard earlier Pietism's emphasis on inward,

79  Toews, *Hegelianism*, p. 245.
80  Ibid., pp. 246–7. See also Robert M. Bigler, "The Social Status and Political Role of the Protestant Clergy in Pre-March Prussia," *Sozialgeschichte Heute. Festschrift für Hans Rosenberg zum 70. Geburtstag,* ed. Hans-Ulrich Wehler (Göttingen, 1974), p. 176.
81  See Bigler, *Politics of German Protestantism*, p. 93.
82  See Shanahan, *German Protestants*, p. 31, and the discussion of Württemberg's "down-to-earth Pietism" in Laurence Dickey, *Hegel*, pp. 40–137.

subjective religious experience as a potentially subversive force. This became a Pietism of the Word, wary of enthusiasm and committed to fostering absolute obedience to church and state by purifying Protestantism in accordance with the Augsburg Confession and the original teachings of the early Protestant reformers.

The sense of urgency that the Pietists attached to their program of doctrinal repristination and subjection to divinely ordained authority was greatly intensified by news of the July Revolution in Paris. One of the immediate products of the reaction against the Revolution of 1830 was the founding of *Das Berliner Politische Wochenblatt*, a journal that came to dominate Prussian conservatism for a decade with its blend of authoritarian theology and the feudalist political theory of Carl Ludwig von Haller. Faced by the specter of revived republicanism, conservative Lutherans, Calvinists, and Pietists converged in the 1820s to form a broad front in Prussia committed to enforcing orthodoxy and linking their theology to a "restorative" political program. The "Christian-German" state that they envisioned was to unify "throne and altar" under the same principle of legitimacy, "authority, not majority," in Friedrich Julius Stahl's pregnant phrase.[83]

Even though divergent tendencies were beginning to appear by 1827, common political and theological enemies held neo-Pietists and orthodox Calvinists and Lutherans together in the 1820s.[84] In theology, the main target of neo-orthodoxy was the tradition of enlightened rationalistic faith that had come to dominate Prussian Protestantism by the end of the eighteenth century. By the 1790s, not only prominent literary figures like Lessing, but also many pastors, including most of the leadership of the Protestant Church in Prussia, had elevated the ethical message of Christianity over the soteriological mysteries of the supernatural faith, and they had mitigated the doctrine of original sin with a belief that human volition could choose the path of goodness.[85] Enlightened rationalism was anathema to the conservative Pietists and other orthodox Protestants, who found it appalling that so many clerical leaders could espouse a creed that in their view was the

83  Welch, *Protestant Thought*, vol. 1, pp. 194–8.
84  Toews, *Hegelianism*, p. 247.
85  On theological rationalism, see Welch, *Protestant Thought*, vol. 1, pp. 30–51. On its political implications, see Hans Rosenberg, "Theologischer Rationalismus und vormärzlicher Vulgärliberalismus," *Politische Denkströmungen im deutschen Vormärz* (Göttingen, 1972). See Dickey, *Hegel*, pp. 17–32, on the "Pelagian" aspect of this *Aufklärung* emphasis on the role played by human will in attaining salvation. On the dissemination of rationalism within the clergy, see Birtsch, "Christian as Subject," p. 315.

source of all evils, including the French Revolution with its subversion of religious, social, and political legitimacy.[86] The conservatives' intense efforts to gain ascendancy within Prussian Protestantism and politics and to drive rationalists from the clergy and the theology faculties of the universities form the background for their increasingly vitriolic attacks on Hegel.

Hegel's rising star made him appear as the chief heir to the Enlightenment and the arch-rationalist of the 1820s. His belief in the rational appropriation of religious dogma by philosophy suggested an arrogant and heretical self-apotheosis, and it made him an extraordinarily unwelcome ally of revealed religion. After all, in the eyes of devout Christians, Hegel's system, in contrast to the bald hostilities of self-professed atheists, threatened to destroy revealed religion in the very act of saving its rational truths. Virtually from the start of his years in Berlin, Hegel recognized just how uncertain his position actually was within Prussia's fractious religious politics. He saw that in fact his influence was quite limited, confined to his academic supporters and a few sympathetic civil servants. In this climate, it is not surprising that his responses to his critics were aggressive and cautious by turns. We have already seen that he did not hesitate to lash out at his theological and political opponents. Yet he also felt constrained to answer their charges, ample evidence that accusations of pantheism and Spinozism had lost none of their force since the "Pantheism Controversy" of the 1780s.

Hence, in essays in the *Jahrbücher für wissenschaftliche Kritik,* the main journal of the Berlin Hegelians, and in the second edition of his *Encyclopedia,* Hegel tried to clarify his religious position. He claimed to be neither an atheist nor a pantheist, and he disavowed the intention of divinizing man or elevating his philosophy above Christianity.[87] Against the charge that his system was a form of panlogism that subordinates freedom to logical necessity, he emphasized the activist and transformative dimension in the struggle to actualize the Christian principle in modern life – that is, the struggle to make the abstract concept of speculative philosophy the concrete principle of ethical life. This orientation established some basis for connections between Hegel and the more progressive of his followers, men like August Cieszkowski, Friedrich Wilhelm Carové, and Friedrich Richter, so-called "old-left Hegelians" who envisioned the Hegelian dialectic as an open-ended progression of the World Spirit and of the historical spirit of humanity.[88] Yet in fact

86   Bigler, "Social Status," p. 181.
87   Laurence Dickey, "Hegel on Religion and Philosophy," p. 309.
88   Toews develops the category of "old-left Hegelianism" in distinction to the "new-left

Hegel revealed considerable ambivalence toward those of his followers who collapsed the identity within difference of humanity and God into a doctrine of the full divinization of human being. To deflate criticisms of his "un-Christian" views, Hegel insisted on the capacity of speculative philosophy to live side-by-side with traditional religion: If he could proclaim boldly the need to carry the Idea into the world, he could also argue blandly for the identical essence of philosophy and religion. His public and private writings include professions of faith in the activist cause of the Idea, but they also include a favorable review of the orthodox presentation of his system offered by his conservative student, the Naumberg jurist Karl F. Göschel.[89] In the late 1820s, Hegel clearly waffled on the progressivist-critical potential of his philosophy of religion, displaying a timidity that was also evident in his last political pronouncements.[90]

Whether this accommodationist stance expressed Hegel's increasing conservatism or an astute political calculation is a matter of some controversy, but whatever his motives, his efforts to defend himself against conservative attacks were not very successful. His ambivalence toward the critical tendencies of his own thought made him appear disingenuous in the eyes of his critics, and his failure to clarify his position added in the mid-1830s to confusion within the Hegelian School itself over the "true" meaning of his system. More important, his responses were characteristically couched in philosophical terms, whereas his Pietist and orthodox critics were interested less in philosophic dialogue than in judging whether his conclusions conformed to Christian dogma, a criterion by which he was found signally wanting. The quality of debate did improve somewhat with the posthumous publication of Hegel's *Lectures on the Philosophy of Religion* in 1832, insofar as henceforth, all parties had to refer to the same textual evidence. However, whereas Hegelians such as Karl Rosenkranz and Philipp Marheinecke, the editor of the *Lectures*, had hoped that the new text would educate Hegel's critics, it served instead to confirm their prejudices.[91]

Hegelians" like Feuerbach or Bruno Bauer who envisioned history in strictly immanent and humanist terms. See *Hegelianism*, esp. pp. 241–3.

89 Hegel's review of Göschel has been translated by Clark Butler in *Clio*, no. 17–18(1988–9). See also *Hegel: The Letters*, trans. and ed. Clark Butler and Christiane Seiler (Bloomington, 1984), pp. 537–8; and Graf and Wagner, "Einleitung," pp. 32–4.

90 See, for example, Hegel's quarrel with his liberal follower Eduard Gans over the Revolution of 1830, discussed in W. R. Beyer, "Gans' Vorrede zur Hegelschen Rechtsphilosophie," *Archiv für Rechts- und Sozialphilosophie*, 45(1959), p. 259.

91 Graf and Wagner, "Einleitung," pp. 36–37.

## The Speculative Theists

Orthodox theists such as August von Tholuck, Ernst Hengstenberg, and the erstwhile Hegelian Heinrich Leo contributed much to the shrillness of the debate about Hegel but little to the substantive discussion of his philosophy of religion. By contrast, the so-called "Speculative Theists" of the 1830s sought more sophisticated philosophic responses to Hegel, although their ultimate goal was in many respects similar to that of their orthodox contemporaries. The leaders of Speculative Theism, C. H. Weisse (1801–66) and Immanuel Hermann Fichte (1796–1862), and the contributors to Fichte's *Zeitschrift für Philosophie und spekulative Theologie*, founded in 1837, did not form a unified "school," but they were united in their demand that philosophy recover the "personal God." In 1868, Fichte recalled that at the height of the philosophic campaign against Hegel's "panlogism" and the "necessity of his dialectical process," he and Weisse "inscribed [our] banner with the principle of individualism, freedom and personality."[92] Prominent in its own day, virtually forgotten in ours, the Speculative Theism of Weisse and Fichte deeply influenced the development of philosophic and academic theological anti-Hegelianism in the 1830s.

Even in the 1820s, both I. H. Fichte and C. H. Weisse regarded knowledge of the personal God as the highest goal of speculation, although they disagreed on the way to reach that goal.[93] Weisse, a professor of philosophy at Leipzig, regarded Hegel in a more positive light than did Fichte.[94] Indeed, Weisse considered himself a follower of Hegel for a time in the late 1820s, but his enthusiasm was short-lived, and his development took him in a different direction. Even when he urged Hegel to adopt a more activist stance *vis à vis* his own dialectical method, he did not really mean what progressive "old-left" Hegelians meant. Whereas the old-left advocated an open-ended view of the dialectic – the ever-closer approximation of the identity of human and divine – Weisse actually pressed Hegel to step outside of the

---

92  I. H. Fichte, "Bericht über meine philosophische Selbstbildung, als Einleitung zu den '*Vermischten Schriften*' und als Beitrag zur Geschichte nachhegel'scher Philosophie," in *Vermischte Schriften zur Philosophie, Theologie und Ethik*, vol. 1 (Leipzig, 1869), p. 62.

93  See Fichte's *Sätze zur Vorschule der Theologie* (1826) quoted in Jaeschke, *Reason in Religion*, p. 368; and Weisse's *Über den gegenwärtigen Standpunct der philosophischen Wissenschaft, in besonderer Beziehung auf das System Hegels* (1829), cited in Graf, "Untergang," p. 285.

94  For biographical information, see Kurt Leese, *Philosophie und Theologie im Spätidealismus. Forschungen zur Auseinandersetzung von Christentum und idealistischer Philosophie im 19. Jahrhundert* (Berlin, 1929), p. 10. See also Albert Hartmann, *Der Spätidealismus und die hegelsche Dialektik* (Berlin, 1937).

logical circuit of his philosophy, to move "to something higher" rather than
to "return to the absolute beginning."[95]

Weisse never pitted himself antithetically against Hegel, but he believed
that it was his responsibility to take the step to something higher and thereby
complete and correct Idealism. While he praised Hegel for describing the
nature of the Absolute as "pure subjectivity," he rejected the equation of the
Absolute of pure thought with the living, personal God. According to Weisse,
Hegel's recognition of God as pure subjectivity created the possibility for the
idea of personality, but he had remained too wedded to his own conception
of "Gottheit" as "spirit in its universality."[96] Against this formal, "negative"
definition of the Absolute, which Weisse believed devalued God's *objective*
existence by reducing Him to universal subjectivity, Weisse tried to develop
a "positive" idea of the personal God. To this end, he adopted Hegel's *Geistesgeschichte* method but traced a different narrative toward a very different
conclusion. He agreed with Hegel that in the history of spirit, men's ideas
of God receive ever-greater clarification. However, where Hegel's system had
led to the self-identification of the human mind with God, Weisse maintained that his own philosophy leads onward to the discovery *within* reason
of an already-existing idea of the transcendental, personal God. His assertion rested on a reading of Hegel wherein he detected the nascent idea of
the personal God in the speculative philosophy of religion. Hence, Weisse
saw in Hegel "an instinct of genuine Christian orthodoxy,"[97] a dubious understanding of Hegel's conception of absolute subjectivity that nonetheless
allowed Weisse to proceed with his own task of yoking the philosophy of religion to orthodox ends.

As Walter Schulz has observed, Weisse's effort to derive the idea of the
personal, living God from within reason did not take him fully beyond the
identity philosophy of Idealism.[98] Weisse's mix of theistic intentions and
residual identity philosophy eventually drew the criticism of other philosophical theists like Schelling; even Weisse's ally I. H. Fichte complained
that, not unlike the Hegelians, Weisse placed the personal God at the *end* of
the world process, whereas Fichte strove to place Him at its *beginning*.[99]

95  Weisse to Hegel, 11 July 1829, *Hegel: The Letters.*
96  C. H. Weisse, "Über die eigentliche Grenze des Pantheismus und des philosophischen
     Theismus (1833)," *Die Flucht in den Begriff*, p. 67. I. H. Fichte also offers a good discussion
     of Weisse in "Bericht," esp. pp. 61–99.
97  Weisse quoted in Jaeschke, *Reason in Religion*, p. 410.
98  Schulz, *Die Vollendung des Deutschen Idealismus in der Spätphilosophie Schellings* (Pfullingen,
     1975), p. 173f.
99  Fichte, "Bericht," p. 102.

Fichte departed from Weisse over the question of the relative roles played by reason and experience in the human confirmation of the personal God. Weisse ascribed a supplementary role to experience, in that the philosophical discovery of the theistic idea of personality is augmented by the conviction of God's living presence within the Christian religious experience. Fichte rejected this quasi-Hegelian attempt to harmonize the truths of reason and faith, and he tried instead to attain the "idea of a *personality* of primordial reason" entirely from experience, which he regarded as the sole source of knowledge.[100] Interestingly, this emphasis upon experience and mental facts anticipated later nineteenth-century empiricism and psychologism, even if the particular facts that Fichte chose to privilege did not.[101] "Religious experience" is, for Fichte, the highest psychological fact, but he argued further that it is also the highest fact of the "world," because it has proven to be the deepest and most creative force in history.[102] Proceeding through an inductive process from these "facts" of psychology and history, Fichte claimed to arrive at the highest absolute, the personal God, which humanity knows only *a posteriori* through His revelation in the world.[103]

Whatever their differences, Fichte and Weisse were united not only in their intense desire to reassert the principle of theistic personality against Hegel's alleged pantheism and panlogism but also in their identification of the principle of personal divinity with a defense of finite human freedom, which they believed Hegel had seriously compromised. We have already encountered Jacobi's defense of a theistic notion of individuality against the nihilism he detected in rationalist philosophy; similarly, a crucial element of the varieties of philosophical anti-Hegelianism was a form of individualism based on the analogy between the personal God and the human individual. God gives His shape to the human person – that is, the divine imparts the unity of conscious will to the human. The Speculative Theists were quick to emphasize that human personality is not identical to that of God, because the personality of God comprises absolutely self-identical Being, or absolute unity of consciousness,[104] and complete freedom requires this divine unity

---

100   Fichte's *Die Idee der Persönlichkeit und der individuellen Fortdauer* (1834) quoted in Jaeschke, *Reason in Religion*, p. 371. See also Schulz, *Vollendung*, p. 170.

101   Hermann Ehret's admiring *Immanuel Hermann Fichte. Ein Denker gegen seine Zeit* (Stuttgart, 1986) seems much too willing to accept Fichte's claim that his emphasis upon the "facts" of experience promised a reconciliation between natural science and theology.

102   Fichte, "Bericht," p. 106.

103   Ibid., p. 115.

104   See ibid., p. 103; Weisse, "Grenze," pp. 84–5; and *Die Idee der Gottheit* (Dresden, 1833), pp. 159f.

of self, for absolute personality experiences no limiting condition upon its will.[105] In contrast to this image of divine personhood, Fichte and Weisse both acknowledged that human beings cannot abstract themselves either from their dependence on God or from the otherness of nature. Nonetheless, they insisted that despite these limitations on human freedom, the distinctness of the human person as a *relatively* self-identical being ensures the integrity of personhood both in this world and in the next.[106]

One must recognize that this concern for the finite person was not merely a repetition of the perennial Christian theme of humanity's creation in the image and likeness of God. It reflects, rather, a specific reaction to post-Kantian philosophy of religion that recoiled from the conclusions of Idealism even as it relied on the pioneering efforts of the Idealist generation. Where Weisse drew substantially from Hegel even as he criticized him, Fichte relied heavily on the critical philosophy of his father and Kant in formulating his own conception of experience. More generally, their view of human personality as free and creative echoed the individualism of German humanists from Goethe and Schiller to Wilhelm von Humboldt, while it also shared the post-Kantian generation's preoccupation with the nature of human subjectivity. This was especially clear in the case of I. H. Fichte, who was influenced by his father's idea of the "I" as the highest expression of the Absolute, the "I" as a self-positing unity of will and action.[107] The older Fichte had remained unclear about the relationship between the finite human subject and the Absolute, never fully embracing the identity thesis of the young Schelling; but by the end of his life, he had moved toward a more fully personalist and transcendent conception of the nature of God. Immanuel Hermann Fichte, it might be said, completed his father's evolution away from identity philosophy when he declared human subjectivity to be a loan from God.

While Weisse and Fichte's conception of personality rested on an analogy between the divine and the human, their assertion of the human personality's freedom required a resolute rejection of identitarian thinking. This fundamental critique of dialectical logic became the nodal point for a widespread revolt against the identity thesis that was at the core of Hegel's logic.[108] It must be acknowledged that Hegel's critics in the 1820s and

105  I. H. Fichte, *Die Idee der Persönlichkeit und der individuellen Fortdauer* (Elberfeld, 1834), pp. 97f. The same theme is central to K.Ph. Fischer's *Die Freiheit des menschlichen Willens* (1833), esp. p. iv.
106  See Weisse, "Grenze," p. 58.
107  See esp. I. H. Fichte, *Sätze zur Vorschule der Theologie* (Stuttgart and Tübingen, 1826), pp. xlvii–xlviii.
108  Max Wundt, "Die Philosophie in der Zeit des Biedermeiers," esp. pp. 122, 130.

1830s were not particularly careful in their terminology when they criticized Hegel, for they routinely conflated pantheism, atheism, and panlogism. Moreover, many of his more sophisticated critics, who engaged him on the level of his logic, actually charged him with a form of acosmism, ironically a term coined by Hegel to criticize Spinoza, even though they then proceeded to confuse acosmism with pantheism.[109] In other words, their charge was not so much that Hegel absolutized or divinized finite being but rather that in asserting the absolute status of spirit, he sublated the specific reality of finite existent beings into a mere moment of spirit's progress.

In a significant way, Weisse and Fichte's criticism of Hegelian logic echoed Jacobi's opposition between theistic *"Realismus"* and rationalist *"Nihilismus."* Believing that dialectical logic subordinates reality to the categories of thought,[110] Weisse and Fichte asserted the non-identity of reason and reality; reason is always abstract and generalizing, reality always particular, concrete, and individual. Indeed, they maintained, reality is pervaded by an individualizing power that escapes rational categorization.[111] This power, identified as the source of freedom, is none other than will itself – in the first instance God's will, in the second, that of His creature. Freedom becomes synonymous with this individualizing power, with the assertion of personality that finds its "Ur-form" in God's will.[112] Freedom thus lies outside or beyond reason, as Weisse made clear in his critique of Hegel's conception of freedom:

> To [Hegel], the essential form of "reconciliation" amounts to "the relationship [of the subject] to an object as to something that is not foreign," with an express "accentuation [Herausheben] of the negation of the difference of the other being [Anderssein]." Freedom exists for him . . . not in the *posited* Positive, but in its *sublation;* it is, as he expressly names it, *Process:* – these words reveal not only that substantiality is yoked to a strict law, but also that substantiality is confined to the moments of this law. In all being there is only the progress from being to knowledge, which is to him the truth as well as freedom. But he knows nothing of the progress from knowledge to being in living action and creation, which is the true freedom for *us*. . . .[113]

---

109   On Hegel's usage, see G.H.R. Parkinson, "Hegel, Pantheism, and Spinoza," pp. 449–59.
110   Weisse described Hegel's *Logic* as "the doctrine of the pure categories or the absolute forms of thought and knowledge, which are at the same time the absolute forms of being and truth," in "Grenze," p. 85.
111   Ibid., p. 61.
112   See, for example, Weisse, *Grundzüge der Metaphysik* (Hamburg, 1835), p. 16, and his assertions in "Grenze," p. 67.
113   Weisse, "Grenze," p. 84.

## Schelling's Positive Philosophy

Weisse's discussion of freedom, with his emphasis upon the facticity of the positive rather than its overcoming, and his frequent recourse to the distinction between "negative" and "positive" philosophies, exemplify two of the many ways in which the Speculative Theists overlapped with the so-called Positive Philosophy of the later Friedrich Wilhelm Schelling. Walter Schulz has cautioned against the tendency to identify Schelling too closely with the Speculative Theists,[114] but it is not my intention here to enter this controversy or the debate over continuities and discontinuities in Schelling's long and checkered career. Rather, Schelling concerns us here because his Positive Philosophy represented for Feuerbach and the other Young Hegelians the consummate example of the "personalist" *Weltanschauung* shared by so many of Hegel's critics. Indeed, despite the fact that Schelling's Positive Philosophy differed in many details from Speculative Theism, it helped decisively to define the philosophic anti-Hegelian discourse of the 1830s and 1840s.

Schelling's Positive Philosophy was known more by hearsay and rumor than by actual study because he had published almost nothing after his *Investigations into the Essence of Human Freedom* of 1809. What the philosophic public learned of Schelling's evolving philosophical system came mainly from reports of his lectures at Erlangen in the early 1820s and his famous lectures on the history of modern philosophy in Munich in the winter semester of 1827–8.[115] The Munich lectures had introduced the distinction between "positive" and "negative" philosophy that was further clarified in his 1834 foreword to a work by the French philosopher Victor Cousin.[116] Even before the publication of this foreword to Cousin, however, Positive Philosophy had already entered the lexicon of German philosophy, in Weisse and I. H. Fichte and most prominently in the first volume of Friedrich Julius Stahl's *Philosophie des Rechts* (1830), which presented the first published commentary on Schelling's new philosophical direction. Ironically, although Schelling regretted what he considered the grievous misunderstanding of his Positive Philosophy by the Speculative Theists and Stahl, lack of understanding had benefits for a philosopher who was very jealous of his public standing. As Erdmann recalled in 1853, "The less that was known about the

---

114 Schulz, *Vollendung*, p. 168.
115 Schelling, *On the History of Modern Philosophy*, trans. Andrew Bowie (New York, 1994).
116 See "Zur Geschichte der neueren Philosophie. Münchener Vorlesungen (Aus dem handschriftlichen Nachlass)," and "Vorrede zu einer philosophischen Schrift des Herrn Victor Cousin" (1834), Schelling's *Sämmtliche Werke, 1833–1850*, vol. 10 (Stuttgart and Augsburg, 1861).

Positive Philosophy and how the transition from the negative to the positive was to be made, the more everyone could fashion a Schelling to his own taste, and there was scarcely a time when Schelling was so valued by so many diverse thinkers as then, when no one knew what he taught."[117]

The Positive Philosophy came as the culmination of Schelling's long journey away from the Idealism that he himself had developed between 1798 and 1804.[118] Schelling had grown steadily less satisfied with his earlier attempts to reconcile thought and being, and by 1827 he could repudiate his youthful position as a sterile panlogism. Claiming that since 1804 he had attempted to replace the philosophy of absolute identity with a new philosophy of freedom, the philosophy of subjective reflection with a philosophy of being, he insisted that henceforth the ground of freedom must be sought in existence, not in reflection. This required the rejection of a dialectical logic that absorbed finite being in ever-higher levels of abstract reflection in favor of a flexible mode of thought that preserved finitude, particularity, contingency, and the discontinuities of crisis and decision.

In an important book, Andrew Bowie has recently emphasized the contemporary relevance of Schelling's philosophical problem, while minimizing the significance of his theological solutions.[119] This is appropriate insofar as one follows Bowie's suggestive efforts to explore the significant affinities between Schelling and late-twentieth-century postmetaphysical thinking; however, from the perspective of both Schelling's historical context and the immediate reception of his philosophy, the theological turn of his later thought cannot be discounted. For the revelation of a complex, living personal God was to be the *sine qua non* of this new effort to grasp existence outside of subjective reflection. This was a dramatic revaluation of his earlier view of personality. As an Idealist, the youthful Schelling had conceived God as a totality that itself knows no consciousness, while he had regarded the finite human personality as a diremption of the absolute Ego. Hence, Schelling wrote to Hegel in 1795, "There is no personal God, and our highest strife is to destroy our personality, passing over into the sphere of absolute Being."[120] As late as 1804, Schelling still co-edited the *Kritisches Journal der Philosophie* with Hegel, but already *Philosophie und Religion* (1804) foreshadowed his repudiation of identity philosophy. His move away from Idealism

---

117   Erdmann quoted in Schulz, *Vollendung*, p. 173.
118   Andrew Bowie argues that even in his Idealist phase, Schelling did not subordinate being to thinking to the same extent that Hegel did. See Bowie, *Schelling and Modern European Philosophy. An Introduction* (New York, 1993).
119   Ibid., p. 14.
120   Schelling quoted in Reardon, *Religion in the Age of Romanticism*, p. 95.

was undoubtedly speeded by Hegel's criticism of him in the *Phenomenology of Spirit* and by his experience at the University of Jena, where he had accepted a professorship at twenty-three in 1798. Jena was the center of German Romanticism, and there, Schelling became closely involved with the circle of Ludwig Tieck, August and Friedrich von Schlegel, and Novalis, all of whom were increasingly attracted to Catholic ultramontanism after 1800. Although Schelling never converted to Catholicism, he moved to Catholic Bavaria in 1803 and spent most of the next forty years there. At the very least, like his Romantic friends, he became increasingly preoccupied with mysticism and Christian spiritualism.

By 1809, influenced by the seventeenth-century Lutheran mystic Jakob Böhme – to whose thought his friend the Catholic philosopher Franz von Baader had introduced him – Schelling pitted the "lifeless abstractions" of Idealism, which had "no concept of personality," against a cosmos animated by personality, itself the sole principle of "life."[121] Although Schelling had found himself in a sharp controversy with Jacobi in 1811–12, by the 1820s, Schelling could even praise that old adversary of systematic reason, detecting in Jacobi "something in him from youth onward that rebelled against a system reducing everything to mere rational relationships, a system excluding freedom and personality."[122] Schelling believed that his 1809 *Investigations into the Essence of Human Freedom* established the "first clear concept of personality."[123] Equally rejecting orthodoxy's anthropomorphic God as well as Idealism's absolute subject, Schelling conceived of God's personality as pure will and free creativity. Yet following the mystic Böhme, Schelling argued that there is something in God that is not Himself. Instead of conceiving of God as a self-identical totality, Schelling postulated that He brings into "living unity" two beings, each of which is a force of will.

On one side, the will of God seeks to "universalize all, to raise all to unity with the light." Against this principle of "light" contends the "dark principle" of the "Ground," a blind, irrational will to "particularize all or to make it creaturely."[124] This is the principle of nature, and though God contains the will of the ground within Himself, He cannot annul it; for personality, like all particular things, depends on the specificity of nature for its expression. Free-

121  Schelling, "Philosophical Investigations into the Essence of Human Freedom and Related Matters," *Philosophy of German Idealism*, pp. 247, 282.
122  Schelling, "Jacobi. Der Theosophismus," *Sämmtliche Werke*, vol. 10, p. 168. On Schelling's controversy with Jacobi, see Dale E. Snow, *Schelling and the End of Idealism* (Albany, N.Y., 1996), pp. 205–13.
123  "Essence of Human Freedom," p. 281.
124  Ibid., pp. 267, 256.

dom, which Schelling defined as the capacity for good and evil, depends, as Bowie writes, "upon a ground from which it can never be wholly separated, lest it lose that via which it can reveal itself and be itself." At the same time as freedom therefore entails a resistance to the ground of being, its dependence on the ground prevents the circular closure implied by identity philosophy's notion of absolute subjectivity.[125] Quite in contrast to Hegel's view, or for that matter, Schelling's earlier *Naturphilosophie,* the God of the *Essence of Freedom* can strive only to impose order on the chaos of the ground, to "overpower it through love and subordinate it to himself for his glorification."[126]

Schelling's system of 1809 is rightly described as a form of "pan-entheism" – that is, as a conception of God as both transcendentally complete but dependent upon appearance in the world.[127] His next major work, *The Ages of the World,* written in 1812 but unpublished in his lifetime, brought him much closer to a transcendent conception of God. Two important themes first elaborated in the *Essence of Freedom* persisted in this work and those of the 1820s and 1830s. First, Schelling continued to define God's personality as pure will, the center of a metaphysics of voluntarism that resists rational explication. Voluntarism explains God's simultaneous immanence and transcendence, because His creation of the world is guided by no necessity but only by an irrational principle of creativity. Accordingly, God reveals Himself in and through the world yet remains eternally separate from the world; and His revelation is strictly voluntary. In lectures and texts after 1809, Schelling's principles of "light" and "dark" evolved into the doctrine of the "two potencies," one potency turning outward to creation, the other turning inward toward God's own unity of self.[128] Thus, suggested Schelling, behind and outside all revelation, Divine Being remains an undisclosed and "irrational principle, resisting differentiation, therefore also contrary to the [world]. . . . It is necessary to acknowledge this principle as the personality of God, his being in himself and for himself. . . ."[129] This conception of divine personality thereby stands in the sharpest contrast to Hegel's, whose God, quipped Schelling, can never celebrate the Sabbath because He is never free from the process of development.

The second persistent theme concerns Schelling's conception of humanity. In his youth, Schelling had shared Romanticism's Promethean ideal,

125 Bowie, *Schelling,* p. 96.
126 "Essence of Human Freedom," p. 270.
127 See Schulz, *Vollendung,* p. 12.
128 Ibid., p. 327.
129 Schelling quoted in R. F. Brown, *The Later Philosophy of Schelling: The Influence of Boehme on the Works of 1809–1815* (London, 1977), p. 248.

wherein freedom consists of the radical overcoming of all otherness through the recognition of the universal presence of spirit in all nature. This idea of freedom entailed at the very least a synergistic conception of the relation of humanity and God but tended more radically toward an assertion of their ultimate identity. In 1804, however, Schelling began to move away from this idea when he introduced the language of the Fall into his account of the human person's freedom. Subsequently, the Augustinian image of man as a rebel from God became a leitmotif of his thought. Schelling took the Fall to be the result of the self-assertion of human will, the result of "aroused selfhood."[130] This was a Fall from divine unity into fragmentation and egoism; however, even though it plunged humanity into sin and suffering, the Fall also revealed the essential relationship between God and man. Echoing orthodox Christian premises, Schelling insisted that because humans are made in God's image, they too have "personal unity" that allows them to raise their creaturely particularity to a principle of conscious self-assertion.[131]

This led Schelling to a conception of freedom sharply at odds with Idealism, based not on the infinite selfhood of spirit but on human personality born of sin and the radical capacity for good and evil in each person – in short, humanity's participation in the metaphysics of voluntarism. It is, as we will see in Chapter 2, an idea of freedom that leads to very different political conclusions from those of Hegel. Moreover, whereas the young Schelling had agreed with Hegel that true salvation lay in the merging of the individual and the Absolute, the older Schelling maintained that the possibility of human salvation depends on the person's potentiality as the *imago dei*.[132] Contrary to his earlier impulses, he now argued that the individual instinctively resists an Absolute that would swallow him, whereas he freely chooses in faith a God who is living, personal, and redeeming. Therefore, the relation between the divine and the human must always be between persons, a relationship of analogy and dependence rather than one of identity. Hence, in 1809, Schelling wrote that "in order to counter personal and spiritual evil, the light of spirit appears likewise in personal, human form and as a medi-

---

130  "Essence of Human Freedom," p. 271.
131  Ibid., p. 249.
132  Schelling shared aspects of Luther's Augustinian view, but they differed fundamentally on several crucial points. Most significantly, Luther believed that the Fall had destroyed man as the image of God; recognition of the utter dissimilarity of man and God, yet faith that God would nonetheless redeem man, was the unitive principle of Luther's theology. See Stephen Ozment, *The Age of Reform, 1250–1550. An Intellectual and Religious History of Late Medieval and Reformation Europe* (New Haven, 1980), p. 243.

ator, in order to restore the rapport between creation and God to the highest level. For only the personal can heal the personal, and God must become man so that man may return to God."[133] More than thirty years later, his message was essentially unchanged: "A person seeks a person. The self, as itself a personality, desires personality; it demands a Person who is outside of the world and above the universal, and who understands – a Heart that is like unto our own."[134]

Schelling's repudiation of his youthful philosophy brought him into close contact with Christian orthodoxy. Along with the Augustinian tenor of his emphasis upon man's sinfulness, he approached full acceptance of the traditional Christian creation myth. Moreover, his defense of a personal God against all pantheisms, including that imputed to Hegel, touched on perennial themes within Christian theology. Indeed, his debate with Hegel has distant roots in the ancient controversy between the Stoic conception of God as *logos* (universal reason or necessity) or *physis* (a universal natural force), and the assertions of early Church fathers of a personal loving God, as well as roots in the late medieval controversy between Scotists who stressed God's will, and hence his freedom, and Thomists who emphasized His reason, and hence his restriction by the laws of his own creation.[135] Nonetheless, it would be a mistake to regard Schelling's later philosophy merely as a repetition of themes that have circled endlessly within Christian culture. For one thing, Schelling's continued, though weakened, affinity with Idealism is signaled by his willingness to probe the nature of divine being, a commitment to philosophical knowledge that set him at odds not only with strict Lutherans but also with Jacobi in their 1811–12 dispute. For another, Schelling's theism, like that of the Speculative Theists, was both an attempt to recover Christian tradition and a specific response to what he regarded as the failure of Idealism: the apparent inability of German philosophy since Kant to explain the relation between the subject and the object of knowledge. The ambition of Schelling's Positive Philosophy was to overcome this failure by grounding reason in the reality of being. Although his solution points both backward to traditional theological motifs and forward to postmetaphysical thinking, his project reveals a continuous engagement with the specific problems of Idealist epistemology.

In his 1834 essay on Victor Cousin, Schelling introduced the Positive

---

133   "Essence of Human Freedom," p. 255.
134   Schelling quoted in Reardon, *Religion*, p. 113.
135   See G. L. Prestige, *God in Patristic Thought* (London, 1981), and on medieval disputes, Ozment, *Age of Reform*, pp. 33f.

Philosophy to the philosophical reading public.[136] The Positive Philosophy
outlined in this work was ostensibly a critique of Cousin's empiricist sensa-
tionism, but it was really the ghost of Hegel whom Schelling engaged. According to Schelling, Hegel's attempt to develop a dialectical logic that com-
prehends all reality was the most overt expression of the ambition of all
modern philosophical systems to substitute a mode of thought for reality.
Hegel's failure to fulfill this ambition, in Schelling's opinion, was thus an open
verdict on the era of "negative philosophy" opened by Descartes. Contrary to
Hegel's assertion of an identity between thought and being, Schelling could
find no adequate reason in the *Logic* to account for the passage of the dialectic into reality, no adequate explanation why there is something and not nothing. In a manner that came to be echoed in Kierkegaard's *Concluding Unsci-
entific Postscripts,* Schelling found at the originary passage from nothingness
to being the emblematic inability of all "purely rational systems" to include
the empirical, the existent, the real.[137] The dialectic, he conceded, might
remain a keen scalpel for the dissection of thought, but it broke on the mass
of reality.

Against philosophies that could negate reality only by denying its autonomy, Schelling sought a "positive explanation of reality," and this demanded
that reality be treated not as the end of thought but as its beginning. The articulation of Positive Philosophy involved a sharpened formulation of Schelling's earlier arguments about the ground of being, understood as God, and
about the limits of fallen man's imperfect knowledge. Whereas negative philosophy discerns the logical structure of the world, or what is necessary, and
discloses order in the world and the rules and laws that bind being, Positive
Philosophy reveals that logical "necessity" in its deeper truth is really the result of God's will, which is unbound by any law. Hence, there is a hiatus between thought and the ground on which it depends, with regularity in being
dependent on the self-constraint of a purely spontaneous will. "Following
the eternal act of self-revelation," Schelling wrote, "all is rule, order, and
form in the world as we now see it. But the ruleless still lies in the ground as
if it could break through once again. . . . This is the incomprehensible basis
of reality in things, the indivisible remainder, that which with the greatest
exertion cannot be resolved in the understanding, but rather remains eternally in the ground."[138] Speculative reason thereby reaches an absolute limit

136   In addition to already cited works on Schelling's Positive Philosophy, see Emil Facken-
      heim, "Schelling's Philosophy of Religion," pp. 1–17, and "Schelling's Conception of Pos-
      itive Philosophy," *Review of Metaphysics,* 1954, pp. 563–82.
137   See especially, *Sämmtliche Werke,* vol. 10, pp. 212–13.
138   "Essence of Freedom," pp. 238–9.

in its confrontation with God, because the groundless ground of all reality eludes purely rational thought.

It is not surprising that Heidegger discovered in Schelling's project affinities with his own attempts to develop fundamental ontology as an alternative to the western metaphysical tradition. Like Heidegger and unlike Jacobi, Schelling took the collapse of identity philosophy to be an invitation not to renounce philosophy in favor of theology but to search for a new way to think of being. Still, despite the prescience of Schelling's attempt to philosophize in a new key, his efforts to evoke the ek-static quality of "positive" knowledge were much more deeply theological than Heidegger's. On Schelling's account, reason, having recognized its limits, must eventually become ek-static, moving outside itself to acknowledge that which is not itself as its own ground and the condition of the possibility of all knowledge. Precipitated by the dilemma of reason, this is an act of will beyond all reason: "The Positive Philosophy is genuinely free philosophy: the person who does not will it may leave it alone."[139] "Positive" knowledge begins with the acceptance of the unknowable God as the beginning and the end of reason. Undoubtedly, Schelling tried to present this "grounding" of knowledge as the new precondition for rationality, and he even contrasted his own "scientific" efforts to the mysticism of Jacobi.[140] In one of the most significant studies of Schelling, Walter Schulz has even argued that Positive Philosophy remains committed to resolving Idealism's problem of the self-mediation of consciousness, because it is to be a *self-restriction* of reason that finally negates negative philosophy. However, Schulz's description of Schelling's conception of the positive ground of reason as a "completion" of Idealism is misleading. Positive Philosophy is, rather, post-Idealist, marking one terminus of the Idealist notion of the autonomy of self-consciousness; and despite Schelling's disavowals, Positive Philosophy circles back to the issues that Jacobi had first raised as he confronted rationalistic "nihilism."

Like the Speculative Theists, it can be said of Schelling that his later philosophy represents a retreat behind Hegel's attempt to reconcile reality and reason, reason and faith. Before the most devastating critiques of the Left Hegelians had been written, Weisse, Fichte, and Schelling unintentionally proved the impossibility of reconciling theology and philosophy, thereby contributing instead to their divorce. If Hegel was a suspicious ally of revealed religion, Weisse, Fichte and Schelling were *frondeurs* in the court of reason. After all, the Positive Philosophy presupposed the capitulation of

139  Schelling, *Philosophie der Offenbarung, Sämmtliche Werke*, vol. 13, p. 132.
140  Ibid., p. 208.

reason's autonomy to something external to it, to the ultimate "positive" fact that comes to be known only through revelation. Chastened reason takes its place in the immanent fallen world and can evoke its transcendental ground only in mystical and mythopoeic language. In contrast, Hegel's dialectic sought to penetrate the positive, to "negate" the positive in precisely the manner that Schelling repudiated. Undoubtedly, late-twentieth-century readers will recognize in Schelling's thinking a foreshadowing of current philosophical concerns. It is one of the ironies of the history of philosophy that a figure reviled by many of his contemporaries as an unregenerate reactionary should appear freshly relevant to a postmodern age. Still, we ignore the reactionary nature of this enterprise at the risk of misunderstanding its broader meaning within its own historical milieu. Schelling, along with Weisse and Fichte, recognized all too clearly that Hegel's was an intrinsically critical procedure, because it granted reason the power to judge reality. Conversely, Schelling's attempt to trace the genesis of reason back to a ground "*beyond* thinking" fatally weakens reason, leaving it impotent before a reality that it cannot penetrate conceptually but must accept as given.[141] This effort to correct the *a priori* abstractions of speculative reason was a profoundly conservative undertaking, indeed a philosophical and theological counterpart to a political Restoration that sought to reassert the authority of personal monarchy and the legitimacy of the given order against the claims of autonomous political reason.

141  Schelling quoted in Snow, *Schelling*, p. 211.

# 2

# THE TRANSCENDENT SOVEREIGN
# AND THE POLITICAL THEOLOGY
# OF RESTORATION

In 1843, Marx remarked to Feuerbach that "Schelling's philosophy is Prussian policy *sub specie philosophiae*."[1] Marx was referring directly to Schelling's
complicity with the reactionary regime of Friedrich Wilhelm IV, who had
summoned him from retirement in 1841 to take Hegel's chair in philosophy at Berlin with the express command to "slay the dragon-seed of Hegelian
pantheism."[2] In a deeper sense, however, Marx was pointing to the profound philosophical affinities between Schelling's Positive Philosophy and
Prussian political theology. As both Marx and Feuerbach knew, Schelling's
assertion of the theistic idea of personality was directly linked to homologous themes in Restoration political thought. At the core of both the theological and political discourses of personality was an intense concern with
the nature and conditions of indivisible unitary will – in short, with the nature of sovereignty. Schelling's philosophy of revelation, for all its metaphysical pathos, arrived at the orthodox conclusion that history reveals the
absolute sovereignty of God. Similarly, the divinely ordained legitimacy of

---

1   Karl Marx to Feuerbach, 3 October 1843, *Ludwig Feuerbach. Briefwechsel*, vol. 2, ed. W. Schuf-
    fenhauer (Berlin, 1985).
2   For an interesting examination of the ideology of the new king from the perspective of mu-
    sic history, see John Toews, "Musical Historicism and the Transcendental Foundations of
    Community: Mendelssohn's *Lobgesang* and the 'Christian-German' Cultural Politics of Fred-
    erick William IV," *Rediscovering History. Culture, Politics, and the Psyche*, ed. Michael S. Roth
    (Stanford, 1994).

personal authority was the leading theme of conservative political thinkers in the era of Restoration after Napoleon's defeat. The Restoration's preoccupation with the transcendent source of personal sovereignty made a clash between conservative political thinkers and Hegel inevitable.

## Secularization and Political Discourse

The ideological association of the personal God with the personal sovereign was anything but new at the dawn of the nineteenth century. The analogy between God and monarch had been central to the sacral idea of kingship in medieval political thought,[3] and early modern theories of sovereignty carried this association forward. This was true not only for the familiar doctrine of divine right but also for sixteenth- and seventeenth-century theorists of the state. Articulating what was to become the modern theory of sovereignty – that the sovereign power of a commonwealth must be inalienable, indivisible, and perpetual – the French jurist Jean Bodin seized on the most potent expression of lordship available when he wrote that the sovereign person is the "earthly image of God."[4] Similarly, Thomas Hobbes, certainly no orthodox theist, spoke of the Leviathan as a "*Mortall God,* to which wee owe under the *Immortall God,* our peace and defence."[5] In an immediate sense, Restoration political theory in the early nineteenth century is surprising only in its anachronistic revival of political theology in the age of modern politics. How are we to understand the relationship between religion and politics in the political theology of Restoration?

We can begin to answer this question by examining the well-known assertion by the controversial German political theorist Carl Schmitt that "all significant concepts of the modern theory of the state are secularized theological concepts not only because of their historical development – in which they were transferred from theology to the theory of the state, whereby, for example, the omnipotent God became the omnipotent lawgiver – but also because of their systematic structure."[6] The fundamental premise of Schmitt's "secularization thesis" is that political concepts derive from ontologically

---

3   See especially the classic study by Ernst H. Kantorowicz, *The King's Two Bodies. A Study in Medieval Political Theology* (Princeton, 1957). Interesting observations on the gendered nature of this sovereign discourse are found in Jean Bethke Elshtain, "Sovereign God, Sovereign State, Sovereign Self."

4   Jean Bodin, *On Sovereignty,* trans. and ed. J. H. Franklin (Cambridge, 1992), p. 46.

5   Thomas Hobbes, *Leviathan,* ed. C. B. Macpherson (New York, 1985), p. 227.

6   Carl Schmitt, *Political Theology. Four Chapters on the Concept of Sovereignty,* trans. George Schwab (Cambridge, Mass., 1988), p. 36.

and epistemologically prior theological concepts, the essential *substance* of which is then transplanted into the political sphere. Suggestive as this thesis is, it is not without weaknesses. For one thing, Schmitt's claim has the consequence of degrading the domain of politics, which is ironic considering his own insistence on the primacy of the political in human life. As an analytical tool, this view of secularization also violates the self-understanding of historical actors for whom the relationship between the theological and the "secular" was not unilinear but porous and reciprocal. Indeed, it could as easily be argued that, contrary to Schmitt, theological concepts are mystified political concepts, a suggestion made in the spirit of the radical Left Hegelians, or that *some* political concepts have nontheological sources. Rather than see political concepts as derivative of theology, one could say that both theology and political thought concern power insofar as they both examine the relationships of creator and created, decision and action, freedom and law.

Hans Blumenberg, perhaps the most prominent critic of the secularization thesis, has emphasized the important difference between conceptual "transformations" and "analogies."[7] Where Schmitt sees the origin of political concepts in the migration of theology into worldly affairs, Blumenberg points to acts of "metaphorical borrowing" from the lexicon of theology and myth to legitimate or empower modern political and social phenomena.[8] This point may be illustrated by returning to Thomas Hobbes, whom Schmitt regards as the consummate theorist of personalist and decisionistic sovereignty.[9] Hobbes invests the sovereign with divine majesty but does so self-consciously when he writes, "Leviathan, or rather (to speake more reverently) that *Mortall God*." The identification of God and sovereign works metaphorically, and this becomes clearer when one remembers that Hobbes was indifferent as to whether power is exercised by one man or by an assembly, so long as sovereign power is held by a sole authority. Such an authority is the "person" of the state, who can be either a "natural person" in a monarchy or an "artificial person" in a conciliar or republican government.[10] In fact, then, the legitimacy of the Leviathan does not depend on

---

7 Hans Blumenberg, *The Legitimacy of the Modern Age*, trans. Robert M. Wallace (Cambridge, Mass., 1991), p. 93.

8 See, for example, Novalis's plea for a state linked "to the heights of heaven": "I refer you to history; search in its instructive continuity for similar moments and learn to use the magic wand of analogy." In "Christendom or Europe" (1797–8), *Romanticism*, ed. John B. Halsted (New York, 1969), p. 132.

9 Schmitt, *Political Theology*, p. 33.

10 The point is made generally in *Leviathan*, esp. p. 228, and more specifically in Thomas Hobbes, "On Artificial Man," *De Homine*, trans. Charles T. Wood (Cambridge, 1991), pp. 83–5.

its sharing a *substantial* identity with the personal God. The analogy between Hobbes's Leviathan and God operates only at the level of signifying analogous unlimited powers within their respective spheres. Hobbes was hardly representative of theorists of absolute sovereignty, many of whom were outraged by his subordination of divine sanction to naturalistic reason, but his example warns against assuming an immediate identity between the concepts of unlimited political power and divine omnipotence.

In assessing the role of theological analogies in political discourse, Blumenberg correctly argues for the importance of context or situation. Schmitt's secularization thesis gives a stamp of inevitability to the use of theological concepts in political terms, as if we must inescapably deploy theological constructs whenever we speak of political power. This approach masks the substantial differences between various political languages by reducing them all to the same essential core structure. It also minimizes the extent to which theological concepts may serve political goals or reflect historical actors' interpretations of the needs of their time, rather than express the deep structure of political concepts themselves. This is evident in the political theory of Carl Schmitt himself, whose *Political Theology* concludes with his insistence on the need for an unbounded dictatorial power standing above the Weimar Republic's constitution. For early-nineteenth-century reactionaries, the recourse to political theology was prompted by clear-sighted recognition of the dynamic forces of the age and the desire to retard or roll them back. This is not to say that political theology was merely a cynical ideological manipulation. Restoration political theory drew on deep resources of belief and religio-political symbolism. Nonetheless, the unity of theology and political thought was the product of political decisions. Indeed, that unity was itself one of the great political issues of the age.

## Personalism and the Politics of Restoration

The natural enemy of the Restoration was the French Revolution, with its regicidal, anti-aristocratic, and democratic impulses. At a broader level, however, the Restoration intensified the complex response of eighteenth-century conservatives to the *Aufklärung*. As Frederick Beiser has argued, not all eighteenth-century conservatives were opposed to the *Aufklärung*,[11] and

---

11   This is a general assumption underlying Klaus Epstein's *The Genesis of German Conservatism* (Princeton, 1966). Nonetheless, Epstein's account of the origins of conservatism is more nuanced than Frederick Beiser suggests. See Beiser, *Enlightenment, Revolution, and Romanticism*, pp. 282f.

he distinguishes usefully between "absolutist" conservatives, many of whom were *Aufklärer* committed to enlightened despotism, and "estatist" conservatives such as Justus Möser, who defended the old feudal *Ständesstaat* as a guarantee against the centripetal force of the absolutist state.[12] To that typology must be added conservatives who defended or reaffirmed the old patriarchal idea of the state, under which, as Klaus Epstein puts it, "the prince promoted the general happiness of his subjects instead of the policy of modern princes of sacrificing this happiness (if necessary) to the impersonal goal of the greatness of the state."[13] This brand of patriarchal conservatism was not, of course, incompatible with *Ständesstaat* conservatism, both of which found a common enemy in "enlightened" absolutism. Indeed, Enlightenment conservatism differed qualitatively from both. Although many moderate *Aufklärer,* appalled by the French Revolution, came to the defense of the old regime monarchy, many of these figures retained their essential faith in political reason. They met the revolutionary challenge not by retreating from reason but by demanding *more* reason. Consequently, the great political reform movements in Prussia, the introduction of the *Allgemeine Landrecht* in the 1790s, and the reforms of Karl Freiherr vom Stein and Karl August von Hardenberg between 1805 and 1815 were all attempts at "revolution from above," products of political rationalism in the service of "conservative" goals.[14]

It was quite different with the heirs of estatist and patriarchal conservatism, who may be called the ideological fathers of the Restoration. Revolutionary events in France greatly sharpened the hostility between the champions of natural rights and rational political reform and the defenders of prescriptive rights and the *status quo* or even the *status quo ante*. Edmund Burke, though read widely in Germany, was less important in shaping this response than was Justus Möser.[15] Möser's polemical articles in the 1790s

---

12  On the conservative element in the *Aufklärung* itself, in addition to Beiser, see the recent studies of A. J. La Vopa, "The Politics of Enlightenment: Friedrich Gedike and German Professional Ideology," *Journal of Modern History,* March 1990, pp. 34–56, and James Schmidt, "The Question of Enlightenment: Kant, Mendelssohn and the *Mittwochsgesellschaft,*" *Journal of the History of Ideas,* April–June 1989, pp. 269–91.

13  Epstein, *Genesis,* p. 264.

14  See, for example, Hardenberg's 1807 claim that "the power of these [revolutionary] principles is so great, so universally recognized and widespread, that a state that does not embrace them must face either their forcible imposition or its own extinction." Quoted in James Sheehan, *German History 1770–1866* (Oxford, 1989), p. 252. The classic account of the Prussian "revolution from above" remains Reinhart Koselleck, *Preussen zwischen Reform und Revolution. Allgemeines Landrecht, Verwaltung und soziale Bewegung von 1791 bis 1848,* 3rd ed. (Munich, 1989).

15  See Beiser, *Enlightenment, Revolution, and Romanticism,* pp. 287f.

established a living connection between the pre-revolutionary *ständische* hostility toward the enlightened rationalist reform of the German dynastic states, most notably Prussia, and the reactionary opposition to the Revolution. German conservative rhetoric after 1800 repeatedly identified the reform of the Prussian state with the same rationalist spirit that had toppled the French monarchy, for they both replaced personal relations of authority with the force of abstract legal norms and an impersonal bureaucratic state.[16]

The tension between personal and impersonal authority dogged the Prussian *Allgemeine Landrecht* in the 1790s, the Reform Era between 1806 and 1816, and attempts like A. J. Thibaut's in 1814 to create a new civil code for the German states. The emancipation of serfs, the removal of corporatist restrictions on trade and vocation, and the lifting of legal barriers between the social estates all had the effect of diminishing the traditional form of aristocratic power, which rested on the old principle of lordship, or *Herrschaft*, over one's personal domains. By replacing personal domination with impersonal legal relations at every level of society, the reduction of the personalist element in the Prussian state posed obvious challenges to noble power.[17] This was true not only in legal matters proper but also in economic relations, where the capitalization of agriculture was transforming personal interactions into the impersonal transactions of the market. Although the shift to impersonal relations actually helped the aristocracy economically over the long term by lifting many of its obligations to the peasantry and in many cases increasing the size of its holdings, the nobility perceived a threat to its own power base.[18] In consequence, resistance to the depersonalization of authority became the chief political aim of the Prussian nobility.

The political agenda of the Prussian *Junkers* was reflected in the evolution of Restorationist political theory. Here, it is useful to distinguish the line of conservative thought best expressed by the Romantic theorist Adam Müller from that embodied by Carl Ludwig von Haller. In *Die Elemente der Staatskunst*

16  Carl Ernst Jarcke, a follower of Haller, claimed in 1833 that "observed from a higher standpoint, absolutism and revolution are *identical*." Jarcke, "Revolution und Absolutismus," *Vermischte Schriften*, Bd. 1 (München, 1839), pp. 166–203.

17  The aristocratic reaction to the depersonalization of political and economic authority is the major theme of Robert M. Berdahl's *Politics*.

18  On balance, the effect of the Reform Era was modest. See the assessment of Hans Rosenberg, *Bureaucracy, Aristocracy and Autocracy. The Prussian Experience, 1660–1815* (Cambridge, Mass., 1958), p. 203. However, the capitalization of agriculture made the old land-owning aristocrats sufficiently prosperous that they were able to maintain a leading role in Prussian politics and society into the twentieth century, according to Hans-Ulrich Wehler, *The German Empire, 1871–1918* (Dover, New Hampshire, 1985), pp. 10–14.

(1809), Müller defined the state as the "totality of human affairs, their combination in a living whole."[19] With equal vigor, he opposed the "mechanistic" rational state and the selfish individualism of commercial society, but while his organic theory of the state and his idealization of the feudal corporatist economy privileged personal, immediate relationships of domination, obligation and exchange, his political theory contains ambiguities that weakened his defense of personal authority and lessened his impact on Restoration theory and politics. After all, his theory subordinates all individuality to the ontologically prior social totality. Indeed, the organic metaphor itself threatens to replace political decision with morphology, thereby lessening the importance of *Herrschaft* – personal sovereignty – as the determining force of political community.

The totalizing impulses of Müller's theory suggest why Romantic organicism was viewed with considerable suspicion by the mainstream of Prussian conservatives in the early nineteenth century. The Swiss jurist Haller was a much more palatable intellectual figure for the Restoration, considering his close links to the traditions of *ständische* and patrimonial conservatism. In contrast to Müller, Haller defined society as a web of private relationships of domination and deference that reached from the lowest social orders to the highest.[20] Reviving a feudalist notion, Haller argued that power is a form of personal property; legitimate power is a property to be exercised only within one's own domain. Sovereignty is therefore not the preserve of the state, but is a function of the personal rights of property ownership. This applies equally to the male head of a household and the lord of a manor, as well as to the monarch, each of whom enjoys indivisible sovereignty within his proper sphere. In this formulation, no state, no public authority, no public law exists as such. Rather, the king exercises his power as a property owner, and his rights and duties, like those of all other property owners, are defined by private law.[21] By privatizing all power, Haller reversed nearly three centuries of thought about the nature of sovereignty. He pushed estatist conservatism to its most extreme conclusions, striking a blow at the centralizing tendencies of the modern state and dispersing sovereign authority into myriad personal social relationships.

Haller's theory of social relations won wide approval among German

---

19   Berdahl, *Politics*, p. 169.
20   Ibid., p. 237. Haller's main work was the multi-volume *Restauration der Staatswissenschaft oder Theorie des natürlich-geselligen Zustandes der Chimära des künstlichen-bürgerlichen entgegensetzt*, the first volume of which appeared in 1816, the fifth in 1834.
21   In addition to Berdahl, *Politics*, pp. 231–63, see C. E. Merriam, *History of the Theory of Sovereignty Since Rousseau* (New York, 1900), pp. 63–72.

nobles and the intimate circle of the Prussian Crown Prince Friedrich Wilhelm, all of whom shared his resistance to the expansion of public authority.[22] He was not accepted uncritically, however. Prominent members of the Pietistic Awakening like the Gerlach brothers taxed him for privileging an essentially naturalistic scheme over the imperatives of Christian principles.[23] For Haller believed that society is the "natural state" of man, beginning in the family and extending into more complex relationships of superordination and obligation: Authority arises in the first instance from the primitive right of conquest and depends only secondarily on a God-given right to the inheritance of property.[24] Somewhat similar criticisms were directed against the leader of the Historical School of Law, Friedrich von Savigny, whose opposition to legal codification has often led historians to place him mistakenly in the reactionary camp.[25] Ludwig von Gerlach, although he had been a student of Savigny's in 1810, rejected his teacher's effort to trace the origin of law to the common spirit of the community.[26] After reading Savigny's famous *Beruf unsrer Zeit für Gesetzgebung und Rechtswissenschaft*, Gerlach wrote in 1814:

> This teaching, which, in pantheistic fashion constructs a system essentially from the individuality and historical evolution of nations without regard for their eternal origins or for universally human, divinely created and therefore permanent institutions (personality, patriarchy), cannot provide adequate defense against the revolutionary essence of our century.[27]

As W. O. Shanahan has written, it was neither Haller nor Savigny but the Pietistic Awakening that provided "the spiritual basis in Germany, particularly in Prussia, for that emphasis upon Christian principles in the social or-

22  Frank-Lothar Kroll, *Friedrich Wilhelm IV. und das Staatsdenken der deutschen Romantik* (Berlin, 1990), pp. 15–61; and Berdahl, *Politics*, p. 242.
23  See the comments of Otto von Gerlach quoted in Ibid., p. 255.
24  Ferdinand Tönnies aptly described Haller's theory seventy years ago: "What it amounts to is that in real life the strong rule the weak. This can indeed be called a 'natural' law; it might even benefit the weak, especially when they accept it and expressly submit to it by covenant; or simply, being the facts of life, it must be considered a 'law' of nature." Tönnies, "The Development of Sociology in Germany," *On Social Ideas and Ideologies*, trans. E. G. Jacoby (New York, 1974), p. 127.
25  John Toews shows that although Savigny's relationship with the progressives of the Reform Era was not unstrained, he was not a reactionary. See "The Immanent Genesis and Transcendent Goal of Law: Savigny, Stahl, and the Ideology of the Christian German State," *The American Journal of Comparative Law*, vol. XXXVII, no. 1 (Winter, 1989), pp. 139–69.
26  Savigny writes that "the State originally, and according to nature, arises in a people, through a people, and for a people." Quoted in Merriam, *Theory of Sovereignty*, p. 96.
27  Gerlach quoted in Toews, "Immanent Genesis," p. 162.

der characteristic of the Restoration."[28] Pietists like Ludwig von Gerlach, who became one of the most prominent reactionaries of the age, embraced Haller's depiction of social relations but replaced all naturalist explanations of the origins of the state with a Christian one. According to Gerlach's view, the state is the consequence of the Fall, which acts as a divine disciplinary agent to regulate the erring, sinful ways of man. In so arguing, Gerlach sought not only to reinvest monarchy with the majesty of divine ordination but also to lend the state a providential role by assigning it the task of curbing sin. The state shares a godly task with the church; but, following orthodox Lutheran doctrine, Gerlach insisted on the ultimate separation of the state from the church. Natural, fallen man belongs to the state, itself a product of sin, whereas the church, the "community of saints," transcends the state and is directed to the last things. "The born-again," Gerlach wrote, "belong to the state only insofar as they do not yet live completely in the realm of the spirit, and therefore, they need the state's laws as a discipline until they die and are freed by God's grace."[29] A synthesis of Christian providentialism and Haller's patrimonial theory of society came to dominate the political perspective of the major reactionary journals of Prussia in the 1830s, Hengstenberg's *Evangelische-Kirchenzeitung* and *Das Berliner Politische Wochenblatt*, and it may be noted in passing that it was also the political view of the later Schelling.[30] This was the chief ideological matrix in which conservative judgment of Hegel's philosophy of religion united with condemnation of his political philosophy.

## Hegel's Secularization of the Christian Idea

In politics, as in religion, Hegel was vilified as the epitome of the rationalist, critical spirit that had spawned both the French Revolution and bureaucratic absolutism. Hegel has often been presented as a conservative apologist for the Prussian state, but that does not do justice to the complexities of his political philosophy, nor does it reflect the extent to which he was associated in the minds of contemporary conservatives with progressive politics and cultural renewal. However, as in the discussion of Hegel's philosophy of religion, what seemed to draw the most vehement denunciations was not simply the apparent progressive tenor of his thought, which conservatives insisted on despite the many German liberals who disavowed Hegelianism

---

28  Shanahan, *German Protestants*, p. 59.
29  Gerlach quoted in Berdahl, *Politics*, p. 256.
30  Gertrud Jäger, *Schellings politische Anschauungen* (Berlin, 1940), pp. 90–1.

as a philosophy of reaction; rather, it was his claim to be a Christian philosopher, to be a philosopher of Christian *politics,* indeed to be a political theologian, that most provoked conservatives who were themselves intent on formulating the idea of a Christian state. What was at stake in the controversy over Hegel's political thought, beyond any straightforward conflict between reaction and liberalism, was the meaning of Christianity in the politics of the postrevolutionary age. Hence, it is revealing that the typical Pietist charge against Hegel was that he collapsed the distinction between church and state and divinized the state.[31] Conservative Protestant political thinkers sought to mobilize religion for the secular purpose of retrenching social and political hierarchies, even as they jealously upheld the distinction between the secular and the sacred. In contrast, Hegel based his political philosophy on a claim for the emerging identity of religion and politics, the sacred and the secular. In order to understand this conflict, as well as the political development of Hegelians like Feuerbach, Ruge, and Marx, it is necessary to explore in some depth Hegel's vision of political secularization.

We saw that Hegel regarded Christianity as the religion of self-conscious freedom; in his view, Christianity was the inner principle of modern history because "world history is the progress of the consciousness of Freedom."[32] Significantly, however, Hegel argued that freedom remains abstract unless the subject recognizes its own inward freedom mirrored in the concrete institutions of the political and social world. Hence, he cautioned that to extend Christianity's original spiritual principle "to the secular realm was a further task, the solution and execution of which required a difficult and long labor, a civilizing process [*Bildung*]."[33] Secularization, in Hegel's particular usage, was precisely this process of *Bildung,* conceived as the gradual conformity of the outer world to the inner, of exoteric political history to esoteric spiritual history. This theory of convergence allowed Hegel to trace an inner relation between the two great upheavals of the modern era, the Protestant Reformation and the French Revolution. The Reformation called into life the essential freedom of Christianity by creating, as Joachim Ritter put it, "the religion of free individuals, who turn to themselves and to their own convictions with their thoughts, their prayers, and their worship

31  For particularly clear examples of this criticism, see K. E. Schubarth and L. A. Carganico, *Über Philosophie überhaupt und Hegels Encyclopädie der philosophischen Wissenschaften insbesondere* (1829) *Materialien,* ed. Riedel, pp. 209–10; Jarcke, *Vermischte Schriften,* vol. 1, pp. 170f; and Heinrich Leo, *Die Hegelingen: Aktenstücke und Belege zu der s.g. Denunciation der ewigen Wahrheit* (Halle, 1838). Leo's own patriarchal, neo-feudalist views are elaborated in his *Studien und Skizzen zu einer Naturlehre des Staates* (Halle, 1833).
32  Hegel, *Werke,* vol. 12, p. 32.    33  Ibid., p. 31.

of God."[34] For Hegel, the freedom of the modern individual was thereby identified with the "Protestant principle"; but it was the French Revolution, albeit in an imperfect and problematic way, that transformed this freedom into the standard of the world, the concrete principle upon which all true political and social order must be built. The inwardly free person, who has discovered his own infinite spiritual worth, may now recognize that his free essence has become the universal principle of the contemporary world. Flight from the world into the heaven of spiritual freedom is no longer necessary or acceptable.

Hegel's frequently repeated claim that freedom is the principle of the modern world did not mean he believed that any state in his time had perfectly actualized freedom. His point was that the principle of freedom has entered into the world in such a way as to make it the essential content of subsequent history and the practical principle by which all subsequent claims on the human being must be measured. This suggests the true meaning of Hegel's controversial claim that "what is real is rational, what is rational is real." Far from apologizing for "actuality," this expression establishes the tension between actuality and a rationality that may judge existing conditions to be contrary to the core content of history. It is true that in his Berlin years, Hegel subdued this potential for critique and emphasized philosophy's comprehension of an actuality that is "already there cut and dried after its process of formation has been completed."[35] Furthermore, in public and private writings during his later years, Hegel congratulated the Prussian state for the political reforms made in the era of Karl Freiherr vom Stein and Karl August von Hardenberg and for its appreciation of the vital role played by the sciences in the life of the state. However, such blandishments notwithstanding, the frequently made charge in Hegel's time and our own that he was an apologist for the reactionary Prussian state is unfounded. With the significant exception of Altenstein, the minister of Education and Culture, the Prussian government kept its distance from him once he was called to Berlin in 1818. Nor did history have to wait for the radical Left

34  Joachim Ritter, "Hegel and the Reformation," *Hegel and the French Revolution*, trans. Richard Dien Winfield (Cambridge, Mass., 1982), p. 191.
35  *Philosophy of Right*, pp. 12–13. See also Toews, *Hegelianism*, p. 62. K.-H. Ilting detects between Hegel's 1818–19 lectures and his 1820 *Philosophy of Right* a shift away from a "republican" to an "authoritarian" conception of the state that he attributes to the Prussian state's rightward shift after its adoption of the Carlsbad Decrees. See Ilting, "Hegel's Concept of the State and Marx's Early Critique," *The State and Civil Society*, ed. Z. A. Pelczynski, esp. pp. 94–104. Hegel's increasing conservativism in the 1820s, noted by a number of earlier interpreters, is given further support in Horst Althaus's new biography *Hegel und die heroischen Jahre der Philosophie* (Munich, 1992).

Hegelians of the 1840s for the critical potential in Hegel's political thought to find expression, because Hegel himself clearly recognized that the institutional structure of Prussia did not conform closely to the theoretical structure elaborated in the *Philosophy of Right*.

Moreover, even some of Hegel's earliest disciples became quite aware of the ambiguous relationship between Hegelian political philosophy and the Prussian state. John Toews has shown that many young men turned to Hegel after 1815 in search of a coherent political ideology. The patriotic struggle against the French, as well as promises of constitutional reform from the Prussian King Friedrich Wilhelm III, had aroused great hopes among many middle-class Germans for national renewal and the nonviolent expansion of the Third Estate's political role. For many, constitutional change seemed but a logical outcome of the Stein and Hardenburg reform program and a well-deserved reward for the national sacrifice of the War of Liberation. Instead of producing constitutional reform, however, the defeat of Napoleon sparked bitter debates among political factions about the nature of postwar German reconstruction. To young men who rejected either the restoration of the old-regime state or the Romantic dream of a chauvinistic *völkisch* community, Hegel's theory of the modern state and ethical life was deeply appealing. In contrast to either of those political alternatives, Hegel's system articulated universal rational-legal norms while promising the reconciliation of individual freedom with communal integration. However, once the hopes of the postwar years had passed into the conservatism of the Restoration, the ranks of the politicized Hegelians fragmented. Hegel had, after all, made his philosophy subject to validation by historical events when he claimed to discover the rational Idea in actuality. One can detect even in the mid-1820s the emergence of divisions over the relevance of Hegelian political philosophy to a contemporary history that had failed to conform neatly to the Idea.

We will return to these political divisions in later chapters, but at present, it is important to emphasize that ambiguities notwithstanding, Hegel's claim that the inwardly free human being does not need to retreat from the world may be understood in progressive, activist terms once the core of Hegel's notion of secularization is uncovered. That is, his identification of the modern world with the "Protestant principle" was a call for the further extension into the world of the Christian idea of freedom. Secularization in Hegel's thought means neither the withdrawal of religion from social and political life, as the term is commonly understood in the late twentieth century, nor the transmigration of religious into profane concepts, as in Schmitt, nor the domination of political and social life by a theocracy, an impulse that Hegel adamantly resisted in the efforts of his reactionary contemporaries to construct a narrowly confessional Christian-German state. What led Hegel to claim that "secular life is the positive and definitive embodiment of the Spiritual Kingdom" was his conviction that the concept of freedom that first entered the world in Christianity had now come to prevail in the principles of politics.[36] He thus viewed secularization in fully *Christian* terms, but only insofar as Christianity is understood here in its philosophically sublated form, not in any one of its narrow confessional manifestations.

This philosophical reconstruction of Christianity forms the basis of *Sittlichkeit*, or ethical life, the key political concept of Hegel's idea of the state. Indeed, the logical structure of ethical life is that of the Idea itself, the mutual interpenetration of subject and the universal. In ethical life, relationships among subjects and between the individual and the universal are characterized by thoroughgoing reciprocity, in which each individual is both a means and an end. Mutual recognition of the individual and the universal ensures that each sees himself confirmed as the *end* of the other even as he is the means to the ends of the other. Or, to return to a theme of Hegel's philosophy of religion, ethical life is the sociopolitical embodiment of his conception of concrete personality. We saw that by the late 1790s, Hegel was already committed to the idea of ethical life, and it remained the unifying concept of his religio-political thought until his death. Yet it was not until the *Philosophy of Right* in 1820 that Hegel fully elaborated the concept of ethical life, articulating it in terms of both analytical categories and institutional embodiments. The notion of *Sittlichkeit* was intended to mediate between the poles of political thought: on the one hand, the atomizing, asocial vision of modern enlightened Understanding, which cannot move beyond the isolated, "abstract" person, and on the other hand, the totalizing substantial vision of the ancient *polis*, which demanded the sacrifice of the individual to the needs of substantial ethical life. In contrast to the ancient *polis*'s negation of individual autonomy, Hegel argued that the modern ethical order fulfills the meaning of history because it permits the expression of free individuality *within* the community. Modern *Sittlichkeit* therefore strives to make explicit what remained only implicit in the ancient ethical order, the dialectical identity of the individual and the community.

In Hegel's thought, this dialectical unity takes the objective form of the

---

36  Hegel, *Werke*, p. 524. See also Dickey, "Hegel on Religion and Philosophy," p. 323. In *The Philosophy of History*, Hegel writes: "Freedom in the State is preserved and established by Religion, since moral rectitude in the State is only the carrying out of that which constitutes the fundamental principle of religion" (*Werke*, vol. 12, p. 405).

mediated relationship between modern civil society and the state. The *Philosophy of Right*'s seminal depiction of the forms and interrelations of state and society was motivated in part because of the logical demands entailed in the aim of actualizing the Christian principle in rational ethical life. However, true to a dialectical method that always attempted to draw its conceptual forms from the concrete tendencies of history, Hegel also based his descriptions of civil society and the state upon his astute understanding of contemporary sociopolitical developments. As Manfred Riedel observes, Hegel recognized "nothing less than the result of the modern revolution: the emergence of a depoliticized society through the centralization of politics in the princely or revolutionary state and the shift of society's focal point towards economics."[37] It was not only the divergence of the state from society that was crucial here, for Hegel also recognized the *convergence* of the expanding market system and the political function of both revolutionary and rationalist-absolutist states. Which is to say, both revolutionary and enlightened absolutist *praxis* had recognized the institutional validity of abstract rights of freedom and thus had opened up a legal sphere in which people could pursue their own interests.[38] It is a crucial assumption of Hegel's political philosophy that a civil society – *uncivil* though the activities of its members may be – is by definition always already a legally structured society, and that presupposes a state which recognizes society's right to exist *as such*.

Hegel understood civil society not only as a crucial "institutional" feature of modernity, standing between the immediate ethical bonds of family love and the mediate ethical life in the state, but also as a crucial context for the formation of modern personal identity. In contrast to the family, where members view one another as parts of a natural ethical whole, in society, people conceive of themselves and others as "individuals with a free will" – in short, as "persons." In important ways, the passage of the individual from

---

37  Manfred Riedel, *Between Tradition and Revolution: The Hegelian Transformation of Political Philosophy* (Cambridge, 1984), p. 148. On the sheer novelty of Hegel's formulation of the idea of civil society and its impact on social thought, see also Riedel's classic essay "Gesellschaft, bürgerliche," *Geschichtliche Grundbegriffe*, vol. 2, ed. Otto Brunner, Werner Conze, and Reinhart Koselleck (Stuttgart, 1975), pp. 719–800. On the historical emergence of this differentiation in Prussia, see Reinhart Koselleck, "Staat und Gesellschaft in Preussen, 1815–1848," *Moderne deutsche Sozialgeschichte*, ed. H.-U. Wehler (Königstein, 1981), pp. 83–4.

38  See Axel Honneth, "Atomism and Ethical Life: On Hegel's Critique of the French Revolution," ed. David Rasmussen, *Universalism vs. Communitarianism. Contemporary Debates in Ethics* (Cambridge, Mass., 1990), p. 361. An interesting perspective on this change in the German context is found in Keith Tribe, *Governing Economy. The Reformation of German Economic Discourse, 1750–1840* (Cambridge, 1988), esp. pp. 149–82.

the family to civil society described by Hegel reprises the transition he traced from the Greek *polis* to Rome, for it is *abstract* personhood – "rigid, reserved, independent, self-centered" – that the modern bourgeois first gains in civil society. Civil society is initially and essentially dominated by self-assertion and self-interest, and within the social sphere, driven by "wants and a mixture of caprice and physical necessity," men act as "burghers" (bourgeois) or "private persons whose end is their own interest."[39] This status finds legal recognition in "abstract right," the guarantee first expressed in Roman law of the rights of persons *qua* persons to security of self and property. We will return in Chapter 3 to the role that property plays in Hegel's account of the formation of personality; but here it may be emphasized that Hegel did not believe that abstract personality, the sense of pure self-determination, could be dispensed with, for to do so would, in his view, fully compromise the modern principle of freedom. However, Hegel recognized that this sense of personhood, important as it is, also threatens to erode the foundations of shared values and practices. Axel Honneth states the problem succinctly:

> For Hegel, . . . the real challenge posed by the age must have been the question generated by the Revolution, namely, how that sphere of abstract freedom which had been won through political struggle could itself be embedded in an overarching context so that it would not unleash its atomizing capacity *ad infinitum*, but rather become a positive formative element in an ethical community.[40]

This was a problem for Hegel precisely because he viewed the purpose of the social whole in ethical terms; hence, he tried to conceptualize the economic and social structures of civil society in such a way that they would contribute to the formation of concrete personality.

Civil society thus became for Hegel a *Bildungsprozeß*, an educational process, that contributed to the cultivation of the person. However, in contrast to eighteenth-century German notions of *Bildung*, which viewed it as a "process of harmonization, progress towards a goal, or unfolding of an internal faculty," Hegel regarded *Bildung* as "a process marked by division, diremption and opposition."[41] Building upon the insights of eighteenth-century Scottish social theorists like Adam Smith, Adam Ferguson, and James Steuart,[42] Hegel recognized that civil society constitutes a "system of needs"

---

39  *Philosophy of Right,* para. 187 and 182.
40  Axel Honneth, "Atomism and Ethical Life," p. 362.
41  See James Schmidt, "A *Paideia* for the '*Bürger als Bourgeois*': The Concept of 'Civil Society' in Hegel's Political Thought," *History of Political Thought,* vol. II, no. 3 (Winter 1981), p. 480.
42  Norbert Waszek, *The Scottish Enlightenment and Hegel's Account of "Civil Society"* (Boston, 1987).

in which the inability of individuals to meet all of their needs alone leads to the growth of a web of social relations. The atomizing effects of competitive individualism is thereby offset by the interdependencies fostered by exchange and the division of labor. A selfish end, Hegel argued, is "*mediated* through the universal which thus *appears* as a *means* to its realization. Consequently, individuals can attain their ends only insofar as they themselves determine their knowing, willing, and acting in a universal way and make themselves links in this chain of social connexions."[43] Departing from the Scottish social thinkers, who were generally contented with the limited forms of sociability and social cohesion fostered by the marketplace, Hegel did not regard the system of needs as the finally desired end-state of humanity. Even if economic interaction educates the bourgeois into a form of universality, civil society nonetheless remains bound to egoism and natural necessity, thus to external dependence. While Hegel respected the sphere of self-determining personhood in civil society, he believed that society's institutional structures, such as vocational corporations and the juridical and administrative branches of the state, must work to "contain" social egoism.

In one of the most original aspects of the *Philosophy of Right*, Hegel identified a clear division between civil society and the state *proper*, which transcends the *instrumental* universality of civil society because it has as its self-conscious object the universal end of all. In distinction to civil society, the Hegelian state performs genuinely political functions because it represents, articulates, and executes the public will, although the state in his conception is not democratic or participatory in any modern sense. It is, instead, a complex institutional structure synthesizing hereditary monarchy, rationalistic bureaucracy, corporatist-estatist social representation, and an established church. This idea of the state seems to be the ambiguous and fragile product of Hegel's conflicting loyalties to the principle of the French Revolution on the one hand, and, on the other, to his conviction that only a reformed constitutional monarchy could realize those principles once the *revolutionary* search for freedom had ended in tyranny.

Whatever the sources of the hybrid character of Hegel's concept of the state, his particular attempt to theorize modern ethical community virtually *demanded* such a state form. One might argue that only the notion of a mediated dialectical totality comprising the immediate bonds of family, individual self-interest, and universal public will could actualize a rational ethical life that would be true to the convergent strands that Hegel followed through history up to his present moment. In Hegel's perspective, in other

43  *Philosophy of Right*, para. 187.

words, the relational form of concrete personality could be fully realized only when the individual experiences his relation to another not as a means to the other's end but discovers that the other wills an end that the individual recognizes as his own. Only then is the self-relation of the self in the other truly non-alienating. "A State," wrote Hegel, "is well constituted and internally powerful, when the private interest of its citizens is one with the common interest of the State; when the one finds its gratification and realization in the other."[44]

Hegel's theory of modern ethical life sought to correct the failings of both the ancient model of community and the liberal reduction of society to the marketplace by integrating the fact of the modern separation of economic society from the political state within the narrative of the unfolding "Christian principle" in the modern world. Juristic and religious concepts of personhood converge in the *Philosophy of Right* to conceive of a new reconciliation of the civic, political, and spiritual dimensions of full, concrete personality. The application of Hegel's philosophically reconstructed notion of Christianity to politics is of the greatest significance for understanding his departure from the tradition of secular political philosophy. This break is perhaps most clearly illustrated by the contrast between Hegel and Rousseau. Rousseau's great influence reveals itself in Hegel's lifelong concern with the general will, the separation of private from public life, and the tension between the ideal of the public-spirited, virtuous citizen and the atomized, egoistical bourgeois of modern civil society. However, the great eighteenth-century republican had placed Christianity alongside commerce as the chief threats to a free citizenry and a virtuous polity. In similar spirit, the Jacobin phase of the French Revolution, when the revival of classical civic virtue was aggressively pursued, directed an onslaught against Christianity as the great enemy of public spirit. Hegel's solution to the problem of the dissolution of ethical life in the modern world deflected Rousseau's animus by ascribing to Christianity a positive role in healing the break between public and private, citizen and bourgeois. In short, Hegel saw in Christianity the foundation for a community not of saints but of citizens.

This reciprocal "Christianization" of politics and politicization of Christianity was to prove highly vulnerable, however. For Hegel's entire system depended on a greatly revised view of Christianity that neither orthodox nor "philosophical" theists were to recognize as an adequate basis for theology, philosophy, or the "Christian" state. To the basic complaint that Hegel divinized the state, Pietists added the charge that Hegel's claim that ethical

life is actualized in the state appeared to rob the church, the domain of the
sacred, of its traditional ethical and spiritual leadership. On this latter point,
a heated debate arose about Hegel's interpretation of the institutional
independence of the church and the proper religious substance of a Christian state. This line of Pietistic critique climaxed in Heinrich Leo's influential denunciation of the Hegelian School in 1838. The Pietistic opposition
to Hegel's politics need not detain us here, however, for the substance of the
critique was absorbed by the most prominent of Hegel's critics in political
philosophy, Friedrich Julius Stahl.[45] More than any of his contemporaries,
Stahl made the critique of Hegel a chief pillar in the construction of his own
political theory. Stahl was the counterpart in political philosophy to Schelling and the Speculative Theists in the philosophy of religion. That is, despite his own profound piety, Stahl based his effort to construct an ideology
of the Christian state upon philosophical precepts rather than on an exclusive appeal to Christian orthodoxy.

### Anti-Hegelian Politics in the 1830s: Friedrich Julius Stahl and the Positive Philosophy of the State

In a letter of 1835, Ludwig Feuerbach described Stahl as the "emissary out
of the land of mystical dreams of the newest Schellingian philosophy."[46]
Stahl was indeed an adept of Schelling's Positive Philosophy; but more than
that, he also embraced most of the conservative trends of the age. He was
deeply influenced by the Awakening and closely allied to the Historical
School of Law, and he hoped his work would set a headstone over the grave
of rationalism.[47] The publication of Stahl's *Die Philosophie des Rechts nach
geschichtlicher Ansicht,* the first volume of which appeared in 1830, began his
rise to prominence within the ranks of the conservative movement that
sought to reassert authority in both the Protestant church and the state. As
was the case with the other Fundamentalists of the Awakening, the French
Revolution of 1830 intensified Stahl's anti-democratic, anti-rationalist sentiments and his resolve to unite theology and political philosophy in defense
of the monarchy.

Stahl was a professor at Erlangen in Bavaria from 1832 until 1840. In

---

45   For further discussion of the Pietist reaction, see John Toews, *Hegelianism*, pp. 226–8; and
     Shlomo Avineri, "Hegel Revisited," *Contemporary History*, III(1968), pp. 133–47.
46   Feuerbach to Christian Kapp, 13 January 1835, *Ludwig Feuerbach. Briefwechsel I (1817–
     1839),* ed. W. Schuffenhauer and E. Voigt (Berlin, 1984).
47   Friedrich Julius Stahl, *Die Philosophie des Rechts,* 5th ed., vol. 1, p. xxviii.

1840, shortly before Schelling took Hegel's chair in philosophy, Stahl assumed the chair in the Berlin Law Faculty left vacant by the death of Eduard Gans, the renowned Hegelian jurist. Stahl's nomination for the appointment in Berlin was eagerly supported by Savigny, who had by then adopted Stahl's political philosophy as a metaphysical basis for his historical legal studies. Hengstenberg's Pietist circle also championed Stahl's appointment.[48] Nonetheless, many Berlin conservatives were not happy with Stahl's call to Berlin, not only because he had been born Jewish but because he was not a supporter of Haller's neo-feudalist theory. In fact, it was only with the publication of *Das monarchische Princip* in the mid-1840s that Stahl really won a preeminent place among Prussian conservatives. In 1840, what seems to have recommended him most strongly to the new king Friedrich Wilhelm IV and the new minister of Education and Culture J.A.F. Eichhorn was his well-known opposition to Hegel. Stahl was summoned to the University of Berlin to unite swords with Schelling against Hegel's ghost. Indeed, it was primarily as a staunch critic of Hegel's political philosophy that Stahl was known to German intellectuals in the 1830s. Stahl's sympathies for the Historical School of Law and its leading figure Savigny associated him with one of Hegel's great rivals; but above all, it was his adaptation of Schelling's Positive Philosophy to political theory that characterized his attack on Hegel.

Stahl was born to a Jewish family in Munich in 1802, but, against the wishes of his parents, he converted to Lutheranism in 1819. Many German Jews found baptism necessary to career advancement, but Stahl seems to have been motivated by genuine conviction.[49] The personal influence of one of his teachers at Munich's Wilhelms Gymnasium, Friedrich Thiersch, helps certify the sincerity of Stahl's conversion. Not only did Thiersch proselytize on behalf of Lutheranism, but significantly, he also introduced his promising student to the writings of Friedrich Heinrich Jacobi. From Jacobi, the young Stahl took one of the central themes of his life's work, the connection of the free personality of man to a personal God.[50] In 1822, Stahl left Munich to study at the University of Erlangen. Schelling had lectured at Erlangen since 1820, and though there is no evidence that Stahl actually heard Schelling at that time, the philosopher's influence was pervasive at the Protestant university. The steady course of Stahl's formal studies was interrupted in 1824 when the Bavarian government discovered his involvement

---

48  See Toews, "Immanent Genesis," p. 162; and Shanahan, *German Protestants*, p. 102.
49  See, by contrast, Heine's famous description of baptism as an *"entrée billet* into civil society."
50  Stahl's early education and the influence of Jacobi are discussed in Dieter Grosser, *Grundlagen und Struktur der Staatslehre Friedrich Julius Stahls* (Köln, 1963), p. 11.

with the *Burschenschaften*. Initially, he was punished with a permanent ban
from university studies, but when it was discovered that he had opposed the
politicization of the student movement, the government commuted the ban
to a two-year suspension.

During those two years, Stahl studied Hegel closely, an encounter that
precipitated a deep personal crisis made all the more severe by the fact that
there were aspects of Hegel that attracted him strongly. Pietistic by temperament, yet drawn to the rigors of philosophy, he regarded Hegel's so-
briety as a worthwhile corrective to Jacobi's mystical flights. Beyond that,
Hegel's apparent belief that the existing state is an objective expression of
spirit seemed to appeal to Stahl's reverence for the political *status quo*.[51]
Nonetheless, Stahl was profoundly disturbed by the metaphysics that underpinned Hegel's political philosophy. Like Schelling or the Speculative
Theists, Stahl asked whether philosophy must lead to a logical dialectic that
consumes even the personal God. In trying to answer that question, he despaired that he had reached an impasse and saw himself before a choice
much like that which Jacobi had described forty years earlier. He could either
choose philosophy, in which case he risked sinking into nihilism, or choose
faith, in which case he forsook the rigors of philosophy for the "realism" of
the personal, living God.

Still troubled by these questions, but undeterred in his diligence, Stahl
returned to his studies in 1826. He quickly completed a degree in law and
accepted a post at the new *Hochschule* in Munich.[52] He was thus able to at-
tend Schelling's famous Munich lectures on the Positive Philosophy in the
winter semester of 1827–8. Stahl was galvanized by what he heard, for in
Schelling's thoughts he glimpsed a way past Jacobi's either/or choice. Schelling's trenchant critique of the "negative" epoch in philosophy that had climaxed in Hegel's absolute Idealism seemed to provide a philosophical affirmation of the freedom of personality, while Schelling's demonstration of
the necessity of belief in a freely creative personal God as the precondition
for "positive" knowledge seemed to offer a much firmer basis for Stahl's own
convictions than had Jacobi's poetic intuitions. As Stahl recalled, Schelling's
"system of freedom" gave him the courage to step boldly into the "new era
in philosophy."[53]

The "discovery" of Schelling in the late 1820s thereby resolved Stahl's

---

51    The underlying affinity between Hegel and Stahl is exaggerated in Arie Nabrings, "Der
      Einfluss Hegels auf die Lehre vom Staat bei Stahl," *Der Staat*, vol. 23 (1983), pp. 169–86.
52    Berdahl, *Politics*, p. 351.
53    Stahl, "Vorrede zur ersten Auflage," *Die Philosophie des Rechts*, 5th ed., vol. 1, p. xvi.

personal intellectual crisis and cleared the way for his first major work, *Die Philosophie des Rechts*. The strength of Schelling's influence is attested to by the fact that the first edition of *Die Philosophie des Rechts* essentially took over the Positive Philosophy unchanged, and although Stahl tried to distinguish himself from Schelling in every subsequent edition, the imprint of Schelling remained indelible.[54] All the elements of Schelling's metaphysics of voluntarism are present in Stahl's basic concepts: the critique of Hegel's logic, the distinction between pantheism and theism, the contrast between necessity and freedom, the separation of concept from being, the emphasis upon contingent, finite individuality and the autonomy of creation. Indeed, even Stahl's *geschichtlicher Ansicht*, his historical perspective, is based directly on Schelling's notions of facticity and freedom.

Stahl's description of his philosophy of law as "historical" is frequently taken to indicate his indebtedness to Savigny and the Historical School, but that relationship was actually quite complicated. He was indeed a supporter of Savigny, but not an uncritical disciple. He endorsed Savigny's preference for positive law, but he worried that Savigny's belief that positive law evolves in accordance with the character of a people or nation implied a dangerous relativism because it failed to provide a transcendent norm for law. When Stahl spoke of his own "historical perspective" he meant to relate the development of law to Schelling's reformulation of the basic theological insight that the world is the free act of God and that by God's allowance, humanity participates in the fate of the world through its own capacity for free action. Advanced in opposition to rationalist political theory, which Stahl believed subordinates the drama of crisis and decision to a determined historical process, the "historical" means an appreciation for the role of freely creative will in the world. In evoking the relationship among the personal God, the free action of the human individual, and the facticity of historical action, Stahl gave an explicitly political inflection to the kind of theistic realism introduced by Jacobi in the 1780s. As a consequence of this theistic realist understanding of history, "positive" law held a rather different meaning from the one it did for Savigny, because Stahl believed that positivity does not rest

---

54  See, for example, his mildly critical comments on Schelling's conception of personality in ibid., vol. 2, pt. 1, pp. xiii, 20. Schelling's influence is clearest in the first edition of *Die Philosophie des Rechts*, which offers the first published commentary on Schelling's Positive Philosophy. Subsequent editions attempted to downplay the connection. Julius Löwenstein's claim that Stahl's biblical fundamentalism distinguishes him from Schelling is less significant than the fact that the metaphysical basis for Stahl's political philosophy remains Schellingian. See Löwenstein, *Hegels Staatsidee. Ihr Doppelgesicht und ihr Einfluss im 19. Jahrhundert* (Berlin, 1927), p. 95.

in the evolution of a people but in the sovereign personality's authority to decree.[55] Significantly, Savigny himself came increasingly to accept Stahl's redefinition of positive law, and during the 1830s, the great legal historian undergirded his own work with Stahl's political metaphysics.

Describing the personality of God as "the principle of the world,"[56] Stahl developed homologous arguments in support of the authority of personal monarchy and, as we will see in the next chapter, the inviolability of private property. These homologies were so self-evident to Stahl that he could allege that Hegel's negation of divine personality threatened all forms of personhood and all authority. "Unpersonal Reason," he contended, subordinates the finite reality and freedom of the individual, the family, and the state to the process of Spirit's self-realization.[57] The result, in Stahl's striking formulation, is that "the person does not know himself in the family, the state, philosophy or God . . .; rather, the system of thought, idea of the family, the state, etc. knows itself in the person. One might say, the mirror contemplates itself in the person."[58] Stahl recognized that personality held a place in Hegel's system, but he lamented that it was given only a secondary importance. He was presumably speaking here of the treatment of personality in the section on "abstract right" in Hegel's *Philosophy of Right*. It is not the purpose of the present discussion to judge the accuracy of Stahl's criticism of Hegel, though it must be observed that his treatment is highly tendentious. To sharpen his critique and bolster the alternative he championed, Stahl ignored both Hegel's assertion that the rights of the person are indispensable to modern ethical life and his efforts to balance personal and collectivist elements. Instead, Stahl repeatedly charged that Hegel disregarded the "real, distinct personality" and recognized only the "personality *in abstracto*" as the vehicle of a spirit whose actual telos leads toward the overcoming of personality.[59] Significantly, in assigning to Hegel a merely abstract notion of personality, Stahl inverted Hegel's own distinction between "concrete" and "abstract," because it was Hegel's belief that precisely the telos of spirit leads away from the abstract personality of the isolated self to the concrete personality stemming from the subject's self-consciousness of the role of relationship in the formation of identity.

In Stahl's view, the worst consequence of Hegel's destruction of the free-

---

55  Herbert Marcuse fails to distinguish between these different meanings of the "historical" when he associates both Schelling and Stahl too closely with Savigny in *Reason and Revolution. Hegel and the Rise of Social Theory* (Boston, 1941), pp. 366–5.

56  Stahl, *Die Philosophie des Rechts*, 5th ed., vol. 2, pt. 1, pp. 7–69.

57  Stahl, "Hegels Naturrecht und Philosophie des Geistes," *Materialien*, ed. Riedel, p. 231.

58  Stahl, *Die Philosophie des Rechts*, vol. 1, p. 68.

59  Stahl in *Materialien*, ed. Riedel, p. 232.

dom of will, which he took to be the essence of both divine and human personality, is the destruction of the "personality of sovereignty."[60] On Hegel's account, the monarch is absorbed by the "substance" of the state, its ethical Idea, whereas real authority resides in the "constitution which has become mature as a realization of rationality."[61] Hegel recognized, however, that legal norms cannot in themselves make decisions, because decisions require an agent, a particular person who can say "I will" and thus cause a transition from discussion to action and actuality. In Hegel's system, the monarch fills this need by binding the various branches of government into a subjective unity capable of decision, thereby lending in his person actuality to the abstract "personality of the state" itself. Hegel thus translated the definitional requirements entailed in the concept of decision making into an argument for the necessary though limited role of the monarch. Hence, he made his famous claim that in a "completely organized state, it is only a question of the culminating point of formal decision. [The monarch] has only to say 'yes' and dot the 'i.'"[62] This led still further to his rather idiosyncratic argument for primogeniture, because precisely the accidental quality of an inherited throne ensured that the actual personal attributes of the monarch would not intrude upon his strictly formal role. These arguments, logically compelling within Hegel's system, pleased almost no one, neither his radical followers in the later 1830s who condemned his defense of hereditary monarchy as merely arbitrary nor his conservative detractors who recognized his revision of the personalist principle for what it was.

In the 1845 edition of his *Philosophie des Rechts,* Stahl observed that the republicanism of Hegel's younger disciples was not at all surprising. Hegel's doctrine could easily slide into popular sovereignty because his "ultra-governmentalism," as Stahl dubbed it, lacks any actual center, any source of ultimate authority. In Stahl's opposing view, social and political life must culminate in one personality who embraces and unifies all, just as the self-identical consciousness of God imparts unity to all creation.[63] The legitimate state thus became, for Stahl, the "Reich der Persönlichkeit," presided over by a monarch whose "majestic personality would be the living unity of all other personalities."[64] At the same time, however, like the transcendent God who cannot be bound by His creation, the ruling person must reveal

---

60  *Philosophie des Rechts,* 2nd ed., vol. 2, pt. 1, p. 16.
61  Hegel, *Philosophy of Right,* trans. T. M. Knox (Oxford, 1967), para. 279.
62  Hegel, *Philosophy of Right,* addition to para. 280.
63  See Christian Wiegand, *Über Friedrich Julius Stahl (1801–1862): Recht, Staat, Kirche* (München, 1981), p. 255.
64  Stahl, *Philosophie des Rechts,* 2nd ed., vol. 2, pt. 2, p. 5. See also Wilhelm Füßl, *Professor in der Politik: Friedrich Julius Stahl (1802–1861)* (Munich, 1988), p. 28.

himself in the totality of social life while remaining above it. In thus insisting that the sovereign transcends social or constitutional limitations, Stahl tried to resolve the dualism between monarch and law that had plagued centuries of thought about sovereign power decidedly in favor of the monarch. This was a position explicitly at odds with all attempts to assign sovereign "personality" to the state itself, and it was aimed not only at Hegel, but at Kant and Fichte's abstract theories of right as well.[65] Where Kantian theorists of the *Rechtsstaat* viewed the state as an abstract "juristic person" bearing rights and duties, Stahl insisted on distinguishing the "juristic person" from the "political person." Only the latter is sovereign, for unlike the abstract personhood of the state, which is merely the ensemble of legal relations binding the state in its passive and active duties, the "political person" bears the capacity to be the agent of "action" and "domination."[66]

Stahl's emphasis distinguished him sharply from Haller, whose theory Stahl attacked as a caricature of feudal relations. For Haller, the "state" was really nothing more than one of innumerable relations among sovereign persons, whereas for Stahl, a sharp separation exists between the rights of private subjects and the sovereignty of the prince. Where Haller had recognized only private law, Stahl set the state under public law. This was a point where Stahl's theory intersected with that of both Hegel and liberals, because they all recognized that the state was not merely the personal property of the monarch but had an objective institutional existence. Stahl was thereby able to draw a conceptual distinction between public and private spheres and, like Hegel, between the state and civil society. Robert Berdahl has suggested that Stahl thereby made a fundamental contribution to German conservatism by "modernizing" its theoretical understanding of the state. Not only did his conception of the state conform more accurately to the actual development of the state in the nineteenth century, but his recognition of public law was also better suited to the social and economic transformations that even the nobility could no longer afford to ignore. Hence, his advance beyond earlier Restoration figures was sufficient to draw praise

---

65  F. H. Hinsley argues that the central line of development in modern thinking about sovereignty has led not to the primacy of the sovereign people but to the idea of the sovereignty of the state itself. See Hinsley, *Sovereignty* (New York, 1966), p. 126. On theorists of the *Rechtsstaat*, see Merriam, *Theory of Sovereignty*, pp. 112f. The idea of the juridical or normative "personality of the state" is the primary target of Carl Schmitt's *Political Theology*. In fact, Schmitt's controversial ideas on sovereignty are largely anticipated in Stahl's "Schellingian" political theology.

66  Stahl, *Philosophie des Rechts*, 5th ed., vol. 2, pt. 2, p. 17. Incidentally, this insistence on the "natural" person of the sovereign even set him apart from Hobbes, who, we remember, was indifferent as to whether the Leviathan is a natural or artificial person.

from the Hegelian liberal H.F.W. Hinrichs in his famous *Politische Vorlesungen.*[67]

Nonetheless, the "modernity" of Stahl's political theory must be strictly qualified. His willingness to grant individuals certain inalienable rights because they all have innate dignity as persons amounted to a minimal conservative concession to the idea of equality before the law. He saw no contradiction in also supporting various legal inequalities as divinely ordained sources of order and authority: "The right must differ in accordance with the vocation of the sex, age, estate or class."[68] Moreover, whatever modern institutional features Stahl endorsed were subordinated to a theological rationale. The state is, according to him, a moral institution, an "ethical kingdom" (*sittliches Reich*) established by divine ordination. The ethical kingdom expresses a vision of legitimate domination and deference, of authority voluntarily recognized and accepted by all subjects. The ethical kingdom exists, however, only in the external form of the state, in its formal legal and constitutional recognition of the human being's essence as a free person.[69] People should strive to fulfill their destiny as *imago dei*, to become complete persons by willing God's will as their own, but they do not. For in reality, the human is *homo lapsus*, a refractory, fallen creature. Hence, Stahl distinguished between *homo noumenon*, the righteous person created in the image of God, and *homo phenomenon*, the real person whose freedom is perverse.[70] For Stahl, there could be no Hegelian optimism about the eventual reconciliation of individual inclination and duty, freedom and virtue, divinity and worldliness. Instead, Stahl followed the Pietist Ludwig von Gerlach in assigning equal weight to the state's providential prefiguration of the ethical kingdom, on the one hand, and to its disciplinary enforcement of absolute norms in human affairs, on the other hand. Stahl thereby made clear the political meaning of Schelling's Augustinian defense of free personality. Freedom, for Stahl, is good and true when it affirms the ordained order, sinful and punishable when it asserts the claims of selfhood against external authority.

---

67  Hinrichs, *Politische Vorlesungen*, vol. 1 (Halle, 1843), p. 327.
68  See Stahl, *Die Philosophie des Rechts*, vol. 1, p. 277; and Berdahl, *Politics*, p. 363. In 1841, Feuerbach doubted the sincerity of even Stahl's minimal guarantee of a basic right of personhood. See Feuerbach, "Ein kurzes Wort gegen die Hypokrisie des liberalen Pietismus," *Ludwig Feuerbach und die Philosophie der Zukunft*, ed. Hans-Jürg Braun, et al. (Berlin, 1990), pp. 771–6.
69  Toews, "Immanent Genesis," p. 166. See also Füßl, *Professor*, p. 32.
70  Stahl in *Materialien*, ed. Riedel, p. 229; and *Die Philosophie des Rechts*, 2nd ed., vol. 2, pt. 2, p. 275.

Among the ranks of recalcitrant humanity, Stahl maintained, it is ultimately only the monarch, through the element of sovereign personality,
who approaches the highest ethical idea. Because the personalist dimension
remained so central to his political theory, Stahl's contribution to the evolution of the German idea of the *Rechtstaat* was strictly limited. Although he
conceived of the state as standing under the rule of law, the indivisibility of
monarchic sovereignty precluded the notion that a parliament or, for that
matter, rational public deliberation could play an effective role in preserv-
ing the stability of legal norms. Instead, Stahl had to rely exclusively on the
self-limitation of the monarch himself.[71] Just as Schelling believed that the
order of the universe depends on the self-constraint of the spontaneous divine will, so Stahl maintained that the entire institutional and constitutional
form of the state is both created and sustained by the sovereign will. The
monarch's authority permeates all political and social institutions but transcends these insofar as monarchic will remains unbounded. In times of
conflict, Stahl insisted, the maxim *In dubio pro rege* takes precedent over all
norms.[72] Like Schelling, then, Stahl could account for law only in its *creatio
ex nihilo* from a chaos that has no intrinsic order itself. Put in different terms,
this makes the central notion of democratic theory, the "people," entirely
unintelligible, because in Stahl's view, the "general will" cannot constitute
itself as a sovereign personality. Nor can a shared political or social life, the
participation of citizens in public affairs, be construed as a formative moment in the actualization of personality. The passive mass of individual persons forms a political community only insofar as the individuals are unified
in the will of the sovereign ruler.[73]

Is Stahl's political theory adequately described as a "secularization" of theological concepts? The union of political and theological concepts is clear
in a thinker who could declare that "the state is to be endowed with the
majesty of the personal God."[74] This would seem to support Carl Schmitt's
insistence upon the structural parallels existing between theological and political concepts. But does Stahl's theory support Schmitt's stronger claim for
the *substantial* identity of theological *cum* political concepts? Here the case

71  Füßl, *Professor*, p. 47.
72  See Wiegand, *Stahl*, p. 255.
73  In this sense, Stahl retreats not only behind democratic theory but also behind the me-
    dieval juridical recognition of dual majesty, the *maiestas realis* of the people and the *maiestas
    personalis* of the emperor. See Kantorowicz, *King's Two Bodies*, p. 20; and Hinsley, *Sovereignty*,
    *passim*.
74  Stahl quoted in Hermann Klenner, "Berliner Rechtsphilosophie in der ersten Hälfte des
    19. Jahrhunderts," *Klassische deutsche Philosophie in Berlin*, W. Förster (Berlin, 1988), p. 297.

is less convincing. It must be emphasized that Stahl himself saw the relationship between earthly and divine majesty as an analogy, not as an identity, not even as a continuum. Although he claimed that the king rules by divine grace, his was not actually a theory of divine right. In fact, particularly in the second and subsequent editions of the *Philosophie des Rechts,* he was at pains to emphasize that the relationship between God and the state is not immediate.[75] Monarchy does not flow directly from God, which would suggest pantheism, but is rather grounded in an analogy between distinct spheres bound by the "principle of the world" and the "Urrecht" of human life, the shared idea of personality. Nor does the political theology of Restoration resemble secularization as Hegel understood it. Hegel believed that modern ethical life entailed the actualization of the Christian principle in the world. Restorationist political theology, whether Stahl's or Gerlach's, insisted on separating the state from the sacred. Far from fulfilling a sacral task, the state is part of the desacralized world, essentially free from religion to pursue worldly ends. The contrast to Hegel's own notion of the "Christian" state could hardly be more stark. Restorationist theory operated within a classically Augustinian-Lutheran view, which rendered secularization in Hegel's sense unintelligible and sacrilegious because of the Augustinian doctrine of the separation of the two kingdoms. The "Christian" state of the Restoration thereby consisted precisely in the state's divorce from spirit.

As we turn now to the Young Hegelian response to religio-political personalism, we may anticipate the double quandry faced by thinkers like Ludwig Feuerbach. The Young Hegelians desired to reverse Restoration theory's desacralization of ethical life without resorting to Hegel's particular conception of secularization. For Hegel's attempt to construct a viable notion of ethical life on the basis of a philosophically reconstructed Christianity foundered once the Young Hegelians came to associate Christianity *as such* with anti-social egoism. In an ironic inversion, Feuerbach and other left-wing Hegelians eventually drew a line of affinity from Hegel to his own erstwhile enemies. This development unfolded during the 1830s in the context of the progressive Hegelians' deep involvements in the frequently polemical interactions between Hegelians and anti-Hegelians against the shifting background of Prussian and German politics. As Hegel's political secularization of Christianity fell into discredit among his most radical followers, their great challenge was to discover a new secular basis for the *sacral* life of society, a new basis for the realization of "concrete personality."

---

75  See *Die Philosophie des Rechts,* 5th ed., vol. 2, pt. 1, p. viii.

3

# LUDWIG FEUERBACH
# AND CHRISTIAN CIVIL SOCIETY

"Protestant morality is and was a carnal mingling of the Christian with the man, the natural, political, civil, social man, or whatever else he may be called in distinction from the Christian."[1] This description in Ludwig Feuerbach's *The Essence of Christianity* suggests the complexity of the Young Hegelians' understanding of the interpenetration of Christian belief, politics, and society. By 1841, when Feuerbach published *The Essence of Christianity*, Young Hegelians like him clearly recognized the need to undo the "carnal mingling" of Christian otherworldliness with the worldly political and social subject. To separate the Christian from the "man" and thereby to liberate political, civil and social life from the distorting effects of Christian belief was one of the central tasks that Feuerbach set himself in his 1841 *magnum opus*. Yet this program did not emerge suddenly for Feuerbach and other Left Hegelians in the 1840s. We shall see in this chapter and the next two that during the 1830s, sociopolitical circumstances, as well as intellectual concerns and influences, led some left-wing Hegelians to criticize aggressively the social and political effects of Christian, particularly Protestant, belief.

Feuerbach was perhaps the first Hegelian to attack the nexus of Christian faith, politics, and society; accordingly, it is to his work during the 1830s that we turn first. Feuerbach's exploration of Christian culture and society

---

1  Ludwig Feuerbach, *Das Wesen des Christentums*, vol. 5 of *Ludwig Feuerbach. Gesammelte Werke*, ed. Werner Schuffenhauer (Berlin, 1973), p. 246.

gained greater and greater clarity and vitriol in a series of critical encounters with the personalism that had come to dominate Protestantism in his own day. This engagement was not merely at the theological or philosophical level, however. For Feuerbach directly confronted the political and social dimension of Protestant efforts to reassert the principle of personality against Hegelian pantheism. Thus, Feuerbach's interventions in the debate about personalism pitted him against the orthodox philosophy and theology of his time, furnished material for his education as a political radical, and, finally, prepared the ground for his seminal critique of Hegel himself.

The prominence given to Feuerbach's political and social concerns in this chapter may upset some readers who are accustomed to regarding Feuerbach in the 1830s as, essentially, a technical philosopher preoccupied with the epistemological, ontological, and theological problems posed by Hegelian Idealism, the modern philosophical tradition, and Christian belief. To repeat a qualification from the Introduction, I do not intend to suggest that Feuerbach's philosophical work was subordinated to or in the service of his political and social engagements. To do so would reintroduce the division between the sociopolitical and the philosophico-theological that I am in fact challenging. However, in emphasizing Feuerbach's religio-philosophical critique of Christian bourgeois society, I do intend to counteract the longstanding neglect of a dimension of Feuerbach's thought that must be considered crucial to an understanding of his own development as well as his impact on Hegelian radicalization in general.

## Feuerbach's Early Hegelianism

Feuerbach was eventually to break from Hegel in a very public way in the late 1830s, but his loyalty was actually never to the letter of the Hegelian system, but to the progressive, rational commitment that he regarded as the animating spirit of Hegelian philosophy. He was probably the most brilliant of Hegel's actual students, and perhaps no other pupil absorbed so much of the teacher's message. Nonetheless, at a remarkably young age, Feuerbach drew consequences from Hegel's teaching that more timid or conservative followers wrapped in tepid compromises, and from his early work onward, he pressed the Hegelian legacy into the service of his own concerns.

Feuerbach's degree of independence may have derived in part from the circumstances of his early family life and education.[2] Ludwig Feuerbach was

---

2    The biographical details of Feuerbach's life are well known. John Toews offers an excellent discussion in *Hegelianism*. See also S. Rawidowicz, *Ludwig Feuerbachs Philosophie. Ursprung und*

born in 1804 into the family of Paul Johann Anselm von Feuerbach. Feuerbach senior, of Prussian Protestant birth, was educated at Jena and Kiel and
made a distinguished career as a jurist and professor in Catholic Bavaria. A
man of the *Aufklärung* by temperament and training, Paul Johann Anselm
Feuerbach not only played a key role in Bavarian legal reform but was the
author of numerous works in jurisprudence and political theory.[3] The Feuerbach household was exceptional by any measure, enlightened and progressive by the standard of the day. The father played a strong hand in the
education of his five sons, and each went on to high scholarly attainment.
Although Ludwig eventually rebelled against his father's brand of rationalism, he was not untouched by his father's skeptical turn of mind, his preference for the *philosophe* over the mystic, and his opposition to the reactionary
Restoration after 1815.

Whatever domestic tranquility existed in a family dominated by such a
strong personality as P.J.A. Feuerbach was shattered when he left his family
for his mistress Nanette Brunner in 1816. Biographers have pointed to this
unhappy situation in accounting for the intensely religious phase through
which Ludwig Feuerbach passed in his early teens.[4] Ludwig's spiritual fervor
may also have been an expression of his receptivity to the general religious-
patriotic mood that prevailed among German students in the early postwar
era.[5] However, this proved to be a short-lived phase. By the time Feuerbach
left the Gymnasium of Ansbach to matriculate in the Theology Department
at Heidelberg in 1823, he had worked his way through to a more reflective
stance toward Christianity. Obeisance to the heavenly Father had failed to
meet either his emotional or intellectual needs, although in his obsessive
search for religious conviction he acquired a profound knowledge of Christian doctrine that was to be a fecund source for his later attacks on theology.[6]

While a Gymnasium student in Ansbach, Feuerbach found a new desire
to comprehend the speculative truth of Christian dogma that was stimulated
by one of his teachers, Theodor Lehmus. Lehmus, a theologian, had begun
to explore Hegel's thought as a possible way to reinvigorate Christian the-

*Schicksal* (Berlin, 1931); Uwe Schott, *Die Jugendentwicklung Ludwig Feuerbachs bis zum
Fakultätswechsel 1825* (Göttingen, 1973); Hans-Martin Sass, *Ludwig Feuerbach* (Hamburg,
1978); and Eugene Kamenka, *The Philosophy of Ludwig Feuerbach* (London, 1970).

3  See the study by the eminent twentieth-century jurist Gustav Radbruch, *Paul Johann Anselm
Feuerbach: Ein Juristenleben,* 2nd ed. (Göttingen, 1957).

4  On Feuerbach's early faith, see Schott, *Jugendentwicklung,* pp. 24–30; and Walter Jaeschke,
"Feuerbach redivivus," *Hegel-Studien,* 13(1978), pp. 213–14.

5  Toews, *Hegelianism,* pp. 179–80.

6  See his comment quoted in Van Harvey, *Feuerbach and the Interpretation of Religion* (Cambridge, 1995), p. 14.

ology. Uwe Schott, the biographer of Feuerbach's youth, speculates that Lehmus may have provided Feuerbach's first introduction to Hegel. Moreover, it was through Lehmus that Feuerbach first learned of Karl Daub, a theologian and philosopher at Heidelberg whose conversion to Hegelianism had been the inspiration for Lehmus's own explorations.[7] So it was that upon matriculating at the University of Heidelberg, Feuerbach quickly turned to the "great" Daub, rejecting the more conventional theological rationalism of H.E.G. Paulus, whose lectures he derided as "cobwebs of sophistry."[8] Because Paulus was a personal friend of Feuerbach's father and shared his rationalist views on religious matters, Ludwig's declaration for the speculative philosophy had the unhappy effect of pitting son against father. Nonetheless, his father acquiesced when Feuerbach announced his desire to move to Berlin, where, he argued, he could better continue his "theological studies."[9]

Arriving in Berlin in the spring of 1824, Feuerbach found that he could not tolerate the "mishmash of freedom and dependence, reason and belief" of the prominent theologians Friedrich Schleiermacher and August Neander.[10] By contrast, he began attending Hegel's lectures and studying speculative philosophy with great concentration. The initial contact with Hegel struck Feuerbach like a bolt of lightning. Four weeks into his courses, he informed his father that "what was still obscure and incomprehensible while I was studying under Daub, I have now understood clearly and grasped in its necessity . . . ; what only smoldered in me like tinder, I see now burst into bright flames."[11] Three months later, he declared breathlessly to Daub that his encounter with Hegel marked the "turning point of my entire life," while he pronounced Berlin the "Bethlehem of a new world" revealed in Hegel's lectures.[12]

In the same letter, Feuerbach also made clear his belief that the speculative philosophy superseded the lower truth of Christian dogma. His growing conviction of the superiority of philosophical truth over revelation led

7   Schott, *Jugendentwicklung*, pp. 31–2.
8   Feuerbach to P.J.A. Feuerbach, Autumn 1823, *Briefwechsel (1817–1839)*, vol. 1, ed. W. Schuffenhauer and E. Voigt (Berlin, 1984).
9   Feuerbach to P.J.A. Feuerbach, 8 January 1824, *Briefwechsel*, vol. 1.
10  Feuerbach quoted in Karl Grün, "Ludwig Feuerbach. Philosophische Charakterentwicklung," in *Ludwig Feuerbach in seinem Briefwechsel und Nachlass*, vol. 1, ed. Karl Grün (Leipzig, 1874), p. 16.
11  Feuerbach, "Fragments Concerning the Characteristics of My Philosophical Development," *The Fiery Brook: Selected Writings of Ludwig Feuerbach*, trans. Zawar Hanfi (New York, 1972), p. 268. See also Feuerbach to P.J.A. Feuerbach, 24 May 1824, *Briefwechsel*, vol. 1.
12  Feuerbach to Karl Daub, September 1824, *Briefwechsel*, vol. 1.

him to transfer from the theology faculty to philosophy in 1825, despite his
father's vigorous objections. "No salvation without philosophy!" he wrote his
brother. "To want me to go back to theology now would be like forcing an
immortal spirit back into its dead and foresaken shell or like converting a
butterfly back into a cocoon."[13] Feuerbach's new wings allowed him to take
spiritual flight above the new Bethlehem, but he was forced to walk away
from this city of revelations early in 1826 when the newly crowned Bavarian
king Ludwig I canceled the young student's royal stipend upon his father's
being suspected of liberal proclivities. However, Feuerbach left Berlin without evident regrets, declaring that he had "gone through the whole of
Hegel," and he returned to Bavaria to live under his father's roof, confident
that he could proceed independently. Sure that he had mastered not only
the "contents" but also the "method" of Hegelian philosophy,[14] he diligently
applied himself to his doctoral dissertation, *Of Reason, One, Universal and Infinite,* which he completed in 1828 for the University of Erlangen.

  There are several things to note in these brief details of Feuerbach's early
exposure to Hegelian philosophy. First, he quickly established himself as a
*critical* disciple of Hegel.[15] In the letter to Hegel that he sent along with a copy
of his dissertation in 1828, he described his tutelage as a "living, so to speak
essential rather than formal assimilation and imagination of ideas or concepts
forming the content of your works and oral lessons."[16] The distinction between the Hegelian system and its method was, of course, to become a standard trope for all Hegelians who wished to turn the critical dialectic against
the constraints of the system's own claim to absolute knowledge, but it is a
sign of Feuerbach's precocious independence that he had drawn this distinction as early as his twenty-second year.[17]

  Second, his "living" assimilation of Hegel ranged him with what John
Toews has called the Hegelian "old-left," men like Christian Kapp and Hermann Hinrichs.[18] Like Kapp, who became his close friend, Feuerbach regarded Hegelian philosophy as nothing less than a new dispensation, the
"germ" of "a new period in world history."[19] Yet his 1828 letter to Hegel,

13  Feuerbach, "Fragments," p. 269. See also Feuerbach to Eduard Feuerbach, 1825,
    *Briefwechsel,* vol. 1.
14  Feuerbach, "Fragments," p. 269.
15  The classic study by Rawidowicz, *Ludwig Feuerbachs Philosophie* (p. 19), errs in calling the
    young Feuerbach an "orthodox Hegelian."
16  Feuerbach to G.W.F. Hegel, 22 November 1828, *Hegel: The Letters.*
17  The distinction between system and method became crucial not only for Left Hegelians
    but also for later Marxist critics of Hegel. See, for example, the comments of Georg Lukács,
    *Hegel's False and His Genuine Ontology,* trans. David Fernbach (London, 1982), p. 55.
18  Toews, *Hegelianism,* p. 328.
19  Feuerbach to Hegel, 22 November 1828, *Hegel: The Letters.*

while expressing the most reverential respect, evinces a clear impatience with the Hegelian philosophy. Hegel's ideas are subtly compared in their "colorless purity, immaculate clarity, beautitude, and unity" with Feuerbach's own "manner of philosophizing," which he claimed descends from heaven and takes "form in an intuition which penetrates the particular, cancels and masters appearance within appearance itself." The specifically Christian dimension in Hegel's idea of secularization is here discarded in favor of the "actualization and secularization of the idea, the *ensarkosis* or Incarnation of the pure *logos*." Philosophy is thus declared triumphantly post-Christian and becomes the affair of all "humanity" whose task it is to found the "Kingdom of the Idea." Besides the prophetic anti-Christian tone in this letter, we note that already Feuerbach has equated the philosophy of the Idea exclusively with the immanent destiny of humanity and that, even though his concepts were clearly Idealist at this stage, he associated his own style of thought with a form of *praxis*. Georg Friedrich Daumer, Feuerbach's close friend, drew a revealing conclusion from his enthusiastic reading of Feuerbach's dissertation: "[T]he entire system of speculation must in my opinion become history, simply the history of spirit and the world. Hegel perceives this to an extent in his method. But it is absurd to permit world history to enter only as one moment of the whole, as he does."[20]

Finally, of significance to our discussion is the fact that at this youthful stage, Feuerbach expressed a decided preference for the "universal" moment in the Hegelian dialectic at the expense of the "particular." He had thanked Daub in 1824 for first lifting him from the confines of "base subjectivity," from the "poor little I of the individual," to the concrete vision of the unity of "life, truth and reality" in spirit.[21] To be sure, a militant desire to overcome subjectivity, negatively associated with Romanticism's emotional and solipsistic indulgences, was not uncommon to the youthful converts to the philosophy of Hegel, who himself had claimed that the speculative philosophy leads us beyond the "standpoint of the individual, particular person."[22] Still, it must be said that Feuerbach was particularly adamant in his rejection of subjectivism, a reaction that might have been closely related to the failure of his adolescent attachment to the ideal of spiritual inwardness to meet his emotional and intellectual needs.

By the time Feuerbach wrote his dissertation, Hegel's nuanced dialectical treatment of the tension between the universal and the particular had sharpened in his mind into a world-historical antithesis between philosophy

20 Georg Friedrich Daumer to Feuerbach, 12 February 1828, *Briefwechsel*, vol. 1.
21 Feuerbach to Daub, September 1824, *Briefwechsel*, vol. 1.
22 Hegel quoted by Butler in *Hegel: The Letters*, p. 547.

and Christianity, between the universality of reason and the particularity of the self. Hence, he declared in a crucial passage of his letter to Hegel that the task of establishing the Kingdom of the Idea demands "overthrowing from its throne the ego, the *self* in general, which, especially since the beginning of Christianity, has dominated the world, which has conceived itself as the only spirit to exist. This spirit, [in asserting itself] as absolute, has validated itself by repressing the true absolute and objective spirit."[23] Feuerbach here inverted Hegel's own assessment, for rather than link Christianity to a new universal idea of shared spirituality, he associated Christianity with the hypostatized spirit of Hellenistic philosophy. By this, he meant that Christianity actually absolutizes the *sensuousness* of Greek philosophy through its elevation of the immortality of the individual self to the highest doctrine of faith. Christianity thus takes the form of "fixed finitude"; it is the religion of "the pure self, of the person taken as a *solitary* spirit."[24]

Feuerbach's letter to Hegel anticipated at a highly abstract level the central themes of his 1830 *Thoughts on Death and Immortality*, and it articulated more clearly than the dissertation what he considered to be at stake in championing philosophy. Indeed, the dissertation scarcely mentioned Christianity and directed its main attack against the tendency of "too many philosophers of our time" to "want to make the single and contingent individual (that is, themselves) into the principle and content of their philosophizing," a trend that he detected not only in Kant and Fichte but in Jacobi and Novalis as well.[25] On Feuerbach's account, this focus on self-consciousness reduces thinking to a self-relation of the thinking individual, which means that all knowing is merely personal. In opposition to this trend toward epistemological individualism, Feuerbach took an extreme position on Hegel's thesis of the reflective universality of Reason. That is, he maintained that whereas mere self-consciousness constitutes the personal identity of the individual self, "thinking" elevates self-consciousness to universality. Reason is thus the sole and proper object of philosophy that must always eschew the particular in favor of the universal. In that Reason is the "substance of the individual," "insofar as I think, I am no longer an individual."[26]

Feuerbach relied explicitly on Hegel's concept of relation in order to articulate this transcendence of individuality, even citing the discussion of the relational formation of concrete personality in Hegel's *Encyclopedia*.[27] Hence,

23  Feuerbach to Hegel, 22 November 1828, *Hegel: The Letters*.
24  Ibid.
25  Feuerbach, "Über die Vernunft," in *Gesammelte Werke*, vol. 1, pp. 145–7.
26  Ibid., p. 18.      27  Ibid., p. 62, n15.

he wrote, not only am "I and the other united in thought in the same act," but "in thought the other I is in myself undifferentiated, I am at the same time I and the other, not as a determinate other, but as the other overall (as species [*Gattung*])."[28] While Feuerbach made a Hegelian argument for identity in difference, however, his concluding mention of the *Gattung* actually signals a departure from Hegel. Although Feuerbach's language at this stage was sufficiently inconsistent and imprecise that he could sometimes speak of "God" or "godly unity," he had in fact already replaced the moment of divinity with the *Gattung* in this self-relation of the self in the other. Feuerbach thus construed universality in strictly human terms, with reason and language constituting the universal essence of humanity.[29]

Two observations on the dissertation are particularly important for our discussion. First, Feuerbach identified individuation (and, incidentally, pure self-consciousness) with unmediated nature, while he associated universality, the "human overall," with spirit. Measured against his subsequent turn toward naturalism, Feuerbach's early commitment to the primacy of spirit over nature is especially striking. Second, he invested his understanding of universality with sociopolitical import. He cited Aristotle's claim that outside "human society" there are only beasts or gods to support his own contention that all thought is social, communicative activity: "Reason is social, neither born in the individual nor private. Only the social person [*Mensch*] can attain to Reason or Thought." Among the consequences that Feuerbach drew from this position was the denial of contract theories of the origin of the state, because he could not accept any notion of a rational state of nature.[30] The antithesis of nature and spirit thus became identical with the antithesis between two conceptions of the human being, the first taking the isolated presocial or asocial person as the basic ontological reality, the second, Feuerbach's, holding that the person is constituted as a social being. The strong Hegelian dimension of Feuerbach's position is clear; yet at the same time, his stress on the social nature of reason seems all the more emphatic because he had silently dropped Hegel's mediation between the immanent and the transcendent.

Feuerbach's dissertation confirms him as the critical disciple he considered himself to be, still operating within a Hegelian framework even if in crucial ways he had already moved outside it. One might say that at this

28 Ibid., p. 21.
29 Feuerbach writes that reason is neither "finite" nor "generally human [*menschliche*]," but here he identifies *menschlich* with individuality, not with the human *per se* (ibid., p. 43).
30 Ibid., p. 73, n60

point, his critical relationship to Hegel consisted not only in his resolute commitment to speculative philosophy over and against Christianity but also in his enthusiasm for precisely that brand of panlogism which critics had attributed to Hegel. Indeed, even though Feuerbach criticized Christianity for its negative attitude toward nature, this was only because Christianity was content to leave nature uncomprehended and unredeemed by spirit. For Feuerbach, the blinding light of pure *logos* was finally to erase the particularity of nature.[31] Further, insofar as the moment of particularity is preserved, it is assigned only negative associations with nature and unfreedom. By thus embracing an extreme form of panlogism at this stage in his development, Feuerbach actually retreated behind the idea of "concrete totality" that had animated Hegel's work. The relation of the self to "objective being" that he tried to describe as an antidote to subjectivism turns out on closer inspection to be a self-relation of reason.

Consequently, while Feuerbach rejected Romantic subjectivism, his monistic view of universal spirit reinscribed subjectivism as the sole principle of the universe. Hence, in his letter to Hegel, he claimed that the founder of the Kingdom of the Idea "will not be an individual, or will be this individual which alone *is*, the World spirit."[32] Although Feuerbach struggled against various forms of personalism and subjectivism throughout the 1830s, he never overcame the residue of personalism that shadowed his attempts to describe the collective essence of humanity. Even his breakthrough to an "anthropological" and materialist position in the late 1830s complicated but did not overcome the dilemma. For his new position contained an unresolved tension between, on the one hand, the definition of humanity as a unified *species-subject,* and, on the other hand, the human individual as a being whose essence is radically undefined once it is emancipated from its theological illusions.

Unsatisfying as Feuerbach's youthful vision of an epochal collectivization of humanity under the sign of the incarnate Idea may be, it is necessary to repeat that from the beginning of his serious philosophical work Feuerbach did not isolate his response to various technical problems posed by speculative philosophy from the project of cultural transformation, although these elements remained largely implicit. In his next major work, *Thoughts on Death and Immortality,* published anonymously in 1830, Feuerbach fully

31  This assertion was at odds with doubts that Feuerbach expressed at the same time about the Hegelian account of the relation between thought and being, logic and nature. See "Fragments," p. 269; and below, pp. 101–2.

32  Feuerbach to Hegel, 22 November 1828, *Hegel: The Letters.*

embraced his role as cultural critic and prophet, turning the critique of individual selfhood into a commentary on the social and political condition of his age.

## Immortality and the Personal God

When Feuerbach published *Thoughts on Death and Immortality* in 1830, he felt that it was only under the cover of anonymity that he could launch an assault on the Christian doctrine of personal immortality. Living in Erlangen at the time and seeking a permanent teaching position at that city's university, where Stahl and other Pietists had gained ascendancy, Feuerbach had reason to publish anonymously.[33] Indeed, the eventual discovery of his authorship contributed decisively to the permanent destruction of his hopes for a professorial career, despite his repeated efforts to gain preferment in both Bavaria and Prussia in the early 1830s. Still, it is not at all surprising that he was found out. For one thing, *Thoughts on Death and Immortality* displayed continuities with the themes of Feuerbach's writings of the 1820s, though these could hardly have been known to more than a few of his friends and teachers. More important, Feuerbach himself appears to have grown more casual about the secret, as increasingly frequent references to the book in his correspondence suggest. It is as if prudence lost a battle of attrition against pride at his independent stance and its historical importance.[34]

*Thoughts on Death and Immortality* is too frequently read as simply an attack on Christian dogma and as an anticipation of themes of Feuerbach's mature critique of religion. The book is, of course, a substantial critique of theology. Indeed, if Carl Ludwig Michelet was correct in noting in 1841 that the "personality of God" had dominated philosophical debate in the previous ten years, then Feuerbach's *Thoughts on Death and Immortality* articulated at the outset of the 1830s a radical rebuttal to the issue that preoccupied theologians and philosophers for the entire decade. Feuerbach's intense concern with the interrelated issues of the personality of God and personal immortality in *Thoughts* contradicts Marx Wartofsky's claim that it was only in 1838 that Feuerbach made his "first clear attack on the concept of personality."[35]

---

33  Toews, *Hegelianism*, p. 252.

34  This is true, I think, even if Feuerbach was evasive in responding to a direct inquiry from the senate of the University of Erlangen as to the authorship of *Thoughts on Death and Immortality*. See Feuerbach to J.G.V. Engelhardt, 2 October 1836, *Briefwechsel*, vol. 1.

35  Wartofsky, *Feuerbach* (Cambridge, 1977), p. 169. Wartofsky passes over *Thoughts* with the comment that it was a "traumatic incident." This is a surprising omission given Wartofsky's genetic approach in his study of Feuerbach. In contrast, see the recent study by Alexis

Feuerbach's target in his dissertation had been the subjective Idealism fashionable among philosophers of his day, and in *Thoughts,* he broadened his target to Christianity in general and more particularly the orthodox, Pietistic, and rationalist strains in Protestantism.

The meaning of the *Thoughts* is seriously compromised if one fails to see that it is also a political tract of considerable force. At the core of Feuerbach's critique of the Christian doctrine of personal immortality is a set of social and political associations that were to gain still greater clarity in his writings of the later 1830s and early 1840s. Parts of *Thoughts on Death and Immortality* had already been sketched while Feuerbach lived in Berlin, but the book's appearance coincided with the brief flurry of passion aroused by the French Revolution of 1830.[36] While direct evidence of Feuerbach's response to the July Revolution is absent, as is most of his correspondence from 1830, his *Thoughts* struck a radically defiant stance against the reactionary forces of the day:

> ... we see how a great multitude of our contemporaries, unconcerned for the exalted teachings of history, paying no attention to the strenuous deeds and painful works of humanity, scorning and insulting the rights and claims that reason has earned over a thousand years of battles, has turned back to the old ways and is concerned to restore them unchanged. They attempt their restoration as if the rivers of blood of past ages had rushed by to no purpose. . . .[37]

Unambiguous declarations for rights and freedoms like this have led one prominent Marxist scholar to describe *Thoughts* as a typical expression of the bourgeois opposition beginning to rise in Germany in 1830.[38] However, although such a characterization at least recognizes a political content in Feuerbach's theological critique, it neglects the fact that Feuerbach's target was not only the Restorationist monarchy. Rather, it is a critique of the bourgeois spirit itself that emerges as an integral element of Feuerbach's examination of the personalist dimension in Christian belief.

Feuerbach's critique of personal immortality centered on a speculative and historical examination of the idea of the personal God of Christianity, "the religion of the pure self, the person as the single spirit." As in his dis-

Philonenko, *La jeunesse de Feuerbach. 1828–1841. Introduction à ses positions fondamentales,* vol. 1 (Paris, 1990), pp. 55–167.

36 Werner Schuffenhauer, "Neue Daten zum Corpus der Schriften Ludwig Feuerbachs," *Ludwig Feuerbach und die Philosophie der Zukunft* (Berlin, 1990), p. 765.

37 Feuerbach, *Thoughts on Death and Immortality,* trans. James Massey (Berkeley, 1980), pp. 15–16.

38 Werner Schuffenhauer, *Feuerbach und der junge Marx. Zur Enstehungsgeschichte der marxistischen Weltanschauung* (Berlin, 1965), p. 16.

sertation, Feuerbach contrasted the Christian personalist view of God as possessing "self-consciousness, freedom, will, decision, and purpose" to his own conception of "God" as universal *logos*.[39] However, the 1830 work marked a decisive shift toward naturalism in Feuerbach's thinking, for the *Thoughts* conceives of God as the infinite unity of all being, a pantheistic spirit of universal activity. In contrast to the panlogism of 1828, in 1830 God appears as a "self-forgetting poet" who brought forth the world in "the back of his consciousness." Nature is thus not simply the latent object of thought, its otherness to be sublated eventually by reason. Rather, nature is equally compounded of the rational and the irrational, the light and the dark that eludes comprehension. For the "night in nature was produced out of the night in God."[40] A "tragic," mystical element came to compete with the panglossian rationalism of Feuerbach's dissertation, for he now considered "God" to be the cyclical process of affirmation and negation in life itself. Life, the living otherness of nature in us and outside us, entered his thinking decisively, and "love," the eros that unifies all being, came to contend with "thought" as the central category of his philosophy.

Feuerbach's language clearly echoes the mystical idea of God articulated by Jakob Böhme and embraced by Schelling in his 1809 *Investigations into the Essence of Human Freedom*. Both Manfred Frank and Peter Cornehl have argued convincingly that Schelling's *Naturphilosophie* played an important role in stimulating Feuerbach's move away from the extreme panlogism of the dissertation. In 1827, Feuerbach was in Erlangen, where Schelling's influence was strong, and he did send him a copy of his dissertation along with a respectful letter. Schelling's attempt to think about the ground of being anticipated Feuerbach's growing preoccupation with the naturalistic base of human rationality. His elevation of the substantiality of nature, of the "night in nature," over subjectivity in his definition of the universal bespeaks the same recognition of an unbridgeable hiatus between consciousness and being that had so troubled Schelling. Moreover, Manfred Frank suggests that Schelling's Munich lectures of 1827–8 may account for the misgivings about the relation between thought and being in Hegelian logic that Feuerbach voiced in his notebooks of the late 1820s.[41] Although these doubts do not fully accord with the tenor of Feuerbach's dissertation or his *Thoughts,* they do anticipate his 1839 critique of Hegel's dialectical logic. In this sense, we

39  Feuerbach, *Thoughts*, p. 23.
40  Ibid., p. 82.
41  Frank, *Der unendliche Mangel an Sein. Schellings Hegelkritik und die Anfänge der Marxschen Dialektik* (Frankfurt, 1975), p. 195.

must acknowledge that Schelling's thought had an early and enduring effect on Feuerbach's development during the 1830s.[42]

Nonetheless, it is equally important to acknowledge, as Frank does not sufficiently, that even at this youthful stage a considerable gulf separated Feuerbach from Schelling. Although he was receptive to Schelling's critique of Hegel's conception of the identity of thought and being, Feuerbach gravitated toward naturalism, Schelling toward theology. Whereas Schelling insisted on the non-identity of universal concepts and existing real beings, Feuerbach resisted the nominalist implications of this critique. His more fully developed notion of "species-being," for all its emphasis on sensuousness and embodiment, was not intended to erase universality but rather to reformulate it in an immanent naturalistic form. Finally, Feuerbach never abandoned his commitment to rationalism, even if reason now consisted in part in recognizing the limits imposed on subjectivity by our life in nature. By the early 1830s, he had grown critical of Jakob Böhme's mysticism, and he was delivering lectures critical of the intuitive orientation of Schelling's early Idealism as well as the irrationalism of his Positive Philosophy.[43] Throughout the 1830s, Schelling's probable influence upon Feuerbach did not prevent him from reaching a radically antithetical position.

Feuerbach's evaluation of the Christian doctrine of immortality rested on psychological and historical arguments that anticipate in many important respects his critique of religion in *The Essence of Christianity*. As he was to do in that later work, he traced the belief in a personal God back to human psychological needs. For, he maintained, although God appears as the "prototype" of personhood, he is in fact a product of the human person's egoistical refusal to recognize his own limits in nature. Hence, the creation of a God in the "exact image of human personhood" satisfies the human person's own sense of unique importance.[44] From faith in the eternal personhood of God, Feuerbach continued, the believer could draw a "sacred certificate and guaranty [*sic*] of himself and his own individual existence." Therefore, the cherished faith in personal immortality rests on the "principle of [the person's] selfish reality," the egoistical desire to affirm the infinite and eternal value of the self in the face of the nullity of physical death.[45]

According to Feuerbach, the basic psychological impulse that creates gods took a particularly egoistical turn in Christianity because of the histor-

42  See also Toews, *Hegelianism*, pp. 196–7; and Ursula Reitmeyer, *Philosophie der Leiblichkeit* (Frankfurt, 1988), p. 140.
43  Feuerbach, "Schelling und die 'intellektuelle Anschauung,'" *Nachlaß*, pp. 326–8.
44  Feuerbach, *Thoughts*, p. 23.    45  Ibid., p. 24.

ical conditions of its emergence as a faith. Feuerbach sounded remarkably like the young Hegel, whom he could not have read, or like Edward Gibbon, the great British historian of ancient Rome, whom he had read in his youth,[46] when he tied the Christian belief in personal immortality to the decline of ancient political life. Where the Greek or Roman conceived of virtue only within the horizons of public life and could face death confident of enduring in the grateful memory of posterity,[47] Feuerbach argued that with the collapse of the Greek *polis* and the Roman Republic, the individual felt compelled to project his quest for personal worth into an afterlife beyond the social and political world that had ceased to be the sustaining medium of the self. Consequently, he wrote that for the Christian, the promised world of infinite existence becomes more "real" than the communal or natural existence of the individual. Seeking to evade the restrictions and threats of earthly life, the Christian invests his hopes and energies in a fantasy of unlimited selfhood that denigrates the concretely existing individual and the world in the name of an abstract idea of personality. Even in *Thoughts on Death and Immortality*, then, alienation was central to Feuerbach's understanding of religious belief; and, significantly, he viewed this alienation as both existential and political. The self is estranged from its social and natural being because it is determined by an atomistic ideal of personhood that cannot be realized in the mundane world. The self is alienated politically, as a result, because the practicable virtues that would relate the individual actively to existing communal life become irrelevant to his self-fulfillment.

In an attempt to transcend the debilitating effects of the Christian conception of the human person, Feuerbach drew very different consequences from his discussion of the nature of the animating spirit of the cosmos. If "spirit" is taken as the constant activity of differentiation and reabsorption of forms into the eternal unity of being, then spirit is both the ground of personhood, in the moment of differentiation, and the negation of "absolute personhood," in the moment of unity.[48] Where the Christian attempted to fix for all eternity the single isolated person, Feuerbach emphasized that the person is comprehensible only as a concretely existing, intersubjectively mediated, limited being. This led him to reassert the social orientation that had dominated his dissertation. Yet, if Feuerbach thus insisted on the "communal"

---

46  See the comments of a childhood friend of Feuerbach quoted in *Ludwig Feuerbach. Werke in Sechs Bänden*, vol. 2, ed. Erich Thies (Frankfurt, 1975), p. 338 n1.

47  See *Thoughts*, esp. p. 6. Feuerbach here sounds strikingly like the young Hegel in his unpublished essays of the 1790s. See Hegel's comments on Roman republicanism and immortality in "The Positivity of the Christian Religion," *Early Theological Writings*, p. 157.

48  Ibid., p. 110.

essence of the human person, it must be emphasized that his aim was not to
erase personality but rather to stress that there are "degrees of personhood."
It was not only this social ontology of the self that led him to qualify the status of the individual. Consistent with the general turn of his thought, he presented this discussion against the background of the cycle of nature as both
the ultimate negation of all finite beings and the most basic source of ontological unity.

Like such "old-left" Hegelians as Christian Kapp, Feuerbach clearly believed that the transition from a religious to a philosophical consciousness
would usher in nothing less than an epochal transformation in the human
spirit. This lent his analysis of Christian personalism an evangelical fervor
and an activist strain. So, for example, he claimed that once the person faces
the limit imposed by death he will "gain the courage to begin a new life and
to experience the pressing need for making that which is absolutely true and
substantial, that which is actually infinite, into the theme and content of his
entire spiritual activity."[49] Feuerbach's 1830 work therefore had the intention of recalling humanity from a fantastical potentiality to actuality, from
egoistical self-worship to the task of realizing humanity's potential as a communal being. As in his 1828 letter to Hegel, we see again that Feuerbach
connected his own form of thought with a form of activism that he expected
would transform the world from the realm of the enthroned "I" into the
"Kingdom of the Idea." Already in Feuerbach's formulation of 1830, we find
in embryo not only the politics of Young Hegelianism but also the philosophical basis for the "philosophy of the deed" and, indeed, for Marxism.[50]

However, unlike Marx's later attempt to explain the false consciousness
of religion by reference to tensions in the secular basis of material life,
Feuerbach was here content to rest at the level of a critique of false beliefs.
Consequently, he remained optimistic that the secular basis, that which is
"absolutely true and substantial," contained in itself the ground for communal union once true consciousness prevailed over false. Feuerbach's
utopian streak was further revealed by his commitment to love as the source
of communal being and as the force that would compel an epochal transformation. Although he tried to identify thinking and love as equally capable of transcending particularity in the affirmation of universality, he clearly

---

49  Ibid., p. 17.
50  For an example of the direct influence of Feuerbach's *Thoughts*, see the discussion of the
    socialist poet and activist Georg Herwegh by Ingrid Pepperle, "Philosophie und kritische
    Literatur im deutschen Vormärz: Ludwig Feuerbach und Georg Herwegh," *Ludwig Feuer-
    bach und die Philosophie der Zukunft*, pp. 575–92.

regarded *eros* as a more powerful bond than *logos*. Indeed, love emerges in his account as both the essence of humanity and the most powerful negation of personality. Whereas Christians egoistically believe that God cherishes their particular selves, Feuerbach contended that the creative principle of the world, which he called love, both affirms and negates the self; hence, "only the genuine pantheist knows what love is."[51] For Feuerbach, human love is the exemplary experience of the loss of self, the sense of placing another above oneself, of being outside oneself in an other, of throwing off the shackles of egoism. He drew a continuum from sexual contact, the most elemental expression of this transcendence of self, to love of humanity as the object of self-sacrifice and devotion. By the mid-1830s, Feuerbach came to identify the universalizing force of love with the *true* essence of Christianity and to associate the particularizing impulse of personalism with a distortion of that essence.

In 1830, Feuerbach had not yet arrived at that insight, but he did nonetheless recognize epochs in the history of Christianity when love contended with egoism as the main impulse of faith. Early Christianity and even medieval Catholicism contained a strong communal dimension that mitigated the tendency toward a fixation on the self.[52] Egoism became the principle of Christianity only in the modern age. Hence, *Thoughts* repeatedly contrasts "ancient, genuine, essential Christianity" or the faith that could create monuments to community such as the cathedrals of Cologne and Strasbourg to the decadent modern faith.[53] On Feuerbach's account, it was Protestantism that destroyed the spiritual community of medieval Catholicism and prompted the turn toward the self, Protestantism that marked a climax in the career of egoistical personhood. Early Protestantism's insistence upon a direct relationship of man to God placed great emphasis upon the "single, world-historical person of Christ" in His role as the redeemer of the faithful.[54] In the Pietism that emerged in the seventeenth century, the cult of the singular person of Christ weakened before a new object of devotion, "each person in himself and in his own interior reality."[55] Indeed, Feuerbach believed that Pietism expressed with particular clarity the central tendency of Protestantism toward an increasing fixation upon one's own pious emotions.

Peter Cornehl has suggested that Feuerbach's sharp criticism of the modern era's preoccupation with subjectivity and individualism drew heavily on Romantic representations of history. The influence of Novalis's depiction of

51 Feuerbach, *Thoughts*, p. 29.     52 Ibid., esp. pp. 7 and 135.
53 Ibid., p. 216.     54 Ibid., p. 10.     55 Ibid., p. 11.

Protestantism as a fall from the communal solidarity of medieval Christendom is readily discernible in Feuerbach's trenchant opposition to the modern cult of the individual, though Feuerbach's hopes for the "Kingdom of the Idea" departed significantly from the reactionary hostility toward Protestant individualism that characterizes Novalis's great paean to the middle ages, "Christianity or Europe."[56] The *Thoughts on Death and Immortality* was resolutely set against any nostalgic dream of a return to the past. At the same time, however, Feuerbach's quasi-eschatological expectation of a coming new age of universality also clarified the challenge he had posed to Hegel in his 1828 letter, because his critique of Protestantism involved a precise inversion of Hegel's "Protestant principle." Where Hegel had regarded Protestantism, the "religion of free individuals," as the vehicle for the secularization of the Christian idea of freedom, Feuerbach implied that far from manifesting an idea of freedom fit for politics, the only conception of freedom operative in Protestantism is that of an egoistical withdrawal from communal life. The future called for a radical overcoming of Protestantism, not its gradual evolution, in Feuerbach's apocalyptic view.

Feuerbach was not alone among his contemporaries in inheriting this critical perspective on Protestantism. In a recent essay, Laurence Dickey calls attention to the "countless examples of negative representations of Protestantism . . . in the writings of Saint-Simon, Comte, and the Saint-Simonians from at least 1820 on." He writes that Protestantism and the forms of introspective Idealism associated with it were "assigned prominent places in a 'critical' era of history that is an *ensemble* of anti-social values – in religion, philosophy, literature, politics, and economics."[57] As in Feuerbach's case, the Saint-Simonians' association of Protestantism with modern egoism seems to have derived from earlier sources, particularly the critique of the modern spirit of individualism and liberalism that one encounters in conservative Catholics like Louis de Bonald, Joseph de Maistre, and the poet Félicité de Lamennais in the 1790s and early 1800s. Noting this genealogy, Dickey makes the important point that the Saint-Simonians mark the "strategic ideological cross-over point whereby 'right-wing' theocratic conceptions of history were appropriated by the self-proclaimed 'apostles' of the 'left.'"[58] The relationship between the Saint-Simonians and German radicals like Feuerbach will be a subject of the next two chapters, but for the moment it may

56  Cornehl, " Feuerbach und die Naturphilosophie," p. 52. See Novalis, "Christendom or Europe."
57  Dickey, "Saint-Simonian Industrialism as the End of History: August Cieszkowski on the Teleology of Universal History," *Apocalypse Theory and the Ends of the World*, ed. M. Bull (Oxford, 1995), p. 178.
58  Ibid., p. 186.

be said that Feuerbach's *Thoughts on Death and Immortality* clearly reveals the same passage of conservative criticisms of modern subjectivism into the lexicon of the nascent Left.

Like the Saint-Simonians, Feuerbach pushed this evaluation of Protestantism beyond a condemnation of religious individualism. Feuerbach's target gains much greater specificity once we realize that he associated the post-Reformation religious idea of personality with modern bourgeois social and political relations. There can be little doubt that in Feuerbach's account, the modern believer, convinced of his infinite self-worth, is in fact the bourgeois of civil society, the sphere of the market and self-interested individualism that Hegel had described in the *Philosophy of Right*. Hence, when Feuerbach had written in December 1828 that the "illusion" of "immediate personality" "could only arise in an age when the single individual takes himself as absolute and infinite,"[59] he meant to signify not only a religious and philosophical but also a social and political feature of modernity. The "individuals of the modern world," Feuerbach wrote in the *Thoughts,* stand isolated in "all-negating nakedness," torn by the reductive, atomizing forces of modern commercial society from community and a personality "rich in relations." This is a critique of the social conditions of Feuerbach's own age that scholars have neglected in the *Thoughts on Death and Immortality,* but it is unmistakably present alongside the more generalized critique of Christian egoism.

Feuerbach's language reveals the association of the Christian idea of personality with bourgeois civil society. With satirical wit, he argued that the comforting images of an eternal life pull

> the great and serious tragedy of nature into the common realm of the bourgeois [and] economic life of the philistine, because the bottomless abyss of nature is turned into a shallow meadow brook near which individuals pick charming forget-me-nots and relax with tea and coffee from the burning sunlight of actual life and reason, and in which they see only themselves reflected.[60]

At a more serious level, Feuerbach's descriptions of the opposition between love and ego, or pantheism and personality, reveal that he merged theistic and juridical definitions of personhood to form a general critique of the modern fixation upon the isolated self. In one revealing passage, for example, he compared the Christian's desire to preserve his finite particular form within the infinity of being to a *"contrat social"* which is not in fact ratified by

59  Feuerbach to Johann Paul Harl, December 1828, *Briefwechsel,* vol. 1.
60  Feuerbach, *Thoughts,* p. 82.

the infinite itself.[61] In his 1828 dissertation, Feuerbach had rejected the idea of the social contract because it presupposes the ontological primacy of the presocial self. In 1830, this metaphor establishes a link between belief in immortality and the desire of the person to establish his relationship to the community on "contractual" – that is, self-serving – terms. By contrast, Feuerbach claimed that love overcomes the "juridical, excluding, distinguishing self"; outside love, "everything is egoism, self-seeking, vanity, greed, mercinariness, idolatry"; in love "you no longer exist in your particular interests, in your affairs, in the many objects in which you used to exist." He contrasted a love that leads to the self-sacrifice of one's being with a love for "that which is single, sensible (money, determinate things)."[62]

In an epigram entitled "Mercantilistic Speculations, together with Complaints about the Bad Times of the Present and the Poor Products of the Christian Lands," Feuerbach wrote:

> Ever since belief became the mode, all business has stagnated,
> Even ideas in the head, even blood in the veins.
> What a solid foundation we had when civic virtue [Bürgertugend]
> And a sure sense for what is right built the cities!
> In those days, when the public was not yet prohibited from access to virtue,
> There were a lot fewer bankruptcies than today!
> These are really bad times; the most oppressive misery in the land
> And yet the Christians won't let us import any foreign product.
> For our spiritual customs officers prohibit the entrance
> Even of good products if they don't have a crucifix on them.[63]

This epigram brings together many of the implicit elements of Feuerbach's social and political critique. The economic metaphors of bankruptcy and protectionism ironically appropriate the Christian culture's own values in order to pronounce that culture spiritually and *politically* defunct. Feuerbach evokes the past in which "virtue" was the public possession of citizens rhetorically and polemically rather than nostalgically to sharpen his critique of the selfish, private, and apolitical values of contemporary Christian society. The epigram also exposes the role played by the Christian state in perpetuating this situation, an observation echoed in Feuerbach's prediction that "soon the police will be the ground of theology."[64] The "foreign prod-

61 Ibid., p. 36.    62 Ibid., p. 122.
63 Ibid., p. 244. I disagree with James Massey's translation of *Bürgertugend* as "bourgeois virtue." Feuerbach undoubtedly uses Bürger in this context to connote civic status, or citizenship, even though elsewhere in *Thoughts*, *bürgerlich* clearly signifies the pejorative adjective "bourgeois."
64 Ibid., p. 189.

uct," left unidentified in this and the other epigrams, could well be the atheistic spirit of the French Enlightenment and the revolutionary fervor that had broken out again in 1830 but was suppressed in the German states.

As he had done in his dissertation, Feuerbach embraced the most radical conclusions that critics had attributed to Hegel himself. We have seen that by 1830, the charge that Hegel's philosophy negated the personality of God and the immortality of the soul had become common currency among his theological and philosophical opponents. In enthusiastically confirming their worst fears, Feuerbach rebuked these critics of the Idea, who were part of the "multitude" that would attempt a "restoration as if the rivers of blood of past ages had rushed by to no purpose."[65] What is more, he politicized his criticism of theological personality by tying it to a critique of the private, self-centered, apolitical German *Bürger*. From that position, it would not be a great leap to demand openly a virtuous citizenry that would be actively engaged in realizing the spirit of the community and to draw a democratic political message from his pantheistic humanism. These conclusions remained implicit in *Thoughts on Death and Immortality*. Nonetheless, they anticipated features of Feuerbach's more radical future and some of the salient elements in the politics of the intellectual Left in the later 1830s and 1840s.[66]

## Feuerbach's Critique of Friedrich Julius Stahl

After the anonymous publication of *Thoughts on Death and Immortality,* Feuerbach turned from radical anti-Christian prophesy to the study of the history

---

65 Ibid., p. 16.
66 Although *Thoughts* had grievous consequences for Feuerbach's career, the book did not receive widespread attention. The 1833 works of another Hegelian, Friedrich Richter, *Die Lehre von den letzten Dingen* and *Die neue Unsterblichkeitslehre,* had greater immediate impact upon the discussion of the Hegelian position on immortality and personality. Walter Jaeschke claims in *Reason in Religion* (p. 366) that Feuerbach's *Thoughts* met with muted response because in 1830 the absence of any published version of Hegel's *Philosophy of Religion* did not permit "reasoned critique" of these issues. This is only a partially convincing explanation for the reception of Feuerbach's work. Hegel's critics had found enough evidence of his stance in other published works to form an opinion by 1830 that was little changed by the publication of the *Lectures on the Philosophy of Religion* in 1832. Moreover, with the exception of serious philosophers such as I. H. Fichte and C. H. Weisse, Hegel's critics were not primarily interested in reasoned critique, as Jaeschke himself says elsewhere. I think Richter provoked more controversy because he identified himself, a known Hegelian, as the author and because he assailed Christian principles from a scrupulously *Hegelian* position, thereby forcing the ambiguities of Hegelianism into the light. Feuerbach diverged in many ways from Hegel, and his work was vilified not as that of a Hegelian but as that of an anonymous blasphemer.

of modern philosophy. Yet far from being merely scholarly studies, his three great historical works were efforts to clarify his own thought through a critique of the course of modern philosophy. His *History of Modern Philosophy from Bacon to Spinoza* (1833) initiated this long reexamination of the historical roots of his own philosophical influences.[67] In this work, he criticized the one-sidedness or abstractness of previous empiricism and atomism, as well as of Idealism. Feuerbach's historical examinations of the tendency of Idealism to reduce the empirical to a reflected moment of self-consciousness articulated an implicit criticism not only of Hegel but also of the thoroughgoing Idealism of his dissertation. Each of Feuerbach's historical studies marked an important step toward the new empiricism and materialism that came to define his philosophy in the 1840s.[68]

The contemplative calm that these historical studies should have offered Feuerbach was dispelled by his growing mood of personal, intellectual, and political frustration. His outspoken opposition to Christianity and his antitheological Hegelianism made him a pariah in the conservative pietistic community of Erlangen. Although he lectured there as an unpaid *Privatdozent,* his applications for a salaried professorship were routinely declined. His sense of isolation in Bavaria growing and his hopes for employment dwindling, he moved to Frankfurt in 1832 and planned to emigrate from there to Paris. Feeling persecuted and unable to speak his mind in Germany, he described Paris as "entirely suited to my character and philosophy."[69] When this plan collapsed because of his father's inability to support him in Paris, he directed his search for academic work to Prussia.

This led him to renew contacts with the Berlin Hegelians, even though he considered them to be "slaves of a great mind."[70] In May 1834, Leopold von Henning, the editor of the Hegelian *Jahrbücher für wissenschaftliche Kritik,* wrote to tell Feuerbach that the response among Berlin Hegelians to his *History of Modern Philosophy* had been so positive that they now invited him to join the major Hegelian organization, the Society for Scientific Criticism. He accepted this invitation, as well as Henning's offer to write several reviews for the *Jahrbücher.* John Toews has persuasively argued that Feuerbach's rapprochement with the Hegelian establishment in 1834 was not simply opportunistic, for he was driven to reaffirm his connections with the Hegelian

---

67  This work was followed by *Geschichte der neueren Philosophie. Darstellung, Entwicklung und Kritik der Leibnitz'schen Philosophie* in 1837 and *Pierre Bayle* in 1838.

68  The most comprehensive discussion of Feuerbach's historical works is found in Wartofsky, *Feuerbach,* pp. 49–134.

69  Feuerbach to Friedrich Feuerbach, 12 March 1832, *Briefwechsel,* vol. 1.

70  Feuerbach quoted in Toews, *Hegelianism,* p. 330.

School by his revulsion for the speculative Christian mysticism that had engulfed Erlangen.[71] He considered Erlangen's mood to be a reflection of a larger phenomenon: "This evil is not provincial. Christianity is once again breaking over Europe with all its barbarism."[72] Among all the signs of recrudescent Christianity, however, Feuerbach was particularly galled by the conflation of speculative philosophy and pietistic theology in his native Bavaria, exemplified by the works of Schelling and Stahl. By late 1833, the sharp attacks that Feuerbach had made against the youthful Schelling's Romantic aestheticism and intuitionism gave way to more vitriolic remarks about the Positive Philosophy of the elderly Schelling. At the same time, Feuerbach's animus was drawn with growing fervor toward Stahl, the "emissary" from the "land of the mystical dreams of the newest Schellingian philosophy."[73]

Compounding the substantive philosophical quarrel that Feuerbach had with Stahl was perhaps a considerable degree of professional envy, for this mystic emissary had taught at Erlangen since 1832 and received a full professorship in 1834. Feuerbach, by contrast, had left Erlangen in disgust and frustration, and after a brief return in the summer of 1834 he wrote to Kapp, "I find no words to describe to you the scandal of this university, the audacity, shamelessness, and ignorance of the obscurantists of contemporary Protestant theology."[74] Later that year, Feuerbach suggested to Henning that he review the second volume of Stahl's *Philosophie des Rechts nach geschichtlicher Ansicht* for the *Jahrbücher für wissenschaftliche Kritik*. Henning accepted the offer when Eduard Gans, who had also expressed a desire to write against Stahl, eventually declined the task. Despite his bitter enmity toward Stahl, Feuerbach had anxieties about attacking such a powerful figure, because he saw that a negative review might destroy any remaining chance he had of securing an academic post in Bavaria. Indeed, at the same time as he offered to review Stahl, he complained to Friedrich Thiersch about his inability to find a teaching post and resolved to "distance myself from all political tendencies."[75] But he also thought that a killing blow

---

71  Ibid., p. 331. However, Toews wrongly claims that the speculative theism of the Erlangen conservatives was derived from the "reactionary political and religious implications of Schelling's philosophy of absolute identity." As we have seen in Chapter 1, it was precisely Schelling's renunciation of absolute identity and his articulation of Positive Philosophy that appealed to reactionaries like Stahl.

72  Feuerbach to Christian Kapp, 3/18 February/3 March 1835, *Briefwechsel*, vol. 1.

73  Feuerbach to Christian Kapp, January 1835, *Briefwechsel*, vol. 1.

74  Feuerbach to Christian Kapp, 1/23 August 1834, *Briefwechsel*, vol. 1.

75  Feuerbach to Friedrich Thiersch, December 1834, *Briefwechsel*, vol. 1.

struck against the "unphilosophy" of Stahl and Schelling might help him secure a post in Prussia.[76] These tactical considerations were ultimately secondary to his conviction that such a critique was an urgently needed intervention that would be at once philosophical and political. Considering the growing influence of Schelling, the vigorous politico-religious program of the orthodox Protestants, and even the growing conservatism of the Berlin Hegelians, there were grounds for Feuerbach's belief that Stahl represented a "more and more pernicious, expanding party."[77] Hence, he wrote to his fiancé, Bertha Löw, that he seized the "sword of critique" not only against Stahl but against "false, perfidious, vain, slanderous Schelling."[78]

Feuerbach took pains to emphasize to prominent Hegelians like Kapp, Gans, and Henning that this was to be the first critique of Positive Philosophy to be written by anyone. This is perhaps one reason why an anonymous article in the *Hallische Jahrbücher* in 1841 claimed that Feuerbach's essay on Stahl was "recognized even at that time [1835] as epoch-making."[79] Yet, there were other possible reasons. For one thing, Feuerbach's critique broke through the gentility of the Berlin Hegelian establishment, exposing in unequivocal terms the folly of confusing theology and speculative philosophy, a folly of which many Hegelians were also guilty. By the late 1830s, the issues that Feuerbach first broached in 1835 were to become central to the internal controversies of the Hegelian School. Second, the polemic against Stahl helped to establish the main line of political critique of the Hegelian Left in the later 1830s and early 1840s. At a more personal level, the critique of Stahl marked a turning point in Feuerbach's vocation. "The spirit of the Xenien of *anno* 1830 comes over me again," he wrote to Kapp as he composed the piece.[80] Even as his radical impulses gained new vigor, the essay committed him irrevocably to his position as a cultural outsider because the attack on Stahl likely helped to scuttle any remaining chances of his securing an academic post. Accepting this fact, Feuerbach married Bertha Löw in 1837 and undertook the management of her family's porcelain factory in the small Bavarian town of Bruckberg. Isolated from the intellectual centers of German life, he presented himself to the reading public as the Bruckberg anchorite, reveling in his freedom even while he clung until the early 1840s to vanishingly small chances for university employment.

76  Toews, *Hegelianism*, pp. 331–2.
77  Feuerbach to Bertha Löw, 12 February 1835, *Briefwechsel*, vol. 1.
78  Feuerbach to Bertha Löw, 3 February 1835, *Briefwechsel*, vol. 1.
79  M-r, "Stahl und die Willkür, nebst Erinnerung an Feuerbach über ihn," *Hallische Jahrbücher*, no. 23, 1841, p. 92.
80  Feuerbach to Christian Kapp, 3/18 February/3 March 1835, *Briefwechsel*, vol. 1.

Feuerbach's essay on Stahl picks up both the theological and the socio-political threads of the critique of personality that he had launched in *Thoughts on Death and Immortality*. Now, however, the attack on theological personality was directed not against Protestantism as such but against the Positive Philosophy's attempt to base speculative philosophy on the idea of a personal, voluntarist God. Feuerbach was to deal with this theme in greater detail in his 1838 essay on Positive Philosophy to which we shall turn later in this chapter. What concerns us here is his critique of Stahl's use of the idea of personality in the sociopolitical domain.

The specific volume of Stahl's *Philosophie des Rechts* that Feuerbach reviewed is that which develops the analogy between the personal God and the personal monarch. Because Feuerbach could not have been ignorant of the significance of the analogy, he surely realized that in denying the personality of God, he undercut Restoration political theory's main support for personal sovereignty. In fact, he likely intended it, because, as he told Marx in 1843, his critique of Stahl was necessitated by political circumstances.[81] Nonetheless, he remained silent on the issue of sovereignty. This was perhaps a sign of prudence or timidity in the face of censorship, but it might also have expressed Feuerbach's stronger association of the issue of personality with social themes; although he did not openly address the nature of sovereignty, the essay on Stahl greatly clarified the implicit association in *Thoughts on Death and Immortality* of the Christian idea of the person with the self-centered bourgeois of civil society. In the *Philosophy of Right*, Hegel had made it clear that he considered this atomistic bourgeois individualism to be only "one principle of civil society." As he claimed, "the particular person is essentially so related to other particular persons that each establishes himself and finds satisfaction by means of the others, and at the same time purely and simply by means of the form of universality, the second principle here."[82] We shall see that the second principle of civil society played a crucial role in Feuerbach's effort to envision a new form of communal association. By contrast, it seems that Feuerbach taxed Stahl's idea of personality for remaining arrested undialectically at Hegel's "first" principle of civil society, the particular person who pursues his selfish interests.

This point is illustrated by Feuerbach's concentration upon Stahl's interpretation of "public" and "private" law. The separation of public from private law had been a major demand of late-eighteenth-century liberal legal reformers, including Feuerbach's father, and in the years after the French

81    Feuerbach to Marx, 25 October 1843, *Briefwechsel*, vol. 2.
82    Hegel, *Philosophy of Right*, para. 187 and 182.

Revolution of 1789, private and public law was codified in German legal theory and practice.[83] This codification represented the adaptation of jurisprudence to the historical emergence of a centralized state that monopolized political power and of a civil society oriented toward private domestic and economic interactions. Accordingly, liberal proponents of legal reform believed that the primary purpose of law was no longer to encourage subjects to lead a virtuous life but rather to demarcate and protect the private freedoms of self-determining persons.[84] Although Stahl shared many of the objections of earlier conservatives like Haller or Müller to the "mechanistic" rationalism of liberalism, he upheld the quintessentially liberal distinction between public and private law. Feuerbach discounted Stahl's gesture toward modern jurisprudence, however, and he insisted that Stahl had essentially turned private law into an absolute, with very paradoxical results. Insofar as Stahl valorized the person as the image (*Ebenbild*) of God, Feuerbach argued, "Every relation in which the person stands because he is the image of God is a relation of private law; a relation in which he stands because he is the creature of God, made to serve Him, . . . is a relation of public law. The archetype of private law is the *essence,* that of public law is the *mastery* of God."[85] In Stahl's theological rendering of the split between public and private law, Feuerbach saw a surprising and important consequence. Insofar as Stahl valorized the person as the image of God, Feuerbach claimed that his "Christian" political theory arrived at the same essential result as earlier "abstract natural law" theory.

> The individual recognized in private law in his isolation as independent, which the early natural law doctrines fixed as an absolute and took as the presupposition of the social contract, is here also fixed as absolute, but under the pious expression of the image of God. The public law, the state, appears against this presupposition as a naked limitation, a negation of the image and likeness of God and therefore as something which in itself is only negative.

Feuerbach believed that this position made social union incomprehensible, for if the individual had to surrender his likeness to God in order to come under the "mastery" of God as a subject of the state, then the individual would be perfectly justified in denying obedience to the state. He remarked

---

83  Dieter Grimm, *Recht und Staat der bürgerlichen Gesellschaft* (Frankfurt, 1987), p. 295.
84  On the relationship between law and virtue in debates over the Prussian *Allgemeine Landrecht,* see Koselleck, "Staat und Gesellschaft," pp. 59f; and more generally Koselleck's *Preussen zwischen Reform und Revolution,* pp. 23–51.
85  Stahl quoted in Feuerbach, "[Über] *Die Philosophie des Rechts nach geschichtlicher Ansicht.* von F. J. Stahl," *Gesammelte Werke,* vol. 8, p. 40.

wryly that it is "easier to see how people in the *status naturalis* of Hobbes submit to the *status civilis* than how these majestic, godly persons could consent to a state and to obedience."[86] Paradoxically, then, instead of *sanctifying* social life by appeals to Christian principle, Stahl's emphasis upon personality led him to support the same principle of egoistic individualism that he himself vilified in the natural law tradition.

Feuerbach's surprising insight echoed Hegel's claim in the *Philosophy of Right* that feudal theories of political rights and social contract theories both make the same mistake of transferring "the characteristics of private property into a sphere of a quite different and higher nature [i.e., the state]."[87] Yet Feuerbach's 1835 observations also recall a critique of Thomas Hobbes's political theory that he had published in his 1833 *History of Modern Philosophy*.[88] After noting that Hobbes had assigned "absolute power" to the Leviathan, who unites the will of all in his "one person," Feuerbach praised the Englishman for seeing that the state must constitute a unity. He remained critical, however, because the unity of the Hobbesian state is based not on reason but on "particularity or arbitrariness." Therefore, Hobbes had elevated the principle of the state of nature, the isolated individual, to the pinnacle of the civil state, while "the *Cives* remain against this *Unio* [of the state] a mere mass, a *multitudo dissoluta*."[89] The rational will of citizens does not constitute the unity of the Hobbesian personal state, and so the citizens are reduced to "mutually indifferent individuals."[90] Thereby denied the great freedom that would come from sharing in the unity of the state, the "mass" claims "only so much freedom as is necessary for a pleasant and peaceful life."[91] Citizens thus remain in their isolated, self-centered natural condition, their natural brutishness curbed but not overcome by the social contract. And precisely because the social contract was initiated in order to end the strife of the state of nature, the peaceful existence of the individual citizen emerges as the goal of the state, even if the individual is excluded from the life of the state. The state, "which should be the existence of reason and objective morality, is again reduced to a mere means, which has its goal only in the physical welfare of the individual."[92]

---

86  Feuerbach, "[Über] *Die Philosophie des Rechts*," p. 41.
87  Hegel, *Philosophy of Right*, para. 75. See also the perceptive comments on Haller in H.F.W. Hinrichs, *Politische Vorlesungen* (Halle, 1843), p. 325.
88  In May 1832, after having advised Christian Kapp to change the title of his proposed journal *Athene* to emphasize politics, Feuerbach offered this critique of Hobbes as an item for publication. See Feuerbach to Christian Kapp, 22 May 1832, *Briefwechsel*, vol. 1.
89  Feuerbach, *Geschichte der neueren Philosophie*, p. 107.
90  Ibid., p. 98.    91  Ibid., p. 97.    92  Ibid., p. 108.

Feuerbach's critique of Hobbes reveals obvious debts to Hegel, particularly in the assumption that the state has the ethical obligation to overcome the selfishness of civil society.[93] What is especially relevant to the political and philosophical context of the mid-1830s, however, is Feuerbach's recognition of the compatibility of an authoritarian theory of sovereignty with a theory of possessive individualism in civil society.[94] This insight into the possible convergence of an authoritarian state and a "liberal" society was of utmost importance to Feuerbach's critique of Stahl and to the larger political stance of the Hegelian Left in the later 1830s and 1840s, as we shall see in later chapters.

Whereas Hobbes had attempted to reconcile individualism as the principle of society and absolute authority as the principle of the state through his appeal to contract theory, Feuerbach maintained that Stahl sought the same goal through Christian personalism. Yet the egoism of the idea of personality, charged Feuerbach, contradicts the entire attempt to ground social law in Christian principles. For, he insisted, the true essence of Christianity is not personality but "Love." Because personality is bound up with particularity, in the social sphere the notion of personality is the origin of private law, grounded in "possession and property," "mine and yours." It "isolates people, concentrates them on themselves, and sets them as single self-subsisting beings against one another." In other words, in Feuerbach's view, law based on personality applies to humanity's condition in the state of nature, not to its spiritual, rational, or social state. In contrast, Feuerbach held, Christianity originally emerged as the purest of religions, free from all external elements and interests. Though early Christianity did not challenge the legal structure of the world, the new faith, by uniting humanity through love, promised to soften the harshness of worldly laws. Therefore, Christianity could not become the basis of property law except by distorting its essential truth. So, Feuerbach reasoned, the true Christian must be indifferent to possessions, whereas the "legal [rechtliche] person regards that which he has as actual Eigentum, as a part of himself; he is bent on it, mad after it. . . ."[95] As

---

93   In a description of civil society (Philosophy of Right, paragraph 289) Hegel alludes to the Hobbesian war of all against all. Hegel's political philosophy is implicitly critical of Hobbes, but his discussion of Hobbes in his Lectures on the History of Philosophy is not as detailed or negative in tone as Feuerbach's. See Hegel, Lectures on the History of Philosophy, trans. E. S. Haldane and F. H. Simson (Atlantic Highlands, N.J., 1983), vol. 3, pp. 318–19.

94   I do not mean to endorse the controversial thesis of C. B. MacPherson's The Political Theory of Possessive Individualism. Hobbes to Locke (Oxford, 1962), although, interestingly, Feuerbach's comments on Hobbes anticipate elements of MacPherson's argument.

95   Feuerbach, "[Über] Die Philosophie des Rechts," p. 38.

early as 1830, Feuerbach had suggested that the true but hidden essence of Christianity is the unifying love of humanity; it is noteworthy that in 1835, he returned to the theme in order to refute a prominent contemporary theory of property.

Stahl's pious words issued from a false view of Christianity, Feuerbach charged. Instead of converting the social world into a truly "Christian" community, the injunctions of Christian personalism cloaked a defense of private property every bit as egoistical as that of "natural law doctrine." Property ownership was, in fact, central to Stahl's concept of personality. Like Hegel, Stahl maintained that the personality first objectifies itself in property when it invests an object with its will. However, Hegel maintained that personality is not fully expressed by the relation of the isolated individual will to an object but rather must involve the mutual recognition of persons through contract and the legal structure that sanctions and upholds contract; ultimately, then, the property relation points beyond a mere act of personal acquisition or possession to a *social relation* among people. Thus, property is incorporated into the same relational structure that we have traced in other moments – religious and political – of Hegel's idea of concrete personality.

Stahl, by contrast, argued that the idea of property is so primordial that it presupposes neither a contract nor a state. Rather, he emphasized the "natural power of the human over nature," the "command over a passive object" that "celebrates [the property-owner's] triumph as a person."[96] Of course, Stahl had to acknowledge that property subsequently becomes the object of contracts and laws, but he insisted that the principal aim of property law must always be to protect the "inviolability of the actual, present relationship to the object."[97] Hence, Stahl's concept of property did not involve a relation among people but strictly a relation of personal dominance over the object-world. In contrast, he judged Hegel's principle, wherein the property relation appears to be subsumed in higher expressions of "unpersonal reason," as being inimical to the concrete mastery of persons over things. Significantly, just as Stahl asserted in 1845 that Hegel's view of sovereignty led to republicanism, so too did he believe that Hegel's idea of property led to communism.[98] In either case, the "magic of unity," the personality, was dissolved by dialectical reason.

Property rights had been a question of paramount importance for the Restoration's ultra-conservatives, who endorsed Haller's view of social and

96   Stahl, *Philosophie des Rechts*, 5th ed., vol. 2, pt. 1, p. 285.
97   Ibid., p. 315.
98   Ibid., p. 80; also Stahl, *Materialien*, ed. Riedel, p. 226.

political power, prerogatives and privileges, as forms of private property.
Stahl departed from this corporatist defense of private property in an important way. For whereas Haller located individual property owners within
hierarchical, patriarchal, estatist categories, Stahl's theory of property began with the relationship of persons *qua* persons to possessions. In this sense,
although deriving the category of personhood from the image of God rather
than from enlightened principles of rational self-determination, Stahl recognized the social transformation described astutely by an anonymous author in 1844: "Society has to do only with the single, with personalities. Before the great revolution [of 1789], society was comprised of estates which
differed according to privileges."[99] It was becoming difficult even for conservatives like Stahl to ignore the historical development of modern civil society and its attendant legal claims. Hence, Stahl's theory endorsed bourgeois property rights and even championed the right of commoners to
acquire noble estates.[100] Nonetheless, his theory of property rested on the
assertion of a continuum of sovereign personhood stretching from God,
through the monarch, to the *Bürger;* and so, he insidiously incorporated the
modern legal claim for individual property rights into an irrationalist authoritarian scheme based on the Christian idea of personality.

Feuerbach ridiculed this attempt to sanctify property ownership on the
ultimate basis of the conception of the personal God, as if the "miserable limits of finite relations" could be deduced from the "infinite being" of God.
Criticizing the analogical foundation of this argument, Feuerbach reasoned
that if God were a mere property holder, free either to "occupy" or "dispose"
of His possessions, then the actual order of the world would be merely the
product of arbitrary choice; God would always be entirely free to reveal the
"inestimable abundance of his essence in other and the most widely varying
ways." Freedom would thus lose all connection to rationality, reduced instead to choice among a plenitude of possibilities. It would not be overly
anachronistic to call such a view of freedom *consumerist,* especially because
Feuerbach himself derided Stahl's conception of freedom as "a childish fantasy" of "endless multiplicity in . . . a confectionary store." The social vision
that Feuerbach attributed to Stahl's metaphysical voluntarism was that of atomized individuals caught in a bad infinity, endlessly and fruitlessly engaged
in the struggle to acquire the manifold of objects.

Significantly, Feuerbach identified this arrested view of unassimilated,
arbitrary multiplicity with "the misery, the need of material existence," thereby

99  Anon., *Über den vierten Stand und die socialen Reformen* (Augsburg, 1844), p. 18.
100  See Berdahl, *Politics,* pp. 364–5.

linking once again the belief in the personal God to the wants, caprice, and physical necessity that Hegel had associated with civil society. By contrast, Feuerbach believed that philosophical comprehension of the true pantheistic nature of the divine reveals the necessity of God's creation of and presence in the world. Plurality and arbitrariness give way to a recognition of ontological unity: "before God, the countless persons make only one essence, that is, the human."[101] Feuerbach did not explore this argument's radical implications for the question of social and property relations until the 1840s, when he identified his philosophy of human species-being with communism. However, we shall see in Chapter 5 that the first socialist book in Germany, Moses Hess's *Die heilige Geschichte der Menschheit*, attacked the institution of private property precisely by criticizing the homology of divine and human personality.

Feuerbach's essay concluded that the idea of personality had tried, but failed, to justify earthly life through an appeal to a transcendent God. In an 1838 essay, he argued that the Schellingians' Positive Philosophy could not explain the immanence of God without lapsing into the pantheism they so strongly eschewed. Consequently, philosophers like Schelling and Stahl were forced to insist on a purely arbitrary relationship between God and the created world.[102] In stipulating the separation of the divine from the worldly, the doctrine of personality thereby had the paradoxical effect of *desacralizing* the immanent relations of humanity. For the Christian perceives his highest task to be the cultivation of his purely private perfection as a person in the image of God. The notion of participation in the collective, of political or social virtues as integral to the self-expression of the whole person, is rendered meaningless. Christian inwardness impels the abandonment of collective human life to the distorted figure of the isolated, self-seeking bourgeois of civil society. As Feuerbach put it, "virtueless, egoistic religiosity" is "poison to [man's] political energy."[103]

## The End of the Religio-Philosophical Debate about Personality

In 1843, Feuerbach wrote to Marx that his 1835 critique of Stahl had been necessitated more by political than by philosophical circumstances; but in

101  Feuerbach, "[Über] *Die Philosophie des Rechts*," p. 29.
102  Feuerbach, "Zur Kritik der positiven Philosophie," *Werke*, vol. 8, p. 189.
103  See Feuerbach, "[Über] Dr. Karl Bayer, *Betrachtungen über den Begriff des sittlichen Geistes und über das Wesen der Tugend*" (1840), *Werke*, vol. 8, p. 96, and "The Necessity of a Reform of Philosophy," *Fiery Brook*, p. 151.

truth, the essay opened a period of intense involvement with the philosophical and theological issues raised by the Schellingian Positive Philosophy. Feuerbach's critique of Stahl was his first work to highlight what he considered to be the folly of conflating theology and philosophy, and this became a central theme in his writings in the later 1830s. In 1835, he had regarded this folly as the cynical attempt of mysticism to grace itself with the mantle of reason; increasingly, he came to see the conflation of theology and philosophy as the fundamental tendency of all speculative metaphysics. Feuerbach developed this negative assessment of modern philosophy in his substantial historical studies of Leibniz and Pierre Bayle, but in 1838, he returned to the Schellingian Positive Philosophy, the most salient example of what he called the "believing unbelief" or "unbelieving belief" that had come to characterize philosophy in contemporary Germany. Many of the themes of the critique of Stahl are repeated in Feuerbach's 1838 essays on Positive Philosophy: the mistaken equation of freedom with the arbitrary exercise of will,[104] the atomizing, anti-social consequences of the theistic view of personhood,[105] and the limitations paradoxically imposed when divinity is conceived in the finite terms of personality. Still, Feuerbach's 1838 "Critique of Positive Philosophy" went far beyond the earlier essay, not only in terms of its denunciation but also in its effort to explain the essence of personalism.

By 1838, Feuerbach had come to consider the principle of personality to be the very antithesis of philosophy. Personality cannot be an object of philosophy, in his view, because "personality *in concreto*" is bound to the particular, and, consequently, it always remains as the precipitate of philosophy's process of conceptual abstraction.[106] Feuerbach argued that by seeking an "absolute self-grounding" in the concrete personality of God, Positive Philosophy renounces the universal, pantheistic, intellectualist God of philosophy in favor of the God of theology and common belief.[107] Positive Philosophy wants to be both philosophy and theology, but it ends up being neither because it binds itself to an irrational principle of belief while trying to elevate that principle unchanged to an object of reason.[108] These observations led Feuerbach to praise the honesty of F. H. Jacobi, whom he had

---

104  Feuerbach, "[Über] Die Idee der Freiheit und der Begriff des Gedankens. von Dr. K. Bayer," *Werke*, vol. 2, p. 141.
105  Feuerbach, "Positive Philosophie," p. 190.
106  Ibid., p. 182.
107  On Feuerbach's discussion of the "God of philosophy," see Wartofsky, *Feuerbach*, p. 122.
108  Feuerbach clearly influenced the critique of Positive Philosophy found in Bruno Bauer's *The Trumpet of the Last Judgement Against Hegel the Atheist and Antichrist* (1841), trans. Lawrence Stepelevich (Berkeley, 1989), pp. 7of.

described in 1837 as the author of a "self-annihilating philosophy."[109] For Jacobi never attempted to make personality an object of science but always left it as the "inexplicable axiom of an immediate, apodictic feeling, that is, a *purely personal* truth and affair."[110] Jacobi's philosophy of feeling was something Feuerbach could agree with, because he too had come to the conclusion that *feeling*, not reason, is the essence of religion.

Feuerbach had already articulated this position in earlier studies, but in his "Critique of Positive Philosophy," he transformed this insight into the theory of projection that was to furnish the main thesis of *The Essence of Christianity*. Reading Jacobi, Feuerbach saw that the great critic of philosophical nihilism had unintentionally exposed the human origin of religious concepts. That is, Jacobi had intuitively recognized that in the human–divine relationship the emotional needs of the human person lead him to conceive of a divine being in his image. However, whereas Jacobi had been content to articulate the sentimental nexus within which emotions call forth religion, Positivism's philosophical ambitions led it to objectify human traits as divine attributes. Hence, Feuerbach claimed that Positive Philosophy had actually retreated *behind* Jacobi's intuitive anthropology of religion and had come to share the illusion of naïve faith, namely the ascription of the attributes of human personality to an autonomous, really existing God.

In 1830 Feuerbach had already made a similar assertion about the human source of belief in a personal God; his 1838 position differed fundamentally insofar as he now claimed that the anthropomorphic God is not simply a *mistake* about the true nature of the divine but is rather a projection of human attributes into *nothingness*. Hence, the thinker speculates strictly about his own nature in speculating on the nature of God, even though he does so unconsciously as long as he does not recognize God as his own objectified essence. In a key statement, Feuerbach drew the consequence for a radically redefined philosophy of religion: "Philosophy of religion is only philosophy when it knows and treats religion as *esoteric* psychology."[111] Thus, the theory of projection that Feuerbach applied to religious doctrine in his masterwork *The Essence of Christianity* of 1841 was first developed as a criticism of Positive Philosophy's delusions. It should not be surprising, then, to find Feuerbach describing his most famous work as a critique of speculative philosophy carried onto the terrain of religion.[112]

109   Feuerbach, *Darstellung, Entwicklung und Kritik der Leibniz'schen Philosophie* in *Gesammelte Werke*, vol. 3, p. 122.
110   Feuerbach, "Positive Philosophie," p. 183.
111   Ibid., p. 205.
112   Feuerbach, draft letter to Otto Wigand, 5 January 1841, Feuerbach. *Briefwechsel*, vol. 2.

Scholars have failed to notice that Feuerbach's "Critique of Positive Philosophy" introduced another new element into his theory of religion. For he took pains to emphasize that the projected human essence that speculative philosophy mistook for the divine was itself based on a distorted conception of humanity that took the isolated, atomized person as the basis of human life.[113] This is the reason why Feuerbach detected a mix of humility and arrogance in the fantastical image of the personal God. As Feuerbach expressed it in this essay, the Speculative Theist, in assigning attributes to the divine being, confuses his individual self, his sense of particular personhood, with his general human essence.[114] That is, the person projects onto God the attributes of humanity's social being but wrongly hypostatizes these as attributes of isolated individual beings in their isolation. Overcoming the negative effects of religion, therefore, would require more than merely reuniting "divine" predicates with their proper subject, "man"; it would also demand the correction of humanity's distorted self-image. We shall see in Chapter 7 that when Marx appropriated Feuerbach's idea of the religious inversion of subject and predicate as a basic tool of social critique, he conceived subject–predicate inversion in the same double sense as Feuerbach.

In this 1838 essay, Feuerbach did not link these observations explicitly to the debates about the Christian doctrine of Incarnation that had raged since the appearance of David Friedrich Strauss's *The Life of Jesus* in 1835.[115] Still, it seems likely that the christological controversy aroused by Strauss provided an important context for Feuerbach's assertions. Like Feuerbach, Strauss had pitted the idea of humanity as a collective essence against the idea of personality. In Strauss, this took the notorious form of an explicit refutation of the doctrine of the unique incarnation of God in Christ. He described this belief as the product of collective myth, the truth of which lies not in the unity of one man with God but in the divinity of humanity itself. Jesus thus symbolizes the divine perfection of humanity. Yet in real terms, the historical Jesus could not *be* that perfection because "in other cases, we never find the ideal [completely] realized in a single individual, but only in an entire cycle of appearances, which reciprocally complete each other."[116] Strauss thereby subordinated the perfection of one person to the perfection

113   Ibid., p. 193.    114   Ibid., p. 195.
115   Particularly good discussions of the theological and philosophical debates over Strauss are found in Jaeschke, *Reason in Religion*, pp. 349–421; Hans-Martin Sass, *Untersuchungen zur Religionsphilosophie in der Hegelschule, 1830–1850* (Munster, 1963); Peter Cornehl, *Die Zukunft der Versöhnung* (Gottingen, 1971); Jürgen Gebhardt, *Politik und Eschatologie* (Munich, 1963); and Toews, *Hegelianism*.
116   D. F. Strauss, *The Life of Jesus*, trans. George Eliot (Philadelphia, 1972), p. 770.

of the species, and, like a good Hegelian, he cast the actualization of the human species in terms of a historical process, what he called the *Gattungsprozeß*. One can readily agree with Walter Jaeschke's claim that Strauss's argument was consistent with Hegel's own interpretation of the God-Man,[117] although it must also be noted that Strauss was less equivocal than Hegel in his conclusions, and he was remarkably original in his use of historical and philological analysis to support his metaphysical convictions.

In *The Essence of Christianity* Feuerbach was to address the doctrine of Incarnation in a far more radical way than Strauss. In the 1838 essay on Positive Philosophy, however, he chose to direct an argument similar to Strauss's against contemporary German philosophy. Oddly enough, in a work that tried to separate Hegel from the Speculative Theism of the Positive Philosophy, Feuerbach concluded with a call for philosophy to surpass Hegel, whom he now painted as the philosophical Christ: "It is speculative superstition to believe in an actual incarnation of philosophy in a specific historical appearance."[118] In configuring Hegel as the Christ of philosophy, Feuerbach established what quickly became one of the central tropes in the Young Hegelians' effort to overcome their erstwhile master's hypostatization of "Absolute philosophy." While the "Critique of Positive Philosophy" resisted the evident temptation to implicate Hegel directly in the attack on Speculative Theism, in 1839 Feuerbach gave in to this inclination. "Towards a Critique of Hegel's Philosophy," the essay that Feuerbach published in Arnold Ruge's *Hallische Jahrbücher*, formally announced his break with Hegel's speculative Idealism, and it proved seminal to the increasingly critical turn that the Young Hegelians took against Hegel.

Undoubtedly, Feuerbach's public repudiation of Hegel articulated an internal process of self-criticism of his Idealist roots and drew on longstanding misgivings about Hegel that he had expressed as early as 1827. Yet, in important ways, his critique of Hegel was also occasioned by his critical reflections on the Positive Philosophy. For one thing, the increasing stridency of the anti-Hegelians made it seem urgent to direct the critical discussion of Hegel into more fruitful channels. Feuerbach had already pursued this tactic in 1835 when he defended Hegel against the Kantian Carl Friedrich

117  Jaeschke, *Reason in Religion*, esp. p. 375.
118  Feuerbach, "Positive Philosophie," p. 207. I do not mean to suggest that Feuerbach derived his view of philosophical or theological incarnation from Strauss. Elements of his critique of incarnation are already intimated in his essay on Carl Friedrich Bachmann, written in 1834. See "Kritik des 'Anti-Hegels.' Zur Einleitung in das Studium der Philosophie," *Gesammelte Werke*, vol. 8, pp. 62–127. Nonetheless, the discussion of incarnation after 1835 undoubtedly sharpened Feuerbach's own formulation.

Bachmann's *Anti-Hegel.* Given the alternatives to Hegel in contemporary German intellectual life, Feuerbach obviously felt it prudent in 1835 to muffle his own doubts about Hegel. Even in early 1839, he was still worried that his own criticism of Hegel might inadvertently amplify the mocking, disdainful chorus of anti-Hegelians. Nonetheless, he wrote to Arnold Ruge, "it is necessary that the critique of Hegel not remain in the hands of his enemies, but should pass into the hands of those who honor him and recognize the *good* spirit of Hegel as the animating genius of their own activity."[119] At another level, Feuerbach's intense preoccupation with Schelling and his coterie had gradually convinced him that far from being an aberration, Positive Philosophy revealed something intrinsic to modern speculative philosophy. Hence, positivism's particularly "shameless" mixing of theology and philosophy exposed the theological core of all metaphysical speculation, including Hegel's. In this sense, the insights developed in Feuerbach's refutation of the Positive Philosophy could be, and were, directly transposed onto Hegel himself.

The analogy between the Christian Incarnation and the idolatry of absolute philosophy, first drawn in the "Critique of Positive Philosophy," became one of the key themes of "Towards a Critique of Hegel's Philosophy." In this important essay, Feuerbach refuted the claims of Hegelian acolytes that Hegel is nothing less than "philosophy itself," that is, the *"absolute reality of the idea* of philosophy."[120] Much like Strauss, Feuerbach rejected the idea of incarnation in any region of human activity and insisted instead on a radically historicized vision of human culture. Whether religious, artistic, or philosophical, every human phenomenon, he claimed, "originates . . . as a manifestation of its time; its origin *presupposes its historical time.*"[121] Thus, against the closure implied by the concept of incarnation, Feuerbach conceived of an open-ended process of development and supersession in which the repudiation of the possibility of incarnation effectively removes the teleological drive toward an end-state of perfection. At first glance, this argument looks much like that made as early as the 1820s by those Hegelians, including the young Feuerbach, who wished to separate Hegel's dynamic dialectical method from the constraints of his system. But Feuerbach's critique in 1839 broke out of the familiar tension between system and method by subjecting both to equally critical scrutiny. To achieve this, he practiced on Hegel the *esoteric psychology* that he had first formulated a year earlier in the

119  Feuerbach to Ruge, 13 February 1839, *Briefwechsel*, vol. 1.
120  Feuerbach, "Towards a Critique of Hegel's Philosophy," *Fiery Brook*, p. 56.
121  Ibid., p. 59.

essay on Positive Philosophy. Esoteric psychology is essentially a science of origins – in Feuerbach's terms, a "genetico-critical" inquiry that must always question "whether an object is a real object, only an idea, or just a psychological phenomenon."[122] This genetic concern led Feuerbach to identify what he thought was a common element in all speculative metaphysics, their origin in the subjective wishes of the thinker. In this view, Hegel's claim for the reconciliation of subject and object in the Idea was as much a product of projection as was the Positive Philosophy's hypostatized notion of personality. Hence, Feuerbach described Hegel's system as "rational mysticism," because it too mistakes a subjective need for an objective absolute.[123]

Feuerbach's 1839 critique of Hegel thereby opened the path toward the complete identification of Hegel with the theologizing mode of philosophy that he had first criticized in Positive Philosophy. In 1839, Feuerbach associated Hegel with this mystifying philosophical style primarily in terms of form – that is, in the deep structure of projection and objectification. However, as Feuerbach clarified his theory of projection in relation to the origin of religious concepts, he came increasingly to recognize in Hegel the same content and goal as those of Speculative Theism and theology. By the 1843 edition of *The Essence of Christianity*, he could ridicule the "learned mob's" failure to recognize Hegel as the ally that he actually was.[124] And in his essays of 1842 and 1843, Feuerbach completed this assimilation of Hegel and his critics by reducing Hegelian philosophy to theology in its form and its goal as the "last magnificent attempt to restore Christianity . . . through philosophy."[125]

By 1843, Feuerbach was firmly committed to the belief that what made Hegel's philosophy irredeemably theological was its reliance on an abstract dialectic that reconciled thought and being one-sidedly in thought. While Feuerbach acknowledged the tendency of modern philosophy to reconceptualize the absolute being of "God" as universal subjectivity, consciousness, or thought itself, he maintained that this "negation" of theology in fact reproduces the theological notion of God as the being whose essence contains existence:

> Speculative philosophy has only generalized and made into an attribute of thought or of the notion in general what theology made into an exclusive attribute of the notion of God. The identity of thought and being is therefore

122 Ibid., p. 86.   123 Ibid., p. 86.
124 Feuerbach, *Gesammelte Werke*, vol. 5, p. 384.
125 Feuerbach, *Principles of the Philosophy of the Future*, trans. Manfred Vogel (Indianapolis, 1986), p. 34.

only the expression of the divinity of reason – that thought or reason is the absolute being, the total of all truth and reality, that there is nothing in contrast to reason, rather that reason is everything just as God is, in strict theology, everything, that is, all essential and true being.[126]

Feuerbach's identification of Hegel's abstract reconciliation of thought and being with "theology" consummated over a decade of doubts about the validity of Hegel's understanding of the relation of thought and being. Not only was this skepticism voiced in 1827, but it was expressed again in his 1835 essay on Bachmann's *Anti-Hegel,* where he defended Hegel's identity thesis even as he in fact undercut it by distinguishing between the identity of thought and being in God and the human representation of this identity in Hegel's *Logic.*[127] Having cast off all vestiges of belief in an Absolute Spirit that achieved this identity of thought and being, by 1839 Feuerbach was ready to regard the Hegelian logic as an arbitrary construction that confused the form or rhetoric of philosophy with the thing itself. In short, he detected a gulf between real being and the Hegelian mediation of thought and being that lay concealed behind the *theological* trope of a thought that thinks all being. From his 1839 critique of Hegel onward, Feuerbach committed himself to the task of replacing the abstract logic with a "new philosophy" that would genuinely reconcile thought and concrete being without subsuming the one in the other.

In thus conceiving his new critical relationship to Hegel, Feuerbach actually echoed the criticisms of Hegelian logic already voiced by I. H. Fichte, Weisse, and Schelling, trenchant though his opposition to these figures remained. In 1841, Feuerbach conceded to Ruge that "when the Anti-Hegel [Bachmann] detected the absence of realism in Hegel, this was based on a crude but correct instinct."[128] However, this grudging concession does not go far enough in disclosing Feuerbach's likely debt to Hegel's earlier critics. It is significant to note that even as he accused Hegel of the same theological tendencies that he had vilified in the Positive Philosophy, he directed a critique against Hegel's logic that was strikingly similar to that expressed by the Speculative Theists and Positive Philosophers. Indeed, Schelling believed that disaffected Hegelians like Feuerbach desired something like his own Positive Philosophy, only they were reluctant to abandon the Hegelian system altogether.[129] Weisse recognized echoes of his own ideas in Feuer-

126 Feuerbach, *Principles,* p. 38.
127 Feuerbach, "Anti-Hegel," p. 72.
128 Feuerbach to Ruge, 20 December 1841, *Briefwechsel,* vol. 2.
129 Schelling, *Sämtliche Werke,* vol. 13, pp. 9of.

bach's 1839 essay, and not surprisingly, he regarded it as Feuerbach's strongest work. I. H. Fichte had reason when he upbraided Feuerbach in the pages of his *Zeitschrift für Philosophie und spekulative Theologie* for not having acknowledged his predecessors in the critique of Hegel's logic.[130] They all had a point. Feuerbach had in fact written to Ruge in 1837 asking him for references to works critical of Idealism, and by 1837, he could have compiled a sizable bibliography.[131] For Feuerbach was truly a late-comer to the revolt against Hegel's logic, and he was undoubtedly influenced by Hegel's earlier critics.

Nonetheless, even though it is important to acknowledge the role of Schelling and the other anti-Hegelian philosophers in Feuerbach's development, it is equally necessary to recall his longstanding ambivalence toward Schelling. The consistency of his opposition to the irrationalist and theologizing tendencies in Schelling's thought challenges Manfred Frank's suggestion that Feuerbach's polemics against Positive Philosophy were motivated by a desire to conceal his actual dependence on Schelling.[132] To be sure, Schelling's critique of Hegel's logic does indeed make him a forerunner of the materialist philosophy of Feuerbach and, later, Marx, because like them, he reversed Hegel's relationship between being and thought and insisted on the autonomy of being from the circuitous self-relation of consciousness. Yet this influence was strictly limited, for Schelling's insistence on the autonomy of being was in fact inseparable from his metaphysical voluntarism and personalist theism. Hence, despite the apparent importance of Feuerbach's exposure to Positive Philosophy, his appropriation of the anti-Hegelian critique of Hegelian logic was mixed with a profound criticism of the metaphysical and theological underpinnings of their position. Schelling was thus flattering himself, or at best contenting himself with a half truth, when he supposed that his positivism had won over even the radical Hegelians. Feuerbach neither wished to ground philosophy in an unmediated "Being" inaccessible to thought, nor did he for a moment overlook the fact that Positive Philosophy was thoroughly dependent on a philosophically reconstructed theology.

Therefore, Feuerbach's call for "realism" as an antidote to Hegel's alleged panlogism did converge with the desire for "real being" that we saw in the Speculative Theists and the Schellingians; but in truth, Feuerbach and the Positive Philosophers chose different forks on the twisting path of early

---

130  See Rawidowicz, *Feuerbachs Philosophie*, p. 79.
131  Feuerbach to Ruge, 5 December 1837, *Briefwechsel*, vol. 1.
132  Frank, *Der unendliche Mangel an Sein*, p. 184.

nineteenth-century German "realism." The positivists had recourse to the kind of realism that had originated in Jacobi's opposition to rationalistic nihilism. The Positive Philosophy appealed to a *nominalistic* realism, based ultimately on the individuating principle of personality and the separation of the created (and fallen) world from the divine creator. This explains why Schelling described his later Positive Philosophy as "metaphysical empiricism."[133] It also accounts for the distinction that David Friedrich Strauss drew in 1837 between a "nominalistic dependence on empirical individualities" and "true realism" in which "the truly real is not this or that human but the universal humanity."[134] It helps, moreover, to explain the complexity of Feuerbach's stance toward empiricism in the 1830s, because he insisted that philosophy must deal seriously with the empirical, while at the same time he resisted both the unreflexive empiricism of the Anglo-French tradition *and* the theistic empiricism of Positive Philosophy, which had merely "the pretense of being the new realistic philosophy."[135]

Feuerbach actually agreed with Jacobi that the task of philosophy is to "disclose existence," but of course he turned from God to nature and sensibility as the ultimate ground of being. For Feuerbach, to disclose existence meant discovering a new mediation between universality and particularity, thought and being, mind and nature. It was to be a mediation that truly recognizes the reality and autonomy of being. This demanded a departure from the "realism" of both the positivists and of Strauss, whose intellectualist notion of realism appeared more and more like a remnant of the Idealist and theological reasoning that Feuerbach rejected. In terms of philo-

133 See also Schelling quoted in Marcuse, *Reason and Revolution*, p. 324: "[I]f we had only a choice between empiricism and the oppressive apriorism of an extreme rationalism, no free mind would hesitate to decide for empiricism."

134 D. F. Strauss, *In Defense of My "Life of Jesus" Against the Hegelians*, trans. Marilyn Chapin Massey (Hamden, Conn., 1983), p. 43.

135 See his letter to Kapp, 27 June 1835, *Briefwechsel*, vol. 1. Marx Wartofsky in *Feuerbach* (Cambridge, 1977), p. 160, neglects the different meanings of empiricism in the 1830s when he identifies two subjects of critical essays by Feuerbach, Carl Friedrich Bachmann and F.L.A. Dorguth, as opponents of Hegel who both attacked him from the "'left'; that is, from the point of view of empiricism and materialism." Dorguth was indeed an exponent of a materialism reminiscent of Helvetius or d'Holbach, and Feuerbach attacked him for his undialectical reduction of reason to physiology ("Zur Kritik des Empirismus" [1838] *Gesammelte Werke*, vol. 8, pp. 149–64). A close reading of Feuerbach's 1835 critique of Bachmann, on the other hand, reveals the similarity between this essay and his critique of Friedrich Julius Stahl, particularly over the question of the relationship between reason and God. Bachmann did in fact participate in the speculative theistic critique of Hegel. See Jaeschke, *Reason in Religion*, pp. 362, 367–8, 370. On the pretenses of Positive Philosophy, see Feuerbach, "Preliminary Theses on the Reform of Philosophy," *Fiery Brook*, p. 167.

sophical anthropology, this entailed the replacement of the abstract ego, the philosophical corollary of the theological notion of personality, with the "truth of the whole man," which he colorfully described as "reason saturated with blood." Thinking, therefore, must be recognized as an activity that cannot be abstracted from the whole human being, and the real, concrete person must be understood as physically embodied. "I am a real, sensuous being and, indeed, the body in its totality is my ego, my essence itself."[136] The real person is delimited in time and space, has a sex, and has physical wants.[137] In "sensuous being," Feuerbach believed he had discovered the principle of individuation that had eluded him in earlier Idealist works like his 1828 dissertation *Of Reason, One, Universal and Infinite*. Sensuous being was to be the vital corrective to the abstract egoism of both theology and the modern philosophical tradition.

Even though Feuerbach's works of the 1850s and 1860s moved toward a "reductive psychologism" strongly akin to seventeenth- and eighteenth-century sensationalism, in the 1840s, he did not mean to reduce human being to the sensuous being of the individual, contingent body.[138] To have done so would have created a personalism based on the particular, individual, contingent body. Instead, he attempted to view the body, the embodiment of the ego, as a point of juncture between the inner and outer, the subjective and objective, the private and the public. Feuerbach thus tried to remain true to an earlier commitment to the communal nature of humanity. This commitment was formed while he was more strongly attached to the Idealist premises of Hegelianism, but from his new perspective he could broaden his view to include the irreducible individuation that is grounded in sensuous being: "The essence of man is contained only in the community and unity of man with man; it is a unity, however, which rests on the reality of the distinction between I and thou."[139] From his new emphasis upon the intermingling of the sensuous and the rational, thought and nonthought, individual and community, Feuerbach derived a "categorical imperative": "Think in existence, in the world as a member of it, not in the vacuum of abstraction as a solitary monad, as an absolute monarch, as an indifferent, otherworldly God; then you can be sure that your ideas are unities of being and thought."[140]

136  Feuerbach, *Principles*, p. 54.
137  See for example, Feuerbach, *Wesen*, pp. 203–5.
138  Wartofsky, *Feuerbach*, p. 3.
139  Feuerbach, *Principles*, p. 71.
140  Ibid., p. 67.

The fundamental innovations of Feuerbach's most creative years closed the religio-philosophical debate about personality that had dominated German philosophy and theology in the 1830s. After *The Essence of Christianity* and *Principles of the Philosophy of the Future* the debate about God's personality ignored Feuerbach's theses only at the risk of anachronism. For the debate about the personality of God as it had developed in the 1830s could persist only so long as Hegelians identified Absolute Spirit with God. Only in that circumstance was a conflict between pantheism and personalism intelligible and meaningful. Even Strauss's *Life of Jesus* (1835) merely intensified the conflict but did not end it, because his identification of human and divine essence simply marked him as the most thoroughgoing of Hegelian pantheists and perhaps the most faithful of Hegel's exegetes.

It was Feuerbach's achievement in the years between 1838 and 1843 to be able to declare "the speculations and controversies concerning the personality or impersonality of God fruitless, idle, uncritical and odious."[141] Feuerbach identified the personal God as humanity's fantastical wish for perfect Being, the alienated essence of humanity itself. He exposed pantheism as atheism articulated on the ground of theology, a lingering theological mystification substituting Nature for God. This was as true for Romantic pantheists as for the Hegelian Strauss, who continued to insist on the *actual* divinity of humanity. In a radical way, Feuerbach thereby reduced the choice between personalism and pantheism to a more basic choice between belief and atheism. Further, he undercut the Hegelian effort to mediate between faith and knowledge by unequivocally placing Hegel's speculative philosophy in the camp of theology. The choice between varieties of speculative philosophy – Hegelian or Schellingian, Idealist or positivist – became a simpler choice between theologizing metaphysics and Feuerbach's new humanist, materialist philosophy.

---

141  Feuerbach, *Wesen*, p. 199.

# 4

## THE SOCIAL AND POLITICAL DISCOURSE OF PERSONALITY, 1835–1840

It was fitting in 1843 that Feuerbach exhorted people to think "in the world as a member of it, not in the vacuum of abstraction as a solitary monad, as an absolute monarch, as an indifferent, otherworldly God." These similes neatly tied together the homologous theological, philosophical, social, and political associations of his long quarrel with personalism. After all, the fundamental tenets of his theory of religion and his break with speculative philosophy drew on themes that he had first probed in theologico-political tracts like *Thoughts on Death and Immortality* and his essay on the political theology of Friedrich Julius Stahl. If anything, the seminal works of the late 1830s and early 1840s expressed an intensified preoccupation with the sociopolitical dimension of his critique of religion and speculative philosophy. For example, in an 1839 essay he described the illogic of belief in miracles by referring to their political analogue: "God gave the laws of nature, as a king gives a constitution; what he gives, he can take away again."[1] And in *The Essence of Christianity*, a book taken up with the refutation of the idea of divine personality, Feuerbach slipped into the appendices the observation that "personality is only an abstract, modern expression for sovereignty."[2]

Feuerbach's engagement with the question of the relationship between

---

1  Feuerbach, "Über das Wunder," *Werke*, vol. 2, p. 223.
2  Feuerbach, *Das Wesen des Christenthums*, p. 578.

Christian personalism, society, and politics intersected with the larger context of the religio-political controversies that splintered the Hegelian School in the later 1830s. If Feuerbach grew bolder and more explicit in his attack on religio-political personalism, this was in large part because the debate over the ramifications of the idea of personality greatly intensified after 1835. This debate in fact followed two separate paths. First, the political meaning of personality became a key point of contention between defenders and opponents of the Christian state in Prussia. By 1841, Friedrich Wilhelm Carové could assert that the idea of personality had become a "Lebensfrage" for Prussian politics, a political judgment that mirrored Michelet's assessment of the religio-philosophical debates of the 1830s.[3] A less prominent but no less important line of debate centered on the social meaning of personality. The main catalyst for this debate was the German encounter with French social thought in the 1830s. The reception and transformation of French ideas intersected directly with the German religio-political controversy between Christian personalists and pantheists. The convergence of theological and social themes in the German reception of socialism in the 1830s amplified the social dimension of the politico-theological discussion of pantheism and personalism.

This chapter will examine the two paths followed by the discourse of personality in the later 1830s. The next two chapters will move from a general level to more detailed analyses of how these themes shaped the thinking of important radicals in the 1830s and early 1840s. Chapter 5 will show how, in the works of Heinrich Heine, Moses Hess, and August Cieszkowski, French social thought could combine with German metaphysics to form a *social* theology, a millennarian prophecy of religious and social conversion. That chapter will end with a reconsideration of Feuerbach's seminal critique of theology and idealism in the light of what I shall call "social pantheism." Chapter 6 will focus on the impact of the politico-theological discussion of sovereignty, constitutionalism, and the nature of the state upon the thought of Arnold Ruge, an Hegelian who was deeply molded by the pressures of political debate. Repeatedly in these chapters, we will see that the political and social dimensions of the discourse of personality were never fully distinct from each other; indeed, the permeable boundary between the social and the political created ambiguities that help account for the ideological transformations of the late 1830s and early 1840s.

---

3  [Carové], *"Hegel, Schubarth und die Idee der Persönlichkeit in ihrem Verhältniss zur preußischen Monarchie,* von Dr. Immanuel Ogienski," p. 269.

## The Strauss Controversy and the Defection
## of the Hegelian Right

In an 1839 essay, the prominent Hegelian philosopher of law Eduard Gans noted an important change in the opposition to Hegel's political philosophy. In his 1832 foreword to the second edition of Hegel's *Philosophy of Right,* Gans had defended Hegel against liberals who accused him of servility to the Prussian state. He now observed that "since 1832, with shifting winds, the attack has come from the other side" and with such vigor that Hegelianism has become "more uncomfortable than liberalism itself."[4] As Gans suggested, Hegelianism was a victim of a general reactionary shift in German politics. In the wake of the French Revolution of 1830, which had stirred great hopes among German liberals and republicans, the movement for constitutional reform in Germany had suffered serious setbacks.[5] The most notorious of these reactions against constitutionalism occurred outside Prussia. In Hesse-Kassel, Elector William II began a campaign in 1832 against the constitution that he had been forced to accept in the tumultuous year 1830. When the Hessian *Landtag* was dissolved and its spokesman Sylvester Jordan arrested, the parliamentarians proved powerless to defend either themselves or the constitution. Likewise, the Saxon government repressed political agitation and emasculated the *Landtag.* In Hannover, when Ernest August ascended the throne in 1837, he adjourned the *Landtag* and declared the constitution invalid. Each of these reactionary measures resonated throughout Germany.[6] The monarchical *coup d'état* in Hannover attracted particularly intense scrutiny in the rest of Germany when seven professors at Göttingen who objected to Ernest August's actions were summarily dismissed and three were driven into exile.[7] Liberals developed a wary sense of the fragility of their hopes and gains, even as persecution furnished martyrs and rallied liberal opinion around *causes célèbre* such as that of the Göttingen Seven. Conservatives, on the other hand, were emboldened to believe that in politics, if not in nature, royal decree could stem a tide.

4 Eduard Gans, "Erwiderung auf Schubarth," *Materialien,* ed. Riedel, p. 269.
5 On the attempt of liberals to build on the monarchically given "constitutions" of the 1820s, see Hartwig Brandt, "Die Julirevolution (1830) und die Rezeption der 'principes de 1789' in Deutschland," Roger Dufraisse, ed. *Revolution und Gegenrevolution, 1789–1830. Zur geistigen Auseinandersetzung in Frankreich und Deutschland* (Munich, 1991), pp. 225–33.
6 Thomas Nipperdey, *Deutsche Geschichte. 1800–1866. Bürgerwelt und starker Staat,* 6th ed. (München, 1993), p. 375.
7 Sheehan, *German History,* pp. 614f.

In Prussia, the Restorationist "counter-offensive" launched in the 1820s against the spirit of the Reform Era bore fruit in the 1830s.[8] The denunciation of Protestant rationalist theologians by Pietists during the Halle Affair of 1830 initiated the practice of rigorous official scrutiny of candidates to academic posts. Prussia took the lead in reinvigorating the Carlsbad Decrees of 1819 when it convinced the German Confederation to ban the writings of the Young Germans in 1835. Then, in 1837, the Prussian government attempted to resolve a longstanding conflict with the Catholic church in the Rhineland by imprisoning the archbishop of Cologne on charges of treason and taking over the archdiocese's administration. The reaction of Prussian liberals to this arbitrary use of state power was mild compared with their outrage at the plight of the Göttingen Seven, demonstrating that liberal principle itself could fall victim to anti-Catholic sentiment. Yet, as with the Hannoverian *coup d'état*, the Cologne Affair revealed the growing contempt of Germany's monarchical regimes for the aspirations of constitutionalists and liberals.

This shift in attitude was reflected in Prussia by the waning influence of reform-minded bureaucrats, while Pietist Fundamentalists like Ernst Hengstenberg and Ludwig von Gerlach came to regard themselves as the spiritual and political counselors of Friedrich Wilhelm III.[9] If the attachments of the king had thus grown somewhat suspicious in the eyes of Prussian progressives, the affiliations of the crown prince left no doubt as to his political sympathies, because he had surrounded himself with a coterie of Pietists, mystics, and Romantics.[10] Despite these unpromising signs, during the 1830s Prussian reformers and liberals did not abandon their optimism that the progressive spirit in Prussia could be rekindled and its "revolution from above" completed. Their willingness to believe Friedrich Wilhelm IV's shortlived promise of constitutional reform upon his accession to the throne in 1840 amply displays the tenacity of a basic liberal faith in the better spirits of the Prussian state. Conversely, like liberals elsewhere in the German states, Prussian liberals in the later 1830s could not remain blind to the setbacks that their cause had suffered or to the fact that the monarchy seemed ever less inclined to honor the promise of constitutional reform that had buoyed progressive hopes in the aftermath of Napoleon's defeat.

8  Berdahl, *Politics*, p. 257.
9  See Bigler, *Politics of German Protestantism*, esp. pp. 106–7.
10 See the recent works by Lothar Kroll, *Friedrich Wilhelm IV und das Staatsdenken der deutschen Romantik* (Berlin, 1990) and Dirk Blasius, *Friedrich Wilhelm IV. 1795–1861: Psychopathologie und Geschichte* (Göttingen, 1992).

Prussian conservatives' more aggressive attacks on Hegel's political philosophy in the second half of the 1830s must be understood as part of this
ongoing, intensifying reaction against constitutionalism. The broader conflicts between defenders of absolute monarchic authority and champions of
alternative ideas of sovereignty, whether it was the people, parliament, or
the law itself that was to be invested with sovereign authority, may explain in
large measure the increasingly strident political debate between Hegelians
and anti-Hegelians over the idea of personality. More specifically, though,
the intensity of the assault on Hegelian political philosophy, as well as the
centrality of the issue of personality in this political debate, was one of the
important products of the storm of controversy that broke over David
Friedrich Strauss's *Life of Jesus* when it appeared in 1835. Non-Hegelians and
Hegelians alike quickly detected revolutionary political implications in
Strauss's denial of the incarnation of Christ and his emphasis on the divinity of humanity. However, as Walter Jaeschke has written, "much of the extensive literature devoted to the Hegelian Left and Right has failed to notice
and has consistently disregarded the fact that it was [the Strauss controversy]
which transformed a debate on the philosophy of religion into a political
debate."[11] Of course, we have seen that Friedrich Julius Stahl had readily
spelled out the political implications of Hegel's philosophy of religion as
early as 1830; and in 1835, Bachmann's *Anti-Hegel* had identified Hegel's alleged pantheism with Jacobinism.[12] Moreover, since the Halle Affair of 1830,
when Protestant theological rationalists had been censured by the government for their deleterious effects upon orthodox belief, politics had never
been far from disputes among Prussian Protestants. Nonetheless, Jaeschke
is correct in suggesting that the controversy over Strauss brought into bold
relief the political dimension of the religio-philosophical debate over the
idea of personality.

   Ironically, it was the most prominent of the conservative Hegelians, the
Naumberg jurist Carl Friedrich Göschel, who first called attention to the
political implications of Strauss's "apolitical" critique of divine personality.[13]
Strauss placed all conservative Hegelians in a profoundly uncomfortable
position because his denial of the God-Man and apotheosis of humanity appeared to confirm the worst suspicions of Hegelianism's opponents. Indeed, Hengstenberg could not conceal his delight that Strauss had finally

---

11  Jaeschke, *Reason in Religion*, p. 377.
12  Cited in Avineri, "Hegel Revisited," p. 138.
13  My discussion of Göschel is based on Walter Jaeschke, "Urmenschheit und Monarchie,"
    *Hegel-Studien*, 14(1979), pp. 73–107.

exposed the intrinsic anti-Christian bias of Hegelianism, thus drawing firm battle lines in the struggle over the faith.[14] From another side, non-Hegelian theological rationalists saw in the controversy over Strauss an opportunity not only to discredit Hegelianism, which had overshadowed their own attempts to develop a rational interpretation of religion in the 1820s and early 1830s, but also to divert attacks against their own creed by joining Pietists and orthodox Lutherans in a chorus of denunciation. In the midst of this clamor, conservative Hegelians saw their own attempts to prove the compatibility of Hegelian philosophy and Christian dogma gravely jeopardized.[15]

By the time Strauss's *Life of Jesus* appeared, Göschel had built a career out of precisely this conciliatory enterprise. Göschel's attempt to reconcile Christian piety with Hegelian speculative Idealism had won praise from Hegel himself in 1829, although Hegel's endorsement of this bland presentation of his views might have been motivated more by his desire to disarm orthodox criticism of his system than by genuine approval of Göschel. In 1834, Göschel published a sharp attack on Friedrich Richter's *Die neue Unsterblichkeitslehre*, a book that anticipated in more arcane language the principal arguments of Strauss's *Life of Jesus*.[16] Göschel followed that in 1835 with his own book on immortality, in which he attempted to answer I. H. Fichte's charge that Hegel had rejected the doctrine of immortality by arguing that it was in fact the Hegelian speculative philosophy that best honored the sacred principle of personality.[17] In 1837, Göschel undertook a critique of Strauss at the personal urging of Karl von Altenstein, the Prussian minister for Religious and Educational Affairs. Altenstein, whose sympathetic support of the Hegelians since the early 1820s had tied his own fate to theirs, was eager to see Hegelianism placed once again on the safe ground of piety.

In the unpublished *Votum* of 1837, found among Altenstein's personal papers, and again in an 1838 book, Göschel undertook to demonstrate that, properly understood, Hegel's speculative philosophy did not support Strauss's iconoclastic conclusion that Christ was the mythic personification

14    Toews, *Hegelianism*, p. 243.

15    See Strauss's description of the impact of his work upon Hegelians and non-Hegelians, *In Defense of My "Life of Jesus" Against the Hegelians*, trans. Marilyn Chapin Massey (Hamden, Conn., 1983), p. 7. Massey's translation is of the third section of Strauss's *Streitschriften zur Vertheidigung meiner Schrift über das Leben Jesu und zur Charakteristik der gegenwärtigen Theologie* (Tübingen, 1837).

16    Göschel, *Jahrbücher für wissenschaftliche Kritik* (Januar 1834).

17    Göschel, *Von den Beweisen für die Unsterblichkeit der menschlichen Seele im Lichte der spekulativen Philosophie: Eine Ostergabe* (Berlin, 1835).

of humanity's own collective divinity but verified the historical and religious truth of Christ.[18] Significantly, however, in attempting to reassert the primacy of the orthodox idea of the personal God-Man over Stauss's subversive species-concept (*Gattungsbegriff*), Göschel based his argument upon analogies between the monarch and the God-Man, on the one hand, and between the body politic and the community of faith on the other. He conceded to Strauss that the species, conceived as a community, enjoys a "moral personality," that is, a unity or oneness; but where Strauss remained with this "mystical, intellectual personality," Göschel argued that collectivities must gain concreteness through one exalted individual. The highest wisdom of philosophy, he continued, is to recognize that just as the body politic remains incomplete unless it is embodied in the "actual personality" of the monarch, so too must the moral personality of the spiritual community find its fulfillment in the single person of Christ.

Göschel's "political christology" essentially revived the medieval distinction between the two bodies of Christ, the *corpus naturale* and the *corpus mysticum*, in order to counter both the pantheistic and the republican implications of Strauss's anti-hierarchical, democratic insistence on the divinity of all humanity.[19] His position bore a striking resemblance to the political theology of Stahl and other restorationist defenders of personalist sovereignty, although Stahl would not have accepted that the "people" as a collective entity has any sort of personality, "moral" or otherwise. What is more, Göschel tried to demonstrate Hegel's politico-theological orthodoxy by interpreting the philosopher's comments on personality in the most authoritarian terms. In Göschel's mind, Hegel's rather tautological comment in the *Philosophy of Right* that "personality" ultimately must be embodied in a person became an inflexible argument for the necessity to acknowledge the unique persons of the monarch and Christ, while Hegel's recognition of the need for a moment

18 Jaeschke's article "Urmenschheit und Monarchie" prints for the first time selections from the *Votum*. Key sections of the *Votum* were later incorporated into Göschel's *Beiträge zur spekulativen Philosophie von Gott und dem Menschen und von dem Gott-Menschen: Mit Rücksicht auf Dr. D. F. Strauss' Christologie* (Berlin, 1838).

19 Ernst Kantorowicz describes the doctrine of Christ's "two bodies" in *The King's Two Bodies* (p. 206): "one, a body natural, individual and personal (*corpus naturale, verum, personale*); the other, a super-individual body politic and collective, the *corpus mysticum*, interpreted also as a *persona mystica*." The persistence of this theological language in the political and juristic discourse of early-nineteenth-century Germany is amply evident in the discussion in Chapter 2. In addition, see Karl Heinz Ludwig Pölitz's 1827 definition of a "Republic" as a state whose "ruler is not a physical person, as in a monarchy, but is a moral (mystical) person. . . ." From Pölitz's *Die Staatswissenschaften im Lichte unsrer Zeit* quoted in Wolfgang Mager, "Republik," *Geschichtliche Grundbegriffe*, vol. 5, p. 619.

of subjective decision in the state became a defense for a personal sovereign
who transcends the state and the constitution altogether. The only remaining
"Hegelian" element was Göschel's attempt to describe a dialectical progression in consciousness's recognition of different modes of personality, from the
abstract plurality to the concrete singular. Through such an account, Strauss's
species-concept could be integrated into and then overcome in a teleological
account of the triumphal recognition of the sovereignty of actual personality
in both the earthly and heavenly kingdoms.

Whereas the other leading right-wing Hegelians, Marheinecke and Johannes Schulze, tried to protect Hegel's political reputation from the attacks of conservatives by expurgating potentially offensive comments from
the second edition of the *Philosophy of Right*,[20] Göschel met the critics by
politicizing the tactic that he had used in his earlier conflict with I. H. Fichte
over personality and immortality. That is, he implied that in both theology
and politics Hegel was the best ally of his worst enemies. This surprising conclusion did little to placate the reactionaries; but Göschel's strategy exem-
plifies the drift of conservative Hegelians toward philosophical and political
positions that were barely distinguishable from those of Positive Philosophers like Schelling and Stahl, or the Speculative Theists I. H. Fichte and
C. H. Weisse. From the outset, Hegelians like Göschel, Gabler, and Henning
had seized upon Hegel's speculative Idealism as a philosophical support of
orthodox faith. Under the pressure of Strauss's use of Hegelian categories
for radical anti-Christian purposes, their general inclination to seek reconciliation between philosophy and orthodoxy gave way to a more specific
process of accommodation of the Hegelian Right to the philosophical critics of the Hegelian system. The implications of this accommodation were
recognized even before the appearance of Strauss's *Life of Jesus* in Ferdinand
Gustav Kühne's remarkably insightful discussion of Göschel and I. H. Fichte's
controversy over personal immortality. Expressing astonishment that Göschel
had attempted to defend personal immortality on Hegelian grounds, Kühne
claimed that "Whoever places the absolute in personality instead of the idea,
dissolves the bands of this system with one blow. . . . If Göschel can be regarded as the current representative of the Hegelian doctrine, then this philosophy has united with its opponents insofar as the absolute is placed in
personality."[21]

The emerging Hegelian Left clearly recognized the gravitation of the

20  See the remembrances of Carl Ludwig Michelet, *Wahrheit aus meinem Leben* (Berlin, 1884),
     p. 171.
21  F. G. Kühne, "Bücherschau," *Literarischer Zodiacus* (Juni, 1835), pp. 472–7.

Hegelian Right toward the philosophers of Christian personalism. Significantly, Feuerbach told Arnold Ruge in 1837 that his critique of Stahl applied "indirectly" to Göschel as well.[22] It is unlikely that he knew of Göschel's 1837 *Votum*, as this was written for Altenstein's private use, and its essential arguments were not published until 1838. His comment was probably directed against Göschel's earlier works, particularly his 1835 book on immortality and perhaps his collection of juristic writings, a text that revealed his sympathies for the political Restoration.[23] In his 1837 *Defense of My "Life of Jesus,"* Strauss, too, accused his conservative Hegelian critics of betraying the spirit of speculative philosophy. Strauss noted that although reason's right to criticize philosophical and religious consciousness should have been self-evident to all Hegelians, in religious matters, Hegelians had merely tried to conceptualize that which is given in immediate belief or intuition, thereby accepting religious positivism rather than criticizing it. Thus, he concluded, the conservative Hegelians had essentially slid into the practice of Schelling's school, which Strauss chose to illustrate by reference to Stahl.[24]

In the first instance, neither Feuerbach nor Strauss construed the defection of the Right Hegelians in political terms. Nonetheless, the fact that both chose to identify the leading Right Hegelian with the most political of all the Positive Philosophers is an indication that for them, the political was closely bound to the theological and philosophical. Indeed, Strauss amplified his criticism of the Hegelian Right by turning directly to the political corollary of their theological positivism. The Schellingians, he insisted, elevate "historical law" over "the law of reason" and cling to the "principle of stability" that girds the Prussian Restoration. Therefore, Strauss concluded, Hegelians who followed Schelling and Stahl into the same political positivism flagrantly disregarded the explicit message of Hegel's political philosophy: "Anyone who has read Hegel's *Philosophy of Right* knows that in it many essential issues are construed quite differently than in the Prussian state."[25] Strauss's bold insistence upon Hegel's liberalism was hardly what conservative Hegelians wanted to hear. It did nothing to disentangle the emerging political debate from the religio-philosophical controversy, nor for that matter did his decision to use the highly charged vocabulary of postrevolutionary European politics to describe a "right," "center," and "left" within the Hegelian School.

22  Feuerbach to Ruge, 15 December 1837, *Briefwechsel*, vol. 1.
23  Göschel, *Zerstreuten Blätter aus den Hand- und Hülfsacten eines Juristen*, 3 Bde. (Erfurt, 1832–42).
24  Strauss, *In Defense of My "Life of Jesus,"* pp. 11–13.
25  Strauss, *Streitschriften zur Vertheidigung meiner Schrift über das Leben Jesu* (New York, 1980), p. 205.

## Denunciation and the Radicalization of the Hegelian Left

Göschel's response to Strauss indicated the intermingling of theology and politics in the question of the nature of divine incarnation, but it was Heinrich Leo's 1838 denunciations of the "Young Hegelian party" that thrust the political implications of the Strauss controversy into the foreground of debate. Leo had been a committed Hegelian in his youth, but by the time he became a professor of history at Halle University, he had embraced legitimism in politics and orthodox Protestant Fundamentalism in religion.[26] This personal defection from Hegelianism lent authority to his claim that, because the right-wing Hegelians had in fact already abandoned the philosophy of Hegel, they could be summarily dismissed as deluded hypocrites. Against the Center and Left Hegelians – the real enemies – he assembled a familiar litany of complaints against their alleged pantheism.[27] Even his insistence upon a direct link between the Young Hegelians' religious heresies and their revolutionary political agenda contained little news.[28] Nonetheless, Leo's polemic had a greater impact than earlier ones, because it came at a time when Strauss had made the Hegelian School exceptionally vulnerable to accusations of irreligion and blasphemy. His charge that the radical Hegelians were the true heirs of Hegel struck directly at the self-doubts raised among right-wing Hegelians by the dangerous developments within the School.[29] Moreover, his insistence that the time had come to replace academic debate with the more persuasive arguments of censors and jailers greatly increased the bitterness of the politico-theological dispute. Coming as it did so soon after the persecution of the Göttingen Seven, Leo's call for police action was cause for alarm among Hegelians.

The appearance of Leo's polemic marked a decisive turning point in the radicalization of the Young Hegelians. His aggressive attack crystallized the emergent Left's feeling of persecution and alienation, as well as its members' willingness to admit that the philosophical and theological conflict must be carried into the political domain. The numerous responses to Leo that appeared in the recently founded journal of progressive Hegelian opinion, *Hallische Jahrbücher,* also revealed an opening breach between their in-

26  Toews, *Hegelianism,* pp. 226–7.
27  Leo, *Die Hegelingen. Actenstücke und Belege zu der s.g. Denunciation der ewigen Wahrheit* (Halle, 1838), pp. 4–5.
28  Similar charges were repeated *ad nauseam* in the major Pietist journal. See Hengstenberg, "Die Hallischen Jahrbüchern für Deutsche Wissenschaft und Kunst," *Evangelische Kirchen-Zeitung,* August–September, 1838, pp. 545–68.
29  Leo, *Die Hegelingen,* p. 14.

herited belief in the rationalism of the Prussian state and their perception of disturbing Prussian realities.[30]

Leo's denunciations also served to encourage other anti-Hegelians.[31] Noting that Hegel's doctrine had come under attack from "all sides," K. E. Schubarth composed in 1839 the most notable polemic against Hegelian politics since the first volume of Stahl's *Philosophie des Rechts*.[32] Schubarth was an academic outsider whose marginality had nothing to do with unorthodox views. Driven to supplement his meager scholarly talents by currying favor with the luminaries of the cultural world, he had somehow won the support of Goethe in the 1820s. Goethe had even asked Hegel in 1827 if he could help Schubarth obtain an academic post in Berlin. Despite expressing distaste at the young *Privatdozent*'s use of personal connections, Hegel did offer to assist him in a job search that ultimately proved unsuccessful.[33] Two years later, in 1829, Schubarth and one L. A. Carganico published an attack on Hegel. This essay expressed a decided preference for what Schubarth called "pure monarchy" over Hegel's constitutional monarchy, but its sharpest criticism was reserved for Hegel's totalizing image of the state. Schubarth and Carganico here voiced the familiar Pietistic objection to Hegel's alleged desire to transfer the church's ethical and religious role to the state.[34] Their criticisms attracted sufficient attention that Hegel felt constrained to publish a response, although he did not so much meet their criticism as catalogue their numerous philosophical confusions.

In 1839, Schubarth returned to Hegel's doctrine of the state in an even more vituperative polemic. In this book, the Pietistic concerns of his earlier work were overshadowed by the unmistakable imprint of Stahl's political

---

30  See, for example, Feuerbach, "Über Philosophie und Christentum in Beziehung auf den Hegelschen Philosophie gemachten Vorwurf der Unchristlichkeit" (1839), *Werke*, vol. 2, pp. 278–87; and Arnold Ruge, "Die Denunciation der *Hallischen Jahrbücher*" (1838), *Die Hegelsche Linke*, ed. H. and I. Pepperle (Leipzig, 1985).

31  See, for example, H. M. Chalybäus, "Philosophie der Geschichte und Geschichte der Philosophie," *Zeitschrift für Philosophie und Spekulative Theologie*, 1 (1837), pp. 301–38; E. Platner, "Über die Bedeutung und Realität des Rechtsbegriffs," *Zeitschrift für Philosophie und Spekulative Theologie*, 3 (1839), pp. 286–311; and K. A. Kahnis, *Dr. Ruge und Hegel* (Quedlinburg, 1838).

32  Schubarth, "Über die Unvereinbarkeit der Hegelschen Staatslehre mit dem obersten Lebens- und Entwicklungsprinzip des Preußischen Staats" (1839), *Materialien*, ed. Riedel, pp. 249–66.

33  See the correspondence between Hegel and Goethe in the spring and summer of 1827 in *Briefe von und an Hegel*, vol. 3, ed. Johannes Hoffmeister (Hamburg, 1961).

34  K. E. Schubarth and L. A. Carganico's 1829 essay and Hegel's response are reprinted in *Materialien*, ed. Riedel, vol. 1. In addition, see Schubarth, *Erklärung in Betreff der Recension des Hrn. Hegel* (Berlin, 1830).

theology. In 1829, Schubarth had insisted that contrary to Hegel, ethical life "establishes in personality, in good will, ultimately in religion, a sphere over which the state has no power."[35] By contrast, in 1839, Schubarth obscured this orthodox Lutheran separation of the worldly state from the ethico-spiritual realm by applying the metaphysics of personalism to the Prussian state. He no longer considered the state simply as a realm of "power and law." Rather, he argued that in the concrete embodiment of the monarch, the state represented the consummate expression of the concept of personality "which Protestantism awakened and created."[36] All forms of constitutionalism, including Hegel's idea of constitutional monarchy, violated this "highest living principle of the Prussian state." Indeed, because "a constitutional monarchy is none other than a republic in monarchic garb," Schubarth concluded his diatribe by seconding Leo's call for police action against Hegelian subversion.[37]

Schubarth's "well-known accusation," as Arnold Ruge called it, prompted a discussion among Hegelians of the idea of personality in relation to both Hegel's political philosophy and the Prussian state.[38] In sharp opposition to the right-wing Hegelians who defected to the legitimist and positivist camps, a minority of progressive Hegelians conceded the arguments of both the anti-Hegelian reactionaries and the conservative Hegelians in order to proceed to a critique of both Prussian conditions and Hegel's accommodationism. So, for example, K. E. Köppen and F. Förster agreed with reactionaries that Prussia was indeed not a constitutional monarchy.[39] Förster went even further when he accepted the Hegelian Right's claim that Hegel's political views pointed necessarily to the personal sovereignty of the monarch. By raising doubts about Hegel's commitment to liberalism and constitutionalism, Förster anticipated the more radical rejection of Hegel's political philosophy that came in the early 1840s from figures like Arnold Ruge, Edgar Bauer, and

35  Schubarth and Carganico, "Zu Hegels Staatsbegriff (1829). Über Philosophie uberhaupt, und Hegel's Encyclopedia der philosophischen Wissenschaften insbesondere," 209. Schubarth and Carganico's polemic is described as "successful in its historical effectiveness" by Graf and Wagner in Die Flucht in den Begriff, p. 32 n89.
36  Schubarth, "Über die Unvereinbarkeit der Hegelschen Staatslehre mit dem obersten Lebens- und Entwicklungsprinzip des Preußischen Staats" (1839), Materialien, ed. Riedel, pp. 249–50.
37  Ibid, p. 252.
38  Arnold Ruge, "Politik und Philosophie" (1840), Die Hegelsche Linke, p. 189.
39  K. F. Köppen, "Über Schubarths Unvereinbarkeit der Hegelschen Lehre mit dem Preußischen Staate" (1839), and F. Förster, "Noch ein Denunziant der Hegelschen Philosophie" (1839), both in Materialien, ed. Riedel. See also Köppen, "Zur Feier der Thronbesteigung Friedrichs II," (1840), Die Hegelsche Linke, pp. 128–46.

Karl Marx. Furthermore, Förster's criticism of the personalist element in Hegel's politics foreshadowed the Left Hegelians' eventual identification of Hegel with the political personalism of the Positive Philosophy.

Few Hegelians in 1839 were as boldly or openly disaffected as Förster. The more common strategy was to meet Schubarth's polemic by insisting that history was on their side. That is, they argued that the fundamental trajectory of European history was away from personal power and toward the sovereignty of the state itself as an assemblage of powers unified by a rational constitution. Eduard Gans did more than any other Hegelian to develop the outlines and details of this account of the modern European state. In lectures and writings throughout the 1830s, Gans traced the origin of the modern state back to Louis XIV's creation of a unified state from the irrational and fractious elements of feudalism. Although this unity was initially conceived as the "*Ichheit*" or subjective identity of the absolute monarch, Gans was convinced that the modern state had subsequently developed into an objective and impersonal unity.[40] In response to Schubarth, Gans insisted that Prussia was already well embarked on this progressive course. Gans stopped short of declaring Prussia a fully modern state, but he argued that a *de facto* constitutionalism existed in the institutions of the Prussian state, its bureaucracy, and its administration of justice. Moreover, he held that Hegel's view of the monarch accurately described the Prussian king's circumscribed yet important role.[41] To support his argument, Gans charged that the "apotheosis of personality" is merely a "representation" (*Vorstellung*) which yields under rational scrutiny to the recognition of the modern state's complex impersonal totality.[42] Significantly, this claim about the difference between the appearance and the reality of power transferred the contrast between "representation" and "concept" from the more familiar terrain of the Hegelian philosophy of religion to the political domain, and Gans's point foreshadowed the critique that Ruge and Marx directed in the 1840s not only against the Christian monarchic principle but against Hegel's own conception of monarchy.

---

40  See Gans, "Vorlesungen über die Geschichte der letzten fünfzig Jahre," *Historisches Taschenbuch*, 1834–5; and "Über die Provinzialgesetze," *Beiträge zur Revision der Preußischen Gesetzgebung* (Berlin, 1831), p. 368. On Gans's interpretation of the role of political absolutism in the development of the modern state, see Reinhard Blänkner, "'Der Absolutismus war ein Glück, der doch nicht zu den Absolutisten gehört.' Eduard Gans und die hegelianischen Ursprünge der Absolutismusforschung in Deutschland," *Historische Zeitschrift*, 256(1993), pp. 31–66.

41  Gans, "Erwiderung auf Schubarth" (1839), *Materialien*, ed. Riedel, pp. 267–75.

42  Ibid., pp. 272–3.

Other progressive Hegelians were equally insistent upon both Hegel's commitment to constitutionalism and the fundamental movement of history away from the type of personal regime espoused by Stahl and Schubarth.[43] In the most detailed response to Schubarth's polemic, Immanuel Ogienski, a teacher at the *Gymnasium* in Trzemeßno, turned Schubarth's claims back on him by arguing that a constitutional monarchy best actualizes the principle of personality. "Pure monarchy" merely fixes personality in one person, but constitutional monarchy depends on the cooperative interaction of many capable persons. Mobilizing Hegel's notion of concrete personality, as well as general assumptions about the formative effects of political participation on the citizen, Ogienski asserted that a constitutional monarchy is a genuinely "personal state" because it guarantees and cultivates the personalities of both the "governor" and the "governed."[44] Whereas Schubarth's idea of personality remains an "aristocratic privilege" denied to the "mass," the true concept of personality demands "the political and spiritual emancipation of all that remains impersonal."[45] This political norm might easily have led Ogienski to criticize the present Prussian system for its failure to overcome the estrangement of citizens from political life; however, he shied away from such conclusions and insisted instead upon the essentially rational and progressive orientation of the Prussian state.

Ogienski was certainly not alone among progressive Hegelians in the late 1830s in his eagerness to vindicate Prussia. However, the responses of other Hegelians to Schubarth reveal more ambivalent evaluations of Prussian conditions. Even Gans's defense of the constitutionality of the Prussian state must be considered a rhetorical tactic when measured against the lifelong oppositional stance of a man eulogized upon his sudden death in 1839 for his "passion for freedom in a time of reaction."[46] Indeed, Gans's true view is probably better expressed by his claim in the early 1830s that Prussia is a "tutelary state."[47] Friedrich Wilhelm Carové, a Hegelian liberal who had long criticized the Prussian state, agreed with the substance of Ogienski's

43  See Varnhagen von Ense, "Hegel und – Schubarth," *Materialien*, ed. Riedel, p. 317; Varnhagen, "Zur Charakteristik C. G. Schubarth's," *Intelligenzblatt zu den Hallischen Jahrbüchern* (1839), pp. 6–11; and [Ludwig Buhl], *Hegels Lehre vom Staat und seine Philosophie der Geschichte in ihren Hauptresultaten* (Berlin, 1837), pp. 16f.

44  Immanuel Ogienski, *Hegel, Schubarth und die Idee der Persönlichkeit in ihrem Verhältnis zur preußischen Monarchie* (Trzemeßno, 1840), pp. 35, 47. In 1853, Ogienski submitted a *Habilitationsschrift* to the philosophy faculty of the University of Breslau titled *Die Idee der Person*.

45  Ogienski, *Idee der Persönlichkeit*, pp. 57, 59.

46  Anon., "Eduard Gans," *Hallische Jahrbücher*, 132 (3. Juni, 1839), p. 1049.

47  Eduard Gans, *Philosophische Schriften* ed. Horst Schroder (Glashutten im Taunus, 1971), p. 308.

reworking of the idea of personality, but he upbraided the teacher from Trzemeßno for backsliding into an acceptance of Prussian conditions.[48] In an anonymously published book, *Hegel und Preußen,* Carové criticized Prussia for failing to honor Friedrich the Great's declaration that he was the first servant of the state, Friedrich's subordination of his arbitrary personal power to the rational state, and he argued stridently that by not acknowledging that "the elevation of the prince is alone the work of the people," Prussia had deviated from western Europe, southwestern Germany, and, indeed, from its own path of development.[49] "What is now demanded of all states of the civilized world is above all the guarantee of law, freedom, and the autonomous development of all against arbitrariness of any kind."[50] Carové tied the realization of these goals in Prussia to the awakening of "German national feeling," but he maintained that more than nationalism was required. Above all, he insisted that the Prussians needed the political freedoms and representative institutions that he claimed were enjoyed by citizens of other German states. Only that could stimulate a "sense of political solidarity."[51] A review of *Hegel und Preußen* by Moritz Carriere further underscored the liberal and republican aspects of Carové's response to Ogienski. Carriere pointedly remarked that a king who rejects the metaphysics of personalism in favor of a theory that limits his own powers becomes the nation's first teacher of freedom.[52]

One Christian Feldmann neatly suggested the continuing interpenetration of religious and political elements in the evolution of the political debate about personality when he wrote in 1842 that a victory of the Young Hegelians would mean that "The monarchic principle would truly make way for the republican, and the perfect sovereignty of the highest God would be distributed among millions of earthly gods."[53] Driven into full daylight by the controversy over Strauss's denial of divine personality, the politicized debate about personality was an important catalyst as well as a vehicle for the articulation of widely differing views of monarchy and the Prussian state. For

48  [Carové], "*Hegel, Schubarth und die Idee der Persönlichkeit in ihrem Verhältniss zur preußischen Monarchie,* von Dr. Immanuel Ogienski," pp. 269–92. Carové's biographer has attributed this anonymous article to him. See Albert Schürmann, *Friedrich Wilhelm Carové. Sein Werk als Beitrag zur Kritik an Staat und Kirche im frühliberalen Hegelianismus* (Bochum, 1971), p. 298.

49  [Carové], *Hegel und Preußen. Principes mortales, res publica aeterna* (Frankfurt, 1841), pp. 62–5. Surprisingly, no one has noted that Carové's review of Ogienski's book is almost identical to the anonymously published *Hegel und Preußen.* Based on this, authorship may be reasonably assigned to Carové.

50  Ibid., p. 69.    51   Ibid., p. 66.

52  M. Carriere, "*Hegel und Preußen,*" *Jahrbücher für wissenschaftliche Kritik,* 1841, pp. 687–8.

53  Feldmann quoted in Eßbach, *Die Junghegelianer,* p. 229.

all Hegelians, the theologico-political polemics of the Christian personalists were decisive in forcing them to articulate their own positions. Until well into the 1840s, the political language of Hegelianism was to carry the stamp of the theological and philosophical debates within which the question of political sovereignty had become embedded. Further, the political debate must be considered as a vital cause of the irrevocable fragmentation of the Hegelian School in the later 1830s. A proper appreciation of the role of this debate offers an important corrective to the emphasis that scholars have usually placed upon putatively apolitical theological and philosophical controversies in explaining that fragmentation.

The dispute over the political meanings of personality helped precipitate a significant shift of allegiances within the Hegelian School. By 1841, some Hegelians had anointed the monarch as the analogue of Christ on earth, while others had enfranchised him as a "fellow citizen" (*Mitbürger*).[54] With the pretense of ideological unity among Hegelians shattered, the notion that Hegelianism itself constituted a sufficient and autonomous political stance yielded to more pointed affiliations of individual Hegelians with the great political movements of the age. Like immigrants to a new land, Hegelian identities henceforth had to be hyphenated. Right-wing Hegelians discovered that their commitment to "Hegelianism" proved weaker than their attraction to the "philosophical" exponents of religious orthodoxy and political conservatism. In fact, the Hegelian Right did not so much accommodate itself to the political theology of personalism as eventually capitulate to it. By 1839, Karl Gutzkow could report that the conflict between Hegelian speculative philosophy and Schellingian Positive Philosophy had provoked bitter complaints among some Hegelians that they could no longer assume the loyalty of their philosophical "brothers" within the Hegelian fraternity.[55] As for the Hegelian Center and the emergent Left, their criticism of arbitrary personal monarchy brought them into a close relationship with other liberal and progressive elements in Germany.

This proved to be a short-lived alliance for the Hegelian Left, but for a time, the rhetoric of progressive Hegelianism overlapped that of liberalism. This convergence manifested itself at the level of practice, as in Gans's vigorous defense of the Göttingen Seven, or in many personal, professional, and political connections among liberals and Hegelians.[56] Furthermore, the parallels at the theoretical level between progressive Hegelians and both

---

54    M. Carriere, "*Hegel und Preußen*," p. 688.
55    Karl Gutzkow, *Beiträge zur Geschichte des neuesten Literatur* (Stuttgart, 1839), p. 212.
56    See, for example, the many non-Hegelian liberals listed among the collaborators of the *Hallische Jahrbücher* in its first two years of publication.

north and south German liberals in the later 1830s are easily overlooked if one accepts the hostile article on Hegelianism in the famous liberal *Staats-Lexikon* as representative of liberal opinion toward Hegelianism.[57] Moderate German liberals shared the centrist Hegelians' desire to avoid the extremes of absolute monarchy and democratic suffrage, and in that moderate spirit, both groups insisted on the sovereignty of the state itself. The liberal insistence that the identification of the state with the personal monarch must yield to an enlightened understanding of the state itself as a "juristic personality" closely resembled Eduard Gans's own understanding of the evolution of the state from the "I" of the monarch to the objective unity of the constitutional state. In addition, the familiar liberal defense of individual rights was an equally vital part of the progressive Hegelian response to the Restorationist offensive against constitutional reform.[58]

Although liberals and Hegelians like Gans, Carové, and Ogienski remained unclear on the precise mechanisms of political participation and representation, their ideal of the state presupposed a citizenry characterized by rationality and autonomy. Both groups pitted their classically "enlightened" model of personhood, based on the intrinsic dignity and rights of the human being, against the theological and hierarchical model of personhood employed by Restorationists. Hence, for example, Carl Ludwig Michelet's 1840 defense of Hegel's idea of Spirit included a scrupulously "liberal" discussion of the equality of human persons and their rights.[59] More surprising is Bruno Bauer's lengthy analysis of the "right of personality" and "civil society" in his 1838 book *The Religion of the Old Testament*. Considering that this was written while Bauer was still a "right-wing" Hegelian opponent of Strauss, his advocacy of a liberal ideal of rational individual autonomy demonstrates that theological and political positions did not always align perfectly.[60] It may also be said that the disjunction between Bauer's theological and political views

57  K. H. Scheidler, "Hegel'sche Philosophie und Schule, insbesondere Hegel's Naturrecht und Staatslehre," *Staatslexikon*, vol. 7, ed. Carl von Rotteck and Carl Welcker (Altona, 1839), pp. 607–47. The classic essays by Gustav Mayer remain excellent sources for the relations of the Hegelians to German liberalism. See "Die Junghegelianer und der preussische Staat" and "Die Anfänge des politischen Radikalismus im vormärzlichen Preussen," *Zeitschrift für Politik*, 6(1913), pp. 1–117. See also Eßbach, *Die Junghegelianer*, pp. 244 n282, and pp. 207f on north and south German liberalism.

58  On these dimensions of German liberal theory, see Ernst Rudolf Huber, *Deutsche Verfassungsgeschichte seit 1789*, vol. 1 (Stuttgart, 1960), pp. 374–7.

59  C. L. Michelet, *Anthropologie und Psychologie, oder die Philosophie des subjectiven Geistes* (Berlin, 1840), pp. 512–40.

60  Bruno Bauer, *Die Religion des Alten Testamentes in der geschichtlichen Entwickelung ihrer Principien*, vol. 1 (Berlin, 1838), pp. 173–266. Surprisingly, the scholarly literature on Bauer has failed to discuss the large section of this book that is explicitly modeled on the distinctions between the family, civil society, and the state made in Hegel's *Philosophy of Right*.

during his early career foreshadowed his move toward the extreme Hegelian Left in the 1840s.

By 1840, it was clear that the reactionary countermovement had won in Prussia. For many Hegelians, the omen of their defeat came with the appointment of Friedrich Julius Stahl to fill the chair in jurisprudence at the University of Berlin left vacant by Eduard Gans's death.[61] Indeed, the highest levels of the Prussian regime engineered the replacement of one of the leading Hegelians with one of the best-known opponents of Hegelianism.[62] Stahl's summons to Berlin was followed quickly by the appointment of Schelling to the chair in philosophy. By the end of 1840, Friedrich Wilhelm III and Altenstein were dead and the Romantic crown prince had acceded to the throne. After passing hints of constitutional reform, Friedrich Wilhelm IV reverted to type. Liberal bureaucrats were replaced by conservatives, and the regulation of political life and discussion was enforced with renewed vigor. The "pernicious party" that Feuerbach had denounced in 1835 had come to power in Prussia.

## Germans and the Social Question in the 1830s

The divisive debate about political personality was an important catalyst for the development of Hegelian radicalism in the later 1830s and 1840s. We have seen that this debate was an expression of larger conflicts in German politics over the nature of sovereignty, constitutional reform, and broader political participation. All of these questions had first been posed in their practical-political form by the French Revolution of 1789. The restoration of monarchic and aristocratic hegemony throughout continental Europe in 1815 had stifled these issues temporarily, but the July Revolution of 1830 revitalized the so-called "party of movement." In Germany, reverberations from the revolution in France did more than shake the liberals and the small number of republicans into wakefulness, however. For the history of socialism in Germany began with the July Revolution – not in the form of proletarian politics, to be sure, but in reports of a Parisian sect prophesying a new age of social equality. Like the constitutional debates of the 1830s, the German reception and expansion of French socialist ideas was a broader phenomenon than the conflict between Hegelians and anti-Hegelians in Prussia. Nonetheless, in the convergence of theological and social themes that

---

61  See, for example, [Carové], *Hegel und Preußen*, p. 41.
62  Hermann Klenner, "Stahls Berufung – Kein Briefwechsel," *Unzeit des Biedermeiers*, ed. H. W. Weise Bode (Leipzig, 1985), pp. 206–16.

characterized the German discussion of socialism, German interest in the new social thought intersected with the political debates about pantheism and personalism in the last half of the 1830s. Alongside that political controversy, the social discourse of pantheism must also be considered a crucial factor in the radicalization of the Hegelian Left.

Hermann Lübbe has written that "at the beginning of the 1830s, the social question was a discovery. By the end of the 1840s, it had become a catchword."[63] The "social question" in Germany was actually a discovery in two senses. First, social observers, journalists, bureaucrats, and intellectuals grew steadily more aware of the pitiable plight of the German lower classes.[64] These observers discovered that what had long been regarded as a static level of misery inherent in the condition of the poor had given way to a steadily worsening problem of mass impoverishment and homelessness. Their observations conformed to the objective situation of millions of Germans in those years. Numerous modern scholars have argued that the crisis of mass poverty was the result of a painful process of social adjustment to the new industrial capitalist order;[65] but, industrialization was then in its first birth pangs in Germany, and the factories that existed could hardly account for the scale of the problem of pauperism. It is now generally agreed that the economic source of this acute crisis lay in too little, not too much, industrialization. The lower classes in the 1830s suffered from the intersection of rapid population growth since the late eighteenth century, the legal emancipation of the lower classes, and a sluggish economy that could not absorb the large number of laborers seeking employment during this initial period of transition from agrarian to industrial society.[66] In the countryside, the mounting population, combined with the emancipation of the peasantry from serfdom, the enclosure of common lands, and new Poor Laws reducing local obligations to the needy, created a new class of landless rural paupers.[67] The assault against the remnants of feudalism in the towns and

---

63 Hermann Lübbe, "Die Politische Theorie der Hegelschen Rechten," *Archiv für Philosophie,* Bd. 10/3–4(1962), p. 218.

64 See the valuable collection, Carl Jantke and Dietrich Hilger, ed., *Die Eigentumslosen. Der deutsche Pauperismus und die Emanzipationskrise in Darstellungen und Deutungen der zeitgenössischen Literatur* (München, 1965).

65 An important expression of this view can be found in Theodore S. Hamerow, *Restoration, Revolution, Reaction. Economics and Politics in Germany, 1815–1871* (Princeton, 1958).

66 The relevant literature is voluminous. For a review of older scholarship, see Frederick D. Marquardt, "*Pauperismus* in Germany during the *Vormärz,*" *Central European History,* 2(1969), pp. 77–88. See, more recently, Sheehan, *German History,* esp. pp. 638–52.

67 The enclosure of woodlands and commons did not merely pit peasants against aristocrats, as the young Marx thought, but benefited many "small and middling peasants" as well. See

cities produced similar results. As the German states abolished the protective status of the guilds, artisans became vulnerable to the pressures of free trade and proto-industrialization. While skilled artisan masters were frequently able to move into relatively secure positions in the new factory hierarchies, a surplus of artisans had to compete against migrants from the countryside for scarce and low-paying factory jobs. No part of Germany had an "industrial" economy before 1850; but a new class of urban workers had made its appearance by the 1830s, workers without connections to the old guilds, laboring now in factories of varying size and mechanization.[68]

Contemporary observers registered these social changes in the growing use of the term "proletariat" to designate this new class. The gradual abandonment of the older term *Pöbel* (rabble) signified an important shift in the analysis of poverty and the onset of the modern German discussion of industrial classes. *Pöbel* had always designated the lower classes within a traditional society of ranks and orders. In this relatively static context, poverty within the lowest ranks was considered a "natural" attribute of society, or as an entailment of humanity's original sinful condition. By contrast, the proletariat, this new class of working poor, was conceived of as a social class produced by new economic forces and new labor and wage relations.[69] The problem of poverty thereby became for some Germans an object of "scientific" analysis; but, more broadly, poverty became historicized when contemporaries related it to a specifically modern crisis, the roots of which they sought in economic dislocation, the ethos of competitiveness, and the collapse of earlier forms of social sympathy and solidarity. By the later 1830s, the problems of pauperism and the new laboring poor had become topics of considerable debate and discussion, even though this concern was not prompted exclusively by observation of German conditions. Serious as these problems may have been in the 1830s, they became acute only in the 1840s,

R. J. Evans, "The 'dangerous classes' in Germany from the Middle Ages to the twentieth century," *Proletarians and Politics. Socialism, Protest and the Working Class in Germany Before the First World War* (New York, 1990), p. 11.

68  Sheehan, *German History*, pp. 493–5.

69  See in particular the classic article by Werner Conze, "Vom 'Pöbel' zum 'Proletariat.' Sozialgeschichtliche Voraussetzungen für den Sozialismus in Deutschland," *Vierteljahrsschrift für Sozial- und Wirtschaftsgeschichte* (1954), esp. p. 340. A similar discursive transformation has been particularly well studied in the British context. See Gertrude Himmelfarb, *The Idea of Poverty: England in the Early Industrial Age* (London, 1984), J. R. Poynter, *Society and Pauperism: English Ideas on Poor Relief, 1795–1834* (London, 1969); and Gregory Claeys, "The Origins of the Rights of Labor: Republicanism, Commerce, and the Construction of Modern Social Theory in Britain, 1796–1805," *Journal of Modern History*, 66 (June 1994), pp. 249–90.

when severe economic depression magnified their cumulative effects. It is necessary to recognize that German perceptions of the social problem in the 1830s were in fact decisively shaped by Germans' awareness of socioeconomic conditions in England,[70] and, above all, by their knowledge of early French socialist theory. In this sense, the social question in Germany was also a discovery of foreign literary sources and conceptual frameworks.

## The New Christianity of Saint-Simonianism

It is somewhat anachronistic to speak of *socialism* in the late 1820s and early 1830s because the substantive noun denoting a discrete and self-conscious ideology was just coming into usage in the mid-1830s.[71] Mindful of this caveat, we may nonetheless identify an important stream of French social theorists who had for some time sought to resolve the problems posed by the rise of the new industrial society in France and England. There was, of course, Charles Fourier, the trenchant critic of commercial society and the inventor of elaborate schemes for the reformation of society through love and communal solidarity.[72] Yet Fourier had labored for twenty-five years since the publication of his masterpiece, the *Théorie des quatre mouvements*, without attracting more than a few followers in the French provinces. By contrast, and much to Fourier's chagrin, the field of social speculation in the late 1820s belonged to the disciples of the Count Henri de Saint-Simon.[73] Saint-Simon's long and checkered career had taken him from soldier in the American Revolution to war profiteer in the French, aristocratic dandy to impoverished social prophet, suicidal despondency to manic self-importance, lunacy to mild craziness. Abandoning the financial schemes that had bankrupted him and nearly cost him his life under France's revolutionary regime, Saint-Simon turned to moral and social speculation after

70  On this theme, see Keith Tribe, *Governing Economy*, as well as his bibliography of older works on the German reception of English political economy. Engels's famous *Conditions of the Working Class in England* (1844) can be said to be a climax rather than the start of a tradition of German reporting on English social conditions.

71  Pierre Leroux used the word "socialism" in this sense in an article of 1834. See R. Picard, "Sur l'origine des mots *socialisme* et *socialiste*," *Revue socialiste*, li(1910), pp. 379–90; and Wolfgang Scheider, "Sozialismus," *Geschichtliche Grundbegriffe*, vol. 5, pp. 923–98. For a still earlier use of the word, although without the specific meaning intended by Leroux, see X. Joncière, "Les Feuilles d'automne, poesies par M. Victor Hugo," *Le Globe*, 13 February 1832.

72  The best book on Fourier is Jonathan Beecher, *Charles Fourier. The Visionary and His World* (Berkeley, 1986).

73  On Fourier's jealous campaign against the Saint-Simonians, see ibid., pp. 418–21.

1800. In the next twenty-five years, he produced a remarkable series of works combining acute insights into social and economic processes with utopian visions of future perfection.[74] By the time of his death in 1825, he had attracted a small band of devout followers, some of whom were students or recent graduates of the *Ecole polytechnique*, others members of the network of activists who haunted the conspiratorial penumbra of Restoration Paris.[75] Immediately after the master's death, the first disciples, led by Olinde Rodrigues, St.-Amand Bazard, Philippe Buchez, and the man destined to become the charismatic leader of the Saint-Simonians, Prosper-Barthélemy Enfantin, formed the Saint-Simonian Society and launched the short-lived journal *Le Producteur* (1825–6). In this and the ensuing journals, *L'Organisateur* (1829–1) and *Le Globe* (1831–2), as well as in well-attended public lectures held in Paris from 1828 to 1830, the Saint-Simonians fashioned a compelling social and ethical doctrine. Even the disciples made clear that they were not simply mouthing their teacher's words but had developed a living doctrine inspired by Saint-Simon's voluminous and eclectic body of writings.[76]

Saint-Simonianism, like other forms of early socialism, cannot be reduced to a set of propositions about the economy. Nor did its analysis of commercial society presuppose the primacy of material interest in history. Although Saint-Simon and his followers believed they had discovered the science of *social physiology*, their science was actually a form of speculative social psychology, because they thought that beliefs and values fundamentally shape human history.[77] The Saint-Simonian philosophy of history fully expresses this essential idealism. European history, in this view, was defined by alternations between "organic" periods of social harmony and unity and "critical" periods of "contest, of protest, of expectation, and transition."[78] In the present critical age, the Saint-Simonians argued, antagonism prevails in the relations between nations, between the sexes, and, most portentously for the history of socialism, between wage earners and employers.[79] They

---

74   The literature on Saint-Simon is immense. Frank E. Manuel's *The New World of Henri Saint-Simon* (Cambridge, Mass., 1956), *The Prophets of Paris* (New York, 1962), and his *Utopian Thought in the Western World* (Cambridge, Mass., 1979) offer engaging discussions of Saint-Simon's life and thought. See also Robert Carlisle's spirited defense of Saint-Simonianism, *The Proffered Crown. Saint-Simonianism and the Doctrine of Hope* (Baltimore, 1987).

75   Alan Spitzer, *The French Generation of 1820* (Princeton, 1987), p. 155.

76   See *The Doctrine of Saint-Simon: An Exposition. First Year, 1828–1829*, trans. G. G. Iggers (New York, 1958).

77   On the use of physiological metaphor in Saint-Simon, see Robert Wokler, "Saint-Simon and the Passage from Political to Social Science," *The Languages of Political Theory in Early Modern Europe*, ed. Anthony Pagden (Cambridge, 1987).

78   *The Doctrine of Saint-Simon*, p. 53.       79   Ibid., p. 80.

denounced the modern wage-relation as a perpetuation of slavery and sought to alleviate the misery of the "poorest and most numerous class" by replacing the inefficient, anarchic, competitive society of the present with rational organization of production and consumption. The Saint-Simonian future was meant to be authentically egalitarian, though not in the sense of equalizing wealth in society. Rather, the Saint-Simonians hoped to make society fully meritocratic by allowing the genuinely competent to rise to positions of leadership in industry and science; to unequal capacities would go unequal rewards, as the famous slogan of the Saint-Simonians proclaimed.[80] Thus, the Saint-Simonians adopted the principle of meritocracy, but they extended this shibboleth of French liberalism far beyond what liberals could accept. For to attain this new social order, the Saint-Simonians insisted on the abolition of the right of inheritance. As the Saint-Simonians themselves were at pains to emphasize, their main target was not private property *per se* but the right to inherit property, because inheritance violates the principle of merit by distributing wealth without regard to the worthiness of the heirs. More than that, they charged, it obstructs social reform because of its irrational and unproductive allocation of wealth. The state must therefore appropriate family wealth and distribute this social capital to truly capable people, whose excellence and industriousness will enrich the general stock of humanity.

The Saint-Simonians stopped far short of demanding the abolition of family wealth, but their attack on the right of inheritance struck deeply at existing social values. Robert Carlisle has written that "the point of the discussion on property . . . was that it made imperative a different view of the family, of marriage, of sex, and of the relations of men and women if the conversion of property to the service of humanity was to be brought about. *Conversion* was the operative word. Nothing short of a transvaluation of all values would suffice."[81] Carlisle's comments are apt, for it was not to changes in material life that the Saint-Simonians looked for the causes of modern egoism but to the dominant spiritual values of the modern epoch. And here, following Saint-Simon in *Le nouveau christianisme*, they traced the immediate origins of the critical age to the effects of the Protestant Reformation. We saw in the preceding chapter that, perhaps influenced by earlier Catholic writers, the Saint-Simonians were extremely critical of what they believed to be the deep relationship between modern bourgeois social and political relations and modern (post-Reformation) religious individualism. This

80   Ibid., p. 89.
81   Carlisle, *Proferred Crown*, p. 74.

judgment of Protestantism was not lost on the Saint-Simonians' contemporaries. As one German student of the French movement reported in 1834,
in Saint-Simon's view, "Luther's insurrection" had "turned the human spirit
from the general standpoint [of medieval Christianity] toward analysis of
particularity. . . . The neglect of universality has produced the feeling of egoism which now rules in all classes of society."[82] As with Feuerbach, much of
the Saint-Simonians' invective against Christianity at large must be read as
really directed against the "anti-social values" that they identified with
Protestantism.[83]

Again like Feuerbach, however, they also believed that the Reformation
had accentuated tendencies present even in earlier Catholicism. That is, although they praised the organic holism and order of medieval Catholicism
and openly drew from the writings of Catholic conservatives like Bonald and
Maistre, nevertheless they believed that Catholicism too had strayed from
the original message of primitive Christianity. Because the Saint-Simonian
goal was nothing less than a radical conversion that would fulfill the truth
of human nature, their ambition put them in direct competition against two
millennia of Christian history, which they considered the only rival to their
own comprehensive understanding of human nature. The supersession of
social antagonism and the achievement of economic justice were dimensions of the much greater task of superseding Christianity, which they hoped
to achieve by enlisting what they believed to be the essence of Christianity
in the struggle against modern social conditions.[84] The Saint-Simonians
found a prophecy of the new millennium in Saint-Simon's last book, *Le nouveau christianisme*. There, Saint-Simon traced the decline of Christianity
from an immanent religion of brotherly love to a dualistic faith that elevates
heaven only to debase earth. Defending the idea of a pantheistic "God of
love," he insisted that "the true Christianity must render men happy on
earth as well as in heaven."[85] "All men must behave as brothers towards one
another," he wrote, reducing the entire content of Christianity to this one
"sublime principle."[86] Saint-Simon prophesied that although this principle

82    Moritz Veit, *Saint Simon und der Saintsimonismus. Allgemeiner Völkerbund und ewiger Friede*
      (Leipzig, 1834), p. 104.
83    Dickey, "Saint-Simonian Industrialism as the End of History," p. 178.
84    This was, of course, a common strategy of early socialists, as Gareth Stedman Jones has em-
      phasized in "Utopian Socialism Reconsidered," *People's History and Socialist Theory*, ed.
      Raphael Samuel (London, 1981).
85    Claude Henri Saint-Simon, "The New Christianity. Dialogues Between a Conservative and
      an Innovator," *Socialist Thought. A Documentary History*, by Albert Fried and Ronald Sanders
      (New York, 1964), p. 91.
86    Ibid., p. 78.

belonged essentially to primitive Christianity, the social bond of love would be "regenerated" in the future as a religious injunction to *"direct society toward the over-all goal of the most rapid possible amelioration of the condition of the poorest class."*[87]

Animated by this vision, Saint-Simon's followers constituted themselves as a "church" in 1829, with Prosper Enfantin and Saint-Amand Bazard anointed as its two "popes." Ironically, along with the papal hierarchy, the Saint-Simonians adjusted various aspects of Catholic ritual to a new faith shorn of all supernatural trappings and directed solely toward sanctifying the social bond. It has been widely argued that the Saint-Simonians betrayed the intentions of Saint-Simon by forming a religion, but if there was any betrayal, it lay in the Saint-Simonians' initial resistance to Saint-Simon's religious ideas out of fear of appearing utopian.[88] Indeed, the first Saint-Simonian journal, the *Producteur*, dedicated itself solely to the technical and instrumental aspects of social organization and reform. It was only in the two years after the collapse of the journal that the inner circle of the movement struck a new path. They grew convinced that the transformation of humanity's material life must be preceded by moral and spiritual change. In a critical epoch of individualism and self-interest, people must be taught to love one another. So the Saint-Simonians came to pin their fervent hopes for the conversion of society from "antagonism" to "association," from the "critical" present to the last and highest "organic" era, on the conversion of Christianity into a humanistic religion of love.[89] After months of doctrinal refinements, this "New Christianity" was unveiled to widespread acclaim in a series of public lectures at a rented hall in the rue Taranne in 1829 and 1830.

The Saint-Simonians exalted Saint-Simon as the messiah of the New Christianity, but like the disciples of Christ, whose example they were keen to follow, they offered more than a doxology of their master's revelation. In their analyses of the connections between the old Christianity – particularly Protestantism – and social disorganization and injustice, as well as in their efforts to enlist artists, scholars, and industrialists in the service of the new faith, they went significantly beyond Saint-Simon. Further, they developed a comprehensive philosophical basis for the New Christianity that centered upon an analysis of a fundamental dualism in orthodox Christianity between "spirit" and "matter." This dualism, the Saint-Simonians maintained, lies at the heart of Christianity's indifference to the happiness of people on this

---

87  Ibid., p. 82.
88  Carlisle, *Proffered Crown*, p. 41.
89  See especially *The Doctrine of Saint-Simon*, pp. 244–62.

earth because it encourages people to mortify the flesh to sanctify the spirit, to turn inward to the cultivation of their own souls at the cost of the human community. The need to overcome the Christian dichotomy of flesh and spirit found succinct expression in one of the most famous slogans of Saint-Simonianism. As Bazard proclaimed in the second exposition of the doctrine: "The Most Striking and Novel, indeed the Most Important, task of general progress that humanity is called upon to perform TODAY consists, gentlemen, in the REHABILITATION OF MATTER. ..."[90] From the diffuse pantheistic faith that was to achieve this reconciliation of flesh and spirit, the Saint-Simonians derived not only arguments supporting the holy bond of society but also theories supporting the androgyny of God, free love, and the equality of the sexes.[91]

The Saint-Simonians' dominance of Parisian intellectual life was almost as complete as it was short-lived. Late in 1831, one of the two "popes" of the movement, Bazard, left the church after bitterly disagreeing with Père Enfantin's views on marriage, free love, and the emancipation of women. Several other important members, including Pierre Leroux, Jules Lechevalier, and Abel Transon, defected to the rival camp of Charles Fourier.[92] The antics of the Saint-Simonian "church" at its Menilmontant commune, the Saint-Simonians' mimicry of the Catholic church's hieratic order, and misadventures like the search in the Middle East for a female messiah drew equal measures of public interest and ridicule. Public attention reached a high point in the summer of 1832 when the Saint-Simonians stood trial for offenses against public morality, but it waned quickly once the charismatic leaders were sent to Saint-Pélagie to serve their one-year jail term. Though the group had dissipated much of its energies by 1832, the follies of the Saint-Simonian church should not distract us from recognizing the influence it had in its heyday and long afterward. Saint-Simonian ideas resonated deeply among young writers and intellectuals who had come of age in the last years of the Napoleonic regime and felt themselves stifled by the reactionary union of throne and altar in Restoration France.[93] Among many members of this generation, an initial commitment to conservative Romanticism broke down under the cumulative pressure of the restored

90  Quoted in E. M. Butler, *The Saint-Simonian Religion in Germany. A Study of the Young German Movement* (Cambridge, 1926), p. 44.

91  On these issues, see Carlisle, *Proferred Crown;* Claire Moses, *French Feminism in the Nineteenth Century* (Albany, 1984), pp. 41–59; and Claire Moses and Leslie Wahl Rabine, ed., *Feminism, Socialism and French Romanticism* (Bloomington, 1994).

92  See Beecher, *Fourier,* pp. 422–30.

93  See Spitzer, *French Generation.*

Bourbon monarchy's ineptitude, economic stagnation, the ideological cacophony of the 1820s, and the July Revolution, which overthrew the old
monarchy but enthroned a new aristocracy of monied bourgeois. The new
"Romanticism" that gripped many of France's most talented young people
in the years immediately after the July Revolution found perfect expression
in the Saint-Simonians' mix of sober criticism, sentimental humanism, and
messianic utopianism.

We can trace this profound change in French Romanticism in two spec-
tacular personal conversions to the ideas of progress and social liberation.
Victor Hugo, not yet thirty in 1830 but already a towering figure among
French Romantics, moved from royalism to liberalism by 1827.[94] By the
early 1830s, he identified the struggle for political freedom with the fight
against ignorance and misery. Embracing the tendency of his age to substitute "social questions for political questions," he proclaimed that literature
"has a national mission, a social mission, a human mission."[95] Hugo's was
not the only poetics that championed social responsibility. Indeed, the
Saint-Simonians' insistence that art must have "social usefulness" was a commonplace among artists and aestheticians in the years of the July Monarchy.[96] In a conversion similar to Hugo's, the older poet Félicité de Lamennais also subscribed to the new ideal of artistic commitment. Abandoning
the ultramontane Catholicism and royalism of his four-volume *Essai sur l'in-
différence en materière de religion* (1817–23), he dedicated his *Paroles d'un croy-
ant* of 1834 to the "tremendous revolution which is going on at the heart of
human society."[97] More powerfully than Hugo, Lamennais united a yearning for social justice with profound religious devotion and a hunger for spiritual and moral renewal. The same marriage of social outrage, soaring idealism, and spiritual credulity defined the views of George Sand, Alphonse
de Lamartine, Eugène Sue, Alfred de Vigny, Sainte-Beuve, Pierre Leroux,
and numerous lesser figures. Romanticism's migration from reaction to the
"party of movement" was arguably the fundamental feature of intellectual
life in France during the 1830s, and this sea change had vast significance

94  Ibid., p. 143.
95  Hugo quoted in D. O. Evans, *Social Romanticism in France, 1830–1848* (Oxford, 1951),
    p. 73, 30.
96  See Neil McWilliam, *Dreams of Happiness: Social Art and the French Left, 1830–1850* (Prince-
    ton, 1993). Spitzer, *French Generation*, pp. 163f, maintains that even French liberals shared
    this utilitarian view of art. Contrast this to the charge that this politicization of art ex-
    pressed the Saint-Simonians' "totalitarian" impulses in F. A. Hayek, *The Counter-Revolution
    of Science. Studies on the Abuse of Reason* (Glencoe, 1952), pp. 145f.
97  Lamennais quoted in Evans, *Social Romanticism*, p. 39.

for French politics in the years leading up to 1848. The Saint-Simonians did not initiate this transformation single-handedly, but their comprehensive ideal of a humanistic religion of love uniquely satisfied the intellectual and emotional needs of this generation of French Romantics.

## Saint-Simonianism in Germany

The first German to report on these shifts in French culture and politics was Friedrich Buchholz, the Berlin historian, political thinker, and editor of the *Neue Monatsschrift für Deutschland*. From 1824 onward, Buccholz published many translations of articles from the Saint-Simonian *Le Producteur,* including Olinde Rodrigues's comprehensive presentation of Saint-Simon's thought.[98] However, it was only after the July Revolution had rekindled great German interest in French politics and ideas that the Saint-Simonians became a topic of broad discussion in Germany. Paris once again became the spiritual home of all European progressives, and in Paris, the Saint-Simonians were the most intriguing of progressive camps. A flood of writings in German books, newspapers, and journals introduced the German reading public to this new sect.[99] Germany's renowned exiles in Paris, Ludwig Börne and Heinrich Heine, wrote of Saint-Simonianism, while the movement crops up in Goethe's conversations with Eckermann and in Hegel's musings shortly before his death.[100]

In the German interest in Saint-Simonianism, one detects much innocent curiosity along with some amusement at French goings-on. From many German churchmen, however, the movement elicited stern denunciations. Such Christians downplayed or ignored the movement's social and political aspirations and seized upon its religious and ethical consequences. In the Saint-Simonians' claim to overcome or transcend Christianity, their rever-

---

98   These translations are collected in *Saint-Simonistische Texte. Abhandlungen von Saint-Simon, Bazard, Blanqui, Buchez, Carnot, Comte, Enfantin, Leroux, Rodrigues, Thierry und Anderen in zeitgenössischen Übersetzungen,* 2 vols., ed. Rütger Schäfer (Aalen, 1975). See also R. Schäfer, *Friedrich Buchholz – ein vergessener Vorläufer der Soziologie,* 2 vols. (Göttingen, 1972).

99   See Butler, *Saint-Simonian Religion,* esp. pp. 52–9, for a bibliography of works on Saint-Simonianism in the German press from 1830 to 1834; Werner Suhge, *Saint-Simonismus und junges Deutschland. Das Saint-Simonistische System in der deutschen Literatur der ersten Hälfte des 19. Jahrhunderts* (Berlin, 1935); Charles Rihs, *L'école des jeunes hegeliens et les penseurs socialistes français* (Paris, 1978), pp. 292–320; Thomas Petermann, *Der Saint-Simonismus in Deutschland. Bemerkungen zur Wirkungsgeschichte* (Frankfurt, 1983); and Hayek's *Counter-Revolution,* pp. 158–67.

100  Börne was more critical of the movement than Heine. See Börne's *Briefe aus Paris* (Wiesbaden, 1986), esp. 30 December 1831.

ence for Henri Saint-Simon as the messiah of the New Christianity, or their
energetic embrace of free love there was more than enough to scandalize
Christians of all denominations, but Catholics and Protestants also found
specific insults tailored to provoke their indignation. The French group's
aping of the structures of the Catholic church, with the carnal pope Enfantin at its head, deeply offended Catholics like the Archbishop of Trier, who
issued a circular against the Saint-Simonians in 1832.[101] For the same reason, Protestants became convinced that the Saint-Simonians were little
more than disguised Jesuits.[102] The Saint-Simonians' special hostility toward
Protestantism as a more egoistical religion than Catholicism only confirmed
German Lutherans and Calvinists in their negative judgment.[103] Behind
their breathless rhetoric, German detractors struck a contradictory stance
toward this beast of the apocalypse. On the one hand, German Christians'
hysterical response and the volume of polemical literature suggest that they
viewed Saint-Simonianism as a real threat to public piety and morality. On
the other hand, they dismissed the Saint-Simonians as a ridiculous sideshow
that only French frivolity could have produced, and they denied that the sect
could take root in German soil.

Some German intellectuals did find substantial inspiration in the Saint-
Simonians, however. As the poet and essayist Heinrich Laube reported, the
new creed stimulated a lively passion for "projects of emancipation" and "social speculation."[104] For some, like Friedrich Buchholz or Eduard Gans, who
was the most eminent Hegelian advocate of Saint-Simonian ideas, their importance lay in their "science of society," not in their religious preten-
sions.[105] Buchholz and Gans notwithstanding, it was not the "secular" and
"scientific" application of Saint-Simonian theories to social problems that accounts for the appeal of the French movement. Rather, Saint-Simonianism
fascinated numerous young German writers precisely because of its Social
Romanticism. This intoxicating formula proved fateful for the poets Heinrich Heine, Varnhagen von Ense, Rahel Varnhagen, Theodor Mundt, Karl
Gutzkow, and Heinrich Laube, the major literary rebels in the years of the

101  See the *Allgemeine Kirchenzeitung*, Darmstadt (March 8, 1832).
102  See especially K. G. Bretschneider, *Der Saintsimonismus und das Christentum. Oder: beur-
     theilende Darstellung der Simonistische Religion, ihres Verhältnisses zur christlichen Kirche, und der
     Lage des Christenthums in unserer Zeit* (Leipzig, 1832).
103  Heinrich Leo, "*Nouveau Christianisme, dialogues entre un conservateur et un novateur,*"
     *Ergänzungsblätter zur Allgemeinen Literatur-Zeitung* (März, 1831), p. 179.
104  Heinrich Laube, *Ausgewählte Werke in zehn Bänden*, vol. 8, ed. H. H. Houben (Leipzig,
     n.d.), p. 186.
105  See, for example, Buchholz, "Was ist von der neuen Lehre zu halten die sich die St. Si-
     monistische nennt" (1832), *Saint-Simonistische Texte*, ed. R. Schäfer, pp. 523–48.

Restoration. The Young Germans, as this loose grouping came to be known, had begun a two-front struggle against the dominant literary forces of the age: conservative Romanticism, with its gothic fascination for throne and altar, and Goethe's monumental presence in German literature; but these campaigns quickly spread beyond a narrow conflict over aesthetic values.[106] In the aftermath of the July Revolution, with its promise of a new epoch of political movement and happiness, these young writers seized upon the social concern and political activism that had come to define the French Left. Against the stifling political, social, and artistic mood east of the Rhine, the Young Germans discovered kinship with the Social Romanticism of Lamennais, Lamartine, Hugo, Sand, and, most important, the Saint-Simonians.

The attraction of Saint-Simonianism for the Young Germans lay less in the specifics of its political or social program than in the moral vision that animated its most grandiose demands. The Young Germans were drawn to the Saint-Simonians' optimistic belief in the progressive evolution of human society. Critical of the constraints of family and sexual convention, they were intrigued by the emancipatory prospects of the doctrine of "free love" and by the New Christianity's call for the "rehabilitation of matter," which the Germans frequently misunderstood as the "rehabilitation of the flesh."[107] Indeed, some of the Young Germans, particularly Heinrich Laube, seemed tantalized by the Saint-Simonians' promise of greater social license, but they also hoped sincerely for a revolution that would be at once erotic, social, political, and religious.[108] Hence, for the Young Germans, a revolution in society and mores was expected to be the ultimate result of the pantheistic New Christianity of the Saint-Simonians. As Karl Gutzkow wrote in 1832: "The truth of the Saint-Simonian doctrine lies in its expression of the need

---

106 On Goethe, see, for example, Theodor Mundt, "Über Bewegungsparteien in der Literatur," *Literarischer Zodiacus,* Januar 1835, pp. 1–20; and Book One of Heinrich Heine's *Die Romantische Schule.* The Young Germans were not alone in their ambivalence toward Goethe. "With the possible exception of the first five years of his public literary career, Goethe was never a model which a whole generation chose to imitate," writes Nicholas Boyle in *Goethe. The Poet and the Age. vol. 1. The Poetry of Desire* (Oxford, 1991), pp. 6–7. Both the Young Germans and the Young Hegelians preferred Schiller for his partisan engagement in the moral and political conflicts of the age. See Else von Eck, *Die Literaturkritik in den Hallischen und Deutschen Jahrbüchern (1838–1842)* (Berlin, 1925), pp. 22f. On a similar case of Schiller worship in Russia, see Martin Malia, *Alexander Herzen and the Birth of Russian Socialism* (Cambridge, Mass., 1961), pp. 38–56.
107 See "Einleitung," to Eduard Gans, *Naturrecht und Universalrechtsgeschichte,* ed. Manfred Riedel (Stuttgart, 1981), p. 239 n40.
108 Werner Suhge rightly criticizes Butler's exclusive emphasis on the religious and moral influence of Saint-Simonianism in *Saint-Simonismus und junges Deutschland,* pp. 91f.

for a coalition of our spiritual and material life. It is a symptom of the *Zeit-geist*. . . ."[109]

Perhaps the most significant reason for the resonance of Saint-Simonianism in Germany, among alienated young rebels, as well as hostile orthodox Christians, is the fact that German writers could immediately integrate the discussion of Saint-Simonianism into the already existing German discourse on pantheism and personality. As one detractor declared in exasperation, for the Saint-Simonians "everything is religion."[110] Of course, in the minds of some Germans, like Heine or some of the other Young Germans, this was the sect's greatest attraction. Conservatives, on the other hand, confronted the new French doctrine with a ready arsenal of invective and denunciation. Quick to attack Saint-Simonianism were some of the sharpest critics of Hegelian pantheism. Schelling dismissed Saint-Simonianism as a "crude scandal," and the movement drew detailed responses from the Speculative Theist C. H. Weisse, the theological rationalist Bretschneider, the Pietist Heinrich Leo, and the circle around Hengstenberg's *Evangelische Kirchenzeitung*.[111] Their criticism of Saint-Simonianism paralleled their opposition to Hegelianism, and they readily pointed to affiliations between the Spinozist-Hegelian pantheist tradition and the French "new Christians." In fact, some of the early German opponents of Saint-Simonianism believed that Germany was immune to this French import precisely because, for better or worse, its themes were already so familiar to German philosophy.[112]

Any traces of complacent dismissal quickly vanished once conservatives realized that Saint-Simonianism had found acolytes among the literary youth of Germany. The denunciations swung rapidly against the materialism, pantheism, and libertinism of the Young Germans. The *Evangelische Kirchenzeitung* launched a particularly vigorous campaign against the exiled

---

109  K. Gutzkow, *Briefe eines Narren an eine Närrin* (Hamburg, 1832), p. 38.

110  Carl M. Kapff, "Der Saint-Simonismus in Frankreich," *Tübinger Zeitschrift für Theologie*, 2. Heft, 1832, p. 89.

111  Schelling, "Vorrede zu einer philosophischen Schrift des Herrn Victor Cousin," p. 223; C. H. Weisse, "[Über] Moritz Veit, *Saint Simon und der Saint Simonismus*," *Jahrbücher für wissenschaftliche Kritik*, no. 120, Juni 1834, pp. 1017–120; Bretschneider, *Der Simonismus und das Christenthum*; Leo, "*Nouveau Christianisme*."

112  See, for example, Carové, *Der Saint-Simonismus und die neuere französische Philosophie* (Leipzig, 1831), pp. 195f; Kapff, "Der Saint-Simonismus in Frankreich," p. 3; Warnkönig, "Rechtsphilosophie in Frankreich. Die Lehre der Anhänger Saint-Simons," *Kritische Zeitschrift für Rechtswissenschaft und Gesetzgebung des Auslandes*, 4. Bd., 1832, p. 79; and Fr. Tappehorn, *Die vollkommene Assoziation, als Vermittlerin der Einheit des Vernunftstaates und der Lehre Jesu. Ein Beitrag zur ruhigen Lösung aller großen Fragen dieser Zeit* (Augsburg, 1834), pp. 40f. Tappehorn's is the first German book on Charles Fourier.

162     DETHRONING THE SELF

Heinrich Heine, whom it considered the leader of the Young Germans.[113] Likewise, Wolfgang Menzel, the editor of the *Literaturblatt*, vigorously denounced Heine, Gutzkow, Wienbarg, and the other Young Germans.[114] By late 1835, the theologian J. P. Lange spoke of an "open war" against the Young Germans' "rehabilitation of the flesh."[115] The war was summarily won in that year, not by Lange, Hengstenberg, Menzel, or their academic allies, but by the actions of the German Confederation. Stirred into action by the publication of Karl Gutzkow's novel *Wally*, the Confederation banned the works of the Young Germans with the charge that they "openly attempted, in belletristic works accessible to all classes of readers, to attack the Christian religion, undermine the existing social order, and destroy all discipline and morality."[116] E. M. Butler has argued persuasively that the association of Young Germany with Saint-Simonianism played a considerable part in mobilizing the repressive machinery of the Prussian state and the German Confederation.[117]

In his long essay on Heine and the Young Germans, Lange maintained that the ground for Saint-Simonianism had been prepared in Germany by Hegel: "Saint-Simonianism overall – its doctrine of the holiness of the here-and-now, and especially its glorification of the flesh – is promoted by the propositions of the currently dominant philosophy.... And even if the meaning and direction of this School is more or less different from that of the Saint-Simonian *Weltkinder*, the emphasis on the here-and-now is the same."[118] One year later, declaring the solemn task of the *Evangelische Kirchenzeitung* to be the monitoring of pantheism in all its guises, Lange was even more insistent on the affinity of Hegelianism and Saint-Simonianism. It was the appearance of Strauss's *Life of Jesus* in the interim that confirmed Lange's judgment of Hegelianism and prompted the more urgent tone of his 1836 piece. Strauss's attack on orthodox christology and his deification of humanity seemed to allow Lange to move easily among Saint-Simonianism, Hegelianism, and Young Germany in his blanket condemnation of the pantheistic tendencies of all three.[119]

113  According to one of Heine's modern editors, the *Evangelische Kirchenzeitung*'s attacks seriously harmed his reputation among German Protestants. See *Heinrich Heine. Historisch-kritische Gesamtausgabe der Werke*, vol. 8/2, ed. Manfred Windfuhr (Hamburg, 1981), p. 576.
114  On Menzel and the Saint-Simonians, see Rihs, *L'école des jeunes hegeliens*, p. 307.
115  J. P. Lange, "Über die Rehabilitation des Fleisches," *Evangelische Kirchenzeitung*, Nov. 1835, p. 729. This essay has been erroneously attributed to Hengstenberg himself.
116  Edict cited in Sheehan, *German History*, p. 579.
117  Butler, *Saint-Simonian Religion*, p. 85. See also Metternich quoted in Suhge, *Saint-Simonismus*, p. 62.
118  Lange, "Über die Rehabilitation des Fleisches," pp. 498–9.
119  Lange, "Bericht über ein pantheistisches Trisolium," *Evangelische Kirchenzeitung*, Oct.–Dec., 1836, pp. 665–782.

Nor was this spokesman for the most prominent pietistic journal in Prussia alone in discovering in Strauss new reasons to conflate these schools. Bretschneider, who had earlier exposed the congruence of French and German pantheism, likewise pursued the connection in an 1837 article on Strauss. He included Hegelians in the same category as the Young Germans and the Saint-Simonians, all of whom "divinize the life of man in not only its spiritual, but also its material side."[120] By 1839, some liberals also believed in a special affinity between Hegelianism and Saint-Simonianism. K. H. Schiedler claimed in the *Staats-Lexikon,* for example, that:

> In France, Saint-Simonianism agitates the people, while among the Germans, fortunately, the theory has appeared only in the form of books supporting Hegelian pantheism and Hegelian divinization of the state. . . . Nonetheless, it is possible that such a doctrine, which complements the general sensuality and demoralization of the age, threatens the gravest practical consequences if no limits are set to its dissemination. Further, the philosophical systems that might be derived from [Saint-Simonianism] would be highly offensive. . . .[121]

Of course, German opponents of Saint-Simonianism had a point when they occasionally attempted to neutralize the sect's impact by discounting its originality. One need not go through France to arrive at the German controversy over pantheism and atheism in the 1830s. These debates remained fundamentally oriented toward the tradition stretching from Spinoza, through the *Aufklärung* and the disputes over Lessing and Fichte at the end of the eighteenth century, to the Hegelians and Young Germans of the 1830s. There is even considerable evidence to suggest that Saint-Simonian pantheism was itself inspired by French exposure to the German Spinozist tradition.[122] Yet as Schiedler's comment reveals, the attempt to disarm Saint-Simonianism by domesticating it proved inadequate to the task because it repeatedly exposed the receptivity of German philosophy to the new French thought. Moreover, critics would not have continued to target Saint-Simonian tendencies within German culture even into the late 1830s – long after the sect had fallen from public prominence in France – had they really believed that the French sect was merely a shadow of the German tradition.

In truth, many contemporaries knew that Saint-Simonianism had

120 Bretschneider quoted in Marilyn Chapin Massey, *Christ Unmasked*, p. 89.
121 Scheidler, "Hegel'sche Philosophie und Schule," p. 619.
122 Victor Cousin's eclectic lectures on modern philosophy helped familiarize French students with this German tradition. Eugène Rodrigues translated Lessing's *Education of the Human Race* in 1832. On Gustave d'Eichtal's role in conveying German ideas to France while he was a student in Berlin, see Mary Pickering, "New Evidence of the Link Between Comte and German Philosophy," *Journal of the History of Ideas*, vol. L, no. 3 (July–Sept., 1989), pp. 443–63. See also Rihs, *L'école*, pp. 297f.

introduced a potent new element into German pantheism by linking the rehabilitation of matter to a vision of social harmony. Hence, Theodor Oelckers declared in 1844 that Saint-Simonianism had transformed Christianity into a "social religion";[123] and Theodor Mundt, one of the Young Germans, astutely observed in 1837 that "the Saint-Simonians had attempted to extend pantheism to social relations, to the position of the sexes, and to political economy [Nationalökonomie]."[124] These German insights corresponded to the self-understanding of the French Saint-Simonians. Friedrich Wilhelm Carové, author of a widely read book on the Saint-Simonians in 1832, reported in 1836 that Enfantin believed France had "inaugurated political and industrial pantheism in Europe." Quoting Enfantin, Carové observed that the "translation of pantheism into political language equals the association of peoples among themselves and of humanity with the earth."[125]

The New Christianity redefined religiosity as brotherly love and enjoined the faithful to aid the poor, replace egoism with altruism, and truly respect individuality by recognizing the social basis of the individual. In Saint-Simonian thought, the conversion of humanity from belief in a transcendent deity to pantheism thus perfectly paralleled the conversion of society from "antagonism" to "association." Indeed, one of the first uses of the word "socialism" treated it as virtually synonymous with "pantheism." In terms that resonate strikingly with German theologico-political discourse, the French Saint-Simonian Joncière wrote that "We do not want to sacrifice *personality* to *socialism*, no more than the latter to personality. The harmonization of these two faces of the life of man is the goal of all our efforts."[126] Likewise, Père Barrault insisted in 1831 that the New Christianity "does not absorb sacred personality."[127] Nonetheless, Barrault, like the other Saint-Simonians, clearly derived "personality" from the more primary socio-theological category of "pantheism." In short, for the Saint-Simonians, as for the Hegelian critics of Christian personalism, personality is the product of society, not its precondition.

## Eduard Gans and the Hegelianization of Saint-Simon

This chapter has traced two paths in the sociopolitical discourse of pantheism and personality in the 1830s. First, the Prussian debate over constitu-

123   Theodor Oelckers, *Die Bewegung des Socialismus und Communismus* (Leipzig, 1844), p. 27.
124   Theodor Mundt, "George Sand und die sociale Speculation," *Charaktere und Situationen* (Leipzig, 1837), p. 201.
125   Enfantin quoted in F. W. Carové, "H. Heine und Prosper Enfantin," *Neorama*, 2. Th. (Leipzig, 1838), p. 154.
126   Joncière, "Les Feuilles d'automne."
127   Barrault quoted in Frank E. Manuel, *The Prophets of Paris* (New York, 1962), p. 176.

tionalism and sovereignty in the later 1830s drew energy and imagery from its intersection with the controversy over Strauss's radicalization of Hegelian philosophy. Second, the emerging German discussion of social problems in the 1830s was strongly influenced by the meeting of Saint-Simonian religio-social themes and the German debate about personality. These two strands intertwined in many ways, as the ensuing chapters will show. Yet it is important also to emphasize the tensions between what we may call the "political" and the "social" critiques of Christian personalism. These will become clearer as we turn to Heine, Hess, Cieszkowski, Feuerbach, Ruge, and Marx in the ensuing chapters. The remaining pages of this chapter will embark on a preliminary exploration of these tensions through a discussion of Eduard Gans, the prominent Hegelian philosopher of law at the University of Berlin. Before his untimely death at forty-two in 1839, Gans was more fully engaged than any other Hegelian in the sociopolitical controversies of the 1830s. His attempt to accommodate both the political and social dimensions of those controversies within a Hegelian framework provides a significant contrast to the more radical approaches that we will encounter in subsequent chapters.

Gans was never formally Hegel's student, but Hegel came to regard Gans as one of his most gifted followers. Once Gans became a professor in the juristic faculty at the University of Berlin in the mid-1820s, it was he, not Hegel, who taught a generation of students the intricacies of Hegelian political philosophy. Among those students, it bears mentioning, was Karl Marx, who took Gans's courses on criminal law in the 1836–7 winter semester and on the Prussian *Landrecht* in 1839.[128] By the time Gans died in 1839, he had written numerous volumes on the history and philosophy of property law, as well as dozens of essays on political and legal issues both in his native Prussia and in Europe, and he had published a posthumous edition of Hegel's *Philosophy of Right*. Gans played a central role in founding the Society for Scientific Criticism in 1826, the Hegelian "counter-academy" established in response to the decision of the Royal Prussian Academy of Sciences to exclude Hegel; and he was a major collaborator in *Die Jahrbücher für wissenschaftliche Kritik*, the Society's journal and the main organ of Hegelianism in Germany.[129] Accustomed to encountering opposition as a Hegelian and a liberal, Gans had in his early years also suffered the official anti-Semitism of the Prussian establishment, because as a Jew he was denied an academic

---

128  H. G. Reissner, *Eduard Gans. Ein Leben im Vormärz* (Tübingen, 1965), p. 157.

129  On the Society for Scientific Criticism, see Toews, *Hegelianism*, p. 60. On Gans's role in conceiving of the journal, see Norbert Waszek, "Eduard Gans, die *Jahrbücher für wissenschaftliche Kritik* und die französische Publizistik der Zeit," *Die "Jahrbücher für wissenschaftliche Kritik." Hegels Berliner Gegenakademie*, ed. Christophe Jamme (Stuttgart, 1994).

post. This was an experience that intensified his sense of Jewish identity, and it helps to explain his role as co-founder and leader of the "Verein zur Verbesserung des Zustandes der Juden im Deutschen Bundesstaat," as well as its successor, the "Verein für Cultur und Wissenschaft der Juden," while he was still a student at the University of Berlin. His professional frustrations continued in 1822, when Friedrich Wilhelm III responded to Gans's situation by issuing a special cabinet order that resolved an ambiguity in the Jewish emancipation edict of 1812 so as to definitively exclude Jews from holding university teaching positions. In lieu of the hoped-for post, Gans was given a government stipend that allowed him to spend much of 1825 in Paris. While abroad, he converted to Protestantism, which was the only path left open to Prussian Jewish academics; upon his return to Berlin, he was finally able to begin teaching at the university. The combination of scholarly attainment and political activism that characterized Gans even in his youth meant that in death he could be eulogized by German democrats and liberals as an "orator for freedom," a man who had used the "lectern as a tribunal" to voice his passion for freedom in a time of reaction."[130]

Friedrich Wilhelm's 1822 decision had been made with the active encouragement of Savigny, who was not only a well-known opponent of Jewish emancipation but also a staunch anti-Hegelian with ample reasons to dread the prospect of such a colleague as Gans.[131] And indeed, in his own time, Gans was probably best known for his campaign against the Historical School of Law. The crux of this long polemical dispute with Savigny and his followers was the question of the relationship between the philosophy and the history of law. Against Savigny's exclusive valorization of the historical development of positive laws, Gans insisted on an identity between the universal history of law and the conceptual evolution of legal philosophy. That is, Gans condemned the Historical School for not being historical enough, because it failed to see the broader pattern of development underlying the disparate facts of historical development. Incidentally, this Hegelian stance also pitted Gans against the *a priorism* and ethical formalism of Kantian natural law theory.[132] Gans's general philosophical objections to the Historical School were distilled into *Über die Grundlage des Besiztes*, a polemical tract on Savigny's *Das Recht des Besitzes*, which had attracted controversy since its first publication in 1803.

130   "Eduard Gans," *Hallische Jahrbücher*, no. 132(3. Juni 1839), pp. 1049–51.
131   See Norbert Waszek, ed., "Einleitung," *Eduard Gans (1797–1839): Hegelianer-Jude-Europaer*. Frankfurt, 1991, pp. 16–18; and Hermann Klenner, "Zwei Savigny-Voten über Eduard Gans nebst Chronologie und Bibliographie," *Topos*, 1(1993), pp. 123–48.
132   Gans, *Naturrecht und Universalrechtsgeschichte*, p. 46.

Significantly, Gans centered his critique on the relationship of persons and property, which, as we have already seen, was an important dimension of the debate over personality. Like Stahl's, Savigny's theory of property rested on the act of will by which a person takes and holds possession of an object. Following Hegel, Gans argued that this primordial appropriation is only the beginning of law; ownership remains insufficient unless the right to property is recognized by all. Thus, against the Historical School's treatment of property as a kind of natural fact, Gans emphasized the relationship between property and the evolving consciousness of society. The crucial point for Gans, as it had been for Hegel, was that if property is not to remain an irrational expression of arbitrary force, it must become an expression of the social and legal relations among people – in short, of the objective spirit of the community.[133]

Gans's objections to Savigny and the Historical School strikingly paralleled Feuerbach's critique of Stahl. In fact, even before Feuerbach resolved to write against the political ramifications of Positive Philosophy, Gans had informed him that he had already composed a "polemic with bombs against Schelling, Stahl, etc.," which he intended to include in the foreword to the posthumous edition of Hegel's *Philosophy of Right*.[134] Although the publication of this piece was blocked by his co-editors and it is now lost, its contents may be guessed at by correlating Feuerbach's attack on Stahl's Christian personalism with Gans's decade-long polemic against Savigny. Like Feuerbach, Gans believed that by the early 1830s, the Historical School had sought to endow its "positivist" view of property with philosophical credibility by borrowing from the later Schelling.[135] Both Feuerbach and Gans detected antisocial and egoistical implications in a theory of property that stopped with the connection between persons *qua* persons and possessions. Neither Feuerbach nor Gans attacked private property *per se*, but both derived the right of private property from society's prior right to rational self-determination. As these thinkers confronted the social question, the latter right took precedence over the former. Finally, Gans and Feuerbach were equally critical of

133   Ibid., pp. 55f; and Gans, *Über die Grundlage des Besitzes* (Berlin, 1839), pp. 6–20. The controversy between Savigny and Gans is discussed briefly in Donald R. Kelley, *The Human Measure. Social Thought in the Western Legal Tradition* (Cambridge, 1990), pp. 246–9. For an excellent contemporary discussion of the controversy, which focuses on the issue of personality, see the anonymous "Eduard Gans und den Besitz, und seine neuesten Gegner," *Hallische Jahrbücher*, 206–7, April 28–29, 1839, pp. 1641–53.

134   Gans to Feuerbach, 4 January 1834, *Feuerbach Briefwechsel*, vol. 1.

135   See Ferdinand Tönnies, "The Development of Sociology in Germany in the Nineteenth Century," *On Social Ideas and Ideologies*, trans. E. G. Jacoby (New York, 1974), p. 134.

the links between this positivistic idea of possession and the personalist view of the state as the property of the monarch.

Although Gans regarded Hegel as the essential philosopher of modernity, he came to believe that Hegel had neglected crucial dynamics in modern life. So he wrote in the preface to the 1833 edition of Hegel's *Philosophy of Right* that "this philosophy belongs to history. A development within philosophy proceeding from the same basic [Hegelian] principles will be necessary to offer a new interpretation of a changed reality."[136] Gans's acute awareness of the revolutionary forces of the age made it difficult for him to accept Hegel's efforts to reconcile tradition and change. The July Days persuaded him that the democratic revolution had not yet come to an end, and the global impact of commerce convinced him that industrialism was the paramount social force shaping the future.

This sensitivity to processes of social transformation led Gans to recognize the full significance of the social question. As with other perceptive Germans in the early 1830s, this was only partly the result of observation of German society. Gans visited England in the early 1830s, and he supplemented his lectures on Hegelian political philosophy with detailed discussions of the British political economists from Smith to Ricardo.[137] More important, his deep interest in French affairs gave him early exposure to the new French social thinking. He visited Paris frequently, spoke fluent French, and was celebrated by his contemporaries as a liason between the two great continental cultures. Acknowledged in the French capital as a major German jurist, he moved comfortably in the city's social and intellectual circles. He knew most of the city's prominent political and intellectual figures, from Victor Cousin, to the moderate liberals Thierry and Guizot, to the socialists and utopians. When revolution broke out in July 1830, he rushed to Paris.

Arguably, no group made a stronger impression on him during that visit than the Saint-Simonians. In Saint-Simonian doctrine, Gans discovered a compelling articulation of the crisis of industrial society, a potential remedy to the problems of industrial society, and a vital corrective to defects in Hegel's philosophy of the state and society. Gans was attracted solely to what he considered the Saint-Simonians' sociological realism and its implications for a "secular" science of society and politics. Consequently, he dismissed the

---

136   Gans, "Vorwort zur 2. Ausgabe der Rechtsphilosophie," p. 248.
137   Gans described his travels in the widely read *Rückblicke auf Personen und Zustände* (Berlin, 1836). His extensive knowledge of French and British political economy is evident throughout his *Naturrecht und Universalrechtsgeschichte*. Another aspect of his wide reading is discussed in Norbert Waszek, "Eduard Gans, die *Jahrbücher für wissenschaftliche Kritik* und die französische Publizistik der Zeit," pp. 93–118.

New Christianity; but tellingly, he did so on the thoroughly Hegelian grounds that through Protestantism, the philosophical truth of Christianity had already entered the practical world as the secular principle of personal freedom. Although Gans was a Prussian Jew who had been compelled to convert to Protestantism in order to qualify for an academic post, he valued Protestantism for precisely the reason Saint-Simonianism condemned it – that is, as the agent that had translated the Christian affirmation of the individual's infinite value into the secularized political principle of individual liberty.[138] This secularization of Christianity's original promise of emancipation and equality made it impossible, in Gans's view, that these principles could be cast back into religious form, even one as diffuse as Saint-Simonianism.

His positive evaluation of Protestantism and modern individualism led him to reject important aspects of the Saint-Simonians' social agenda as well. Against their desire to eradicate all the contradictions of an egoistical and competitive society, Gans defended the notion of subjective autonomy that underpins the Hegelian conception of civil society. "Antiquity worked with slaves. We work with our own person," he argued in 1835. "Therefore, the person belongs to himself, as well as his happiness or unhappiness, success or failure. The negative side also belongs to life: just as good presupposes evil, so too must a complete unhappiness be possible, in order to make happiness concrete."[139] This Hegelian emphasis on subjective freedom further explains his objection to the Saint-Simonian demand for the abolition of private inheritance, although he united a defense of people's right to dispose of their own goods with an argument that inheritance is in truth the sole ethical element in modern property, because it brings the individual back from the egoism of the marketplace to the larger needs of the family.

This lukewarm opinion reveals that behind Gans's defense of the basic principle of civil society was a deep concern about the social and ethical effects of unfettered competition. In the most politically and socially advanced of European nations, he believed, the compromised outcome of the July Revolution made future conflict almost inevitable. Desirable as Gans had found the overthrow of the Bourbon monarchy, the Orleanist *juste-milieu* had in his opinion made the political nation identical with the "sovereign bourgeoisie" and "shop-keepers." In the face of the apparent triumph of the bourgeoisie, Gans pointed to the growing disparities of wealth and poverty in the societies of western Europe. To have underscored the urgency of this

---

138  *Rückblicke*, pp. 92f; and "Vorlesungen über die Geschichte der letzten fünfzig Jahre," pp. 290–2.
139  See especially Gans, *Rückblicke*, p. 99.

social crisis was, he believed, the Saint-Simonians' fundamental contribution to the spirit of the age. "Must the penurious *Pöbel* remain?" Gans asked in his 1832 lectures. "Is it necessary? Here I subscribe to the opinion of the Saint-Simonians, who alone are correct in this matter."[140] In 1836, he insisted that "the Saint-Simonians have said something great and put their finger on an open sore of the present age." For they have recognized that slavery persists in the form of the tyranny of the capitalist over the worker. "Visit the factories of England," he urged his readers,

> and there you will see hundreds of men and women, starving and miserable, who have sacrificed their health and enjoyment of life to a single person, in exchange for mere subsistence. Is it not slavery when one exploits people like animals, even when they are otherwise free to choose to die of hunger? . . . Future history will more than once have to speak of the struggle of the proletariat against the middle classes of society.[141]

Gans's denunciation of wage-labor and class division expressed not only his critical stance toward industrial society, but also his departure from Hegel's approach to social problems. Of course, Hegel had not remained unaware of the problem of poverty in modern society. Indeed, as early as the *System der Sittlichkeit* (1802–3), Hegel offered acute insights into the deleterious effects of modern society's division of labor and private property relations. The *Philosophy of Right* resumed this early diagnosis of civil society's tendency toward the concentration of "disproportionate wealth in a few hands" and the concomitant production of "a rabble of paupers." Despite the deepening perspicuity of Hegel's discussion of social problems, however, he grew increasingly pessimistic about the potential of resolving the dilemma of poverty. The welfare assistance that he envisioned as one of the obligations of the corporations extended only to their members, but in Hegel's scheme, the abjectly poor, people without vocation or corporate membership, were "rabble" by definition precisely because they fell through the welfare net as he conceived it. Hegel believed that to an extent these unfortunates could be aided through private charity or assistance from public institutions; but he judged charity to be an inadequate solution, because it violates the principle of civil society by depriving people of their "feeling of individual independence and self-respect." Nor could poverty be alleviated by creating work for the unemployed, because that would simply create an imbalance between supply and demand. Hence, Hegel concluded his dis-

140  Gans, *Naturrecht*, p. 92.      141  Gans, *Rückblicke*, p. 100.

cussion of poverty with uncharacteristic resignation: "It . . . becomes apparent that despite an excess of wealth, civil society is not rich enough, that is, its own resources are insufficient to check excessive poverty and the creation of a penurious rabble." His most concrete proposal was to urge the poor to emigrate to overseas colonies.[142]

Norbert Waszek has shown that prior to 1830, Gans accepted Hegel's discussion of the problem of poverty with almost no revision. In his 1832–3 lectures, by contrast, a new tone of moral condemnation sharpened his discussion of poverty, making it impossible for him to remain satisfied with Hegel's answers.[143] Saint-Simonianism had proven crucial for Gans not only in articulating the problem but also in outlining the solution. For one thing, Gans drew from the French sect an argument for a much higher level of state intervention than Hegel would have tolerated: "Is it true that no spark of ethical life can be brought to this suffering proletariat? . . . It is a great insight into our age that the state must care for the poorest and most numerous class, that if they wish to work, they must never be denied, that great attention must be given to removing this scab of civil society, that is commonly called the *Pöbel*." Gans proceeded to identify what he considered to be an even more significant Saint-Simonian insight. "The Middle Ages," Gans wrote, "with their guilds had an organic structure for labor. The guilds are now destroyed, and can never be revived. But should emancipated labor now fall from the guild into despotism, from the domination of the master into the domination of the factory owner? Is there no means against this? To the contrary. It is the free corporation, it is association [*Vergesellschaftung*]."[144]

In advocating the association of working people in defense of their interests, Gans borrowed the central strategy of early French socialists like the Saint-Simonians and Charles Fourier. Waszek rightly emphasizes that Gans's idea of the "free corporations" anticipates the basic form of trade unionism.[145] Yet in trying to understand this development, it is essential to go further toward recognizing how Gans's idea significantly modernized Hegel's understanding of corporations. Gans shared Hegel's conviction that corporations not only organize the modern division of labor into productive and profitable units but also serve an ethical function by involving the otherwise

142 See Hegel, *Philosophy of Right*, para. 244–5. For an illuminating discussion of this issue, see R. Treichgraeber, "Hegel on Property and Poverty," *Journal of the History of Ideas*, 38(1977), pp. 47–64.
143 Norbert Waszek, "Eduard Gans on Poverty: Between Hegel and Saint-Simon," *The Owl of Minerva*, 18, 2(Spring 1987), pp. 171–2.
144 Gans, *Rückblicke*, pp. 100–1.
145 Waszek, "Eduard Gans on Poverty."

isolated individual in a "comparatively disinterested end;"[146] but his exposure
to modern political economics and radical social thought, as well as his vis-
its to English factories, convinced him that the image of the corporation as
an organization embracing masters and journeymen, owners and workers,
bound together by their shared vocational practice, was no longer adequate
to the division of labor within industrial societies. Such a community of interest could not be assumed in a society driven by the profit motive. Thus,
Gans fundamentally realigned Hegel's idea. He no longer conceived of the
corporation as a structure integrating the members of civil society vertically
but rather as a horizontal mode of association that corresponds to the division of industrial society into classes and the different interests of wage-
laborers and employers. Although Gans continued to insist on the ethical
functions of corporations, his insights into the industrial age made Hegel's
hybrid structure untenable. Hence, he urged the idea of "free corporations"
because "workers must seek a basis within society." Otherwise, "the determination of wages is placed in the hands of the factory owner, and the reciprocity of the work relationship is destroyed."[147]

Gans's notion of the "free corporation" clearly responded to the breakdown of the old corporatist organization of labor, and it also reflected the
increasing dominance of German bourgeois life by informal and formal social organizations that were themselves possible only because of the development of a more open and flexible social structure since the late eighteenth
century. Thomas Nipperdey has spoken of a "passion" for such *Vereine* that
had reached a point by 1840 where virtually all bourgeois activities were so
organized.[148] Given what had become an almost reflexive tendency toward
this form of sociability, it is hardly surprising that by the mid-1840s, even
some conservatives were ready to invoke various forms of "associationism"
as the antidote to the atomized individualism of a competitive commercial
society.[149] Gans was in the vanguard of this turn to association as a panacea
to social ills; moreover, his conception of "free corporations" of working
people carried the associational structure of civil society significantly be-

146  Hegel, *Philosophy of Right*, para. 253.
147  Gans, *Rückblicke*, p. 101.
148  Thomas Nipperdey, "Verein als soziale Struktur in Deutschland in späten 18. und 19.
     Jahrhundert. Eine Fallstudie zur Modernisierung," *Gesellschaft, Kultur, Theorie. Gesammelte
     Aufsätze zur neueren Geschichte* (Göttingen, 1976), p. 175.
149  See Werner Conze, "Staat und Gesellschaft in der Frührevolutionären Epoche Deutsch-
     lands," *Historische Zeitschrift*, 186(1958), pp. 1–34; and Herman Beck, *Authoritarian Wel-
     fare State. Conservatives, Bureaucracy, and the Social Question, 1815–70* (Ann Arbor, 1995),
     p. 60. As Beck makes clear, conservative visions of association remained attached to the
     neo-feudalist categories of family, social hierarchy, estates, and corporations.

yond what liberal advocates of voluntary association would have accepted. Indeed, in arguing for workers' right of association within "free corporations," Gans represented a specifically "Hegelian" appropriation of a significant move made by early French and English socialists when they adapted a liberal rhetoric supporting the *individual* right of voluntary association for the purposes of advancing the *collective* right of the working class to defend their common interests within civil society.[150]

Receptive as Gans was to French social thought, he refused to accept the Saint-Simonians' connection between New Christian pantheism and social associationism. In the conjunction of pantheism and association, Gans detected a threat to the main feature of modern civil society, the freedom of individual subjectivity. This wariness set him apart from many early western European socialists, including Germans like Moses Hess and Wilhelm Weitling, who quickly pushed beyond the liberal model of associationism to an ideal of holistic community. Gans's position more closely resembles that of one of the talented young men who left the Saint-Simonian church in 1831, Pierre Leroux, who wrote in 1834 that "we are neither individualist nor socialist. We believe in individuality, personality, and liberty; but also in society."[151] A similar desire to preserve the sphere of individuality within a cohesive society prompted Gans to situate the social question *as such* within a broader conception of political association.

This impulse helps to account for Gans's interest in Alexis de Tocqueville, whom he met in 1835. However, his ideas about political association are not explained by his encounter with Tocqueville, not only because they predate that meeting and the publication of the first volume of *Democracy in America* in 1835 but also because there is no proof that Gans actually read the book, even though he was obviously aware of its main arguments.[152] The general penchant for association that Nipperdey described may help explain Gans's ideas about political association, but he may also have been influenced by yet another dimension of French political thinking. When Gans resided in Paris during 1825, he came to admire deeply the writers involved in the

150 This process has been convincingly analyzed in the French context by William Sewell in *Work & Revolution in France: The Language of Labor from the Old Regime to 1848* (Cambridge, 1980) and in the English context by Gareth Stedman Jones in "Rethinking Chartism," *Languages of Class. Studies in English Working Class History* (Cambridge, 1983) and Gregory Claeys, *Citizens and Saints. Politics and Anti-Politics in Early British Socialism* (New York, 1989).
151 Leroux quoted in Horst Stuke, *Philosophie der Tat: Studien zur "Verwirklichung der Philosophie" bei den Junghegelianern und wahren Sozialisten* (Stuttgart, 1963), p. 87.
152 Reissner, *Eduard Gans*, p. 154, remarks on Gans's enthusiasm for Tocqueville, but he is unsure that he actually read him. On his meeting with Tocqueville, see Gans, *Rückblicke*, pp. 133f, 156f.

journal *Le Globe*. In the years before the Saint-Simonians took over the journal, it was stridently committed to the creation of a form of "new" liberalism. Figures like Pierre Leroux (prior to his conversion to Saint-Simonianism), Théodore Jouffroy, and Paul-François Dubois embodied for Gans "all
that belongs to the young and striving generation in France."[153] These men
had embarked on a public criticism of the Restoration and boldly championed the principle of liberty, but at the same time, they declared themselves
to be a new generation of liberals, freed because of their youth from the ideological polarities dividing older liberals like Guizot and Constant and reactionaries who were still carrying on the battles of the 1790s.[154] This was
perhaps a "hazy" liberalism, as George Armstrong Kelly recently claimed,[155]
but it seems to have helped focus Gans's thinking. Though the liberals of *Le
Globe* had misgivings about democracy, figures like Jouffroy and Dubois did
move away from the monarchist and elitist principles typical of the liberalism enshrined in the *Charte* of 1814 toward approval of a "liberalized, di-
versified society, requiring a new and difficult legitimation consonant with
the new-won liberties."[156]

   Norbert Waszek has argued that from the example of *Le Globe*, Gans drew
the model for *Die Jahrbücher für wissenschaftliche Kritik*, which he was instrumental in establishing in 1826. He was inspired not only by the measured
tone of *Le Globe* but also by the idea of a journal as the voice of a society of
intellectuals.[157] The image of autonomous intellectuals forming a journal
to express their partisan position stood in direct contrast to Hegel's own conception of the *Jahrbücher* as a "*Staatsanstalt,*" an officially state-sanctioned and
supported publication. Waszek neglects the deeper significance of this difference between Gans and Hegel, however; for in it, we see an example of
Gans's endorsement of political discussion within the public sphere, as well
as his belief that civil society has a vital political role to play. In short, for
Gans, the partisan intellectual journal was an instance of association for the
purpose not only of advancing a philosophical creed, but of pursuing civic
and political objectives. Given the parallels between this view and that of
Jouffroy and the other leaders of *Le Globe*, it seems reasonable to assume that

153  Gans quoted in Waszek, "Eduard Gans, die *Jahrbücher für wissenschaftliche Kritik* und die
     französische Publizistik der Zeit," p. 111.
154  See Alan Spitzer, *The French Generation of 1820* (Princeton, 1987), p. 108.
155  George Armstrong Kelly, *The Humane Comedy: Constant, Tocqueville and French Liberalism*
     (Cambridge, 1992), p. 137.
156  Ibid., p. 138.
157  Waszek, "Eduard Gans, die *Jahrbücher für wissenschaftliche Kritik* und die französische Pub-
     lizistik der Zeit," pp. 115–16.

in addition to Saint-Simonianism there was another French influence upon Gans's conception of associationism. If so, this might be a point of contact between Gans and Tocqueville, whose views of democracy and social inter-action may also have been influenced by Jouffroy and the liberal milieu of *Le Globe* in the later 1820s.[158]

The distance that Gans had moved from Hegel may be measured by the extent to which he conceived associationism as the "educator" of political society. This was more in the spirit of French liberals like Jouffroy and Toc-queville than of Hegel, because Gans thereby advocated a more direct in-teraction between society and the political life of the state – precisely an in-teraction that Hegel had taken pains to deflect through a series of complex mediations between society and state. Thus, it was a dramatic departure from Hegel when Gans described society as an adolescent who was already well embarked on a political *"Bildungsprozess."* Judging society's *"Lehrjahre"* to be nearing their end, he predicted that society would soon outgrow "tute-lary" states like Prussia.[159] Such forecasts not only made him a permanent suspect in the eyes of some officials of the Prussian state but also set him at odds with Hegel's views. After all, Gans's belief that civil society could constitute itself as a *political* society assigned vital importance to public opin-ion, an oppositional public sphere, and representative government, all in-stitutions that Hegel had mistrusted.[160] His insistence that sociability and association could generate freer forms of civic life also underlay his attempts to reform the Prussian legal code by devolving more legal powers from the central state to the cities.[161] Finally, the same conviction led him to reject voting by estates and instead to champion an open-ended manhood suffrage based on the minimal qualification that the voter be a tax-payer.[162] This, he argued, was the only defensible position in the wake of the French Revolu-tion of 1789, which had irreversibly elevated "men as men to citizens."[163]

We may identify in Gans's writings on society and politics a paradoxical chal-lenge posed to all progressive German intellectuals in the 1830s; for Gans's task within his Prussian context was to reconcile an industrial revolution that

---

158 Kelly, *Humane Comedy*, p. 34.
159 Gans, *Philosophische Schriften*, p. 317.
160 Gans defends the partisan nature of the Parisian press in "Briefe aus Paris und Frankre-ich im Jahre 1830 von Friedrich von Raumer," *Vermischte Schriften*, vol. ii (Berlin, 1834), pp. 161–2. See also Gans, "Über Opposition," *Eduard Gans*, ed. Waszek.
161 Gans, *Beiträge zur Revision der Preußischen Gesetzgebung* (Berlin, 1830–2), pp. 277–8.
162 Gans, *Naturrecht*, pp. 102–4.
163 Gans, "Vorlesungen über die Geschichte der letzten fünfzig Jahre," *Raumers Historisches Taschenbuch*, 4(1833), p. 292.

had not yet occurred with a political revolution that was not yet complete. To this end, he embraced a twofold idea of association. He conceived association first as a means of addressing the problems of industrial society, and second as a means of developing a more democratic polity. "*Vergesellschaftung,*" the social formation of the working class, thus stood in conceptual unity with the enfranchisement of all citizens within a mature political association. Although Gans preserved Hegel's distinction between the state and civil society and continued to view the state *as such* as a higher sphere of reconciliation and universality, his belief in the dynamic and constructive powers of sociability and association within civil society narrowed the distance that Hegel had set between the state and society.

Saint-Simonianism's sociological insights were crucial to Gans's reorientation of Hegelian political philosophy toward the intersecting challenges of political and social equality. However, the Saint-Simonians were only one source for Gans's broader conception of association in modern politics and society. In fact, his work verifies the intellectual eclecticism of the 1830s, as well as the ideological cacophony of the 1820s to 1840s. For Gans attempted to synthesize an eclectic combination of early socialist, liberal, democratic, and Hegelian ideas. Without doubt, his commitment to Hegelianism remained paramount not only to the mediated terms of Hegelian political philosophy but also to a stridently "secularist" reading of the relationship between Christianity and the Hegelian idea of freedom. The latter conviction prevented him from conjoining pantheism and social association in a Saint-Simonian manner; the former, perhaps, led him to uphold the pluralism of civil society while attempting to alleviate the misery of its largest class and to defend the modern political revolution against both a personalist reaction and a more thoroughgoing social revolution.

# 5

## PANTHEISM, SOCIAL QUESTION, AND THE THIRD AGE

Eduard Gans rejected the Saint-Simonians' conversion of the science of society into a new social religion. In the 1830s, however, such reticence was unusual among those progressive Germans who felt themselves attracted to the teachings of the early French socialists. Indeed, for some of the most significant left-wing intellectuals of that decade, the convergence of German philosophy, the Saint-Simonian rehabilitation of matter, and the French tradition of revolutionary egalitarianism provoked a profound reassessment of their German philosophical inheritance. As we saw in the previous chapter, the combination of German metaphysics and French social thought helped to move the German debate about pantheism and personalism toward a new set of social concerns. Under the pressure of this ideological amalgam, the misgivings about the politico-social effects of Christian inwardness that we first found in Feuerbach's early works became sharpened into an explicit attack on Christian culture's egoism and its indifference to material need; moreover, under its sway, a number of radical German intellectuals were prompted to cast their thought in the form of social theology. In addition to giving these Germans a compelling prophecy of religious and social "conversion," the New Christianity led them to search for an activist principle that would make philosophy a force of change in the world. In what follows, this overlapping of French and German themes will be pursued in the works of Heinrich Heine, Moses Hess, and August Cieszkowski. The chapter will end with a reconsideration of Feuerbach's seminal critique of theology and Idealism in the light of the social pantheism that is encountered in Heine, Hess, and Cieszkowski.

## Pantheism and Social Prophecy

This discussion will emphasize the common elements in the thought of Heine, Hess, and Cieszkowski, but it must begin by acknowledging their differences. For the moment, it suffices to describe the very different circumstances of each. Heine first encountered Saint-Simonian ideas while he still lived in Germany, but the period of his intense engagement with the sect began when circumstances drove him into exile in Paris in May 1831. Of the three men, Heine had the earliest and most intimate relationship with Saint-Simonianism, and it most deeply influenced his thinking. Conversely, skepticism and disillusionment came earliest to Heine. By 1836, he could no longer ignore those aspects of Saint-Simonian doctrine that contradicted his own antipathy toward hierarchy and authority and his sympathies for democratic republicanism and the critical rationalism of the Protestant tradition. In contrast to Heine, Moses Hess and August von Cieszkowski knew French ideas solely from the pages of books and journals, and this may be one reason why Saint-Simonianism could influence both figures several years after the movement had lost its momentum in France, as well as its appeal for Heine.[1] Moses Hess, the son of a Jewish merchant in the Rhineland, never had the benefit of an advanced formal education, and the weaknesses of the autodidact are evident in his first book, *The Holy History of Mankind* (1837). Nonetheless, *The Holy History*, often called the first socialist book written in Germany, is a significant work that integrates key elements of Saint-Simonianism into an idiosyncratic prophecy of historical redemption through socialism. Although Cieszkowski also sounded a prophetic tone in his 1838 work *Prolegomena to Historiosophy*, he disavowed any revolutionary yearnings.[2] Further, his situation could hardly have been more different from Hess's. A Polish Catholic aristocrat, Cieszkowski enjoyed an enviable

1   On Hess's biography, see Isaiah Berlin, "The Life and Opinions of Moses Hess," *Against the Current* (New York, 1980); and Shlomo Avineri, *Moses Hess: Prophet of Communism and Zionism* (New York, 1985). On Cieszkowski, see Walter Kühne, *Graf August Cieszkowski, ein Schüler Hegels und des deutschen Geistes. Ein Beitrag zur Geschichte des deutschen Geisteseinflusses auf die Polen* (Leipzig, 1938); and Liebich, *Between Ideology and Utopia. The Politics and Philosophy of August Cieszkowski.*
2   Against the tendency of many scholars to associate Cieszkowski directly with Marx, because of his emphasis upon social *praxis*, Horst Stuke characterizes Cieszkowski as "conservative" in *Philosophie der Tat*, p. 86. This is a useful qualification, but as a label, it does not do justice to the progressivist, socially transformative aspects of Cieszkowski's view.

education, first in the library of his father's estate and then at the University of Berlin. The rigors of Cieszkowski's education as well as his immersion in Hegelian philosophy as a student in Berlin stamp the *Prolegomena* as a book that pivots almost exclusively on problems posed by Hegel and German Idealism. Saint-Simonianism was an important but ancillary element of Cieszkowski's efforts to break an impasse in German philosophy.[3]

These figures are united by an acute consciousness of an epochal crisis in Christian culture and by a belief that only a future-oriented philosophy of action can transcend the dilemmas of the present. A sense of crisis was, of course, common among German intellectuals in the early nineteenth century, most prominently in Hegel himself, who did more than any other thinker to introduce the theme of alienation into the philosophical investigation of modern life. However, Hegel had sought to overcome alienation through the reconciliation of tradition and modernity, of orthodox belief and the modern claims for the rational, autonomous subject. By contrast, Heine, Cieszkowski, and Hess traced modern humanity's unhappiness to tensions within Christianity itself. Hegel could no longer stand as a sufficient guide to their thinking, because each judged Hegel to be an expression of a Christian culture that was itself the source of the troubling dualisms of modern life. Hence, where Hegel had claimed that reconciliation occurred in a present fulfillment or secularization of Christianity, they shifted to a post-Christian future.

Cieszkowski, Hess, and Heine each relied on a tripartite division of history in trying to imagine this future resolution. Accordingly, pagan antiquity or, in Hess's case, ancient Jewish monotheism represented a period of immediate unity that was broken by the more self-reflexive Christian era. The third period belongs to the future, although for each thinker, the outlines of its higher reconciliation of immediacy and self-reflexivity are already discernible in the present. This forecast of a future dispensation strongly suggests the influence of the millennarian tradition derived from Joachim of Fiore, the twelfth-century sage who prophesied a coming Third Age that would fully realize the promise of the ages of men embodied in the Old and the New Testaments. Many claims have been made for the profound

---

3 Liebich notes that although Cieszkowski referred often to the Saint-Simonians in his diaries, it is Fourier whom he recommends to his readers in the *Prolegomena*. Liebich seems correct, however, in maintaining that Saint-Simonianism and not Fourierism was the central French influence on Cieszkowski. He speculates that Cieszkowski chose to praise Fourier because by 1838 Saint-Simonianism was already old news, whereas mention of the relatively unknown Fourier would be more striking to German readers (*Between Ideology and Utopia*, p. 332 n61).

influence of this tripartite scheme upon all subsequent millennarian and utopian thought in Europe, but Marjorie Reeves and Warwick Gould caution against assuming that every scheme dividing history into three ages is Joachimite in inspiration, because the habit of thinking in "threes" seems to have a much more ubiquitous ancestry in western culture. Still, according to Reeves and Gould's two criteria for assessing the influence of Joachim, Heine, Hess, and Cieszkowski must be counted among the Joachimite millennarians of the nineteenth century. First, each linked the tripartite division of history to the Trinity, with the ages of the Father, the Son, and, coming at the end of history, the Holy Ghost.[4] Hess divided *The Holy History* into chapters identifying the ages of humanity with the Persons of the Trinity, promising that the age of the Holy Ghost would witness the building of the Kingdom of God on earth. Cieszkowski rejected Hegel's fourfold division of history in favor of a threefold one, and he prophesied that in the future, "organic mankind" would be a "church in its highest sense."[5] Heine's adoption of the trinitarian division was less systematic, but he too foresaw the coming age of the Holy Ghost, as in the visionary poem in the *Harzreise*.[6] Second, Reeves and Gould's other criterion, the idea of a spiritual fraternity called upon to "participate in the great design of the last days,"[7] forms an important motif of their thought. The narrator of Heine's *Harzreise* poem identifies himself as a "stalwart Champion of the Holy Ghost," whereas Hess and Cieszkowski clearly saw themselves as possessors of a spiritual wisdom that had come to fullness in themselves but must now be "popularized" in order to initiate the Third Age.

This form of chiliasm is a structural feature of the writings of Heine, Cieszkowski, and Hess from the 1830s. Yet in sharp contrast to classical Joachimism, they conceived of the age of the Holy Ghost as a *post-Christian* epoch in which the religion of humanity would supplant the supernatural faith of the New Testament. The reformulation of the Joachimite schema as a humanistic overcoming of Christianity did not originate with these three figures. It was enunciated as early as Lessing and picked up by J. G. Fichte, Hegel, and the young Schelling.[8] We have already encountered a fully humanist form of the schema in Feuerbach's audacious 1828 letter to Hegel,

4  Marjorie Reeves and Warwick Gould, *Joachim of Fiore and the Myth of the Eternal Evangel in the Nineteenth Century* (Oxford, 1987), p. 11.
5  August Cieszkowski, *Prolegomena zur Historiosophie*, 2nd ed. (Posen, 1908), p. 149.
6  Heinrich Heine, *Historisch-kritische Gesamtausgabe der Werke*, vol. 6, ed. Manfred Windfuhr (Hamburg, 1981), pp. 109–10. (Hereafter *Werke*.)
7  Reeves and Gould, *Joachim of Fiore*, pp. 27–31.
8  Ibid., pp. 59–83.

with its prediction of a coming "Kingdom of the Idea." Nonetheless, even though this chiliastic expectation had a wide impact upon the historical and philosophical imagination of early-nineteenth-century Germans, its specific articulation in Hess, Heine, and Cieszkowski was decisively influenced by Saint-Simonianism. For it was the New Christianity that led each man to conceive modern history as a struggle against the debilitating spiritual and social effects of Christianity.

Even before his first exposure to Saint-Simonianism, Heine had already depicted the history of Europe as a perennial contest between "Hellenism" and "Nazarenism," between pagan sensualism and Christian otherworldly spiritualism.[9] Heine argued that the "unnatural enmity" between body and soul in Christian doctrine forced believers to repress their sensual side in the name of a promised paradise. In more explicit terms than the young Feuerbach, he claimed that Christianity's postponement of equality and fulfillment until the afterlife supported inequality and oppression in the world. However firmly planted the seeds of Heine's theological and political views may already have been, when he encountered the Saint-Simonian's "rehabilitation of matter" in 1830, he recast his insights into Christian dualism in the form of a religious and sociopolitical *program*.[10] Moved by the Saint-Simonians' "science of society," Heine came to identify sensualism and spiritualism not merely as structures of belief but as rival systems of social organization. In the 1820s, he had lamented the complicity of the priest and the aristocracy in denying political equality to the majority of people, and he had predicted a catastrophe wherein the revolutionary tide would finally overflow the banks of reaction. In the 1830s, his emphasis shifted to spiritualism's indifference to material human needs – that is, to its complicity in the social crisis of modern commercial and industrial society.

Like Heine, Moses Hess believed that Christian otherworldliness relegated mortal existence to alienation, social cleavages, and a struggle for scarce resources.[11] Hess added a still deeper argument about the role played by Christian dualism in generating the exploitative egoism of the "aristocracy of money" and the misery of the new working class. He argued that because Christianity's sharp division between spirit and matter reduces humanity in its external aspect to material nature, Christianity could abandon the "natural" human being to a state of degradation without believing that

9 A good discussion of Heine's works of the later 1820s is found in J. L. Sammons, *Heinrich Heine. A Modern Biography* (Princeton, 1979), pp. 147f.
10 See, for example, *Werke*, vol. 8/1, p. 17.
11 Avineri, *Moses Hess*, p. 42.

the essential spiritual person is thereby violated. Cieszkowski meant exactly the same thing when he charged that Christianity "doubles the person."[12] From that assertion, it was relatively easy for him to link Christian dualism to the "social contradictions" of modern life.[13] Christianity has "set free only one-half of man, revealing the equality and the eternal privilege of the souls of men. But the soul, set free, did not at the same time concern itself for the emancipation of the body – rather, despising it, left it in subjection."[14] Cieszkowski wrote in his personal diaries that the full realization of Christianity – and, by implication, of freedom – depended on the rehabilitation of matter and the restoration of the dignity of the body.[15]

Whatever the differences between Hess, Heine, and Cieszkowski, they would have agreed that Christianity's absolute valorization of the individual soul violates the social essence of human being. Much in the spirit of Feuerbach's objections to Christian personalism, Cieszkowski argued that Christianity's abstract egoism means that "in all human relations we observe a radical lack of real society, and on the other hand an exalting of the power of the individual."[16] Hess claimed that Christianity's sole focus on the inner person separates "religion from politics. The Christians have no social order based on God, neither a holy state nor a divine law."[17] While this charge was directed against Christianity in general, Hess, Heine, and Cieszkowski – in common with Feuerbach and the Saint-Simonians – believed that although Catholic Christendom had initiated the era of abstract subjectivity, modern Protestantism had consummated it. As Heine put it, Protestantism swept away medieval Catholicism's complex "concordat between God and the devil, between spirit and matter," and established a religion of pure spirit.[18]

Significantly, these three thinkers also associated Protestant individualism with modern political liberalism, because both valorize the asocial, atomized, and monadic self.[19] In their hostility to Protestantism and what they considered its political corollary, Hess, Heine, and Cieszkowski may be taken as further examples of what Laurence Dickey calls the "strategic ideological

12  Moses Hess, "Die heilige Geschichte der Menschheit. Von einem Jünger Spinoza's," *Philosophische und sozialistische Schriften 1837–1850. Eine Auswahl*, ed. Wolfgang Mönke (Vaduz/ Liechtenstein, 1980), p. 49. Cieszkowski quoted in Stuke, *Philosophie der Tat*, p. 101.
13  See Cieszkowski, *Prolegomena*, p. 145; *Du crédit et de la circulation* (Paris, 1839).
14  Quoted in Stuke, *Philosophie der Tat*, p. 99.
15  Quoted in Liebich, *Between Ideology and Utopia*, p. 78.
16  Quoted in Stuke, *Philosophie der Tat*, p. 100. See also *Prolegomena*, p. 28.
17  Hess, "Heilige Geschichte," p. 71.
18  Heine, *Werke*, vol. 8/1, pp. 27–8.
19  Cieszkowski, *Prolegomena*, p. 138. On Cieszkowski's view of Protestantism and liberalism, see Jürgen Gebhardt, *Politik und Eschatologie*, p. 148. On Hess, see Avineri, *Moses Hess*, p. 34.

cross-over" of originally right-wing Catholic criticisms of Protestantism into the rhetoric of the "self-proclaimed 'apostles' of the 'left.'"[20] Given these conceptual linkages between the Christian (particularly Protestant) idea of the self, the modern bourgeois, and political liberalism, it is important to emphasize here that the nascent German Left arrived at its critique of liberal atomization and egoism *through* a critique of Christian personalism. By the time Marx described political democracy as "Christian since in it man, not merely one man but every man, ranks as *sovereign,* as the highest being," the Left's identification of theological and "secular" liberal notions of personhood was essentially complete.[21]

The association of political liberalism with the Christian dualism of spirit and matter had an immediately significant consequence for Heine, Cieszkowski, and Hess, because it provided them with a *religious* motive for devaluing merely "political" solutions to the problem of human misery. Like the French Social Romantics, Heine insisted that the deepest question of revolution is not the form or personnel of government, not the introduction of a republic or the constitutional limitation of a monarch. The only real question is the material well-being of the people.[22] Hence, Heine wrote in 1833 that the "political revolution" must strike an alliance with "pantheism" if it is truly to liberate humanity in its spiritual and material totality.[23] Hess argued that the search for a "healthy, social constitution" demands both "inner" and "external" equality, by which he meant equality of both spirit and body.[24] It was this need for reconciliation of body and spirit, more than a specific concept of economic justice, that furnished a basis for Hess's demand for a *Gütergemeinschaft,* a community of goods. Cieszkowski, by contrast, offered no concrete suggesions for political or social reform, least of all for a *Gütergemeinschaft.*[25] Nonetheless, he equated emancipation with nothing short of the resolution of the contradictions of human life in their totality. "Abstract freedom," he claimed, is the "actual social original sin." "Concrete freedom" must be the goal of human action and of all political *and* social institutions. These three social prophets clearly believed that liberation from every form of oppression depended ultimately on the reestablishment of harmony between sensualism and spiritualism. However, even

20 Dickey, "Saint-Simonian Industrialism as the End of History," p. 186.
21 Marx, "On the Jewish Question," *Collected Works,* vol. 3, p. 159.
22 Heine to Heinrich Laube, 23 November 1835, *Heinrich Heine. Sakularausgabe; Werke, Briefwechsel, Lebenszeugnisse,* vol. 21/1, ed. Fritz H. Eisner (Berlin, 1970).
23 Heine, *Werke,* vol. 8/1, p. 61.
24 Hess, "Heilige Geschichte," pp. 55, 51.
25 See Liebich, *Between Ideology and Utopia,* p. 333.

though the social, political, and theological importance assigned to the restoration of this harmony is common to their works, they differed significantly in its application. It is to these differences that we now turn.

## Cieszkowski: Sensuousness and Idealism

The Saint-Simonian critique of Christianity and the idea of the rehabilitation of matter helped Cieszkowski to identify his own philosophical project with an epochal overcoming of the conflict between spirit and matter. Despite this connection to the French sect, however, the *Prolegomena* is held firmly in the orbit of Hegelian philosophy. The book recasts the Saint-Simonian dualism between spiritualism and sensualism in the formal terms of German Idealism as the dichotomy between "thought" and "being," "subject" and "object"; and the global task of overcoming the abstract personalism of Christianity here merges with the more local task of completing and superseding Hegel's speculative Idealism. Cieszkowski thereby joined the ranks of progressive Hegelians, among them Feuerbach, Karl Ludwig Michelet, and Eduard Gans, who believed that Hegel had prematurely announced the fulfillment of history in his own philosophical attainment of absolute knowledge. Indeed, the central argument of the *Prolegomena* is that Hegel's speculative recognition of human history as a process of divine self-realization allows the thinker to project this divine process into the course of future history. Therefore, Hegel's retrospective philosophy must yield to "historiosophy," the knowledge of future history as the metaphysical basis for "absolute activity."

According to this reasoning, if the fulfillment of history entails the overcoming of the division between thought and being, God and man, self-consciousness and consciousness, then Hegel attained only a one-sided unity in thought. Cieszkowski hoped to carry this one-sided speculative reconciliation of thought and being into reality, thereby translating philosophy's abstract knowledge into concrete forms of human life. Coming as it did in the late 1830s, Cieszkowski's assessment of Hegel's abstract one-sidedness suggests that Feuerbach was not alone in finding some guidance in the writings of the many German critics of Hegel's dialectical logic. However, as in Feuerbach's case, Cieszkowski stood at a considerable distance from the theistic personalists and Positive Philosophers despite whatever influence they might have exercised upon him. For one thing, the *Prolegomena* does not seek to remove divinity from the world. Nor, for another, did any of Hegel's Christian critics ever accuse him of quietism or of Protestant inwardness and indifference toward the world. But these were precisely the charges that Cieszkowski brought against Hegel. In this crucial judgment against the master of German Idealism, the influence of the Saint-Simonians may have been decisive. For Cieszkowski's criticism of Hegel exposed the Idealist tradition to the same criteria by which Saint-Simonianism had judged Christianity. Measured by those standards, Idealism suffers from the same dualism of spirit and matter that the Saint-Simonians believed had plagued Christian culture.

Although French sensualism may have guided Cieszkowski's criticism of German Idealism, it was from the heart of the German tradition that he found the thread leading toward the future. He believed that Hegel had brought human consciousness to the stage where philosophy could pass over into action in the real world, because, having recognized history as the process whereby God attains self-actualization, humanity could now become the self-conscious accomplice of God.[26] In this synergistic relationship, collective human action becomes self-consciously divine action:

> To realize the idea of *beauty* and *truth* in practical life, in the already conscious world of objectivity, to grasp and regroup in lively co-operation all one-sided and apparently detached elements in the life of mankind, finally to realize the idea of the absolute Good and of absolute teleology in this world – such is the great task of the future.[27]

Commentators have rightly emphasized the contradiction in this conception of humanity's participation in the divine telos: If the philosopher can know the course and end of history as the fulfillment of an immanent divine teleology, then it seems odd that Cieszkowski should make history dependent upon voluntary human action.[28] Yet it is important to recognize that Cieszkowski did not insist on the absolute identity of thought and action. Despite his attempt to describe the transition from knowledge to action as a rational development out of Hegel's one-sided contemplativeness, the transition depends ultimately on an arbitrary moment of decision. For Cieszkowski, as much as for Schelling, the transition from thought to being remains underdetermined without the intervening force of "will." We may apprehend the future in "feeling" and "thought," but only will is "truly and effectively practical, applied, complete, spontaneous, voluntary and free. Thus, it embraces the whole sphere of the deed, facts and their meaning, theory and praxis, the concept and its reality; it produces the executors of

---

26    In this sense, Hegel is "the beginning of the end of philosophy" (*Prolegomena*, p. 99).
27    Ibid., p. 29. On synergism in the earlier German Idealists, see Dickey, *Hegel*.
28    See, for example, Gebhardt, *Politik und Eschatologie*, p. 131.

history."[29] Noting the prominence of will in the *Prolegomena*, André Liebich has made the important observation that for Cieszkowski, although the deed follows upon the attainments of theory, it is an "ethical and not an epistemological act."[30] In thus shifting from contemplativeness to active will, from epistemology to ethics, Cieszkowski used J. G. Fichte's idea of the active and creative will, as scholars have long recognized.[31]

Having supplemented Hegel's rational cognition of the divine process with the activist principle of will, Cieszkowski believed that he had overcome the one-sidedness of Idealism, but also that he had answered the theological controversy over the personality of Christ then raging in Germany. Through the "*active* elevation of mankind to God," he reasoned, "the unity of human divine nature ceases to be . . . merely a sensibly individual one (which standpoint has already long since been overcome)."[32] Cieszkowski's formulation resembles that of David Friedrich Strauss insofar as he claimed that the divine is incarnate in human history as a whole, in the progressive development of the human species. But in choosing to follow Fichte, who considered will and action to be the consummate expression of the identity of humanity and divinity,[33] Cieszkowski departed from Strauss's contemplative notion in favor of an activist-synergistic principle to explain the presence of the divine in human history.[34]

The question remains whether Cieszkowski succeeded in his attempt to overcome both the one-sidedness of Idealism and the hypostatization of divinity in the person of Christ. Or did his use of Fichte's idea of will expose him to the pitfalls of subjective Idealism? Certainly, his intention was to transcend all abstraction by genuinely bringing philosophy into life and reality. Nevertheless, Cieszkowski's intentions remained captive to the basic presuppositions of Idealism. Because he still viewed history as the identity of

29   Cieszkowski, *Prolegomena*, p. 16.
30   Liebich, *Between Ideology and Utopia*, p. 46.
31   See Georg Lukàcs, "Moses Hess and the Problem of the Idealist Dialectic," *Telos*, 10, 1971, pp. 23–35; Liebich, *Between Ideology and Utopia*, pp. 42f.
32   Cieszkowski, *Prolegomena*, pp. 69 and 123.
33   See, especially, J. G. Fichte, *The Vocation of Man*, trans. Peter Preuss (Indianapolis, 1987).
34   It is this view of human history and action that is important in the *Prolegomena*. It must be noted, however, that unlike Strauss, Cieszkowski was actually a "pan-en-theist." At roughly the time he wrote the *Prolegomena*, he clarified the ultimate relation between God and world in his diaries: "The world is the body of God; God is the body of the world. In this way, speculative transcendence and divine immanence, pantheism and personalism, are reconciled in God. The divine ego is separate from the world and yet it embraces the world as the soul embraces the body. The ego without the world would be an abstraction. It is thus a personal pantheism and a pantheistic personalism" (quoted in Liebich, *Between Ideology and Utopia*, p. 78).

human and divine spirit, all "objectivity" is ultimately a product of subjectivity. Cieszkowski's "self-creating agent" differs from the self-conscious subject of traditional Idealism only in the substitution of "practice" for "cognition." To the self-creating agent, as to the practical subject, the content of history must appear as "a content produced by itself." Furthermore, Cieszkowski believed that along with history, nature too is part of the spiritual process, and so it is also an object of the will. Consequently, the conquest of objectivity by the absolute activity of spirit "will be the true rehabilitation of matter."[35]

Cieszkowski recast the famous slogan of the Saint-Simonians in distinctly Idealist terms. He was well within the parameters of Hegelian philosophy when he insisted on the essentially social nature of human life. His demand that man move from abstract to "concrete" personality, from the "naked $I$" to the "concrete person rich in relations," corresponds in both form and expression to Hegel's own ideas about freedom and personality. Yet French social thought gave these Hegelian ideals a more specific content,[36] and the future he envisioned belonged to French social theory. After all, even as the emergence of the "social individual" is, for Cieszkowski, the consummation of a religious process, it is also the "true solution of the social contradictions in reality."[37] Shrouded though it is by the forbidding language of Idealism and Christian mysticism, the *Prolegomena*'s vision of the human–divine unity is a response to the social question. Like the Saint-Simonians, Cieszkowski offered a vision of the future in which cooperative "social life and work" will overcome the competitive egoism and anarchy of modern commercial society.[38]

## Heine's Democracy of Terrestrial Gods

Heine and Hess also equated the restoration of religious harmony with the social redemption of humanity, but they differed from Cieszkowski in their pursuit of these interrelated goals. Whereas Cieszkowski used Saint-Simonianism to overcome an impasse in Hegelian philosophy, Heine and Hess saw the future primarily as an apocalyptic convergence of Spinozist and Saint-Simonian principles. The role of the historical development of consciousness was not absent from either man's thoughts; still, Spinoza's strong influence made them more truly pantheistic than Cieszkowski and, by extension,

35   Cieszkowski, *Prolegomena*, p. 124.
36   See Liebich, *Between Ideology and Utopia*, p. 49.
37   Cieszkowski, *Prolegomena*, pp. 148, 145.
38   Ibid., p. 132.

inclined them to interpret the rehabilitation of matter in more directly sensualist terms.

In the late 1820s, Heine's humanistic pantheism appears to have been influenced almost exclusively by his eclectic reading of Spinoza, Lessing, Goethe, Hegel, and the young Schelling. This German tradition continued to anchor Heine's reflections in the 1830s. Indeed, in his famous book written at Prosper Enfantin's request to explain the development of German thought to a French audience, Heine identified pantheism as the "open secret" of the history of philosophy and religion in Germany, as identifiable in old "Teutonic" paganism as it was in Spinoza or Schelling's philosophy of nature. Without doubt, the narrative of *Religion and Philosophy in Germany* made for tendentious history, but it served Heine's religio-political goals very well, for it enabled him to graft Saint-Simonianism onto the stem of Germany's indigenous pantheism. In fact, he went so far as to describe the development of Saint-Simonianism on French soil as a deviation from France's own native traditions. Because the essential French challenge to Catholic theism had come from the materialist atheism of the *philosophes,* according to Heine, this cast authentic French sensualism into an alliance with atheism: "French sensualists being ordinarily materialists, the erroneous notion came to obtain that sensualism was but a product of materialism. No; sensualism may with equal right claim to be the result of pantheism, and as such it appears beautiful and imposing."[39] Heine's point was that French sensualism reduced reality to matter, whereas pantheism, as Spinoza had recognized, identified "infinite thought" and "infinite substance" as the attributes of the "absolute substance."[40] Thus, the hybrid plant of spirit and matter should first take root in German soil, where the greatest thinkers had long honored both attributes of absolute substance.

Although Heine insisted on a thoroughgoing pantheism, the key to his religio-political project actually involved a more discriminating belief. That is, he never failed to emphasize the privileged status of spirit as the highest incarnation of the divine: "sensualism . . . has for its aim the rehabilitation of matter and the vindication of the inalienable rights of the senses, without thereby denying to the spirit its rights or even its supremacy."[41] From the vantage point of this refined pantheism, he criticized the naturalistic pantheism of at least some of his German predecessors:

. . . pantheism has not rarely turned people into indifferentists. They thought if everything is God, it does not matter what we concern ourselves with,

39  Heine, *Werke,* vol. 8/1, p. 50.
40  Ibid., pp. 55–6.    41  Ibid., p. 49.

whether with clouds or with antique gems, whether with folksongs or with the bones of apes, whether with human beings or with actors. But herein lies the fallacy; everything is not God, but God is everything. God does not manifest Himself in like manner in all things; on the contrary, He manifests Himself in various degrees in various things, and each bears within it the urge to attain a higher degree of divinity; and this is the great law of progress in nature. The recognition of this law, most profoundly revealed by the Saint-Simonists, transforms pantheism into a philosophy of life which certainly does not lead to indifferentism but to forging ahead by means of the most passionate self-sacrifice.[42]

According to Heine's self-understanding, it was Saint-Simonianism above all that prompted his own transition from quietistic to activist pantheism. Heine's claim for the French provenance of his convictions is important, but we must approach it with reservations because his activist idea of pantheism does draw heavily from the German tradition. It is difficult and probably fruitless to isolate these elements in a mercurial thinker who demanded the rehabilitation of the flesh at the same time as he proclaimed that God is "the real hero of universal history;"[43] nonetheless, Heine's activation of pantheism as a "philosophy of life" remained closely affiliated with Hegel's account of the movement of human consciousness toward recognition of its identity with God. After all, Heine placed German philosophy at the vanguard in the modern struggle for human emancipation not merely because it perpetuated Spinoza's monistic ideas but because German Idealism most fully developed the philosophy of consciousness. Hence, he argued that Kant's "philosophical revolution," which subjected all constituted authority to the sovereign judgment of reason, had initiated a liberation in thought that equaled in magnitude the French revolution in politics.[44] By closing his intellectual history of Germany with Hegel and ranking him higher than the young Schelling, Heine implied that it was Hegel's historical dialectic which prepared Germany for the coming revolution in religion, politics, and society.[45]

---

42  Ibid., pp. 153–4.    43  Ibid., p. 60. See also Sammons, *Heine*, p. 159.

44  Heine traced this spiritual emancipation ultimately back to Luther. It has already been noted that Heine's positive estimation of Protestantism set him apart from the Saint-Simonians, who saw in the Reformation only the poisoned seeds of the modern "critical" era. Heine's attitude was not unambiguous, however, because he recognized that the free conscience and private faith of the Protestant demanded a more rigorous attitude toward sensualism than that of the medieval Catholic, who had established a *modus vivendi* in the fallen world. See Heine, *Werke*, vol. 8/1, pp. 29f.

45  Heine was one of the first Germans to distinguish between Hegel's apparent conservatism and the revolutionary potential implicit in his doctrine. See Toews, *Hegelianism*, pp. 95–6. On Heine's efforts to portray Germany as the site of future revolution through the homology between German philosophical and French political modernity, see Harold Mah, "The French Revolution and the Problem of German Modernity: Hegel, Heine and Marx," *New German Critique*, 50(1990), pp. 3–20.

Heine's claim for the significance of the Saint-Simonians must be weighed against this "Germanic" faith in spirit's advance toward freedom; but his contrast between German "indifference" and French "activism," questionable as it is, did lead him to the important conclusion that only an alliance with French praxis could fulfill German philosophy's inward liberation of the subject. The need for a mutually reinforcing alliance of French social thought and the German philosophical avant-garde was to become a central theme in Moses Hess's *Holy History of Mankind;* such an alliance informs Cieszkowski's *Prolegomena zur Historiosophie;* and in the early 1840s, it became a preoccupation of German radicals like Feuerbach, Ruge, and Marx, who wanted to forge links between the Hegelian Left and the French socialists. Through his exposure to the radical traditions of France, Heine thus arrived at the demand that German philosophy be translated into action several years before August Cieszkowski or Moses Hess spoke of the "philosophy of the deed." "Thought strives to become action," he wrote, "the word to become flesh, and, marvellous to relate, man, like God in the Bible, needs only to express his thought and the world takes form."[46]

This description of practice clearly reveals Heine's presumption about the primacy of consciousness. However, unlike Cieszkowski, Heine did not pursue this Idealist presupposition consistently or rigorously. Whereas Cieszkowski's 1838 work performed a typically Hegelian *Aufhebung* on the Saint-Simonian rehabilitation of matter by imagining it as spirit's active sublation of objectivity, Heine's writings in the early 1830s left matter and spirit standing, as it were, side-by-side. That is, even though he elevated spirit over matter, he did not make the rehabilitation of matter depend on an appropriative act of consciousness. He insisted instead on the equal rights of spirit and flesh against the long tyranny of Christianity's spiritual regime. Heine's acceptance of the main elements of the Saint-Simonian program thereby furnished the metaphysical foundation for his revolutionary social demands: "We promote the welfare of matter, the material happiness of nations, not, like the materialists, from a contempt for the spirit, but because we know that the divinity of man reveals itself also in his corporeal form, that misery destroys or debases the body, God's image, and that thereby the spirit likewise is involved in ruin."[47] This belief converted "equality" and "political brotherhood" from the slogans of a secular politics into the creed of a social pantheism whose redemptive aim is the attainment of "bliss on earth during our own lifetime."[48]

---

46  Heine, *Werke,* vol. 8/1, pp. 79–80.
47  Ibid., p. 61.    48  Ibid., p. 160.

Heine's insistence on the reality of matter as an attribute of divine substance helps to explain his vision of the future, which along with spiritual
liberation entails the emancipation of the body and the senses. In valoriz-
ing pleasure as an inalienable part of human liberation, Heine had more
in common with the Saint-Simonians or the Fourierists than with Cieszkowski, or, for that matter, with Marx, both of whom perpetuated older Idealist suspicions about sensualism as a naturalistic restriction on human
freedom. The Saint-Simonians' optimistic association of industrial and economic advances with the progressive alleviation of human misery appeared
to support Heine's conviction that the world is materially ready for the on-
coming age of earthly happiness. He proclaimed his "belief in progress, a
belief that originated from science"; and in terms heavily indebted to the
Saint-Simonians, he identified progress with the end of scarcity:

> We have surveyed the lands, weighed the forces of nature, calculated the re-
> sources of industry, and behold, we have discovered that this earth is large
> enough; that it offers sufficient space for everyone to build on it the shelter
> for his happiness; that this earth can nourish all of us properly if we all work
> and no one tries to live at another's expense; and that it is not necessary for
> us to refer the larger and poorer class to Heaven.[49]

A future of abundance and pleasure would bring a definitive end to the repressive spiritual and political regimes that had until now regulated popu-
lations whose material needs could not be met by the low levels of current
industrial development.[50] With this vision of the future, Heine broke ranks
with the austere revolutionaries of the past:

> The great word of the revolution pronounced by St. Just, "Bread is the right
> of the people," is translated by us, "Bread is the divine right of man." We are
> fighting not for the human rights of the people, but for the divine rights of
> humanity. In this and in much else we differ from the men of the revolution.
> We do not wish to be sans-culottists, nor frugal citizens, nor unassuming pres-
> idents; we are for founding a democracy of terrestrial gods, equal in glory, in
> blessedness, and in sanctity. You demand simple modes of dress, austere
> morals, and unspiced pleasures; we, on the contrary, desire nectar and am-
> brosia, purple mantles, costly perfumes, luxury and splendour, dances of
> laughing nymphs, music and comedies. Be not therefore angry with us, virtu-
> ous republicans![51]

49   Ibid., p. 218.
50   See Sammons, *Heine*, p. 165.
51   Heine, *Werke*, vol. 8/1, p. 61.

Heine appropriated the language of republicanism but redirected it in crucial ways. His evocation of "divine right" recalls earlier republican dissent from the theory of monarchic sovereignty. Yet whereas the Jacobins had transferred sovereign political right from the single person of the monarch to the multitude of sovereign individuals constituting the people, Heine construed this new sovereign entity as "humanity"; and whereas the republicans' asceticism and frugality revealed their continued bondage to an abstract spiritualist language, Heine broadened the idea of sovereign personhood to include the body and its needs. Once again, we are reminded of Marx's later claim that political democracy is Christian, for to remain with the merely political emancipation of the people is to honor a Christian scale of values. True democracy, Heine seemed to imply, must oppose any political regime that ignores or represses material needs, the *divine rights* of sovereign humanity. In the image of a "democracy of terrestrial gods," Heine thereby fully embedded the early socialist ideal of a universal association of "workers" in a vision of the greater salvific progress of humanity toward the reconciliation of spirit and matter in the social pantheism of the future age.

## The Spinozist Communism of Moses Hess

Moses Hess's *Holy History of Mankind,* published in 1837, outlines a very similar metaphysic – not surprisingly, it must be added, given that Hess sent a copy of the book to Heine, with a note claiming that "without you I would not have become what I am – without you I could not have continued my spiritual life."[52] The experience of Jewish intellectuals in Prussia surely helps explain Hess's identification with the older poet, but common influences from German Idealism, the Saint-Simonians, and, above all, Spinoza are probably more important reasons for the parallels between Hess's peculiar book, with its grandiose and naïve depiction of sacred history, and Heine's works of the early 1830s. Still, despite their affinities, they differed significantly in their emphases. Whereas Heine sought to reestablish harmony or balance between thought and being, spirit and matter, Hess aimed to assert their identity. Heine had a more or less mediated notion of the relationship between the subject and object, spirit and matter; and this was true even of Cieszkowski, despite his tendency toward an idealist theory of identity. By contrast, Hess, the self-avowed disciple of Spinoza, collapsed this relationship into the identity of absolute substance. Even though in the 1840s, Hess

---

52  Moses Hess to Heinrich Heine, 19 October 1837, in *International Review of Social History,*
    vol. vi, 3 (1961), p. 459.

went on to develop a more dialectical conception of communism under the influence of Cieszkowski, Bruno Bauer, and Feuerbach, in *The Holy History of Mankind,* Hess's rigorous application of Spinoza's idea of absolute substance led to a monism that colored every aspect of his theory of "communism."

Hess's sacred history traces the providential course of God in the world from an originary state when man and God had enjoyed perfect, if unreflective, union, to an era of division and conflict beginning with Christian monotheism. Hess regarded Spinoza as the herald of a new age in which man will recognize his unity with God; monotheism, "the God of nations," is currently yielding to pantheism, "the God of humanity."[53] To German intellectuals long accustomed to thinking of history in these providentialist terms, none of this would have been particularly new. By contrast, the account of social life that Hess incorporated into this millennarian scheme was genuinely novel, for he related the sacred history to the successive property regimes that have shaped human life: from an original state of natural equality and common ownership, through the long reign of private property under Christian monotheism, to a future *Gütergemeinschaft.* The community of goods is the "final goal of social life," and it must be attained when humanity recognizes the incarnation of the divine in the "holy bond" of its social life.[54] This turn to property as the core of social life and the key to sacred history surely reflects the influence of French thinkers, including Rousseau and, above all, the Saint-Simonians, especially because Hess identified the abolition of inheritance laws as the key to creating the *Gütergemeinschaft.*[55]

We will return to the issue of property shortly, but it is important first to consider Hess's providential scheme in a comparative perspective. Of course, this holy history has much in common with the ideas of Cieszkowski and Heine and the background of Joachimite millennarianism that they all shared. However, Hess carried the idea of immanence further. Cieszkowski was actually a pan-en-theist; and Heine, despite his pantheist language, implied a certain tension between God and world when he distinguished between a pantheism for which "everything is God" and one for which "God is everything." The latter suggests – correctly, in Heine's opinion – that divinity is not exhausted by its presence in all things. Hess, by contrast, viewed the divine in wholly immanent terms. If it is not entirely surprising that Cieszkowski repudiated the immanentism of his *Prolegomena* within a few years, or even, for that matter, that Heine late in life professed belief in a

53   Hess, "Heilige Geschichte," p. 49.
54   Ibid., pp. 49–51.
55   See esp. ibid., pp. 7–8, 53.

personal God, it is also consistent that Hess professed his atheism in the
1840s and readily embraced Feuerbach's radical anthropological perspective.[56]

Esoteric as this contrast may seem, it nonetheless led these writers to different conceptions of society, consciousness, and action. Because Hess believed human society to be one divine substance, he hypostatized humanity
in the form of one unitary "individual." Where Heine envisioned a future
democracy of "terrestrial gods," Hess imagined the realization of *Gesammt-
menschheit*, collective humanity, in a future of perfect unity and equality. In
the grammatical difference between Heine's plural and Hess's singular, we
see reflected the philosophical difference between a vision of harmony that
contains a notion of individuality and one that depends on its erasure.
Monism defined Hess's position on consciousness and action as well, as
comparison with Cieszkowski illustrates. For Cieszkowski, the precise relationship between consciousness and the teleological course of history was
problematic. Even though there is the suggestion in Cieszkowski that the divine process determines human consciousness, his philosophy of the deed
ultimately depends on a caesura between knowing and acting that preserves
some tension between necessity and freedom. This caesura makes humanity a "participant" in the divine plan, but not absolutely identical with it. Hess
was more rigid on this issue, because he considered consciousness to be an
immanent part of the divine telos in history. Hess did allow that the more
humanity becomes conscious of this progressive movement, the more "humanized" its actions become, but this conception of action differs fundamentally from Cieszkowski's, because Hess envisioned action as an extrusion
of humanity's identity with God necessarily pressing toward its full realization in the external world. Here, the narrow gap between freedom and necessity vanishes: "The freedom of humans exists not in their arbitrariness,
but in conscious obedience to the divine law. Obedience is the virtue of the
pure human."[57]

Once Hess had defined humanity as a single unitary essence, he could
readily define the *Gütergemeinschaft* as the absolute expression of the inner
and external unity and equality of all human beings. Hess's adoption of the
Saint-Simonians' campaign against inheritance was the practical center-
piece of his argument against private property, although his desire for a

56  On Cieszkowski, see n34 (this chapter) and Cieszkowski, *Gott und Palingenesie* (Berlin, 1842).
    On Heine, see the retraction of his pantheist views in the 1852 preface to the second Ger-
    man edition of *Religion and Philosophy in Germany;* and Butler, *Saint-Simonian Religion*, p. 119.
57  Hess, "Heilige Geschichte," p. 45.

*Gütergemeinschaft* took him beyond the French group. In fact, his monistic understanding of the metaphysical reality of social life gave Hess an argument against inheritance law that is nowhere found in the Saint-Simonians. He did not base his deepest argument against private property on economic justice or the need to distribute society's productive wealth to the truly talented for the improvement of everyone. Rather, he attacked inheritance because it depends on the personalist theology of monotheism:

> Since the time of the patriarchs, the belief has ruled that the individual, upon dying, returns not to the general creator, to God, but to *his father.* This fantasy inverts the eternal and the temporal; it assigns finite attributes to the infinite, and infinite to the finite. The same inversion spiritually consecrates the system of inheritance with its whole range of attendant consequences.

Inheritance depends, that is, on the belief in personal immortality, on the belief in the eternal integrity of the person who may thus rule over his property equally in life and death. The modern age, Hess continued, should know better, because it is growing more and more conscious of the true nature of divinity. Genuine self-consciousness tells us that our individual lives are in fact a "loan of capital" which will revert to the creditor upon our deaths: "the eternal right of property belongs to the eternal God alone – the great whole; individuals and even specific nations, by contrast, can acquire nothing for eternity, insofar as they are temporary and limited."[58]

The theological debate between pantheism and personality runs straight into the issue of property in Germany's first "socialist" book. Hess's negation of personality and property contradicted not only the Saint-Simonians but virtually all his German contemporaries as well, including the equally visionary Cieszkowski. For Cieszkowski adhered to the Hegelian idea that concrete personality depends on property for its first objectification. Therefore, he wrote, "It is not a question of abolishing property but of renewing and universalizing it."[59] Whereas Cieszkowski championed the extension of private property to the hitherto propertyless as the precondition of their development as persons, Hess's demand for the abolition of private property as the prerequisite of the realization of human essence fully discloses the proximity of the radical social discourse of the 1830s to the theologico-philosophical challenge to Christian beliefs about the personal God and the individual soul.

---

58   Ibid., pp. 56–7.
59   Quoted in Liebich, *Between Ideology and Utopia*, p. 333 n64.

### Was Feuerbach a Saint-Simonian?

In 1845, Hess wrote that German socialism had emerged out of religious struggles.[60] He had in mind the immediate context of the early 1840s, when he and a small number of radicals, the so-called True Socialists, perceived the socialist implications of Feuerbach's atheistic humanism. Yet Hess's *Holy History of Mankind* is important proof that the convergence of religious and socialist themes had already occurred in the 1830s. Moreover, Hess apparently did not know that in linking a critique of Christian personalism directly to a critique of private property, his ideas already bore an essential kinship to those of Feuerbach. For, in his 1835 critique of Stahl, Feuerbach also rejected the attempt to legitimate private property through the homology between divine and human personality. In terms not unlike Hess's, Feuerbach attacked the theists' mistaken identification of property rights with the sovereign domain of God, or as he put it, the confusion of "the miserable limits of finite relations" with "infinite being."

Contemporaries entirely ignored Hess's bold attack on private property, but Feuerbach was rebuked in 1835 for undermining the sacred basis of private property. When Leopold von Henning, the editor of the *Jahrbücher für wissenschaftliche Kritik*, read Feuerbach's article on Stahl, he sent the author a stern and pedantic reprimand. Although Henning found much to criticize, he was particularly upset to discern in Feuerbach's definition of Christianity a challenge to public morality, marriage, criminal law, even the state itself. Above all, however, he detected a threat to property rights. Henning conceded to Feuerbach that the essence of Christianity is love, but, he cautioned, not in a sense that "excludes freedom and the independent personality," the latter being the "express basis . . . of private property." He urged Feuerbach to acknowledge Christianity as the religion of Absolute Spirit that lifts and preserves the finite spirit within it. A correct Hegelian view of Christianity, Henning concluded, would make it impossible to assert, as Feuerbach had, that "'property has no basis in Christianity.' *So say the Saint-Simonians, but not the Christians.*"[61]

What of this implied affinity between Feuerbach's position and that of Saint-Simonianism? Was his negative association of private property with the Christian idea of personality Saint-Simonian? Although a number of scholars have raised the possibility of a Saint-Simonian influence upon Feuer-

60  Hess, "Über die sozialistische Bewegung in Deutschland," *Philosophische und sozialistische Schriften*, p. 305.
61  Henning to Feuerbach, 17 April 1835, *Briefwechsel*, vol. 1 (emphasis added).

bach, no one has picked up on the implications of Henning's comment to consider the question seriously.[62] Yet the question is worth dwelling on, even if the answer remains inconclusive. It must be immediately acknowledged that there is considerable reason to be skeptical of a Saint-Simonian influence because there is no reference to Saint-Simonianism or, for that matter, socialism in his correspondence until 1844, when he expressed delight at reading about French social radicalism in Lorenz von Stein's *Socialism and Communism in Present-Day France*.[63] Nonetheless, circumstantial evidence suggests a much earlier acquaintance with Saint-Simonianism.

Feuerbach might have read about the Saint-Simonians in any number of journals, including detailed articles published in 1831 in *Das Ausland*, the editorship of which he sought in that year.[64] Nor would he have had to rely on such German sources for news on French developments. Feuerbach shared the young generations' enthusiasm for the July Revolution, and he revered France as the land of Enlightenment and revolution. Indeed, as Feuerbach's frustration with German conditions grew after 1830, he dreamed of emigrating to Paris. Preparing for his move, he read voraciously in French literature and periodicals during the summer of 1832. He was sufficiently well informed of the Parisian intellectual scene to appeal for assistance directly to Victor Cousin, the young doyen of French philosophy.[65] Only financial hardship and the death of his father prevented him from making the move to Paris. In 1834, moreover, he knew that his book *Thoughts on Death and Immortality* had received a notice in the *Revue du progrès social*, the journal edited by Jules Lechevalier, the talented Saint-Simonian who had defected to Fourier in 1831.[66] Feuerbach was also personally acquainted with the two Hegelians most intensively engaged with Saint-Simonianism in the early 1830s, Gans and Carové. Feuerbach's correspondence reveals that he met Carové in 1834 and discussed theological and philosophical matters with him.[67] Carové was primarily interested in Saint-Simonian religious views, and it seems highly unlikely that he and the young iconoclastic philosopher would not have touched on the Saint-Simonian New Christianity. As for the

62 See G. Gurvitch, *La vocation actuelle de la Sociologie* (Paris, 1950), pp. 576–7; Alfred Schmidt, *Emanzipatorische Sinnlichkeit: Ludwig Feuerbachs anthropologischer Materialismus* (Munich, 1973), p. 14; and Hayek's *Counter-Revolution of Science*, pp. 161–2.
63 Feuerbach to F. A. Kapp, 15 October 1844, *Briefwechsel*, vol. 2.
64 Feuerbach to Johann Friedrich Cotta, 11 September 1831, *Briefwechsel*, vol. 1.
65 Feuerbach to C. Kapp, 27 September 1832, *Briefwechsel*, vol. 1. On Cousin's remarkable position in Parisian intellectual life in the 1820s and 1830s, see Spitzer, *French Generation*, pp. 71–96.
66 Feuerbach to Ludwig I., König von Bayern, 23 July 1836, *Briefwechsel*, vol. 1.
67 See Feuerbach to C. Kapp, 16 May 1834, *Briefwechsel*, vol. 1.

Young Germans, Feuerbach remained silent when the Diet of the German Confederation banned their writings, though having himself suffered from the censors, he could not have remained unmoved by their plight. Several years later, in an open letter to Karl Riedel in which he insisted on his own philosophy's practical tendencies, Feuerbach approved the Young Germans' desire to carry the "ideas of new philosophy" into life, even if he also questioned their impetuousness and willingness to subordinate scientific objectivity to the demands of their cause.[68]

Saint-Simonianism was "in the air" in the early 1830s. The widespread German discussion of Saint-Simonianism, Feuerbach's personal acquaintances, and his own temperament make it virtually impossible that he could have remained ignorant of the French socialist sect. But what of Saint-Simonian doctrine and its possible influence on Feuerbach? Before all else, we must address Henning's specific allegation. His suggestion that Feuerbach's view of Christian personalism undermined the basis of property essentially implied that Feuerbach questioned property rights *per se*, because a conservative Christian was unlikely to believe that property could have any other than a Christian basis. Henning's charge reflects the widespread misconception among German intellectuals that the Saint-Simonians advocated a *Gütergemeinschaft*.[69] Was it Feuerbach's intention to negate the institution of private property? In reading the essay on Stahl and even in his most radical writings of the early 1840s, one must say no. His aim was rather to replace the Christian basis for social and political institutions with "rational," "just," and "human" criteria of political right.[70] Frustratingly, Feuerbach never specified just what those criteria were, but he did stop short of ever calling for the total abolition of private property. Nonetheless, the "social" tenor of his thought clearly implied something other than a society based on the exclusive right of private property. And indeed, in 1848, he did call for the radical redistribution of property.[71]

Henning may have misrepresented Feuerbach's own intentions, but he insightfully recognized that criticism of the personal God could easily slide into dangerous attacks on the social and political homologies drawn from

68  Feuerbach, "An Karl Riedel. Zur Berechtigung seiner Skizze" (1839), *Werke*, vol. 2, p. 211.
69  Buchholz struggled vainly to correct this misunderstanding. See "Was ist von der neuen Lehre zu halten die sich die St. Simonistische nennt," p. 545. See also Charles Rihs, *L'ecole*, esp. pp. 292–320.
70  See, for example, Feuerbach, "Über Philosophie und Christentum," pp. 278–87; and *Wesen*, pp. 449–50.
71  Feuerbach, *Lectures on the Essence of Religion*, trans. Ralph Manheim (New York, 1967), p. 307.

divine personality, including that of the sovereign personhood of the property owner. Moses Hess certainly illustrated this danger when he united the German discourse on pantheism and personalism with the Saint-Simonian critique of private property. A similar Saint-Simonian influence might have moved Feuerbach to associate the Christian fixation on personalism with the "misery, the need of material existence," and to insist on a humanistic pantheism of love as a counterweight to the egoism of Christianity. Certainly, like Hess, Heine, or Cieszkowski, Feuerbach had ample German precedents for his doctrine of love: the strong Joachimite tradition in Germany, the mystic Jakob Böhme, the ethical sentimentalism of the German Enlightenment, Schiller and Goethe, Novalis, and the young Hegel. If French social thought did indeed influence him, it did not preempt his preoccupation with the German philosophical and theological tradition. Yet this was also true of Hess, Cieszkowski, and Heine, men whose attraction to Saint-Simonianism is beyond doubt. Influence is, after all, a more complex phenomenon than conversion precisely because it leaves primary engagements in place even as it may subtly recast them.

There is reason to assume that Saint-Simonianism influenced Feuerbach in this subtle way. The social embeddedness of human being was Feuerbach's constant thought from his student days onward, and his deepest political concern lay in the task of recovering humanity's social being from the alienating and atomizing effects of Christian personalism. As Chapter 3 showed, his initial conception of human social being was rooted in the Idealist notion of the universality of spirit or thought, but during the 1830s, he moved further and further from that early formulation. Having seen how Cieszkowski, Heine, and Hess sought to achieve the rehabilitation of matter, it is possible that Feuerbach's attempt to incorporate sensuousness into his thinking about social life may have been motivated in part by the Saint-Simonians' critique of Christian dualism. Whereas the young Feuerbach condemned sensualism as mere "particularity," to be transcended by the universality of reason, the more mature thinker sought to reconcile thought and sensuous being in the "community and unity of man with man."[72] The need to accommodate sensuousness in a thoroughly immanent concept of human social being became the leitmotif of his seminal critique of Christian personalism and speculative Idealism in the years between 1838 and 1843. A search for that accommodation became the dominant task of the "philosophy of the future" that Feuerbach enunciated in the early 1840s.

72  Feuerbach, *Principles*, p. 71.

### Protestantism and Pathological Secularization

The possible impact of Saint-Simonianism upon Feuerbach does not stop with his turn to sensuousness. The concluding pages of this chapter will reconsider Feuerbach's seminal writings of the late 1830s and early 1840s from the vantage point of the social pantheism that we have traced in Heine, Hess, and Cieszkowski. Two themes warrant particular attention: first, Feuerbach's growing insistence on the practical tendencies of his philosophy and, second, what we may call his implicit philosophy of history. Undoubtedly, his "practical" orientation was in part a defensive response to the calls from other leaders of Left Hegelianism that he address political topics more explicitly. However, the larger context that we have discussed – the religious and political debates over personality in the later 1830s, the success of conservative political Romanticism, and the emergence of a discourse about "social" pantheism – all seemed to contribute to Feuerbach's conviction that his critique of theology was linked to a political mission. This emphasis upon *praxis* was, in turn, deeply rooted in Feuerbach's understanding of modern European historical development and his assessment of the processes whereby humanity might enter a new and more liberated age.

Feuerbach borrowed from the vocabulary of the Saint-Simonian philosophy of history when he described the present as a "critical" period, in which the clash of antithetical principles awaited a revolutionary resolution.[73] The conflict as he saw it was between religion and modernity; but rather than merely identify a simple confrontation, Feuerbach traced a subtle dialectical relationship between these contending forces. While he had to acknowledge that religion still dominated Europe, Feuerbach in fact regarded modernity as the practical negation of Christianity. That is, the modern era had already shifted in practice to an immanent, this-worldly orientation, and man had already displaced God as the center of religious devotion. Feuerbach was enough of a Hegelian always to claim that these features of modernity had first entered the world through Protestantism, but he believed that as soon as one conceded that Protestantism's spiritual individualism, affirmation of daily life, and validation of both nature and the powers of the worldly state had borne fruit in the new philosophy and the physical sciences of modern Europe, one had already confirmed the fundamental tendency of the modern age to render Christianity obsolete in practice. Hence, Feuerbach argued that the chief source of modern unbelief lay not in critiques like his own but in the contradiction between contemporary life and belief.[74]

---

73  Ibid., p. 25.
74  Feuerbach, "Philosophie und Christentum," p. 318.

In this sense, a "religious revolution" had already occurred,[75] leaving to the critic of religion the comparatively modest task of transforming "the indirect, unconscious, and negative negation of theology into a direct, positive, and conscious negation."[76] This judgment of Protestantism expressed an adamant rejection of Hegel's notion of the secularization of the Protestant principle. Already in 1830, Feuerbach had challenged Hegel's optimism about the emancipatory potential of Protestantism. Once he had discovered what he believed to be the anthropological truth of religion, he was in a better position to launch a much sharper attack on the inadequacy of Protestantism as a vehicle of secularization. For he was now able to argue that the process of secularization begun by the Reformation was in fact deeply distorted, because Protestantism preserved the religious consciousness even as it inaugurated political, social, and philosophical changes that were destined to contradict religion in practice. "Humanity no longer has religion, and the worst is, it does not confront this, but imagines it still has religion. This most pernicious of illusions poisons all relations."[77]

An appendix added to the 1843 edition of *The Essence of Christianity* elaborated on this conclusion. There, Feuerbach argued that medieval Catholicism had known no strict dualism between earth and heaven: "What it denies in heaven, i.e., in faith, it denies, also, as far as possible, on earth, i.e., in morality." Protestantism directed humanity toward this-worldly practice but divested this world of the sanctity that it had held in earlier Catholicism. By separating the worldly from the spiritual kingdom, Protestantism relegated the commandments of Christian morality to the strictly "private" sphere and channeled our most essential selves, our souls, into an isolated relation to God. It limited humanity's existence as "public persons," by contrast, to the worldly, to "the sword, war, litigation." The "carnal mingling of the Christian and the man" that Feuerbach identified as Protestant morality reveals upon closer inspection a "division," a "chasm," a "disunity": "Here we are half heathens, half Christians; half citizens of the earth, half citizens of heaven."[78] To the "Christian" is promised heaven; to the "man," earth. Feuerbach's hope in his own work was to replace fully the Christian with the man, but to do so in such a way that the alienated species-being of the Christian is returned to humanity. For insofar as Protestantism itself separated the Christian from the man, it left him to a natural existence – that

---

75  Feuerbach, "The Necessity of a Reform of Philosophy," p. 146.
76  Feuerbach, *Principles*, p. 25.
77  Feuerbach to Emilie Kapp, 14 May 1842, *Briefwechsel*, vol. 2.
78  Feuerbach, *Wesen*, p. 594.

is, to the natural egoism of life, without reuniting that natural existence with "species life."[79]

Feuerbach's scattered reflections on Protestantism's imperfect secularization echo Saint-Simonianism's preoccupation with the deleterious effects of Christianity's, especially Protestantism's, dualistic separation of spiritual from natural being. Moreover, his mature criticism of this distorted secularization intersected neatly with his longstanding association of Christian personalism with civil society. In *The Essence of Christianity*, Feuerbach described the specific effects of the insidious convergence of Protestantism's worldliness and its fixation on the spiritual relationship of the isolated person to God. As he had in 1830, Feuerbach denied the fitness of Protestantism as such for any valid idea of political freedom. Protestantism, he wrote, preaches only an internal "spiritual freedom, i.e., a freedom which demands no sacrifice, no energy, – an illusory, self-deceptive freedom; – a freedom from earthly good, which consists in its possession and enjoyment!" Modern Christianity, by deferring the genuine actualization of freedom until the afterlife, makes no demand on the present, on the world, and so this "freedom" conveniently "allots to our spontaneous activity the acquisition and enjoyment of earthly possessions."[80]

The two moments of civil society are conceptually joined in this observation on the effects of post-Reformation Christianity – the depoliticization of individual life and the consequent deflection of activity into the pursuit of private gain. Hence, Feuerbach asserted, the typical modern Christian is a "hypocrite" and a "liar," with a "crucifix in one hand and the banner of free trade in the other": "You want to enjoy the fruit of the old belief in the beyond, but in the here and now, you relish the fruits of modern unbelief."[81] He chose to describe this balance between belief and modern "epicureanism" as a "juste-milieu," thereby associating his observation, perhaps deliberately, with the French regime of the "bourgeois-king" established in the Revolution of 1830.

It must be acknowledged, however, that Feuerbach failed to link his insights into the connection between Christianity and civil society to a more concrete social analysis. Important as the social dimension was in all of Feuerbach's work on religion, he did not attempt to develop a sociology of religion. Not that he was unaware of the need for such an undertaking. Indeed, in 1844, he commended his brother Friedrich for his work on the "so-

---

79 See, for example, "Philosophie und Christentum," p. 326; and "An Karl Riedel," p. 211.
80 Feuerbach, *Wesen*, pp. 284-5.
81 Feuerbach, "Philosophie und Christentum," p. 318.

cial relations of Christianity," and he even promised to supply material from his own observations on the "anti-socialism" of Christianity.[82] Friedrich's *Religion of the Future* does read like a gloss on his brother's fragmentary insights into the relationship between Christianity and civil society.[83] As for his own work, Ludwig told Otto Wigand that "politics and sociality operate only in the background. And these operations do not appear directly to the eye."[84] Nor did Feuerbach dwell on the possible ideological uses of religious belief, even though he was clearly not oblivious to them. As he wrote,

> What idleness it is to wish to set the steam engines and sugar beet factories in motion, while wishing to set the great thinking machine, the mind, in eternal stillness. What a notion – to wish to perpetuate religious confusion so that no one will think any longer about religion; that is, that it is in the best national interest of the Germans, that is of the steam engines and the sugar beet factories, to degrade oneself to a beast in religious matters. . . . Whoever is a slave of his religious feeling deserves nothing other than to be a political slave. Whoever lacks the power to take himself in hand will also lack the power and the right to liberate himself from material and political suppression.[85]

It appears that Feuerbach militantly connected his own battle against Christianity to the class struggle only after he was emboldened by his contacts with communists, both through his personal acquaintance with a left-wing artisan and through the writings of Wilhelm Weitling, Lorenz von Stein, and Karl Marx. For example, two months after Marx wrote to Feuerbach that in France "religiosity has now passed to the middle and upper classes while on the other hand irreligiosity – but an irreligiosity of men regarding themselves as men – has descended to the French proletariat,"[86] we find Feuerbach virtually repeating Marx's words: "the artisans rise to atheism, to be sure not in the sense of the old, say-nothing, empty, skeptical atheism, but the modern, positive, energetic, religious atheism."[87]

As willing as Feuerbach was to connect his critique of religion to socialism, the Marxian identification of socialism with the proletariat's struggle actually militated against the core of his emancipatory project. Feuerbach

82 Feuerbach to Friedrich Feuerbach, February 1844, *Briefwechsel*, vol. 2.
83 Friedrich Feuerbach, *Die Religion der Zukunft*, 2 vols. (Zürich und Winterthur, 1843; Nürnberg, 1845).
84 Feuerbach to Otto Wigand, 5 March 1844, *Briefwechsel*, vol. 2.
85 Feuerbach, "Zur Beurteilung der Schrift 'Das Wesen des Christentums'" (1842), *Werke*, vol. 2, pp. 213–14.
86 Marx to Feuerbach, 11 August 1844, *Briefwechsel*, vol. 2.
87 Feuerbach to Friedrich Alexander Kapp, 15 October 1844, *Briefwechsel*, vol. 2.

never identified the proletariat as the universal class whose emancipation would liberate all mankind. Instead, he remained committed to the task of the universal emancipation of humanity as such. Even though he was sensitive to the miserable condition of the poor, he was also convinced that all humanity was in misery and need. He recognized clearly enough that Christian personalism touched different social groups differently, but he believed even more strongly that it dehumanized all humanity equally. Though he offered no analysis of economic oppression or the means to overcome it, he clearly included emancipation from material suffering along with the spiritual, political, even libidinal liberation that he yearned to achieve all at once. The means he sought to reach this goal were undoubtedly *socialist*, if we conceive socialism in the broad moral terms that are most appropriate to this fluid moment in its history. Ignoring this socialism in Feuerbach, Marx was soon to condemn it as sentimental utopianism in Feuerbach's followers, the "True Socialists."

## Overcoming Christian Civil Society

Feuerbach is too frequently presented as a strictly negative thinker, identified solely with his critical stand against religion. However, when we consider him in the context of the politicized and socialized debates about personalism and pantheism in the late 1830s, it is clear that a constructive, positive side also belongs essentially to Feuerbach's intentions and to his significance in his own time. Like Cieszkowski, Hess, and Heine, or, indeed, the prophets of early French socialism, Feuerbach attempted to transcend the debilitating social and political effects of Christian culture. Like them, he searched in the present for seeds of an epochal transformation of human society. If we may define Feuerbach as a "socialist" – again, in the moral sense and, one might say, almost *avant la lettre* – of what did his positive socialist "program" consist? What were the seeds of the future? What was Feuerbach's vision of *socialized* politics?

Feuerbach's recognition of the role played by modern Christianity in the creation of a private, selfish society articulated a central theme of French and German radicalism in the 1830s and early 1840s. But behind this sociopolitical critique we may also discern echoes of eighteenth-century concerns about the political effects of Christianity. These originated in Enlightenment discussions about Christianity's role in precipitating the fall of Rome. Both Voltaire and Gibbon blamed Christianity for the destruction of public spirit in ancient political life, but it was Rousseau who linked a condemnation of Christianity with a critique of commerce by making both responsible for the development of modern egoistical society.[88] Not only had Christianity destroyed ancient civic virtue, he argued, but it was also an obstacle to a "civic ethos" in the present because of its otherworldly egoism.[89] The civil religion that Rousseau envisaged as a vital part of a genuine republic was intended to be a precise inversion of Christianity, public and active where the Christian faith was private and passive.

Rousseau's pessimistic view of modern Christianity had weighed heavily on the young Hegel.[90] Hegel too sought to create a "civil religion," although his *Volksreligion* was to be built on the truths of early Christianity. In contrast to the historical form taken by the faith, which Hegel believed had degenerated into a "positive" external authority, the essence of Christianity as he viewed it in the mid-1790s was "the commands of virtue which are essential in the faith, not the practices it orders or the positive doctrines it enjoins or may entail."[91] Christ's original message, Hegel claimed, urged people to a "free virtue springing from *man's own being*."[92] Hence, Christ's words took the form not of a decree or injunction but of an appeal to the indwelling capacity of "our hearts" to respond to "the challenge of virtue."[93] Laurence Dickey has argued convincingly that Hegel's main intention in analyzing Christianity's decline from a "virtue religion" into a "positive religion" was to revive the virtue and activism inherent in Christianity as potential resources for reform in a modern world where collective life was increasingly organized "along the socioeconomic lines of a commercial society."[94]

Feuerbach could not have known much, if anything, about Hegel's essays of the 1790s, as they remained unpublished until 1907. Nonetheless, as Feuerbach faced the cultural and intellectual situation of his age, where a new spirit of Protestant "positivism" sanctioned both authoritarian politics and self-seeking individualism in society, he pursued a strategy which bore striking similarity to that of the young Hegel. Against a doctrine that separated transcendental divinity from the world, Feuerbach sought to develop an immanent principle of social union, a principle that would at once overcome the alienation imposed on humanity by theological and political personalism and ground human action and freedom in a meaningful social

---

88   See Rousseau, *The Social Contract*, Book III, Ch. xv, and Book IV, Ch. viii.
89   Lucio Colletti, "Rousseau as Critic of Civil Society," *From Rousseau to Lenin: Studies in Ideology and Society* (London, 1972), p. 175; and Judith Shklar, *Men and Citizens. A Study of Rousseau's Social Theory* (Cambridge, 1985), pp. 118–20.
90   Schmidt, "*Paideia*," p. 477.
91   Hegel, "The Positivity of the Christian Religion," p. 75.
92   Ibid., p. 71 (emphasis added).     93   Ibid., p. 73.
94   Dickey, *Hegel*, pp. 184, 175–9.

context. In this task, he could not rely on the mature Hegel's idea of *Sitt-lichkeit*, ethical life, because that depended on the very Protestantism that Feuerbach criticized as the ultimate source of modern society's atomized egoism and political apathy.

In the mid-1830s, as in *Thoughts on Death and Immortality*, Feuerbach could still appeal to pantheism as the basis for such a social union.[95] Like Heine, Hess, Cieszkowski, or David Friedrich Strauss, he recognized the nonhierarchical, egalitarian, democratic, and emancipatory possibilities of the pantheistic dissolution of personalism. As Feuerbach developed his anthropological theory of religion, he traced the principle of human collectivity not to Absolute Spirit but to species-being. Species-being had been a minor category in Hegel's *Encyclopedia,* used by him to refer to the "natural" component of human life, in particular its sexual and reproductive aspects. When Feuerbach elevated this to the organizing principle of his own thought, he clearly meant to signal the naturalization of Hegel's thought, the return of consciousness from the illusory domain of Spirit to the concrete life of man as a natural and social being. However, whether in the Idealist form in which he introduced species-being in *Thoughts on Death and Immortality* or in the naturalist form that the concept took in his later thought, species-being remained a principle of collective identity that Feuerbach advanced as the antidote to the atomized notion of personality.

There was a clear ambiguity in this challenge to personalism. In identifying a shared human essence and in positing a vision of radical collectivization based on this essence, Feuerbach risked the reintroduction of the notion of a perfectly unified subject in the form of a hypostatized meta-person, "man" as species-subject. This was the gist of Max Stirner's criticism, from whose anarchistic-individualist perspective species-being could be condemned as a covert theological construct.[96] Indeed, the species-concept did tempt Feuerbach with dreams of the unity of man, transferred from the single self of Christian personhood to the collective self of the atheist species-subject. There were, however, important aspects of Feuerbach's thought that conflicted with a monistic or essentialist idea of humanity. First, and most important, the crucial dimension of his conception of emancipation involves the human recovery of powers that are alienated in religious consciousness. Once humanity recognizes these powers as its own, it can embark on a process of self-creation. Freed of the constraints of a Christian teleology, this process is radically undetermined in its form and content. Hence,

95  See Toews, *Hegelianism*, p. 344.
96  See Max Stirner, *The Ego and Its Own,* trans. David Leopold (Cambridge, 1995).

Feuerbach wrote that properly understood, "man" deserves the predicate "many-named."[97] Although Feuerbach certainly envisioned the actualization of human essence as a collective process, he held to an emphasis on diversity within unity. It might be said that species-being is not a substance but rather a standpoint of autonomy, from which people are to recognize themselves as both the subjects and objects of their own development.

Second, as we saw in Chapter 3, Feuerbach's mature work went well beyond his earlier intellectualist idea of universality. Once Feuerbach reached his insights into the sensuous, embodied nature of the ego, he could develop a much more nuanced view of the relationship between particularity and universality, nature and spirit, the "personal" and the "impersonal." In this view, the human body is not a natural obstacle to the spiritual collectivization of humanity. Rather, the body becomes an integral part of the dialectical relationship between the individual and the collective. Therefore, the idea of species-being is not simply an intellectualist construct that replaces an atomized concept of personhood with a collectivist meta-subjective one. Instead, species-being involves relation and non-relation, the latter of which resides in the particularity necessarily entailed in individual embodiment. In this sense, Marx and many critics of Feuerbach have been mistaken in ascribing to him an exclusively intellectualist model of human essence. For example, Wartofsky errs when he writes that "Feuerbach's sense of 'practical'. . . is removed from the context of practice in which man engages not himself, but a world external to himself, which he has to transform, abide, understand, in order to meet his needs."[98] Without question, Feuerbach did not even remotely approach the concrete level of analysis of practice that Marx reached by the mid-1840s, nor, it bears mentioning, was it ever his intention to do so. Nonetheless, far from ignoring "need" in a practical sense, Feuerbach conceived need as the crucial, immanent principle of social integration by which human species-being is to be actualized. Moreover, because both psychological and bodily needs figure in his account, he did not arrive at a monistic conception of a meta-subjective species-being. For the body demands the presence of others for the satisfaction of its needs, but because of the specificity of its needs in time and space, it resists absorption by a collective subject or person.

As early as his essay on Stahl, Feuerbach had attacked the Christian personalists because their belief in the perfection of the single individual contradicted what he considered to be the true essence of humanity. For

97  Feuerbach, "Preliminary Theses," p. 171.
98  Wartofsky, *Feuerbach,* p. 326.

Feuerbach, the perfection of the species depended precisely on the imperfection of each individual: "because no single individual, due to his limitations, is the adequate expression of the Idea, the species, nature seeks to complete the defect of the single existence through the creation of another being."[99] *Need* or *lack* thereby replaces the self-sufficiency of personhood as the defining moment in the life of the individual and the species. This became an enduring theme in Feuerbach's work, and it formed the concrete basis for his insistence upon the social character of species-being. Hence, in 1844, Feuerbach criticized the Christian valorization of blessedness, finding in the image of individual redemption an expression of asocial self-love, while he saw in the Fall from a paradisal state of plenitude into sin a symbol of the dependency and need that are the foundations of all sociality.[100]

In an earlier essay, Feuerbach regretted philosophy's exclusion of the idea of "need" from its concepts of freedom and love. Need is an expression of freedom, he maintained, because unlike those of animals, the needs of humans are unlimited. The defect of individuals draws them out of themselves in a constant striving after completion; therefore, "it is precisely through the concept of need that a being is elevated above the limitations of its subjectivity." Moreover, need explains love. "Love stemming from an overabundance of perfection is luxury"; however, genuine love is "the need for another. . . . Through love a being reveals that it in itself is not enough, that only in connection with another different being is it satisfied."[101] Love, the primary social bond, is therefore inseparable from lack and need; as Feuerbach would repeat many times, the truly *concrete* person is comprehensible only in terms of interaction and interdependency. This sense of neediness and its attendant desire for completion in another is the ultimate source of religious feelings, according to Feuerbach, in that the imagination satisfies this felt need through the creation of divine beings. But it is also the ground for the profoundly social orientation of Feuerbach's atheistic humanism, the famous "I-Thou" that was to replace the authoritarian relation of man to a fictive God.

Scholars have ignored the relationship between Feuerbach's conception of the role of needs in the realization of species-being and earlier discussions of the social dynamics of civil society. To consider the most likely influence first, in the *Philosophy of Right*, Hegel had argued that the inability of individuals to meet all their needs alone draws them into a web of social re-

99 Feuerbach, "*Die Philosophie des Rechts,*" p. 29.
100 Feuerbach, "Das Wesen des Glauben im Sinne Luthers," pp. 66–8.
101 Feuerbach, "[Über] Dr. Karl Bayer," pp. 98–9.

lations.[102] Pure egoism and the atomizing effects of civil society are thereby countered by the interdependencies fostered by the division of labor and exchange. Chapter 3 suggested that Friedrich Julius Stahl and the Christian personalists remained arrested at what Hegel had called the "first principle" of civil society, the particular "person who is himself the object of his particular aims." It may be said in contrast that Feuerbach seems to have based the social union of love upon Hegel's "second principle," the form of universality that arises within civil society as a result of human need and interdependency.[103]

This is not to say that Feuerbach was any more trusting of the dynamics of civil society than was Hegel. In fact, Feuerbach was more hostile to the egoism and self-seeking of modern commercial society and much less concerned with the preservation of the individual right of self-determination than with fulfilling his vision of social harmony. Ironically, however, he was ultimately much more optimistic than Hegel about the transformative power of civil society itself because he believed that egoism could evolve into loving union once the theological roots of egoism were extirpated.[104] Hence, Feuerbach adapted Hegel's system of needs to the utopian task of actualizing species-being. He developed what we may call a political economy of love, complete with a system of needs and a division of labor.

In Feuerbach's conception, the development of species-being involves a vital dialectical interplay between the egoism of need and the cooperation necessary to its satisfaction, between the natural egoism of the embodied subject and social relatedness. "I am an 'I' for myself," he wrote, "and simultaneously a 'thou' for others."[105] Therefore, he rejected the extreme egoism of his harsh critic Max Stirner, who took the isolated individual to be the only reality. "To be an individual," conceded Feuerbach, "is certainly, of course, to be an 'Egoist,' but it is also at the same time and indeed unintentionally to be a 'communist.'"[106] For in his view, the ego, which initially seeks its archetype in the absolute Self of God, overcomes this impulse toward

102  Hegel, *Philosophy of Right*, para. 189–98.
103  Ibid., para. 182.
104  Feuerbach's faith in the integrative powers latent in society can be contrasted to the stance of Right Hegelians in the 1840s, whose belief that the divisiveness of civil society is the essence of society led them to support an authoritarian regulative state. See Jürgen Habermas, *The Philosophical Discourse of Modernity. Twelve Lectures*, trans. F. G. Lawrence (Cambridge, Mass., 1991), pp. 70–1.
105  Feuerbach, *Principles*, p. 52.
106  Feuerbach, "*The Essence of Christianity* in Relation to *The Ego and Its Own*" (1845), *The Philosophical Forum*, vol. VIII, 2–4(1978), p. 85. See also Feuerbach's letters to his brother Friedrich, 2 and 8 December 1844.

"unlimitedness" through its encounter with another like it, "the first stone against which the pride of egoism stumbles." The encounter with the "*thou, the alter ego*" subdues egoism and cultivates recognition of the dependence of the self upon other humans. Interaction and interdependency become the preconditions for the growth of individual self-consciousness, for the self-awareness of people as human beings is inseparable from the awareness that they exist only in the interrelations of social life. Feuerbach did not consider species-being to be a perfectly harmonious, *a priori* given. It is rather the product of "contact and friction" between men; "hence there is more wit in the town than in the country, more in great towns than in small ones."[107]

If parallels to Hegel's account of the development of civil society can be discovered in Feuerbach, we may also detect the influence of another great Idealist account of the rise of civil society, Kant's "Idea for a Universal History from a Cosmopolitan Point of View." In the 1839 essay wherein Feuerbach first introduced the concept of species in the naturalistic form it would hold throughout his later work, he regretted that Hegel had not been more forthcoming in his use of the species-concept. He suggested that the species-concept which Hegel mystified was much more boldly articulated by Kant, whom Feuerbach praised as the first philosopher to introduce the concept. In fact, the "Idea for a Universal History" does contain many of the crucial elements of Feuerbach's own species-concept, including, most important, Kant's contention that humanity is perfected not in the individual but in the race.[108] What is less obvious, but of great importance, is the fact that Kant develops a conjectural history in which "antagonism" and "association," the conflicting impulses of mankind, work to bring about the development of all the capacities of humanity. Natural egoism brings individuals into contact and cooperation with one another, thereby leading to the higher achievements of culture and eventually to the development of a "universal civic society." Kant construed this as a teleological process in which Nature has so constituted humanity that even its faults ensure its transformation from natural being to universal species-being.[109] Feuerbach would have rejected the thinly veiled providentialism of Kant's conjectural history, but his own claim that "nature seeks to complete the defect of the single existence through the

---

107    Feuerbach, *Wesen*, p. 166.
108    Kant, "Idea for a Universal History from a Cosmopolitan Point of View," in *On History. Immanuel Kant,* ed. Lewis White Beck (Indianapolis, 1980), p. 13. See also John Zammito, *The Genesis of Kant's Critique of Judgment* (Chicago, 1992), pp. 333–5.
109    A similar construction can be seen in Schiller's *Aesthetic Education,* written a decade later.

creation of another being" gives an unmistakable teleological form to his concept of species-being.[110] Hence, Feuerbach's assertion that the individual is "unintentionally" communistic echoes Kant's "unsocial sociability," his compressed and ironic formulation of the teleological process that transforms the "bad" qualities of the natural man into the "good" progress of the species. Significantly, this perfectionist telos complicates Feuerbach's attempt at a truly naturalistic transformation of Hegelianism, and it contrasts profoundly with the nonperfectionist evolutionary concept of species that Charles Darwin was developing in those same years.

The inspiration that Feuerbach found in Kant's utopian sketch of humanity's movement toward ethical collectivity presents another striking point of contact with the Saint-Simonians. For they too were strongly impressed by Kant's essay. Auguste Comte was introduced to the essay by the ardent Saint-Simonian Gustave d'Eichtal, whose studies had taken him to Berlin in the 1820s. In the hands of Comte and later Bazard and Enfantin, Kant's two contending principles, antagonism and association, became the key terms of the Saint-Simonian philosophy of history.[111] As one student of the Saint-Simonians notes, Kant's conjectural sketch was "endowed by the Saint-Simonians with an easy optimism which the philosopher of Königsberg never expressed."[112] The same might be said of Feuerbach, who clearly identified his concept of species-being with the possibility of harmonious social association. Indeed, Feuerbach seems to belong among the numerous German writers who, by the early 1840s, had embraced the French idea of association as a remedy for the contradictions of social life.[113]

Because, in Feuerbach's view, "want" and the "sense of poverty" are the "impulse to all culture,"[114] it should not be surprising to see that the division of labor appears as the structure that underlies and enables the progressive development of species-being:

> [S]piritually as well as physically [man] can achieve nothing without his fellow-man. Four hands can do more than two, but also four eyes can see more than two. And this combined power is distinguished not only in quantity but also in quality from that which is solitary. In isolation human power is limited, in combination it is infinite.

---

110  Wartofsky's discussion of Feuerbach's reference to Kant ignores this dimension (*Feuerbach*, p. 163).

111  *The Doctrine of Saint-Simon*, esp. pp. 58–79. See also Carlisle, *Proffered Crown*, p. 101.

112  Manuel, *Prophets of Paris*, p. 169.

113  The interest was not restricted to progressive German thinkers. On the wider German use of the concept of "association," see Conze, "Vom 'Pöbel' zum 'Proletariat,'" p. 356.

114  Feuerbach, *Wesen*, p. 364.

Through the division of labor within a system of interdependency, people produce the very qualities that define the human, not only their material life but also the perfections of culture, art, and rational speech: "Wit, acumen, imagination, feeling as distinguished from sensation, reason as a subjective faculty, – all these so-called powers of the soul are powers of humanity, not of man as an individual; they are products of culture, products of human society."[115] To be sure, Marx's complaints that Feuerbach remained at a very abstract level are well-founded.[116] He never described specific forms of social organization, nor the forms of alienation peculiar to them, nor finally the practical means to overcome them. Although a conjectural historical structure underlies his account of man's production of species-being, Feuerbach did not cast this account in explicitly historical terms. Nor did he criticize the division of labor itself or property as such but only the ends to which they are mistakenly directed in Christian civil society. Furthermore, he overestimated the transformative power and practical significance of critique. He remained wedded to the conviction that enlightenment, or *Bildung,* is the most potent weapon in the revolutionary's arsenal. Therefore, he believed that alienation would be overcome in the first instance when people reclaim the essence of their humanity, their "infinite power," from an illusory God.

Accurate as Marx's criticism is, it has tended to blind us to the model of sociability that underlies Feuerbach's discussion of species-being. When he is viewed in the company of socially minded contemporaries like Hess, Heine, and Cieszkowski, the sociopolitical implications of Feuerbach's effort to overcome the alienation of religious belief are much harder to ignore. Judged from the perspective of Christian personalism – a belief system that separates transcendence from immanence and absolutizes the isolated person – human needs remained arrested at the level of egoism, selfishness, and atomization; from this standpoint, Feuerbach believed, the system of social interdependency created in the satisfaction of needs appeared extraneous, or even hostile, to the perfection of humanity, rather than as its actual source. Conversely, Feuerbach maintained that once the secret of religious belief is exposed, once people no longer squander their energy on an illusory God, the system of social interdependence will become the site of humanity's self-conscious devotion and activity. For it is within such an association that humanity produces its perfection; and perfection of the species

115   Ibid., p. 166.
116   See *The German Ideology,* 3rd ed. (Moscow, 1976), pp. 44f.

consists in overcoming limitations or, in other words, in the satisfaction of needs, both physical and spiritual.[117]

"Activity," "making," and "creation" are "divine," therefore, because production relates the individual to society; and it is precisely because activity brings the individual into relation with his species-being that "activity is the positive sense of one's personality."[118] Not surprising, then, is Feuerbach's expectation, as Karl Löwith put it, that "when the man, poor in earthly goods, replaces the Christian, the fellowship of work must replace the fellowship of prayer."[119] The paradoxes that characterize "civil society," as in Mandeville's *private vices* and *public benefits* or Kant's *unsocial sociability*, are transformed into the means by which perfection is to be actualized:

> Work is worship. But how can I worship or serve an object, how can I subject myself to it, if it does not hold a high place in my mind? In brief, the occupations of men determine their judgment, their mode of thought, their sentiments. And the higher the occupation, the more completely does a man identify himself with it. In general, whatever a man makes the essential aim of his life, he proclaims to be his soul; for it is the principle of motion in him. But through his aim, through the activity in which he realises this aim, man is not only something for himself, but also something for others, for the general life. He therefore who lives in the consciousness of the species as a reality, regards his existence for others, his relation to society, his utility to the public, as that existence which is one with the existence of his own essence – as his immortal existence. He lives with his whole soul, with his whole heart, for humanity.[120]

The parallel to the "New Christianity" is here striking. As one of the German students of Saint-Simonianism wrote in 1834:

> [T]he Saint-Simonians do not ignore the fact that Christianity is against the world, and therefore is unfit to organize it. Saint-Simonianism is to become a religion of this world, in order to spiritualize the worldly and finite expressions of human activity, i.e. work, through connecting them to a higher and general goal. Then work itself is divine service. It is a great service of Saint-Simonianism to have spoken with such energy of this "sanctification of work."[121]

---

117  The holistic impulse of both Feuerbach's "pantheism" and his "atheism" did not make the needs of the body equal to those of the spirit but rather *spiritualized* the needs of the body as integral to the "whole" person. Compare the concluding passage of *The Essence of Christianity* with Heinrich Heine's Saint-Simonian pronouncements in his 1832 *Religion and Philosophy in Germany*.

118  Feuerbach, *Wesen*, p. 365.

119  Löwith, *From Hegel to Nietzsche*, p. 81.    120  Ibid., p. 295.

121  Moritz Veit, *Saint Simon und der Saint Simonismus*, p. 152.

From the standpoint of atheism, need will ultimately unify the natural and spiritual man and, most important, the community of men. Feuerbach derived a political economy of love from *within* the principle of civil society; and this "economy," with its process of collectivization, was to be the means by which civil society would be overcome and the true human society created.

## Feuerbach's Politics

Feuerbach's principle of social union replaces the pursuit of private gain with work for the collective. However, in common with the early socialists, his principle also implies a conceptual continuum between socialized work and politics, because both are equally forms of activity directed toward the actualization of humanity's essence. The attempt to overcome the *depoliticization* of Christian civil society by grounding all human activity in a meaningful communal context had the same effect in Feuerbach as it did in the Saint-Simonians or their German supporters: the devaluation of the notion – traceable to Aristotle and discernible in modern liberal thought – of politics as a sphere of human activity separate from the social. Hence, when Feuerbach called for a republic that would ensure "active participation in the affairs of the state" and the "abolition of political hierarchy and the unreason of the people,"[122] this political stance reveals upon closer inspection an interpenetration of republican and social themes much like that which we saw in Heine. The politics of the species must necessarily be total, because Feuerbach was as unwilling as Heine to separate the "spiritual" from the "material" needs of humanity. Such a politics was intended to replace religion as the self-conscious activity of men directing their energies toward the perfection of humanity. Or, in an ironic inversion of Rousseau, "politics" must become the civic religion of the new humanist culture that Feuerbach anticipated.[123] Yet, if non-alienated love of humanity culminates in politics as its highest practice, then we must confront the paradox posed by Feuerbach's claim in *The Essence of Christianity* that "the highest idea, the God of *unpolitical*, unworldly feeling is Love."[124] To understand this paradox and gain a deeper insight into Feuerbach's conception of politics, we must briefly examine his presentation of Christian history.

Like his Enlightenment predecessors, Feuerbach viewed the Christian principle of universal love as antithetical to the spirit of the Roman Empire.

---

122   Feuerbach, "Necessity," p. 151.
123   Ibid., p. 149.
124   Feuerbach, *Wesen,* p. 219 (emphasis added).

However, he regarded the demise of imperial Rome without regret: "The empire of policy which united men after a manner corresponding with its own idea, was coming to its necessary end. Political unity is a unity of force. . . . [With Christianity] in the place of Rome appeared the idea of humanity; to the idea of domination [*Herrschaft*] succeeded the idea of love."[125] Like the young Hegel, Feuerbach lamented the subsequent decline of Christianity from this principle of love into the dogmatism of "faith" and political alliances with worldly powers. Only with Protestantism did love once again resume its central position in Christianity. However, Feuerbach also argued that Protestantism's faith in the redemptive power of Christ, the God-Man, as well as its belief in a direct relationship between the individual and the divine, had fatefully exposed the anthropological secret of religion that had lain hidden by the rigors of medieval Catholicism.

We have seen that Feuerbach, in common with the left wing of the 1830s, assigned debilitating social and political effects to Protestantism, even going so far as to hold Luther partly responsible for the "political incapacity" of the Germans.[126] Nonetheless, he believed that Protestantism's revival of love and its implicit recognition of the divinity of humanity made it the potential ally of the true human society once the intensity of its inward feeling could be converted into external, this-worldly activity. Hence he wrote, "A Protestant is a religious republican. That is why Protestantism naturally leads to political republicanism once its religious content has disappeared; that is, has been exposed, unveiled."[127] Feuerbach therefore contrasted two forms of politics – one represented by Rome, a unity secured only by force of law, the other represented by a Protestantism transformed by the new awareness of the quasi-divinity of human species-being and the activism enjoined by the recognition that men *produce* this divinity. Once liberated from subjection to a transcendental authority, humanity would be free to act virtuously in the service of a new politics that demands both "external [*sinnliche*] freedom" and "spiritual freedom."[128] Indeed, the quality of virtue itself would change. Whereas Christians are led to virtue by the power of "example" or "imitation" of Christ, the atheist acts because he has internalized the standard of virtue itself as the self-sufficient spring to action. No divine personification of virtue stands between the atheist and his commitment to the common duties and morality of humanity. Virtue ceases to be a private matter –

125  Ibid., p. 440.
126  Feuerbach to Otto Wigand, 26 April 1844, *Briefwechsel*, vol. 2.
127  Feuerbach, "Necessity," p. 152.
128  *Wesen*, p. 283.

what Feuerbach once dismissed as "*spießbürgerliche*" virtue[129] – and becomes
something "social, communal" because the "fundament of virtue is the sense
for the species, for the general."[130] We are reminded forcefully of the young
Hegel's Rousseauian image of Christ calling forth "the free virtue springing
from man's own being."

Feuerbach reached conclusions that were strikingly similar to those of the
young Hegel only by renouncing the "mature" Hegel. For Feuerbach's desire to establish the direct unity of a community bound by love led him to
collapse the conceptual distinction between "civil society" and the "state" that
was so central to Hegel's *Philosophy of Right*. This outcome was an extension
of Feuerbach's general conclusion that Hegel's dialectical mediation is a formal operation of thought but not a structure of the objective world. By 1842,
he resolutely identified the effects of mediation with those of religion. "The
Hegelian philosophy has alienated man *from himself* insofar as its whole system is based on these acts of abstraction. Although it again identifies what
it separates, it does so only in a *separate* and *mediated* way. The Hegelian philosophy lacks *immediate unity, immediate certainty, immediate truth.*"[131] In the
same essay, Feuerbach turned this critique specifically against Hegel's *Philosophy of Right*, noting that it "fixed the separation of the essential qualities
of man from man, thus deifying purely abstract qualities as independent beings." Hence, he rejected Hegel's important paragraph 190, which, as Feuerbach paraphrased it, claimed that

> In right, what we have before us is the *person;* in the sphere of morality, the *sub-
> ject;* in the family, the family-member; in civil society as a whole, the [citizen]
> (as bourgeois). Here at the standpoint of needs what we have before us is the
> composite *idea* which we call *man*. It is thus here for the first time, and indeed
> properly only here, that we speak of man in this sense.

In contrast, Feuerbach insisted that "We speak in truth only and always of
*one* and the *same* being; i.e., of man, even if we do so in a different sense and
in a different quality, when we speak of the [citizen], the subject, the family
member, and the person."[132] Because Feuerbach defined *man* by his *needs*,
it is clear that whereas Hegel delimited the area in which man as a "com-
posite of needs" operates, Feuerbach universalized the category of needs.

---

129  Feuerbach, "[Über] Dr. Karl Bayer," p. 95.
130  Feuerbach quoted in Hans-Martin Sass, "Ludwig Feuerbach und die Zukunft der Philoso-
     phie," *Ludwig Feuerbach und die Philosophie der Zukunft*, p. 21.
131  Feuerbach, "Preliminary Theses," p. 157.
132  Ibid., p. 171.

For it was from the "standpoint of needs" that he fashioned his model of authentic community.

Feuerbach was quite aware that in reducing Hegel's categories to the immediate unity of man, he had overturned the distinction between "man as man" and "man as citizen" that was common in eighteenth-century and early nineteenth-century political discussion.[133] Adhering to a conception of politics that had distant roots in Aristotle, many thinkers of those decades considered political capacities to depend on the citizens' independence from need and self-interest.[134] For as Aristotle had argued, only autonomy from the realm of necessity, from the *oikos*, could ensure the freedom of participants in a community whose telos is the good and just life. However, whereas the original Aristotelian division between necessity and freedom had been literally embodied in the separation of laboring slaves and women from a free political class of men, by the eighteenth century, the division had been internalized as representing different moments or capacities within the same person. This was not an easy duality to sustain, what with the assumption that as "man," the individual is likely to act egoistically, whereas as "citizen," he is obligated to act selflessly for the good of the public. Nonetheless, despite the inherent instability in this separation of private interest from public duty, social from political man, and the inconclusive debates over this issue in the American and French Revolutions and in the thought of Germans like Kant, Moses Mendelssohn, and Hegel, the distinction proved remarkably persistent.

Feuerbach did not reject the effort to distinguish among different civic and social capacities, but the implication of his critique of Hegel's political philosophy is clear. From the standpoint of Feuerbach's humanism, the whole tradition that separates "man" from "citizen" must appear as *theological,* because it alienates the "public qualities" of man from man.[135] Feuerbach's critique of the separation of the "man" from the "Christian" in the religious sphere thus converges with a critique in the sociopolitical domain of the separation of "man" from "citizen," and, by extension, of the separation of work from politics. The longstanding dichotomy between man and citizen had lost its credibility because in his perspective, needs no longer appear as threats to political virtue but rather as the means to humanity's pursuit of the good – that is, the full development of human capacities.

---

133   See, for example, Shklar, *Men and Citizens,* and Manfred Riedel, *Between Tradition and Revolution,* esp. pp. 140f.

134   Manfred Riedel, "Bürgerliche Gesellschaft," *Geschichtliche Grundbegriffe,* vol. 2.

135   Feuerbach, "Preliminary Theses," p. 171.

Because need stands at the heart of Feuerbach's conception of authentic community, he spoke of the state in radically different terms from those of Hegel. Hegel's state relates to society only through complex mediations, and it aims to contain within a higher unity the inherent divisiveness of civil society, the realm of necessity. For Feuerbach, who believed he had discovered the principle of social union within civil society, the state is the universal term that describes the totality of social relations and activities. What is more, the political economy of love and its cooperative division of labor structure this totality:

> Within the state, the powers of man differentiate and unfold themselves in or-
> der, through this differentiation and synthesis, to constitute an infinite being;
> for the multitude of men and the multitude of forces form one single power.
> The state comprehends all realities and is man's providence for him. . . . I am
> surrounded by a universal being; I am part of a whole.[136]

If the true state is the "unlimited, infinite, true, perfect, and divine man," Feuerbach nonetheless retained a *person* at the pinnacle of the "state" because he did not want to erect yet another alienating abstraction: "In the state, the essential qualities or activities of man are realized in particular estates (Ständen), but in the person of the head of state they are again resolved into an identity."[137] This head of state bears some resemblance to Hegel's idea of the monarch; but just as Feuerbach reconceived the state, he also radically altered the conception of the head of state. Whereas Hegel's monarch personifies the *constitutional* totality of the state, Feuerbach wrote that the head of state represents "all estates without distinction; to him they are all equally necessary and equally entitled before him. [He] represents universal man."[138] The head of state thus does not represent merely the *political* unity of the state but rather the unity of the social forces of humanity as it produces itself in the system of interdependency.

Feuerbach's explicit remarks on the nature of the state once again reveal the difficulty of the radical democrat in escaping the language of personalist identity and subjective decision making. Feuerbach's head of state is imagined as the exact antithesis of Stahl's. Feuerbach's head of state is a "man," "as good a man as we all," presumably an elected executive. Stahl's monarch is wrapped in the *arcana* of political theology. Stahl's transcendental sover-

136  Feuerbach, "Necessity," p. 150.
137  Feuerbach's rejection of Hegel's separation of state and civil society is again revealed if
      this representation of the relation of the Estates to the state is compared with Hegel's in
      *Philosophy of Right,* para. 302.
138  Feuerbach, "Preliminary Theses," p. 172.

eign introduces unity from above to a social mass that is otherwise chaotic. Feuerbach's head of state is the hypostatization or manifestation of an immanent process wherein the sovereign people constitute themselves as a unity. Stahl's sovereign is a will *sui generis*. Feuerbach's head of state is a *species subject*, whose will and activity are the emergent will and activity of the people. However, even if the contrast between these transcendental and immanent conceptions of authority is real enough, they meet at the point where both undertake to redeem plurality by unity. In both, this leads to a strong conception of sovereign identity, that of an anointed physical person in Stahl's case; in Feurbach's, that of a *species subject* who is the direct heir of Rousseau's "public person," the artificial person formed by the union of individuals in the commonwealth.[139]

Feuerbach's yearning for a true human society, for an ethical community that overcomes the depoliticization of humanity and the fixation of activity upon private gain, for a virtue that self-consciously directs activity toward the perfection of the species, produced a demand for a transparent, immediate unity of man with man. Whereas Hegel believed that the individual could identify himself with the totality only in a mediated manner, Feuerbach grew impatient with the whole Hegelian project. His impatience expressed a general conviction among the Hegelian Left of the early 1840s that Hegelian philosophy could no longer satisfy the demands of the time. The prevailing mood of conservatism, the apparent success of reaction in political life, and sharpening social tensions seemed to call for more direct and more radical solutions. Where Hegel had envisaged a dialectical unity, Feuerbach began to perceive a debilitating dualism. Indeed he came to see the separation of political life from social activity as an expression of man's real alienation. This suggestion remained cryptic in Feuerbach. It became an article of faith for the young Marx as he worked in 1843 to articulate his own critical stance. But that is a theme for a later chapter.

Rather than emphasize the full extent to which Feuerbach's social and political concerns anticipated those of the young Marx, it is more appropriate to conclude this chapter by underscoring Feuerbach's affinities with the currents of radical thought that we have traced in the 1830s. The parallels between Feuerbach's humanist atheism and the Saint-Simonians' social pantheism, between his sensuousness and their rehabilitation of matter, are strong enough to suggest that Feuerbach shared the Social Romanticism that spread among German progressives in the 1830s. For many young German

---

139  Rousseau, "The Social Contract," in *Social Contract. Essays by Locke, Hume and Rousseau* (Oxford, 1948), p. 257.

intellectuals, Saint-Simonianism suggested a novel way to naturalize their yearnings for religious harmony in the newly discovered continent of social injustice and misery. The influence of the Saint-Simonians introduced an important new social dimension to the German debate between Christian personalists and pantheists. It sharpened the negative association of the idea of personality with civil society; and from the meeting of German and French traditions issued a new pantheism of love that sought to overcome the egoism of Christian personalism and of modern commercial society. This new social pantheism was essentially identical to "socialism," which in that transitional time before "scientific socialism" meant an ethical commitment to the practical consequences of a proper understanding of humanity's collective being. It was a sentimental radicalism, naïve and romantic, but freighted with serious political and social consequences in the repressive world of *vormärz* Germany. This ethereal compound rapidly condensed into more militant calls for action when it met the heavy fronts of political repression and worsening social conditions. The future, Heine proclaimed in 1840, belongs to "steel-clad men."[140] By that time he himself had long since broken off his association with the Saint-Simonians. Evanescent as this style of radicalism may have been, it indelibly stamped the religious, philosophical, and social hopes of Heine, Cieszkowski, Hess, Feuerbach, and many of their progressive German contemporaries.

140   Heine, *Sämtliche Werke,* vol. VI, ed. Ernst Elster (Leipzig/Wien, 1890), p. 536.

# 6

## ARNOLD RUGE: RADICAL DEMOCRACY AND THE POLITICS OF PERSONHOOD, 1838–1843

Reporting on political literature in Germany for the *Revue des deux mondes* in 1844, the French writer René Taillandier complained of the Young Hegelians' "bizarre, half-theological, half-republican speech."[1] Taillandier's dyspeptic description applied particularly well to Arnold Ruge, who viewed himself as undertaking in politics the same kind of critique that Strauss and Feuerbach had pursued in theology.[2] Indeed, as these figures had done in the domain of theology, Ruge set the political agenda of the short-lived Young Hegelian movement. From the death of Eduard Gans in 1839 until the suppression of the *Deutsche Jahrbücher* in 1843, Ruge was inarguably the most prominent progressive Hegelian political writer; but, unlike Gans, Ruge launched a fundamental assault on Hegel's political system. Again in contrast to Gans, the path of Ruge's thinking also led him away from the main tenets of liberalism. More forcefully and clearly than any other Left Hegelian prior to Marx, Ruge marked the departure of the radical Left from liberalism. However, because Ruge was a tireless champion of freedom of the press and representative government, many earlier scholars have chosen to label him a liberal, one of the leading figures of a German "bourgeoisie"

---

1  René Taillandier quoted in A. Schwegler, "Die *Revue des deux mondes* über die Junghegelsche Schule," *Jahrbücher der Gegenwart* (1844), p. 475.
2  Arnold Ruge, "Politik und Philosophie" (1840), *Die Hegelsche Linke,* p. 191.

struggling for emancipation. Assimilated to the German liberal tradition by this view, he has also thereby come to share in its great putative flaw, its trust in power and its willingness to identify freedom with the state. Ruge's idea of the "absolute state" and his support of Bismarck in the last years of his life would seem to place him in the vilified tradition of nineteenth-century German liberals who became idolators of the *Machtstaat* after the failure of the Revolution of 1848.[3]

It is true that Ruge, like many other *vormärz* radicals, frequently identified himself with "liberalism" as the salient movement of opposition against Prussian absolutism.[4] But Ruge was neither statist nor liberal in any unqualified sense. Instead, during the period of his most intense and significant activity, the years from 1838 to 1843 when he edited the *Hallische Jahrbücher* and its successor the *Deutsche Jahrbücher,* Ruge moved toward a more thoroughgoing radicalism that mixed classical democratic republicanism with a collectivist social dimension. This chapter will show how the theologico-political debate over personality in the late 1830s served as a crucial medium for the articulation of Ruge's increasingly radical stance. Given this common rhetorical and ideological context, Ruge's development resembles in many important respects the trajectory that we traced in the preceding two chapters. However, where Feuerbach's sociopolitical commitments remained embedded in his critique of theology and speculative philosophy, Ruge's political thought rested on an explicit formulation of the social and political implications of the theological critique of personality. Ruge's writings were thus like a prism in whose refracted light the theologico-political preoccupations of Strauss and Feuerbach were transmuted into directly political and social terms.

3   The classic statement of this view of German liberalism is found in Leonard Krieger, *The German Idea of Freedom. History of a Political Tradition from the Reformation to 1871* (Chicago, 1957). On Ruge as a "liberal," see Sidney Hook, *From Hegel to Marx* (Ann Arbor, 1962); James Willard Moore, *Arnold Ruge: A Study in Democratic Caesarism* (Ph.D. Diss., University of California, Berkeley, 1977); H. and I. Pepperle, "Einleitung," *Hegelsche Linke*, p. 23; Hans Rosenberg, "Arnold Ruge und die *Hallischen Jahrbücher,*" *Politische Denkströmungen im deutschen Vormärz* (Göttingen, 1972), p. 99; and Herbert Strauß, "Zur Sozial- und ideengeschichtlichen Einordnung Arnold Ruges," *Schweitzer Beiträge zur allgemeine Geschichte,* 12(1954), p. 165.
4   The terminological instabilities in *Vormärz* whereby the distinction between radicals and liberals was frequently obscured by a language of common opposition are traced by Peter Wende in *Radikalismus im Vormärz. Untersuchungen zur politischen Theorie der frühen deutschen Demokratie* (Wiesbaden, 1975), pp. 1–30. See also Wolfgang Eßbach, *Die Junghegelianer,* pp. 184–5.

## Aesthetics and Republicanism

The biographical details of Ruge's early life are now readily available, and it is not my intention to dwell on them.[5] I wish here merely to emphasize certain considerations relevant to our theme. Born in 1802 on the island of Rügen, then a Swedish territory, Ruge as a child experienced the occupation of his island by Napoleon's troops. While still a youth, he secretly committed himself to the "national awakening," the patriotic enthusiasm that flamed into life throughout northeastern Germany in response to the French invasion and occupation. Ruge's patriotic sentiments revived as a young student at Halle and Jena, where he became involved in the *Jünglingsbund*, a conspiratorial wing of the *Burschenschaften*, the German student movement. The *Burschenschaften* had spearheaded resistance to the French during the years of struggle against Napoleon, but their mix of Romantic nationalism and constitutional demands made them a nuisance in the era of Restoration. Consequently, the *Burschenschaften* were outlawed in the Carlsbad Decrees of 1819. For his involvement in the *Jünglingsbund*, Ruge was arrested in 1824 and sentenced to fifteen years in Köpenick prison. He served six years before Friedrich Wilhelm III pardoned him. Ruge later recognized that the *Freiheitskrieg* had been waged not only against Napoleon but also against the French Revolution, the principles of which he never impugned. In the 1840s, he became a trenchant opponent of reactionary German patriotism, and he traced the lineage of anti-French German chauvinism to the youth groups of the 1810s. Nonetheless, even in the late 1830s and 1840s, he continued to find in the enthusiastic sacrifices of the *Freiheitskrieg* an example of active civic virtue that expressed his own ideal of authentic public spirit and political life.[6]

If imprisonment had not cooled his Romantic ardor, undoubtedly other aspects of his background and developing intellectual interests would have sufficed. First, as Ruge tells us in his autobiography, he was reared in an atmosphere of Protestant rationalism. His father and the local pastor on Rügen

5 See especially Moore, *Ruge*; Mah, *End of Philosophy;* and Beatrix Mesmer-Strupp, *Arnold Ruges Plan einer Alliance intellectuelle zwischen Deutschen und Franzosen* (Bern, 1963).
6 This dual image of the *Freiheitskrieg* is clearly expressed in Ruge's 1840 review of Ernst Moritz Arndt's *Erinnerungen aus dem äußeren Leben*. See *Hegelsche Linke*, pp. 172–88. On the variety of myths about the *Freiheitskrieg*, see James Sheehan, *German History*, p. 387; and Christopher Clark, "The Wars of Liberation in Prussian Memory: Reflections on the Memorialization of War in Early Nineteenth-Century Germany," *Journal of Modern History*, 68, 3 (Sept. 1996), pp. 550–76.

were rationalists, and his teacher at the Stralsund *Gymnasium* was a Kantian.[7]
Long before his encounter with Hegelianism, Ruge imbibed the Enlightenment's conviction that religion in its core is compatible with reason, as well
as its distrust of revealed religion as a merely "positive" form of belief. As
Ruge said in 1838, the kernel of the movement of Reformation is the power
of spirit "to establish itself on its own ground and to give itself its own relationship to God."[8] In the nineteenth century, this kind of rationalistic individualism could easily support liberal politics.[9] However, as Hegel had done,
Ruge steered away from the individualistic and subjectivist potentialities
of Protestantism and emphasized instead the possibility that Protestantism
might form the basis of a renewed sense of collective life. As late as 1841,
Ruge upheld Hegel's vision of the secularization of the Protestant idea of
freedom; even after he had accepted the radical anti-theologies of Strauss,
Bauer, and Feuerbach, Ruge continued to believe that the anti-social impulses of Protestantism might be counterbalanced by a "humanized" Protestantism's concern for the ethical life of the collectivity.

The impact of classical studies upon Ruge also weakened whatever at-
tractions Romanticism might have held for him. While at Halle in the early
1820s, Ruge turned to the classics after a brief foray into theological studies. This interest was strengthened at Jena by the personal influence of Heinrich Luden, the scholar of ancient history and philosophy, a political liberal
and popular lecturer.[10] During his imprisonment in Köpenick, Ruge translated Sophocles and Thucydides and studied intently Pericles' speech to the
Athenians. Ruge's fascination with the Greeks placed him firmly in the tradition of German Hellenism, whose idealization of the ancient *polis* had
become a commonplace among German intellectuals by the late 1700s.[11]
Eighteenth-century Hellenism tended to be hostile toward orthodox positive religion, but it stood in a complementary relation to the *Aufklärers'* efforts
to reform Christianity and society. The virtues of the ancients were taken to
counter the narrow chauvinism and pride of Christians, while the image of
free and responsible citizens reinforced the *Aufklärers'* potentially subversive
message of rational freedom and individual responsibility. Indeed, in the

---

7   Moore, *Ruge*, p. 23.
8   Ruge quoted in Mesmer-Strupp, *Ruges Plan*, p. 26.
9   Hans Rosenberg, "Theologischer Rationalismus und Vormärzlicher Vulgärliberalismus,"
    pp. 18–50.
10  See Ralph Marks, *Die Entwicklung nationaler Geschichtsschreibung. Luden und seine Zeit* (Frank-
    furt, 1987). On Ruge's relationship to Luden, see Moore, *Ruge*, pp. 35f.
11  See E. M. Butler, *The Tyranny of Greece Over Germany* (Cambridge, 1935); and Josef Chytry,
    *The Aesthetic State. A Quest in Modern German Thought* (Berkeley, 1989).

wake of the self-conscious appropriation of classical images by French revolutionaries, Restoration authorities correctly feared that classical education
might inspire students with republican ideas.[12]

There was more to this German fascination with Greece than merely an
idealized image of unitary community. As Josef Chytry has recently shown,
German Hellenism centered upon the ideal connection between aesthetic
freedom and political freedom. In this vein, most powerfully expressed in
Schiller's *Letters on the Aesthetic Education of Man*, the artist working on matter in accordance with a form freely conceived by him presents the archetypal image of a freedom that reconciles the individual to the world of sensuous objects and to the world of humanity, the *polis*. In the former, the
creation of beauty proves that "moral freedom is not abrogated by natural
causality"; in the latter, "moral freedom is obedience to a law one prescribes
to oneself, and political freedom is that freedom granted to each individual
of a social whole compatible with the freedom granted the others." Hence,
Schiller wrote that the "most perfect of artworks" is the "construction of genuine political freedom."[13] This "aesthetic" ideal of freedom, which German
intellectuals came to believe had been embodied in the "beautiful" Athenian *polis* of the fifth century B.C., rested on the image of the community of
individuals consciously willing to create the state. It has little to do with liberalism and even less to do with the conservative Romantic image of the personal God or the monarch acting as an artist to create the state as a work of
art. Rather, Schiller stands within an important continuum including the
radical contract theory of Rousseau, Kant, and such neglected nineteenth-
century figures as Arnold Ruge.

The testimony of a friend and admirer of Ruge gives ample evidence of
this continuity. In an 1847 article, Hermann Francke wrote that Ruge combined "Greek aesthetic freedom" and "French political freedom." Francke
recounted how, after his release from prison, Ruge turned to Platonic aesthetics, only to find that Platonism's transcendentalism and quietism could
not satisfy his interest in the human world. He first sought to reconcile the
Forms of the Platonic realm with the real world within aesthetics itself,
Francke tells us, by invoking the "aesthetic view."[14] This is none other than
Schiller's "play impulse," that impulse by which Schiller believed human

---

12    Franz Schnabel, *Deutsche Geschichte im neunzehnten Jahrhundert*, vol. 2 (Freiburg, 1933),
      pp. 360–5.
13    Chytry, *Aesthetic State*, pp. 90, 85, 77.
14    Hermann Francke, "Arnold Ruge und der Humanismus," *Die Epigonen*, 4(1847), pp. 98,
      112–13.

beings could achieve wholeness by balancing in indifference the "formal" condition of personality and the drive toward the sensuous "content" of life. Admittedly, the Young Hegelians of the late 1830s and 1840s celebrated Schiller more for his vivid, restless, and rebellious dramatic characters than for his ideas on aesthetic politics. Moreover, Ruge's insistence on rationality and classical balance restricted his openness to the full legacy of Schiller's aesthetics – namely, the unity of sensuous activity and freedom that came to form one component of Marx's theory of labor. As his criticism of Heine's "frivolity" displays, Ruge's mature writings reveal a preference for overtly political art over aesthetic "playfulness." Still, despite the limitations imposed by Ruge's mix of revolutionary earnestness and bourgeois priggishness, Schiller's ideal reconciliation of beauty and freedom is an essential background for Ruge's own ideal of the free state. Nor did he ever abandon this vision of free citizens, each his own self-determining master yet each participating fully in the political life of the community, or renounce his conviction that the Greeks were the "thoroughly political people."[15]

Thus, there is an essential continuity from Ruge's conspiratorial actions in the early 1820s, to his articles at the time of the French Revolution of 1830 in which he called himself a "republican" and described world history as "an eternal struggle of freedom against usurpation,"[16] to his radical stance in the early 1840s. To be sure, Ruge's classicism and his adherence to Protestant rationalism were modulated in the early 1830s by his reading of Hegel. But we cannot remain deaf to these earlier tones even in Ruge's most committed Hegelian writings. To a greater extent than Feuerbach, Bruno Bauer, or Strauss, each of whom was a youthful acolyte of the Hegelian philosophy, Ruge drew eclectically from the *Aufklärung* and German Idealism. He was a man in his thirties when he first seriously studied Hegel, and he had already read and experienced much that helped to shape his views. This observation suggests some caution in relying too heavily upon conversion imagery to describe the encounter with Hegelianism, that of Ruge and many other young intellectuals of the 1820s and 1830s. Not only does the image of "conversion" immediately privilege the emotive over the rational attraction of Hegel's thought, but it also precludes consideration of the continuing influence of other intellectual traditions.

---

15   On the first point, see *Aus früherer Zeit*, vol. 3 (Berlin, 1863), p. 160. On the second, "Die Hegelsche Rechtsphilosophie und die Politik unsrer Zeit" (1842), *Hegelsche Linke*, p. 444. Even in his memoirs, Ruge still maintained that "We owe everything which is still good and human in the world to the Athenian Republic." Quoted in Moore, *Ruge*, p. 427.
16   Ruge quoted in ibid., p. 54.

## Prussian Loyalty and the Critical Spirit

The most recent work in English to discuss Arnold Ruge, Harold Mah's *The End of Philosophy, The Origin of "Ideology,"* relies heavily upon the process of conversion and disillusionment to explain the collapse of the Young Hegelian movement. Mah argues that Ruge, Bruno Bauer, and Marx each suffered a crisis of faith that forced him to reevaluate his relationship to Hegel and the Prussian state when that state revealed its hostility to philosophy and freedom. In Ruge's case, Mah claims, his conversion to Hegelianism in the early 1830s had made him into a Prussian apologist, for whom the identity of the free philosophical self-consciousness, the Prussian state, and the Protestant faith was "solidly established in the political reality of 1838."[17] In Mah's view, only Ruge's personal disappointment over the failure of Altenstein and the Prussian state to advocate the cause of reason and freedom from 1838 onward, culminating in the suppression of the *Hallische Jahrbücher* in 1841, forced him to renounce his loyalty to Prussia. Without question, the repressive action of the state intensified Ruge's sense of alienation and even prompted him to despair. However, Mah's thesis places the Young Hegelians in a passive, reactive relation to their sociopolitical environment. It neglects the fact that Ruge's early career was marked by a commitment to criticism that predates the most repressive actions of the Prussian state. Furthermore, it does not acknowledge that Young Hegelian radicalism helped to create the political climate even as it was shaped by it.

That is not to say that Ruge was unequivocally opposed to the Prussian state. In fact, his attitude to the state was highly ambivalent. Despite his incarceration by the Prussian state as a youth, he obviously strained to conform to Biedermeier society and sought accommodation with the state, although such efforts must be weighed against the fact that all Prussian academics were dependent upon the state for any professional preferment. Declarations of loyalty to Prussia were frequent in Ruge's essays of 1838 and 1839, and he insisted that he was defending Prussia against reactionaries like Heinrich Leo who aimed to distort its true essence. Leo had emerged in the mid-1830s as a self-styled champion of the Protestant Prussian state against the claims of Prussia's Catholic population, but Ruge associated Leo's Pietistic mysticism and slavish orthodoxy with a graver threat than any posed by Catholicism. This conclusion is revealing, because it derives from Ruge's allegiance to Hegel's optimistic belief in Protestantism as the essential vehicle of the spirit of freedom insofar as Protestantism's religious truth is

17   Mah, *End of Philosophy*, p. 110.

transformed and "secularized" by philosophical comprehension. That view
was to end decisively when Ruge encountered Feuerbach's critical writings,
but in 1838, still committed to the progressivist implications of Hegel's dialectic of Christian secularization, he expressed contempt for Leo's "inverted
interpretation" of the Reformation, which insisted upon the Lutheran's
"obedience to dogma" instead of the "freedom of spirit."[18] In the face of
charges of atheism and radicalism directed at him by Leo and other authors
in the *Evangelische Kirchenzeitung*, Ruge defended the image of Prussia as an
essentially progressive and rational state, an image that had begun with
Hegel's descriptions of the Prussian Reform Era and had become a commonplace among Hegelians.[19]

However sincere his protestations of loyalty might have been, Ruge's efforts to be a "good Prussian" were clearly at odds with other, more disrup-
tive impulses. His youthful participation in the *Burschenschaften* had already
expressed an ambivalent relationship to the status quo, as had his articles in
support of the July Revolution. Even his attempts to curry favor with state officials attest as much to the stifling lack of alternatives for intellectuals in this
period as to a fervent love for the realities of Prussian life. Moreover, even
though Ruge hoped that founding the *Hallische Jahrbücher* with Theodor
Echtermeyer in 1838 would quicken his sluggish academic career, his prospects were hindered largely because of past involvements that had already
made authorities regard him with some suspicion. And the *Jahrbücher* were
from the outset conceived in a critical spirit as an antidote to what Ruge
considered the sorry state of German public discourse, a condition that he
boldly attributed to the "narrow public sphere in Germany."[20] Ruge was al-
luding here to the effects of the Confederation of German States' censorship of political debate, an authority exercised with renewed vigor after the
Revolution of 1830. The *Hallische Jahrbücher* aimed to nurture this repressed
public sphere, but as Ruge recalled in 1845, "direct political critique was
even more dangerous than directly religious, and it had to be avoided in the
beginning."[21]

Ruge initially believed that an eclectic openness would best draw the

18  Ruge, "Gegen Heinrich Leo bei Gelegenheit seines Sendschreibens an Joseph Görres,"
     *GW,* vol. 4, p. 132.
19  Ruge, "Die Denunziation," pp. 76–84.
20  Ruge, "Unsere gelehrte kritische Journalistik," *Blätter für literarische Unterhaltung,* 223–4
     11–12 Aug. (1837), pp. 905–10; and "Gründung und erster Jahrgang der *Hallischen Jahr-
     bücher.* Vorwort zum zweiten Jahrgang" (1839) *GW,* vol. 3, p. 11.
21  Ruge, "Unsre letzten zehn Jahre" (1845), *Sämmtliche Werke,* vol. 6 (Mannheim, 1848),
     p. 79.

"writing" and "reading" public into critical discussion, but from the outset he was open to non-Hegelian philosophical positions in the same way Hegel had been.[22] That is, committed to a progressive view of the dialectical method, Ruge believed that recapitulation of inadequate positions was a necessary preliminary to their *Aufhebung* in a higher truth. The *Jahrbücher* were to provide a forum in which the contradictions of the age could do battle, but this did not imply impartiality, because the journal was charged with achieving the "work of the *Zeitgeist*."[23] As battle lines were drawn more firmly, the *Jahrbücher* abandoned their pretense at eclecticism, and Ruge embraced the challenge of shaping the journal into the organ of an organized Young Hegelian movement. Even before establishing the *Hallische Jahrbücher,* Ruge had already declared his support for what was at that time developing into the "party line" of the Young Hegelians, David Friedrich Strauss's theological critique.[24] Strauss's argument reinforced and confirmed Ruge's insights into the critical political impulses of the Hegelian dialectic. For even in his first readings of Hegel in the early 1830s, Ruge had immediately seen that Hegel's logic was "a two-edged sword which will violently cleave dumb despotism."[25] Inspired by Strauss's example, Ruge now pitted "Spirit, which criticizes all authority," against the authority of the existent, the merely positive.[26] Just as Strauss had argued in his *Streitschriften,* Ruge defended Prussia in 1838 and 1839 only by establishing a certain tension between Prussia's true essence and a political reality that was so amenable to reactionaries that their power was waxing perceptibly in the later 1830s.

Even allowing for Ruge's basic optimism about Prussia in 1838, it is plausible to regard his association of Prussia with the principle of free self-consciousness not as a simple description of "fact" but rather as a rhetorical exhortation to the state to commit itself to progressive reform. The force of this injunction should be coupled with the rhetorical effect of his equally frequent warnings that revolution threatened if the state reneged on its obligation to change. The effects of censorship should also be taken into account when weighing his loyalty to Prussia against his commitment to critique. That said, it would be misguided to argue that Ruge concealed a

---

22   See, for example, Ruge, "Die Denunziation der *Hallischen Jahrbücher*" (1838), *Hegelsche Linke,* p. 78.
23   Ruge, "Gründung und erster Jahrgang der *Hallischen Jahrbücher,*" p. 12. See also "Die Denunziation," p. 78.
24   Ruge, "Strauss und seine Gegner," *Blätter für literarische Unterhaltung,* 9–12 June (1837), pp. 645–57.
25   Ruge, *Aus früherer Zeit,* vol. 3, p. 287.
26   Ruge, "Gegen Heinrich Leo," pp. 133–7.

revolutionary political agenda in 1838. His belief that Prussia shared his interest in rational reform was sincere; but it would be equally misleading to
view him as a Prussian apologist whose faith was broken only when the state
repudiated him. In the face of Prussian repression, the Young Hegelians did
become more strident, but not only because faith in the rationality of the
state became untenable. Rather, as the state grew more intransigent, there
was less and less to gain by moderating their rhetoric and acting as "diplo-
mats," to use one of Ruge's own terms.

### Ruge's Critique of Personalism: From Romanticism to Hegel

The conflict between Ruge's commitments becomes evident when he is
viewed from within the ideological context traced in preceding chapters. In
the politicized debates sparked by Strauss's *Life of Jesus,* progressive Hegelianism had already been reviled as republican and democratic by parties and
individuals who, by the late 1830s, stood in higher favor with the Prussian
royal court than did any Hegelian. Ruge made his support of Strauss widely
known, and he clearly regarded the anti-Hegelian theological debate as
part of a "larger process" that included the conservative campaign against
Hegelian political thought.[27] As Ruge's 1838 articles on Heinrich Leo indicate, he was fully aware of the ready association that reactionaries made between Strauss's critique of divine personality and revolutionary politics. Indeed, all of Ruge's writings during the late 1830s reveal his intent desire to
address directly the political issues thrust into relief by the Strauss controversy.
    Ruge fused his involvement in the theological and political debate with
his earlier aesthetic interests in his first major work, the 1839 manifesto *Der
Protestantismus und die Romantik,* which he co-wrote with Theodor Echtermeyer.[28] In this sustained attack on political reaction, Ruge almost entirely
subordinated aesthetic judgments to politics. The literary Romanticism of
the 1790s and early 1800s concerned him only so far as it shed light on the
reactionary political forces of the 1830s. Like Heine, whose essay "The Romantic School" influenced him, Ruge believed that the gothic tastes of the
Romantics, their nostalgia for the Middle Ages, and their love of sublime
mysteries and shrouded ceremony all bespoke a Catholic sensibility that was
quite at odds with the spiritual independence and simplicity of Protes-

---

27  Ruge, "Unsere gelehrte kritische Journalistik," pp. 905–6. See also Ruge to M. Carriere, 1
    Feb. 1839, *Briefwechsel und Tägeblätter,* ed. P. Nerrlich (Berlin, 1886).
28  Hans Rosenberg claims that their manifesto shaped the "vulgar liberal" interpretation of
    Romanticism for decades. Rosenberg, "Arnold Ruge," p. 111.

tantism. As in his articles on Leo's Pietism, Romanticism's corruption of the Protestant principle of freedom was the real object of Ruge's manifesto.[29] In basic agreement with Hegel's critique of Romanticism in the "Preface" to the *Phenomenology* but sensitized by the politicized debates about personality since 1835, Ruge attributed this distortion of Protestantism to the Romantic fixation on "subjective genius."

Ruge acknowledged that the *Sturm und Drang* poets had revitalized literature with their passionate subjectivity, but he maintained that under the influence of Fichte, the Romantic poets had elevated subjectivity to an "Ich-Kult" that permitted the most unrestrained "arbitrariness." Ruge's point is not dissimilar to Feuerbach's objection to Positive Philosophy. For both Ruge and Feuerbach, the object of criticism is the idea of a self or person whose essence exists outside of its relationship to other humans. According to Ruge, such egoism made the Romantic poets indifferent to the world, leading them into a "Catholic" dualism of spirit and world that accounted for their sentimental sense of alienation and their arrogant disregard for the situation of humanity.[30] In contrast, Ruge defended Hegelian philosophy for its realism and its orientation toward the world. Philosophy unifies, it leads from subjectivity to objectivity, and, most important, it teaches the individual that "his best qualities are not his alone, but are general."[31] In place of the isolated egoism of the Romantics, Ruge defended the ideal of "spiritual democracy" – that is, participation in the creation of a political world in which freedom will be concretely and objectively actualized.[32] The image of the artist that Ruge embraced in this highly politicized view is distinctly Schillerian, for the true artist, having transcended his own egoism, must regard the creation of the free polity as the highest aesthetic act.

In contrast to this ideal of the artist, Romanticism's cult of genius was decidedly undemocratic in Ruge's assessment because its extreme subjectivity located poetic freedom and agency outside the community. He immediately drew out the political implications when he argued that the political analogue to this "spiritual aristocracy" was the personal monarch. The weight

---

29  Ruge and Echtermeyer, *Der Protestantismus und die Romantik* (1839–40), ed. Norbert Ollers (Hildesheim, 1972), p. 2. This work is also published in Walter Jaeschke, ed., *Philosophie und Literatur im Vormärz. Der Streit um die Romantik (1820–1854)*, vol. 2 (Hamburg, 1995).
30  Ibid., p. 6. Ruge extended this criticism to the Young Germans, whom he regarded as a coterie of egoists.
31  Ibid., p. 3.
32  Ibid., p. 23: "This realization can only occur if Germany works through to a free openness in its political relations, if the reformative process moves beyond the subjectivity of feeling and the inwardness of thinking still caught in one-sided theory."

of the intersecting debates about theology and politics was sufficient to lead
Ruge to rebuke Strauss himself for straying too close to the Romantic camp
in the 1838 edition of *The Life of Jesus*. Under pressure from his critics, Strauss
had moderated his original contention that the personal Christ was the
product of the collective consciousness of the Jewish people. Hence, in the
new edition, Strauss portrayed Christ as a genius, just as Schleiermacher had
done in his own *Life of Jesus*. This alteration did not re-divinize Christ, but it
weakened the collectivist impulse of his original 1835 theory. Consequently,
Ruge criticized Strauss for compromising his democratic views with the "aristocratic" idea of genius. From the worship of individual genius, the community could not hope to recognize its own divinity.[33]

At the same time as he wrote the manifesto against Romanticism, Ruge
also moved from the relative safety of aesthetic critique to a sustained campaign against the Prussian government, which, he contended, had betrayed
the rational essence of the state. Ruge had tried to persuade Strauss to write
what he deemed to be a much-needed critique of the Prussian monarchy.
When Strauss refused, Ruge adopted the pseudonym "ein Württemberger"
for the article that he wrote in response to Karl Streckfuß's widely discussed
defense of the personal sovereignty of the Prussian king against constitu-
tionalist demands.[34] Ruge's choice of pseudonyms accomplished several
tasks, protecting him from the censors, expressing approval of Württemberg – not only a Protestant constitutional state that presented an instructive foil to Prussia but also the birthplace of Schiller, Hegel, and Strauss –
and, finally, identifying the author with the line of critique opened by
Strauss.[35] In this critique of Karl Streckfuß's paean to the personal power of
the monarchy, as well as in other articles in 1840 and 1841, Ruge turned his
attention to the social and political effects of an authoritarian regime that
had embraced the "Ich-Kult" of Romantic egoism in the form of the monarchic principle. Following other progressive Hegelians like Gans, Köppen,
and Förster, Ruge criticized a familiar gallery of conservatives – including
Karl Streckfuß, Friedrich Julius Stahl, Schelling, Schubarth, and the Berlin
"old" Hegelians – for adhering to this personalist idea of sovereign power.

Ruge went further, however, when he included Hegel in their ranks. As
we saw in Chapter 4, in 1839 Förster had already suggested that Hegel's po-

---

This paragraph follows Chapin Massey, *Christ Unmasked*, pp. 118–22, 137–40.

34 Karl Streckfuß, *Über die Garantien der preußischen Zustände* (Halle, 1839; first published in
the *Augsburger Allgemeine Zeitung* in 1838).

35 Moore, *Ruge*, p. 128. Adolf Stahr wrote that this article "made an unbelievable sensation.
There was astonishment at the boldness which suddenly dared to say what had been an
open secret." Quoted in ibid., p. 446.

litical thought contained a potentially damaging personalist element, but Ruge more boldly aligned Hegel with the political personalism of the Positive Philosophers. Ruge's first major critique of Hegel's *Rechtsphilosophie* thus represents a significant transformation in the terms of the discourse on Christian personalism. For it is a direct application to Hegel's political philosophy of the criticism of theological personality that had already made Strauss and Feuerbach notorious. Strauss had attacked the Christian doctrine of Incarnation, Feuerbach had attacked the idolatrous belief of some Hegelians in the incarnation of "philosophy as such" in one philosopher, and now Ruge leveled the same critique not only against Hegel's own standing but also against the Prussian conditions that, he believed, Hegel had absolutized as the incarnation of political rationality.[36] Proceeding from what had by then become a familiar left-wing claim that Hegel's disciples were truest to him in overcoming him, Ruge introduced the bold new contention that Prussians were most loyal in seeking to overcome the present state through the creation of a better one. Consistent with this reasoning, Ruge exchanged Hegel's "Absolute" with the new phrase "relative Absolute" to suggest the imperfection of every phenomenon, philosophical or political, and its inevitable supersession in history.[37]

The first major Left Hegelian critique of Hegel's political philosophy followed, as it were, a script already rehearsed in Strauss's critical stance and, equally important, in the arguments that Feuerbach had first expressed as a "Hegelian" critic of the later Schelling and the Positive Philosophers. Just as the process whereby Feuerbach subsequently associated Hegel with his Christian positivist critics was vital to the evolution of Feuerbach's atheistic humanism, a similar assimilation lay at the heart of Ruge's emerging break with Hegel's political philosophy. Although the mental act whereby Hegel was made to share the vice of his own most vigorous enemies may seem questionable to us, it is important to note that Right Hegelians like Göschel had made this elective affinity seem much more convincing to their engaged contemporaries. After all, much to the dismay of a range of observers, from the Young German Ferdinand Gustav Kühne to the Young Hegelians Strauss and Feuerbach, the Right Hegelians had responded to the Strauss controversy by ceding nearly everything to the Christian personalists. Once the

36  Ruge, "Zur Kritik des gegenwärtigen Staats- und Völkerrechts" (1840), *Hegelsche Linke*, p. 152. (The version of this essay published in *Hegelsche Linke* is abridged. Where necessary, the original essay from the *Hallische Jahrbücher* will be cited.)

37  Ibid., p. 154. An interesting discussion of the Left Hegelians' historicization of philosophy is found in Jürgen Habermas, *The Philosophical Discourse of Modernity*, trans. F. G. Lawrence (Cambridge, Mass., 1987), pp. 51–74.

Young Hegelians grew disillusioned with the political conditions that Hegel had allegedly considered absolute, it was relatively easy for them to extend the identification of Hegel and positivism into the domain of political philosophy.

Nowhere is this important process of identification better illustrated than in Ruge's criticism of Hegel's concept of sovereignty. Whereas such anti-Hegelians as Stahl had attacked Hegel for subordinating the personality of the monarch to the logic of the constitutional state, Ruge now accused him of reaching the same result as the "Schellingian Positivists," namely the concentration of all state power in the person of the monarch. For Hegel, as for the Schellingians, the monarch, the natural man, was the "*Staatsperson*" who encompassed the totality of the state in the "immediate unity of his person."[38] Hegel was thus exposed as a "positivist," for he accepted the merely *given* as such. If anything, in Ruge's judgment, Hegel stood condemned of a worse offense than the Positive Philosophers. For the latter sanctioned the given political conditions by appeal to brute *facticity*, while Hegel appeared ready to endorse it with an exculpatory and backward-looking rationality. Ruge asserted that in either case, "positivity" blocked the further development of rational freedom; but Hegel affected to "derive" existing relations such as primogeniture from the logical demands of the Concept, rather than from a concrete, rational analysis of historical processes. Hence, in Ruge's estimation, Hegel had contributed to the decline of the very standard of rationality that he had ostensibly promoted.

Hegel's concessions to the historically given compromised what Ruge regarded as his greatest contribution to political theory, his attempt to establish the sovereignty of the state on the self-determination of the rational human subject. This was the true source of political will in Ruge's view, but he contended that Hegel had mystified the role of self-determination by continuing to insist on personal sovereignty. In contrast, Ruge echoed earlier progressive Hegelians like Gans in arguing that the state should be understood as a mediated totality, which at this point in his thinking meant a constitutional monarchy subordinating the executive to the legislative.[39]

It is evidence of the strong influence of the Young Hegelians' polemical interactions with the Schellingian Positivists that Ruge could consign Hegel to a form of reactionary personalism that Hegel himself had also rejected, while at the same time Ruge could espouse a view of constitutional monarchy that actually seems to differ little from Hegel's. The immediate ideological context may have led Ruge to a tendentious judgment of Hegel, but the quarrel with personalism did sharpen his insight into the undemocratic

---

38  Ruge is here paraphrasing para. 280 of Hegel's *Rechtsphilosophie.* Ruge, "Zur Kritik," p. 163.
39  Ibid., p. 166.

nature of Hegel's political philosophy. Thus, he criticized Hegel for failing to show how the "historical person" of the monarch is determined by the totality of the state and, by extension, how this totality is itself determined by the majority will of the sovereign people. Although Ruge acknowledged that Hegel had assigned the sovereign only minimal duties, he insisted that Hegel's neglect of the democratic basis of sovereign will produced the same effect as Stahl's claim for the transcendent authority of the monarch. Hegel too was guilty of subordinating the collective self-determination of autonomous subjects to an "empty concept," the arbitrary, willful personality of the transcendent sovereign.

Having challenged Stahl's and Hegel's personification of sovereign will, Ruge faced the same temptation as Feuerbach to personify the "people" as the higher source of unitary will. Yet, this temptation was clearly at odds with his general historical sense. On the one hand, he insisted that the will of the majority is never absolute. It may even be mistaken, and it is always corrigible in the future if the process remains dynamic and open-ended. Moreover, he was cautious about universal suffrage, regarding it not as an immediate goal but as a desirable endpoint of a process of broadening political inclusion. Ruge expressed here for the first time his concern for the social question, pointing to the processes that had created a dehumanized class that he deemed incapable of political involvement in its present circumstances. Education, he argued, could correct this and create the conditions for universal suffrage in the future. On the other hand, Ruge believed that education would foster the inherent rationality of the collective and ensure their ultimate infallibility.[40] Later, in 1843, after the German people failed to defend the Young Hegelians against the repressive measures of the Prussian and Saxon governments, he succumbed to the familiar resentments of the radical democrat when a breach opened between his ideal representation of the people and the failure of the real people to recognize their putative rational interests. At that moment, he both despaired of them and dreamed of creating a "new" people.[41]

### The Private and the Public, the Christian and the Humanist

Until the end of 1842, Ruge was reticent about openly declaring a commitment to republicanism. Nor, for that matter, was he unequivocally republican,

---

40  Ibid., pp. 168–71.
41  Ruge to Fleischer, 18 June 1843, *Briefwechsel.* See the comments of Rousseau quoted in Norman Hampson, "The Enlightenment in France," *The Enlightenment in National Context,* ed. Roy Porter and Mikulas Teich (Cambridge, 1981), p. 50.

for his break with Hegel was by no means complete. That said, however, Ruge's attack on the political consequences of Christian personalism centered on a classic republican theme, the tension between private and public life. According to him, the Prussian state's adherence to the principle of personalist monarchy meant that the state operated much like the hierarchy of the Catholic Church. The monarch and his highest aides enjoyed priestlike access to the "absolute state," while the rest of the population were mere "*Staatslaien*" denied any self-conscious insight into the workings of the state and all participation in the "*Staatsleben*."[42] Excluded from the public life of politics, Ruge argued, subjects are restricted to the status of private persons in civil society.[43] The Prussian political system thereby ensures that the people languish in a condition of "tutelage," unable to rise above the egoistical private interests of the marketplace. The legacy of the "absolute police state," Ruge lamented in 1841, was thus a land of *Spiessbürgertum*, a political, apathetic philistinism.[44] While he could praise the Reform Era for attempting to mobilize the people in order to convert them from "*Spiessbürgern* into *Staatsbürgern*," he insisted that the monarchy had since regressed. It was now content to rule over "*Spiessbürgern* and egoists" rather than "republicans and free men."[45] Seeing that the state had failed, Ruge perceived the task of the Young Hegelians to be the emancipation of the Germans from "*Spiessbürgertum*."[46] These concerns suggest that Ruge's political program was not simply a fight for democratic political participation against a despotic monarchy. Rather, in his understanding, the primary goal of Young Hegelian politics was to liberate the citizenry from the narrowness of civil society through the creation of a genuine public life. Ruge's political thought thus explicitly thematized the tension between public and private life that we have already observed in attacks by the likes of Feuerbach, Hess, and Cieszkowski on the theologico-political idea of personality.

Significantly, Ruge did not simply draw a distinction between a privatized civil society and a political state that monopolizes the public interest. Instead, it is important to recognize that Ruge insisted that the same private

---

42 Ruge, "Karl Streckfuß und das Preußentum," *Hegelsche Linke*, pp. 115–16.
43 Hegel's approval of the restriction of citizens ("Bürgers") to civil society led Ruge to criticize the *Philosophy of Right* as a "Prussian Book." See ibid., p. 115.
44 Ruge, "Der preußische Absolutismus und seine Entwickelung" (1841), *GW*, vol. 4, p. 46. For a brief discussion of the history of the word *Spießbürger*, see Warren Breckman, "Diagnosing the 'German Misery': Radicalism and the Problem of National Character, 1830–1848," *Between Reform and Revolution: Studies in the History of German Socialism and Communism from 1840–1990*, ed. D. Barclay and E. D. Weitz (Oxford, 1998).
45 Ruge, "Der preußische Absolutismus," p. 20.
46 Ibid., pp. 48–9.

ethos penetrated *both* Prussian society and the state. That is, he argued, despite the state's claim to embody public life, it was in fact dominated by the same private values as its citizens. By making an empirical person the goal and principle of the state, Romantics, Hallerian Restorationists, Positivists, and even Hegel had ensured that the state could not appear as the expression of a self-conscious community but rather as the private dominion of one man.[47] This "unfortunate private law interpretation, that the state is the domain of the sovereign," contended Ruge, meant that the egoism of the monarch merely confronted the egos of other property owners.[48] In a very revealing claim made in 1845, Ruge insisted that ironically "this State-God, the King, is only the private and acquisitive person (*Privat- und Erwerbsmensch*), but represented as a transcendental essence (*Majestät Divus Augustus*) separated from the common human world."[49] Ruge's remarks demonstrate just how easily left-wing Hegelians moved between a republican critique of personal political sovereignty and a socialized critique of the self-seeking individualism of civil society. We encounter a striking example of the same conceptual overlap in Friedrich Engels's 1847 suggestion that the German "autocrats" must be obliged to say: "*la societé civile, c'est moi.*"[50] In Engels's alteration of the Sun King's famous motto, the sovereign individual of the monarchic state and the sovereign individual of civil society have become virtually identical.

From this vantage point, Ruge could argue that the defect of the "absolute state" is that in fact it is *not* absolute. The current state is a "*res privata,*" whereas the absolute state must be a "*res publica,*" or better still, reasoned Ruge, because the state "is no *res,* no thing, but rather an affair," the absolute state must be synonymous with "public life." As the concern of the "self-determining people," the state should "fill their whole life with its self-consciousness."[51] The absolute state should inculcate an awareness in all citizens of their "ethical autonomy," an autonomy that is based in the recognition of the constituting role of each individual in creating the "public life." The current state, however, appears as a "merely external union with merely worldly goals"; it is a mere guarantee for "external life and comfort."[52] In other words, Ruge

47  Ibid., p. 125.
48  Ruge, "Der schöne Journalismus und die Tagesfragen" (1841), *GW,* vol. 4, p. 279.
49  Ruge, "Unsere letzten zehn Jahre" (1845), *GW,* vol. 6, p. 62. See also Ruge, "Vorwort zur Verständigung der Deutschen und Franzosen, von einem deutschen Publizisten in der Fremde," in Louis Blanc, *Geschichte der zehn Jahre, 1830 bis 1840,* trans. G. Fink (Zürich, 1843), p. xxiv.
50  Engels, "German Socialism in Verse and Prose," *Collected Works,* vol. 6, p. 253.
51  Ruge, "Vorwort zum Jahrgang 1841 der *Hallischen Jahrbücher,*" *Hegelsche Linke,* p. 204, and "Karl Streckfuß," pp. 120–1.
52  Ibid., pp. 124, 126.

judged the Prussian state in both theory and practice to be merely a "state of civil society." Ruge was here employing the distinction between the "absolute state" and the "state of civil society" developed by Hegel in the *Philosophy of Right*. For Hegel, the absolute state is the concrete embodiment of *Sittlichkeit*, whereas the "state of civil society" is essentially nothing more than the guarantor of the order of individual intercourse in the market; in other words, such a state never rises above civil society but is rather the administrative-juridical organization of civil society. This was, according to Hegel, the paradigmatic understanding of the state in liberal contract theory.

It is one of the most significant and counterintuitive features of the ideological context of the 1830s and 1840s that the Young Hegelians saw in Restorationist political theory the same implications as those contained in liberal theory. The conflation of what we would typically regard as two utterly distinct political paradigms – on the one hand, a liberal tradition based on individualism, and, on the other, a reactionary tradition based on neofeudalism and authoritarianism – was possible because of the Left Hegelians' identification of orthodox Protestantism with egoism. Indeed, in the first instance, their criticisms of "individualist" society were articulated, paradoxically, as criticisms of conservative political Romanticism. We have seen that this slippage between liberal individualism and Protestant personalism was a common feature of the nascent Left in both Germany and France. It is an important element in Saint-Simonianism and in German writers like Cieszkowski and Hess, while Feuerbach's critique of Friedrich Julius Stahl rested on the association of authoritarian Christian personalism with individualistic civil society. During these fluid years in the history of leftist social criticism, *aristocratic* individualism, *theistic* individualism, and *bourgeois* or *acquisitive* individualism all overlapped. Hence, given this convergence of various forms of "individualism," Arnold Ruge could charge that the egoistical autonomy envisioned by conservative Romantics would require the situation of "Robinson Crusoe," whereas in subsequent years, Crusoe was to serve German leftists as the archetype of liberal bourgeois man.[53] The next chapter will show that even Marx did not distinguish clearly between these various individualisms until mid-1843, when he turned his critical attention self-consciously to liberalism; but even then, earlier ambiguities continued to have an important influence on the young Marx's emerging critique of individualism.

Ruge maintained that, being a mere "state of civil society," Prussia could

---

53  Ruge "Der preußische Absolutismus," p. 56.

not truly express the "unity of a differentiated totality."[54] It could not, in Ruge's Hegelian language, lead the citizen to "God" – that is, to consciousness of the incarnation of spirit in the community. Ruge thus applied concretely to politics a general insight at which Feuerbach had arrived in the mid-1830s: The monarchic principle of the "Christian state" actually desacralized communal life by locating authority in transcendent personality.[55] We would miss a vital dimension of Ruge's politics if we failed to recognize that until mid-1841, when Ruge fully abandoned Hegel's idea of the secularization of the Protestant principle under the influence of Feuerbach's *Essence of Christianity*, his political aim was to bring his readers to consciousness of the *sacral* dimension of political community. Occasionally, he used eschatological language to invoke the image of a future kingdom of God on earth. More frequently, he spoke of the need for Protestants to be true Christians in the state, or in other words, the need for the state – if it is to be a state of freedom – to channel the truth of religion into its own "inner life."[56]

Of course, this was not at all the same as the conservative desire to maintain the clerical hierarchy, the authority of doctrine, or the privileges of the official state church. Consistent with Strauss and Feuerbach's substitution of *Logos*, or universal Reason, for the old transcendent divinity, Ruge argued as early as 1839 that the true form of religion is the immanent principle of Reason as it is manifested in human community.[57] As the highest expression of community, the state thereby achieves a potentially "divine" status, if divinity is conceived in the sense of an incarnation of Reason. Hence, the state, understood in this collectivist way, is the true "image of God."[58] This view of the state dovetailed perfectly with Ruge's support for the critique of personalist theology launched by Strauss, Feuerbach, and, later, Bruno Bauer. For Ruge believed that once Protestant subjects recognized that the truth of religion lies in philosophical reason, the state could itself absorb their religious impulses; by that, he meant that the principle of spiritual freedom, which had been the most revolutionary and liberating discovery of Protestantism, could

54 Ibid., p. 57.
55 The same thematic constellation is evident in Bruno Bauer's critique of Stahl, written at Ruge's urging. See Bruno Bauer, "Der christliche Staat und unsere Zeit" (1841), *Feldzüge der reinen Kritik*, ed. Hans-Martin Sass (Frankfurt, 1968), p. 17.
56 Ruge, "Über Gegenwart und Zukunft der Hauptmächte Europa's" (1840), *GW*, vol. 3, p. 381; Ruge, "Die Hegelsche Rechtsphilosophie und die Politik unsrer Zeit" (1842), *Hegelsche Linke*, pp. 467–8.
57 Ruge, "Der Pietismus und die Jesuiten" (1839), *GW*, vol. 4, p. 212.
58 Ruge, "Karl Streckfuß," p. 126; and "Zur Kritik des gegenwärtigen Staats- und Völkerrechts," *Hallische Jahrbücher*, 155 (Juni, 1840), p. 1237.

be translated from its excessively inward pietistic form into an external political and social form.[59] Freedom itself could then become the "religion" of the "political" person.[60] Just as Feuerbach had argued that "Protestantism naturally leads to political republicanism once its religious content has disappeared," Ruge hoped that the characteristics that he reviled in the Christian and Romantic might be transmuted into those of civic activism. "*Gemüt*," a Christian and Romantic fixation on personal temperament, would become "*Tapferkeit*," a mental state of courage.[61] The "virtue" of the Christian, an otherworldly, passive, and private quality, would become "public virtue." In short, the Christian bourgeois would be transformed into a citizen.

Ruge emphasized that the "religion" of politics carried with it active responsibilities. "The more worthy the person is," Ruge wrote, "the more duties will he accept, the more duties, the more freedom, right and enjoyment of freedom."[62] Ruge's politics sound least "liberal" at this point, where the absorption of religion by the state entails the fusion of freedom and duty. Nonetheless, it would be anachronistic to associate him with a totalitarian idea of politics, as Jürgen Gebhardt has done for the politics of the Hegelians as a whole.[63] Certainly, Ruge was unwilling to accept Hegel's argument that civil society, with its ethos of private interests, constituted a legitimate sphere of individualism. Like Feuerbach or Marx, he desired to overcome the dualism between society and the state, private and public life, through the "politicization of all humanity."[64] However, his goal was equally the "humanization of the state." And this would require the active participation of the citizenry, both to achieve freedom, if necessary through revolution, and to sustain it through the vigilance arising from their acute sense of ethical autonomy. Therefore, Ruge believed that political rights are not "natural" but are rather "*Bildungsrechte*," the fruits of a civic education gained through

59  See the excellent article by James A. Massey, "The Hegelians, the Pietists, and the Nature of Religion," *Journal of Religion* (1978), pp. 108–29.

60  Ruge, "Vorwort zum Jahrgang 1841 der Hallischen Jahrbücher," p. 205.

61  See Ruge, "Hegelsche Rechtsphilosophie," and "Die Presse und die Freiheit," *Anekdota zur neuesten deutschen Philosophie und Publicistik* (Zürich, 1843), p. 111. On the ambiguities of the word *Gemüt* in the late eighteenth century, see Dickey, *Hegel*, p. 224. Significantly, Hegel chose to use *Tapferkeit* over *Gemüt* in his 1802 essay "Natural Law." Dickey suggests that Hegel might have been influenced by Christian Garve's translation of Aristotle's *Ethics*, where *Tapferkeit* signified "the reflective sense of courage that is a unique characteristic of human political association."

62  Ruge, "Karl Streckfuß," p. 126.

63  Gebhardt, *Politik und Eschatologie*. Gebhardt's analysis is clearly influenced by J. L. Talmon's polemic against all forms of communitarianism in *Origins of Totalitarian Democracy* (New York, 1969).

64  Ruge, "Unsre letzten zehn Jahre," p. 63. See also p. 95.

struggle.[65] This was neither "liberal" nor did it express the idea of the *Rechts-staat*, that view of the state as an abstract "juristic person" bearing rights and duties as defined by public law.

Rather, Ruge presents us with an example of the continuing influence in the nineteenth century of the classic republican tradition, which regarded freedoms as actively won and measured the integrity of public institutions by their effects on the civic virtues upon whose strength the preservation of those freedoms depended.[66] Yet, in common with Feuerbach or the young Marx, Ruge embraced a radicalized Rousseauian version of that republican tradition, which stressed the reconciliation of individual freedom and the community through the act of will by which the individual prescribes law to himself. For Ruge, this was the only conception of freedom commensurate with the development of full moral and civic personality. In other words, only republicanism could adequately realize the original conception of concrete personality that Hegel himself had first offered up as an antidote to the truncated egoistical personality embraced by Romanticism and subjectivistic Protestantism.

Concrete personality, Ruge suggested, had best been actualized in the ancient Greek *polis*. However, this idealization of an integrated "total" life was in tension with other rationalistic, cosmopolitan ideas he held. He never envisioned a Rousseauian "civil religion" aimed at arousing loyalty and virtue in the citizenry of a republic. Ruge's "political religion" implied only the translation of the spiritual freedom of the Protestant into a "secular" political form. The rational recognition of freedom, he believed, would in itself inspire political "pathos" without the need for ritual.[67] Moreover, his belief in the universality of Reason made him a bitter opponent of narrow

65   Ruge expressed this view as early as 1831 in articles supporting the revolution in Paris. See Mesmer-Strupp, *Ruges Plan*, pp. 16–17.
66   The classic work on the republican tradition is J.G.A. Pocock's *The Machiavellian Moment. Florentine Political Thought and the Atlantic Republican Tradition* (Princeton, 1975). Certainly the model of civic humanism that Pocock develops for seventeenth- and eighteenth-century England and Scotland cannot be simply transposed onto Germany, but recent research suggests that in part through the reception of English and Scottish republican writings by eighteenth-century German writers and in part by Germans' exposure to the classical tradition itself, the civic humanist tradition found such prominent proponents as Schiller, Christian Garve, and the young Hegel. In addition to Dickey, *Hegel;* and Chytry, *Aesthetic State,* see Oz-Salzberger, *Translating the Enlightenment;* and Waszek, *Scottish Enlightenment and Hegel's Account of "Civil Society."*
67   It is wrong, therefore, to equate Ruge's appropriation of religion with Rousseau's, as Wende does in *Radikalismus im Vormärz,* p. 176. Rousseau lacked the philosophical means by which to move from religion *per se* to its *Aufhebung,* whereas Ruge's view was predicated precisely on this Hegelian move.

chauvinism and nationalism. Hence, he rejected the Romantics' organic conception of the state, siding instead with the cosmopolitan impulses of the German Enlightenment. Patriotism he accepted only when its aim was to protect a free republic against despotism.[68] Furthermore, like Feuerbach, he qualified his enthusiasm for the ancient city-state. In an 1841 essay, he judged the "old republics" inadequate because they had only special interests that did not extend beyond the city walls, while he criticized the *agora* – the marketplace and "public sphere" of the ancient city-state – because the "eye and ear" do not reach far enough to achieve anything other than unity within the restricted confines of the "city-commune."[69] Ruge challenged a long tradition of civic humanist speculation when he claimed it was not only "corruption" that had led to the collapse of the republics and the emergence of the Roman Empire but also a laudable evolution of consciousness toward universality and cosmopolitanism. Nonetheless, even as he acknowledged gains in modern processes of centralization and state building, he did not unequivocally celebrate the modern state-form. Ultimately, he warned, centralization and the greater abstraction of public life in a large state impede the development of political spirit among citizens, a threat to freedom that can be avoided only if citizens "internalize" and undertake the task of creating a republic.[70]

Ruge sought to retain the positive gains of political modernity – the modern principle of individual freedom and the rational state of rights – but to

---

68  Ruge's most extensive commentary on this issue is found in his tract *Der Patriotismus*, ed. Peter Wende (Frankfurt, 1968). Ruge rejected standing armies as incompatible with freedom and believed that a national citizen militia fostered the spirit of freedom. See Ruge, "A Self-Critique of Liberalism" (1843), *The Young Hegelians. An Anthology*, ed. Lawrence Stepelevich (Cambridge, 1983), p. 258.

69  Ruge's concept of the public sphere, central as it was to his fight for political freedom, was not synonymous with a liberal demand for freedom of the press, nor is it easily reconciled with Jürgen Habermas's understanding of the classic bourgeois "public sphere." Ruge identified the authentic press as the literal incarnation of the "public" conceived as general spirit. In this process by which humanity (the "Gattung") objectifies itself, "accidents" are overcome through the "judgment of publicity," and many voices gradually become one voice. See "Die Presse und die Freiheit," pp. 96–8. This vision weakens the idea of the public sphere as a "neutral" conceptual and institutional space in which the conditions of freedom are established consensually through dialogue and the arts of persuasion. As with his general views on the rationality of the voting public, Ruge's conception of the public sphere contained conflicting impulses toward, on the one hand, an open contestation for truth and, on the other, a rationality that is always already given by the Concept. In this sense, Mah's remark (*End of Philosophy*, p. 259) about the similarity of Ruge and Habermas's idea of the public sphere requires considerable qualification.

70  Ruge, "Zur Charakteristik Savigny's" (1841), *GW*, vol. 4, pp. 231–3. See also "Der preußische Absolutismus und seine Entwickelung," p. 57.

invigorate them with the public spirit of ancient Greece. One might expect that this commitment to public, activist virtues would lead Ruge to denigrate the activities of civil society, which he held partly responsible for the political tutelage in which the majority of Germans remained. Significantly, however, that was not the course he took. Instead, he followed the same conceptual trail as other opponents of the theological and political effects of Christian personalism, because by embracing an immanent conception of human essence, Ruge could no more elevate one dimension of human social activity than could Feuerbach or Heine. Ruge thereby represents a particularly clear example of the important transitional moment when democratic republicanism became permeated with social concerns. Deeply influenced by Aristotle's ancient distinction between *polis* and *oikos*, earlier civic humanists and republicans, including Rousseau, privileged a normative domain of public political discourse and action, while they essentially regarded the economic sphere solely as a source of corrupt private values. By contrast, Ruge attempted to incorporate civil society's productive activities within the community of spirit. Once people recognized the immanent universality of spirit in the community, he maintained, they would realize that not only politics *per se* but "also the life of civil society and the individual represent the work of spirit."[71] Hence, the self-conscious citizen would set aside the egoism of the "natural man" and commit himself freely to the community of spirit.[72] Ruge tapped a rich vein in German Idealism here, for the distinction between a world bound by necessity and one legislated by humanity's conscious will was a governing concept of the political philosophies of Kant, Schiller, Fichte, and Hegel. Not surprisingly, as John Toews notes, all the Young Hegelians shared the Idealist view that nature gains its true reality only when it is "incorporated into the world of human culture as a self-determination of spirit."[73]

Ruge clearly considered industry to be an integral part of this transition from "nature" to "spirit." The inner task of the state, he wrote, consists in the "mastery of nature and the liberation of spirit."[74] "With or without the steam engine, spirit has the task ever more to subject nature, the rawness of land and people, to itself. Industry has no other sense than the work of spirit overall."[75]

---

71 Ruge, "Zur Kritik des gegenwärtigen Staats- und Völkerrechts," *Hallische Jahrbücher*, p. 1238.
72 Ruge, "Zur Kritik des gegenwärtigen Staats- und Völkerrechts," *Hegelsche Linke*, p. 171.
73 Toews, *Hegelianism*, p. 326.
74 Ruge, "Zur Kritik des gegenwärtigen Staats- und Völkerrechts," *Hallische Jahrbücher*, p. 1238.
75 Ruge, "Errinerungen aus dem äußeren Leben, von Ernst Moritz Arndt" (1840), *Hegelsche Linke*, pp. 183–4. See also "Über Gegenwart und Zukunft der Hauptmächte Europa's," p. 352.

The persistent strains of Idealism are evident in this conception of the relationship of spirit to nature. Evident also is the defect of an Idealist conception of freedom wherein spirit gains autonomy only by dominating nature, by reclaiming it as spirit's domain. We may also note that Ruge's new appreciation for the power of modern technology to extend the project of spirit foreshadowed Marx's own productivist bias and his problematic view of the relationship between nature and human emancipation.

Ruge's association of industry with spirit led him to praise money over barter as a more universal form of trade, the bourgeoisie over the "substantial" agricultural estate, and the commercial economy over the old corporatist guild economy. It should be obvious that these preferences did not make Ruge a straightforward spokesman of the "rising bourgeoisie," as some commentators have claimed. He advocated commerce and free trade not because they generated prosperity or enshrined liberty, but rather because they held greater promise of extending the domain of spirit over the material sphere. Ruge thus endorsed the dynamism of modern civil society, which dissolves all old corporate estate barriers, but he immediately assimilated the individualistic potential of this new personal mobility into a more collectivist social conception of humanity:

> What is now the estate (Stand), the determination, the differentiation by which the human determines himself? It is a difference of work, and work is either in nature or in spirit; but whoever stands outside this labor in idleness or vegetating pleasure is part of the *Pöbel*, not of an estate, whether he commands a million Thaler or a million lice; if humanity is spirit, only the working spirit is real.[76]

Idealist as this association of industry with the overcoming of nature may be, it also recalls the Saint-Simonian division of society into two classes, the productive and the idle. Ruge was critical of the Saint-Simonians' main followers in Germany, the Young Germans, for their "frivolity" and feminist views, and he made no mention of the Saint-Simonians until he actually traveled to Paris. Still, it is possible to detect in Ruge's comments on industry a Saint-Simonian provenance, especially if we consider Thomas Petermann's argument that by the early 1840s, the influence of Saint-Simonianism in Germany was no longer direct but rather mixed with other elements.[77] The Saint-Simonian belief that industry must be directed toward public, rational goals instead of egoistical "anarchic" ends is not dissimilar to Ruge's views

76 Ruge, "Errinerungen," p. 186.
77 Petermann, *Der Saint-Simonismus in Deutschland*, p. 95.

in 1840. Moreover, the Saint-Simonians' spiritualization of worldly human activities, the "sanctification of work," parallels Ruge's vision of the convergence of material and spiritual pursuits. Undoubtedly, Ruge always remained more political than the Saint-Simonians, who were the first writers to propose the now familiar idea that under socialism politics would become administration. The difference is evident in Ruge's insistence that the plight of the impoverished *Pöbel,* which he noted had emerged only in the previous thirty-five years, "will only be overcome through democracy, the courageous [*tapfere*] realization of the state *as the public essence.*"[78]

The important point is that Ruge incorporated industrial activity into spirit, conceived as the true content of public life. Hence, economic activity, which liberals, Hegel, and the political Romantics had all consigned to the private lives of citizens, became for Ruge a *res publica.* Economy became inseparable from polity. In 1840, Ruge called for an active public virtue demanding the action of citizens in the economic sphere and enjoining them to actualize spirit equally in "politics" and "economics." By the mid-1840s, this convergence of political republicanism and social concern would lead Ruge to advocate public ownership of the means of production. Ruge's rejection of the general distinction between economics and politics also led him to the point where he could essentially jettison Hegel's distinction between civil society and the state. In place of the dualistic perception of humans performing in their capacities as "men" and "citizens," Ruge insisted on a continuum of human effort toward a freedom that must be at once "spiritual, social, and political."[79] Or, as he was to put this idea in 1863, essentially unchanged despite the apparent Marxian influence, "The difficulty lies in constituting the state of bourgeois [civil] society, based on need, as a state based on freedom, making of the substructure a superstructure, that is, making it the only structure."[80]

Ruge's political thought up to 1842 pursued two aims: to invigorate civil society with public political spirit, on the one hand, and to spiritualize sensuousness, on the other. In Ruge's own development and in the broader history of radical thought during these years, these were aims pursued on converging paths. Even before the period of Ruge's explicit engagement with French and German socialist thinkers, he had already begun to incorporate

78  Ruge, "Errinerungen," p. 186.
79  Ruge, "Über Gegenwart und Zukunft der Hauptmächte Europa's" (1840), *GW,* vol. 3, p. 374. See also "Errinerungen," p. 183.
80  Ruge, *Aus früherer Zeit,* vol. 4, pp. 105f. Löwith quotes this passage at length in *From Hegel to Nietszche,* pp. 212–13.

the social question into his thought.[81] The emancipation of the *Spiessbürger* was thus for him inseparable from the emancipation of the *Pöbel*. In Ruge's philosophical republicanism, participatory politics and work were to be equal partners in the creation of the republic of spirit.

## Ruge's Humanist Republicanism

Ruge's writings during 1840 and 1841 articulated themes that continued to dominate his political thought in the ensuing years. His subsequent development represents successive attempts to adapt his basic premises to new sociopolitical conditions and, even more important, to new intellectual influences. If Ruge's writings from 1840 to 1843 display a fundamental thematic continuity, however, the worsening climate of political reaction in Prussia ensured that these themes were expressed with ever-increasing vigor. With good reason, Ruge charged that the forces of reaction were actively hunting down the Young Hegelians. Ruge had been outraged when, in 1839, residents of Zürich prevented David Friedrich Strauss from accepting a professorship there, but he had regarded this as an isolated insurrection of Pietists against reason and philosophy.[82] He was much less confident about the attitude of the government and the established academic world when the theology faculty at Bonn moved to dismiss Bruno Bauer because of his atheistic writings.[83] Not only did the Prussian government fail to protect Bauer, but Friedrich Wilhelm IV's recently appointed minister of Education, Eichhorn, resolved to drive Bauer out of the university after reading the first volume of his *Critique of the Synoptic Gospels* in June 1841. Bauer was not dismissed until March 1842, but through much of 1841, the conflict in Bonn was a *cause célèbre* for the Hegelian Left. This was true in part because Bauer himself was determined not to compromise and in part because Ruge devoted the pages of the *Jahrbücher* to Bauer's "affair." Throughout 1841 and part of 1842, Ruge labored in defense of Bauer, first against the Bonn theology faculty and then against the Prussian government.[84]

Ruge's attention was distracted by more immediate concerns, however, when the *Hallische Jahrbücher* itself fell victim to the aggressive cultural poli-

81  Indeed, in his actions as an elected city councillor in Halle in 1838, Ruge had worked to enact reforms to counter the poverty that he found there. See Moore, *Ruge*, p. 123.
82  Ruge, "Die gute Revolution" (1840), *GW*, vol. 4, p. 215.
83  Ruge, "Die Politik des Christen K.H. Sack in Bonn. Eine Polemik gegen diesen Apologeten" (1841), *GW*, vol. 3, p. 194.
84  Moore, *Ruge*, p. 153. See also Bauer's letter to his brother Edgar, 10 March 1841, *Briefwechsel zwischen Bruno Bauer und Edgar Bauer während der Jahre 1839–1842 aus Bonn und Berlin* (Charlottenberg, 1844).

tics of the new regime. Following a March 1841 Cabinet order that the journal transfer its office from Leipzig to Halle, where it was to be submitted to
the censor, Ruge instead moved his operation to Dresden in Saxony. The re-
named *Deutsche Jahrbücher* appeared on July 1; the new name signaled not
only the physical move but also the repudiation of Prussia in favor of the
larger German world. As is well known, however, "Germany" did not prove
much more hospitable. Under pressure from Prussia, Saxon censors ha-
rassed the *Deutsche Jahrbücher,* and throughout 1842, the relationship between
the journal and the authorities worsened. Finally in January 1843, Saxony
suppressed the *Deutsche Jahrbücher* at the same time that Prussia closed Marx's
*Rheinische Zeitung.* The experience of Prussian repression and the deterio-
rating relationship with Saxony worked to crush any lingering hopes that
Ruge had held for Prussia and constitutional monarchy. Though he sometimes hoped unrealistically that, despite its actions to the contrary, Prussia
might still follow a progressive path, the general tenor of his writings in 1842
expressed his hostility to the regime. He now opposed monarchy *per se,*
openly espoused republicanism, and criticized German liberals for continuing to believe in the reconcilability of Christian monarchy and political
freedom. What is more, the indifference of Germans to the repressive actions of their governments against the free press made Ruge despair that the
Germans could ever be anything more than a nation of *Spiessbürger.*

Ruge frequently warned that reaction begets revolution. Certainly, the relationship between the Young Hegelians and the Prussian state confirmed
this prophecy. However, the political context cannot entirely account for the
appearance of a number of fundamental Young Hegelian works on religion
in 1841. Intense personal contacts, regular correspondence, and the chan-
neling of so much critical debate into the *Jahrbücher* all ensured a hothouse
atmosphere and an increasingly extreme tone in the movement. Early in the
year, Strauss's *Christian Dogma in Its Historical Development and in Conflict with
Modern Science* appeared. It was almost immediately overshadowed by Feuerbach's *Essence of Christianity,* published in June. Between June and October
came the first two volumes of Bauer's *Critique of the Synoptic Gospels,* which
was, among other things, highly critical of Strauss, as well as Bauer's *Trumpet of the Last Judgement Against Hegel the Atheist and Antichrist.* The critique of
religion shifted with such speed in 1841 that by November, Strauss felt himself so maligned by the journal he had helped to found that he refused to
contribute further to the *Deutsche Jahrbücher.*[85] Strauss's defection marked a
parting of the ways for radical and moderate Young Hegelians. The *Deutsche*

---

85   See Strauss to Vischer, 13 November and 5 December 1841, *Briefwechsel zwischen Strauss
und Vischer,* ed. Adolf Rapp (Stuttgart, 1952).

*Jahrbücher* lost many collaborators and readers;[86] henceforth it grew increasingly marginal even as it grew more vociferous.

During the first months of 1841, Bruno Bauer's philosophy of self-consciousness enjoyed the zenith of its brief influence within the Young Hegelian movement. Significantly, as Ruge and Feuerbach had already done in their criticisms of Hegel, Bauer attacked his chief rival on the Hegelian Left, Strauss, by arguing that he had gravitated toward the Positive Philosophers.[87] Bauer based this surprising accusation on Strauss's reliance upon a mystical substance, the mythic collective consciousness of the community, in order to explain the genesis of the New Testament. The idea of collective consciousness, according to Bauer, is as alienating as the orthodox idea of revelation, for in both cases a transcendent explanation of Scripture conceals its true origin in human self-consciousness. In contrast, Bauer tried to show that the Synoptic Gospels were, in both form and content, the products of individual authors responding freely and pragmatically to the needs of their age. In this critical undertaking, Bauer was motivated by the more ambitious philosophical project of redeeming the "positive" by exposing it not as a mere "given and naked reality" but as the objectified creation of self-consciousness.[88] Self-consciousness is thus revealed as the "only power of the world and history."[89] True to the basic form of Hegel's philosophy of history, Bauer insisted that self-consciousness is not arbitrary, for it develops in a succession of antithetical stages toward recognition of its agency in history. Because Bauer believed that this stage had been reached in his time, he concluded that the self-consciousness of the critic, namely himself, was identical to the movement of history itself. His work declared the triumphant freedom of the critic from all external constraints, and he claimed the power of criticism to dissolve all merely given phenomena, chief among which, we must note, is "personality."[90] In *The Trumpet of the Last Judgement Against Hegel the Atheist and Antichrist,* he brilliantly adopted the persona of an anti-Hegelian Pietist to argue that Hegel was in truth a revolutionary philosopher of self-consciousness. Hence, he argued that "personality, real-

86   Andre Spies, "Towards a Prosopography of Young Hegelians," *German Studies Review,* XIX, 2(May 1996), p. 332.
87   Bruno Bauer, *Kritik der evangelischen Geschichte der Synoptiker,* vol. 1 (Leipzig, 1841), pp. viii–x.
88   Ibid., p. xv.
89   Bauer, *The Trumpet of the Last Judgement Against Hegel the Atheist and Antichrist* (1841), trans. Lawrence Stepelevich (Berkeley, 1989), p. 115.
90   Personality, along with its foundational incarnation in the God-Man, was to be overcome through its sublation into the "universal essence of self-consciousness" (*The Trumpet,* pp. 193–200).

ity and everything positive can in fact be gobbled up and consumed by the Hegelian idea."[91] Bauer thus tried to legitimize his own position by anointing himself Hegel's authentic successor. In truth, however, Bauer had come to share as much with the monistic subjective Idealism of J. G. Fichte as with Hegel.[92]

The "terrorism of reason" that Bauer announced in 1841 eventuated by 1844 in the idea of "pure criticism," a concept that proved so sterile as to ensure almost universal defection from the Bauerian camp, including Bauer himself by 1848.[93] But in 1841, it was a call to battle. Late in 1840, Ruge met Bauer personally and judged his work superior to Strauss's. Strauss, Ruge wrote in 1845, still advocated an "*allpersönliche Gott*," which was an intelligent universal being; not only did the idea of God remain as such, but also the idea of humanity remained abstract.[94] In contrast, Bauer had revealed the origins of the Gospels in human creativity, thereby exposing the role of human activity in history. Thus, Ruge concluded, despite Bauer's theoretical and esoteric preoccupations, his appreciation of the role of human agency gave the Young Hegelian movement a practical turn.[95]

Persuaded of the fruitfulness of Bauer's approach, Ruge swiftly adapted Bauer's terms to his own concerns. Bauer's influence is evident in the strident claim with which Ruge prefaced the first issue of the *Jahrbücher* in 1841: "the awakening to self-consciousness characterizes our age."[96] Similarly, opening the *Deutsche Jahrbücher* in July, he argued for a "new Idealism" comprising Fichte's self-determining "I" and Hegel's historicized interpretation of the development of this "intelligence": this would produce a "true *monism of spirit,* in that it rests on the insight that the process of history cannot be separated from the process of self-consciousness."[97] Further, Bauer's hostility to organized religion led Ruge to see religion and philosophy in more oppositional terms than he had before, although this was mitigated by his continuing belief that philosophy had originated in the "true principle of Christianity" – namely, Christianity's intuitive grasp of the incarnate divinity of

91  Ibid., p. 67.
92  See Zwi Rosen, *Bruno Bauer and Karl Marx: The Influence of Bruno Bauer on Marx's Thought* (The Hague, 1977), p. 82.
93  The key article is Bauer's "Was ist jetzt der Gegenstand der Kritik?" *Allgemeine Literatur-Zeitung,* vol. 8, 1844. See Marx's sarcastic comment in a letter to Feuerbach, 11 August 1844, *Collected Works,* vol. 3, p. 356: "It seems that Bauer has fought against *Christ* out of rivalry."
94  Ruge, "Unsere letzten zehn Jahre," p. 43.
95  Ibid., pp. 50f.
96  Ruge, "Vorwort zum Jahrgang 1841 der *Hallischen Jahrbücher,*" p. 200.
97  Ruge, "Vorwort zum Jahrgang 1841 der *Deutschen Jahrbücher,*" *Hegelsche Linke,* p. 227.

mankind.[98] Finally, though already an adept polemicist, Ruge took a leaf
from Bauer's combative rhetoric, particularly his strategy of wielding his
claim to possess the authentic interpretation of Hegel like a club with which
to beat the "old Hegelians."

Bauer's influence on Ruge was, nonetheless, short-lived and relatively superficial. By late 1842, Ruge had denounced what he considered to be the
self-indulgence, frivolity, and solipsism of Bauer and his Berlin circle, "The
Free."[99] During the time of their collaboration, moreover, it is in fact possible that the influence was reciprocal, at least on political questions. In 1840,
after Ruge's article "Karl Streckfuß," Bauer too launched a critique of the
present "Christian state" as a spiritless, merely coercive external *"Anstalt,"*[100]
and, like Ruge, he came to associate the Christian state with civil society.[101]
It was at Ruge's behest that Bauer undertook a critique of F. J. Stahl in "The
Christian State and Our Time." The themes of that and other essays by
Bauer echo concerns that Ruge had already expressed with great insistence – the distinction between the "government" and the essence of the
"state,"[102] the condemnation of the political cowardice of the German people, the demand for a genuine "public sphere" and public life, the contrast
between the conception of work held by the "businessman" and that held
by the self-conscious,[103] and the desire to emancipate the "bourgeois helots"
from the narrowness of their apolitical lives.[104]

Ruge never fully abandoned Bauer's tenets, but Feuerbach's *Essence of
Christianity* influenced him far more profoundly. Ruge's contacts with Feuerbach were deep and longstanding. He had corresponded with Feuerbach
regularly for several years, and he had also acted as something of a middle-
man between Feuerbach and his Leipzig publisher, Otto Wigand. Moreover,
not only did Feuerbach publish some of his most important essays in the
pages of Ruge's journal, but Ruge also assisted in the editing of *The Essence*

98   Ibid., p. 234.
99   See Ruge to Prutz, 18 November 1842, and to Fleischer, 12 December 1842, *Briefwech-
     sel.* The most comprehensive treatment of the radical Berlin Hegelians is R. J. Hellman,
     *Die Freien: The Young Hegelians of Berlin and the Religious Politics of 1840 Prussia* (Ph.D. Diss.,
     Columbia University, 1976).
100  Bruno Bauer, *Die evangelische Landeskirche Preußens und die Wissenschaft* (Leipzig, 1840),
     p. 104. See also his "Der christliche Staat," p. 17.
101  See, in particular, Bruno Bauer, *The Jewish Problem* (1843), trans. Helen Lederer (Cincin-
     nati, 1958), pp. 58–9.
102  Bauer, "Der christliche Staat," p. 19.
103  Bauer, "Die gute Sache der Freiheit und meine eigene Angelegenheit" (1842), *Hegelsche
     Linke*, p. 511.
104  Bauer, "Der christliche Staat," p. 33.

*of Christianity.*[105] A mere month after its publication, he included an approving discussion of the book's thesis in his introduction to the new *Deutsche Jahrbücher.*[106] And in 1845, he judged it the most important German philosophical work in his time. Ruge maintained that its significance lay in the fact that Feuerbach had not limited himself to an inquiry into the origins of early Christianity and its sacred texts, as Bauer had, nor to Strauss's efforts to determine the scientific worth of dogma. Rather, Ruge emphasized, Feuerbach had exposed the origin of Christianity, indeed of religion generally, in real human needs and aspirations.[107]

There was yet another reason why Ruge preferred Feuerbach over Bauer. Whereas Bauer's condemnation of Christianity was total, Feuerbach's was qualified. Bauer believed that man's subordination to his own religious fantasies dehumanizes him totally, reduces him to an animal. To overcome absolute alienation, in Bauer's unyielding verdict, the free self-consciousness must break with religion "absolutely."[108] Feuerbach, by contrast, though hostile to abstract theology, regarded the religious impulse as an essentially worthy expression of love. The task, as he saw it, was to transfer this misplaced love to mankind, an undertaking that Bauer categorically rejected.[109] Feuerbach's emphasis upon love as the unifying force in human life and his efforts to "sanctify" the community through the exposure of the anthropological truth of religion appealed more directly to Ruge, who continued to view the desire for freedom as the true expression of religious pathos.[110]

Ruge recognized the practical implications of Feuerbach's *Essence of Christianity* immediately upon reading the book.[111] In his major essays of 1842, Ruge translated his political views into the language of Feuerbach's new philosophical anthropology. Most significantly, Feuerbach's theory of alienation gave Ruge a new and more sophisticated explanation for the separation of the people from politics. Ruge's 1839 article on Karl Streckfuß had associated Protestantism with freedom and blamed the authoritarian tendencies of the Prussian state on the incursion of conservative "Catholic" Romanticism. This view was explicitly renounced in his 1842 essay "The Christian State." Now he condemned Christianity itself, and Protestantism in

---

105  See Ruge's correspondence with Feuerbach in *Feuerbach. Briefwechsel,* vol. 2.
106  Ruge, "Vorwort zum Jahrgang 1841 der *Deutschen Jahrbücher,*" p. 232.
107  Ruge, "Unsere letzten zehn Jahre," pp. 57–8.
108  See Bauer's letter to Ruge in 1841 quoted in Rosen, *Bruno Bauer and Karl Marx,* p. 50.
109  Ibid., p. 101.
110  See, for example, Ruge, "Die Hegelsche Rechtsphilosophie und die Politik unsrer Zeit" (1842), *Hegelsche Linke,* p. 468, and "A Self-critique of Liberalism," p. 249.
111  Ruge to Feuerbach, 14 December 1841, *Feuerbach. Briefwechsel,* vol. 2.

particular, for being antithetical to political freedom, because in Feuerbachean terms, it alienates humanity from its essence. Hence, for Ruge, the
Christian subject experiences the state as a transcendent entity, with the universal or general as such fixed in the alienated form of a personal *"Staats-
Gott."*[112] We shall see in the next chapter that Marx's Feuerbachian critique
of the Christian state followed along strikingly similar lines. As Eduard Gans
had done in his 1839 response to K. E. Schubarth, Ruge also attacked the
ideology of the Christian state by associating it with religion's "representa-
tional" mode of consciousness. Hence, he denounced the Christian monarchy's personalized representation of the political spirit of the community as
an extension of Christianity's illusory representation of the "divine Person."
Under the dual influence of Feuerbach and Bauer, he viewed the represen-
tational consciousness of Christian political theology as an instance of the
habit of abstraction that he believed to be the fundament of Christianity.

Ruge followed other earlier left-wing critics, including, of course, Feuerbach, when he proceeded to claim that Protestantism is even more perni-
ciously abstract than Catholicism, because it had made the earthly kingdom
a matter of indifference to the believer by driving a wedge between the
church and the state, which in medieval Christendom had been parts of an
indivisible godly kingdom.[113] The Protestant Reformation was thus assigned
blame for what Ruge, along with many German radicals, considered to be
the de-politicization of the German national character.[114] Seeing no connection between himself and the state, the Protestant turned to his private
affairs. "Outside political life," Ruge wrote, "there are no free people, only
resigned Christians."[115] From being a Hegelian defender of Protestantism's
philosophical truth against the incursions of Catholic irrationality and authoritarianism, Ruge had rapidly come to accept the left-wing condemnation of Protestantism's anti-social and anti-political individualism.

Ruge developed more fully and explicitly two aspects of Feuerbach's account. He extended Feuerbach's analysis of the political effect of Protestantism's distorted and incomplete secularization process, and he built on
Feuerbach's identification of the Christian believer, with his faith in the per-

---

112   Ruge, "Der christliche Staat. Gegen den Wirtemberger über das Preußenthum," *GW*,
vol. 3, pp. 455f. In an 1843 letter to Saxon authorities appealing the decision to close
the *Deutsche Jahrbücher*, Ruge emphasized that in using the term "Staats-Gott" he was simply borrowing directly from the restorationist language of the age. See Ruge, *Polemische
Briefe* (Mannheim, 1847), p. 182.
113   Ruge, "Der christliche Staat," p. 464.
114   Ibid., p. 461. See also Breckman, "Diagnosing the 'German Misery.'"
115   "Der christliche Staat," p. 475.

sonal God and in his own immortality, as the apolitical and acquisitive *Spiess-bürger*. Like Feuerbach, Ruge argued that the Christian's belief in personal immortality fed his egoism, but he was even more adamant than Feuerbach in emphasizing the role of belief in reconciling the Christian to a "bad reality."[116] Protestantism became for Ruge synonymous with the private, and that was true not only for subjects but also for the state itself. Hence, in his view, the Protestant state "is merely the state of need. It concerns the citizen only insofar as it protects him. The people are solely concerned with their private affairs, and religion attends only to subjective private needs (*Privatgemütsbedürfnisse*), to the bliss of the single soul, to the well-being of the private subject in the beyond. Religion no longer concerns itself with a common life."[117] Within the Protestant state, the subjects could at best exercise private virtues, "morality." They could not rise to public virtue, or as Ruge put it, the "ethical life of citizens."[118]

This general critique of the Protestant Christian state animated the second of Ruge's major articles on Hegel's political philosophy, as well as his denunciation of German liberalism. Many of the themes of his 1840 criticism of Hegel were repeated in "The Hegelian Philosophy of Right and the Politics of Our Time." He added a substantial new element, however, when he attempted to explain both Hegel and Kant by developing what amounted to a sociology of knowledge that accounted for their political quietism and philosophical abstractness by reference to the social and political conditions of Germany. Ruge contended that, when faced by a hostile state and an indifferent public, both Kant and Hegel retreated from politics to a position of Protestant inwardness and "narrowmindedness." He judged Kant to be the philosopher of the *Spiessbürger*, a thinker who had praised private virtues over public, counseled political quietism in the name of freedom of conscience, and portrayed the philosopher himself as a mere "private person."[119] Kant, despite his insistence on critical reason and autonomy, had thus fallen prey to the private ethos of Protestant personalism. Yet in Ruge's harsh assessment, Hegel outdid even Kant's abstraction by subordinating history to the one-sided theoretical standpoint of philosophy.[120] Consequently, for Hegel, the theoretical development of freedom obviated the need to realize freedom concretely and indeed compensated for the absence of political freedom. Even at this late stage in Ruge's defection from Hegelian political

116   Ibid., pp. 463, 460.
117   Ruge, "Die Hegelsche Rechtsphilosophie und die Politik unsrer Zeit," p. 471.
118   Ibid., pp. 454–5. The original reads the "Sittlichkeit des Staatsbürgers."
119   Ibid., p. 455.    120   Ibid., p. 458.

philosophy, he still maintained that Hegel had withheld a more radical critique of the patriarchal and bureaucratic state because of the unfriendly climate of his "unpolitical" time.[121] Nonetheless, his sense of the urgent need to translate Hegel's theoretical insights into political *praxis* fully aligns him with progressive Hegelians who, from at least Cieszkowski's *Prolegomena* and Feuerbach's "Towards a Critique of Hegel's Philosophy" onward, had upbraided the master for his abstract one-sidedness.

In Ruge's view, Kant and Hegel suffered the weaknesses of Protestant culture in their time, and in his own age, Ruge insisted in 1843, German liberals were the heirs of these defects. In 1841, Ruge had equated "liberalism" literally with "the emancipation of *Spiessbürgertum*" from the narrowness of private life.[122] By 1843, however, the kind of alliance that Hegelians like himself or Eduard Gans had maintained with German liberals grew less and less possible for radicals who sought to abolish the division between political and civil life. When liberals seemed willing to compromise with repressive German monarchies, left-wing radicals began to suspect liberalism of indifference toward the form of the state so long as it guaranteed the security of the private sphere.[123] Ruge brought this conflict between the liberal core of the so-called *Bewegungspartei* and its leftist fringe into sharp focus in his "Self-Critique of Liberalism," the essay that finally led the Saxon government to yield to Prussian pressures to ban the *Deutsche Jahrbücher*. Significantly, in this piece, Ruge did not seek the roots of liberalism's indifference to public life in the general nature of liberal ideology as it had developed in western Europe. Rather, he denounced liberalism as a product of the "old moralistic Spirit of Protestantism, the empty good will." This "free-thinking mood, this sympathy with democracy 'in intention,'" Ruge wrote, must yield to revolutionary *praxis*. A robust public life must replace the anemic privacy that German liberalism served only to enhance. In a slogan that inflamed the Saxon authorities, Ruge demanded that "Liberalism be dissolved into Democratism."[124]

Ruge's criticism of German liberalism helped to crystallize the disaffection of left-wing Hegelians from their erstwhile allies in the *Bewegungspartei*. In late 1842, for example, Bruno Bauer's younger brother Edgar assailed the western European "juste-milieu" and liberalism in numerous articles for

121  Ruge, "Die Hegelsche Rechtsphilosophie," p. 448.
122  Ruge, "Der preußische Absolutismus," pp. 48–9.
123  See, for example, Edgar Bauer, *Die liberalen Bestrebungen in Deutschland. Volume I: Die Irrthümer der Ostpreußischen Opposition* (Zürich und Winterthur, 1843), p. 26; and [Edgar Bauer], *Staat, Religion und Partei* (Leipzig, 1843), pp. 9–10.
124  Ruge, "A Self-critique of Liberalism," p. 259.

the *Rheinische Zeitung* and in his books *Die liberalen Bestrebungen in Deutschland* and *Der Streit der Kritik mit Kirche und Staat.* The latter work, published in 1844, devotes several chapters to criticizing the *"spießbürgerliche"* consciousness of Germany and repeatedly contrasts liberalism to Rousseauian-style democratic republicanism. Like Ruge, Edgar Bauer traced liberalism's private apolitical values to its provenance in Protestant beliefs about the primacy of spiritual freedom and the inviolable sanctity of the atomized person.[125] This was the time, too, when the young Marx criticized liberalism on similar grounds.

In associating liberalism with Protestantism, Ruge, Bauer, and Marx followed the familiar pattern that reached as far back as Catholic counterrevolutionaries like Joseph de Maistre and ran through the Saint-Simonians, Feuerbach, Hess, and Cieszkowski. Far from weakening with time, this association had strengthened. In Left Hegelian writings of the early 1840s, this theologizing mode of critique became central to the radical assault on liberalism. Hence, Edgar Bauer's *Streit der Kritik* denounced as "theological" any politics short of the radical overthrow of all existing social relations, including the state form itself, while in 1843, Moses Hess traced a direct line from Christianity's collapse into spiritual subjectivism to liberalism's "abstract rights of man or the equal right of the abstract personality, the reflected 'I,' the mathematical point."[126] The process of "theologizing" liberalism reached its consummation in Marx's writings in mid-1843; but that is a theme for the next chapter.

In this vein, having denounced liberalism's compromised constitutionalism and its tolerance of the monarchy as manifestations of Protestantism, Ruge insisted that only the self-conscious sovereignty of the people is compatible with freedom. Just as Feuerbach's critique dissolves the illusion of the personal God into recognition of the sanctity of humanity, Ruge argued, the illusion of the personal sovereign dissolves into popular sovereignty once such abstractions are recognized as human projections. He claimed that both the republicanism of the French Revolution of 1789 and the popular mobilization of the *Freiheitskrieg* represented the return of alienated consciousness from an abstract political heaven to recognition of the immanent majesty of the community. However, the Revolution had been

125  See Bauer's comments on "theological liberalism" in "Der Streit der Kritik mit Kirche und Staat" *Hegelsche Linke,* pp. 657–60.
126  Bauer, "Der Streit der Kritik mit Kirche und Staat," p. 628; Hess, "Philosophy of the Act," *Socialist Thought. A Documentary History,* ed. Albert Fried and Ronald Sanders (New York, 1964), pp. 260–1.

crushed, and the "patriotic-political religiosity" of the German Liberation had subsequently relapsed into the private religiosity of "old Christianity." Thus, Ruge predicted that the apolitical Germans would be mobilized again only when criticism exposed the illusory nature of all abstractions and revealed the state as the people's own "product."[127] In Ruge's thinking, Feuerbachian humanism became synonymous with true public life, the very antithesis of Protestant privacy. The unity of quasi-religious and political moments in Ruge's humanist republicanism was perfectly expressed in his adoption of a cardinal maxim of early democratic theory: "The people's voice is the voice of God."[128]

The 1845 edition of Stahl's *Philosophy of Right in Historical Perspective* claimed that given Hegel's own devaluation of personality, the republicanism of his younger disciples was not at all surprising.[129] Arnold Ruge provides perhaps the most graphic example of the connection between theological criticism and the development of a uniquely Left Hegelian form of democratic republicanism. Before the suppression of the *Deutsche Jahrbücher* in the aftermath of the publication of his "Self-critique of Liberalism," Ruge played a crucial role in shaping the politics of the Hegelian Left. From 1838 onward, he showed great acuity in recognizing the political implications of the theological debates provoked by the likes of Strauss and Feuerbach, and he displayed equally striking originality in articulating those implications in the realm of political theory. In his works, the associations in Young Hegelian thought between the Christian idea of personhood, the egoistical sphere of civil society, and the authoritarian state emerged with unprecedented clarity. With greater emphasis than Feuerbach, Ruge linked the critique of the authoritarian doctrine of sovereignty to the critique of civil society. Again, like Feuerbach, he placed his hopes for emancipation in the possibility of overcoming the dualism of civil society and the state, economics and politics, private and public. For Ruge, by the early 1840s, the integration of social and political power had become the only path to the full realization of human essence in its true universal expression; and this goal was inseparable from, indeed predicated upon, overcoming the atomized form of personhood that had been the target of repeated attack from the philosophical Left during the 1830s. Against this philosophical and anti-theological background, Ruge forcefully articulated the convergence of dem-

127   Ruge, "Der christliche Staat," p. 466.
128   Ruge, "Die Presse und die Freiheit," *Anekdota zur neuesten deutschen Philosophie und Publicistik* (Zürich, 1843), p. 96.
129   Stahl, *Die Philosophie des Rechts nach geschichtlicher Ansicht*, vol. 2, 2nd ed., p. 5.

ocratic republicanism and social radicalism, arguably one of the central phenomena in the transformation of radical German political and social theory
in the watershed years of the early 1840s.

Ruge's social republicanism thereby vindicated many of the worst fears of
conservatives like Schelling, Stahl, and Schubarth when they had first attacked Hegel for his panlogical philosophy and later descried the political
meaning of Strauss's attack on the personal God. However, along with his
claim about the origins of Young Hegelian republicanism, Stahl also insisted
in 1845 that Hegel's idea of property bore responsibility for the development of communism in Germany.[130] In both Hegel's thought and in communism, Stahl argued, the "magic of unity," the personality, is destroyed by
the dialectic. In a similar vein, Lorenz von Stein described communism as
the "negation of the single personality in the material world," and he foresaw a more volatile form of socialism in Germany than in France because of
the power of the Hegelian dialectic.[131] Ruge did not fully bear out this part
of Stahl or Stein's prediction, because he ended up an opponent of communism; nor, it must be emphasized, did the development of communist
theory in Germany unfold from Hegel's alleged pantheism in this automatic
way. Nonetheless, as we turn to Karl Marx, it will be evident just how vital the
theological, political, and social conflicts over the idea of personality were
to his development.

---

130  Stahl, *Philosophie des Rechts*, 2nd. ed., vol. 2, pt. 1, p. 80. For an effort to reconcile the
     Hegelian association of personality and property with the new French social thought, see
     H. W. Kaiser, *Die Persönlichkeit des Eigenthums in Bezug auf den Socialismus und Communismus
     in heutigen Frankreich* (Bremen, 1843).
131  Lorenz von Stein, "Blicke auf den Socialismus und Communismus in Deutschland, und
     ihre Zukunft," *Deutsche Vierteljahrsschrift*, 2(1844), esp. pp. 12 and 59.

# 7

## KARL MARX:
## FROM SOCIAL REPUBLICANISM
## TO COMMUNISM

"Political democracy is Christian since in it man, not merely one man, but every man, ranks as *sovereign,* as the highest being, but it is man in his un-civilised, unsocial form, man in his fortuitous existence, man just as he is, man as he has been corrupted by the whole organisation of our society."[1] Read against the background of our discussion, these famous lines from Marx's "On the Jewish Question" are strikingly resonant. Arguably Marx's first great work of social and political critique, "On the Jewish Question" contains all the sociopolitical elements of the radical Hegelian critique of personalism: the association of Christianity with egoism, egoism with per-sonalist sovereignty, personalist sovereignty with civil society. Familiar as the essay's rhetoric, themes, and conceptual configuration are, however, the object of critique has apparently shifted. For the target of Marx's attack is no longer Christian personalism or the restorationist theory of monarchic sovereignty but rather political modernity in the form of liberal democracy and its concept of individual autonomy. We have already seen that a num-ber of radical Hegelians turned against liberalism in the period 1840 to 1843. In Marx's specific case, the critique of liberalism marked a crucial turning point in his development and in the history of political thought. Nonetheless, vital questions about this pivotal period in the emergence of Marxian socialism still lack satisfying answers. How did the transition from

1 Marx, "On the Jewish Question," *Collected Works*, vol. 3, p. 159.

the critique of theologico-political conceptions of personality to the critique of liberal selfhood occur? How is it that Marx came to denounce not only individualist egoism but also the individual rights and liberties that were the fruits of the modern political revolution? What does it mean to call these rights and liberties "Christian"?

The attempt to answer these questions about Marx's early development must be guided by two assumptions. First, much is lost to our understanding if we overlook the profound affinity between the radical Hegelian critique of Restoration Christian personalism and Marx's critique of "political democracy." Second, much remains obscure if we assume that the *object* of Marx's critique – liberalism – was simply given, and if we assume, by extension, that the terms of his critique were merely derived from that object. Rather, what follows will show that "liberalism" as an object of radical criticism emerged from Marx's prior engagement with the constellation of issues stemming from the Left Hegelians' resistance to the political theology that had come to dominate Prussian political discourse in the early 1840s. How this transition from political theology to liberalism occurred and its effects on Marx's thought during these formative years will be the central concerns of this final chapter.

## Marx's Dissertation: Atomism and the Theological Intellect

In November 1837, Marx wrote at length to his father detailing his first year of studies since he had transferred from the University of Bonn to the University of Berlin. In a tone that was both assertive and supplicatory, the nineteen-year-old Marx revealed his decision not to follow his father in a legal career but to pursue philosophical study instead. Having as an early adolescent moved from an enthusiasm for Romantic poetry to a commitment to his father's brand of Kantian-Fichtian Idealism, he now chronicled the collapse of this filial attachment and his delivery into the "arms of the enemy," the Berlin Hegelians.[2] Donald Kelley has correctly emphasized that this intellectual crisis and conversion were precipitated by Marx's critical engagement with the issues of early-nineteenth-century German jurisprudence.[3] For it was in the course of a precocious attempt to frame a comprehensive philosophy of law that the "very young" Marx recognized the

2 On the strained relationship between Marx and his father, see Jerrold Seigel, *Marx's Fate. The Shape of a Life* (Princeton, 1978), esp. pp. 38–64.
3 Donald Kelley, "The Metaphysics of Law: An Essay on the Very Young Marx," *American Historical Review*, 83 (1978), pp. 350–67.

"serious defect" of Idealism, its characteristic "opposition between what is and what ought to be."[4] As Marx tried to develop a "metaphysics of law" along Kantian lines, Kant and Fichte's separation of normative legal concepts from positive law began to look more and more like a species of "mathematical dogmatism." Marx took from this failed undertaking a new determination to form his concepts as the "concrete expression of a living world of ideas" – in short, to seek "the idea in reality itself."[5] In the 1830s, particularly for a student in Berlin, a resolution like this led almost inevitably to Hegel. Imagining himself as Odysseus, Marx described to his father how his own failure to compose an alternative to Hegel's "craggy melody" had proved to be a "false siren" that finally lured him to Hegelianism.

Marx implied that Hegel's "grotesque" tone had bruised his tender poetic ear, a response not uncommon to young students upon first reading Hegel; but beyond that, Marx's letter does not indicate the reasons for his initial resistance to Hegel. We will see presently that from the outset of his career as a Hegelian, Marx, like Feuerbach or Gans, maintained a critical stance toward the Master. What must be emphasized here is the fact that Marx's letter reveals his relation to the personality debate even at this early date. Having outlined for his father his disaffection for Kantian legal philosophy, Marx went on to describe his attempt to examine "the development of ideas in positive Roman law." This part of his project took him from the purview of Kantian Idealism to that of the Historical School of Law. This was already familiar ground for Marx, traversed during his two semesters at Bonn, where his law professors had all been adherents of the Historical School. This was even more true in Berlin, where Eduard Gans was the only notable exception in a law faculty dominated by Savigny and his followers.[6] Marx's choice of courses in his first year at Berlin thrust him into the center of the controversy that divided the law faculty. For along with Savigny's lectures on the Pandects in the winter semester of 1836–7, he also took Eduard Gans's course on criminal law and, in the summer term of 1838, his lectures on Prussian civil law. Along with these official contacts with Gans, Marx also frequented the Doctors' Club, the gathering of Berlin progressive Hegelians of which Gans was perhaps the most prominent member.

Gans's impact on his young student may be measured by the fact that Marx wholly laid claim to his teacher's objections against both Kantianism and the

4  Karl Marx to his father, November 10[-11, 1837], *CW*, vol. 1, p. 12.
5  Ibid., pp. 12 and 18.
6  Hermann Klenner, "Hegel und die Götterdammerung des Absolutismus," *Deutsche Rechtsphilosophie im 19. Jahrhundert. Essays* (Berlin, 1991), p. 157.

Historical School. Exactly like Gans, Marx argued for mediations between philosophical norm and historical fact, between the "form" and "content" of law. In a manner fashioned on Gans, Marx rejected his own earlier attempts to treat these two separately, "as if positive law in its conceptual development . . . could ever be something different from the formation of the concept of law. . . ."[7] Marx went on to tell his father that when he read Savigny's *Das Recht des Besitzes,* he had discovered that he shared this error with the great historical legal scholar. Without mentioning Gans, Marx had thereby resolutely sided with him in his controversy with Savigny. Significantly, Marx abandoned his precocious attempt at a comprehensive philosophy of law, having reached the end of a section on "material private law" – that is, the laws of "persons," of "things," and "of persons in relation to property." As he told his father, he could no longer force "the Roman concepts" – the facts of possession, use, and disposal, as Savigny had derived them from his historical study of Roman law – into the Kantian "system" that he had tried to construct. The immanent development of the concept of law, the historical dialectic of Gans's legal philosophy, now appeared to Marx as the only path out of the impasse posed by the confrontation of legal facts and legal norms. This conclusion implied a commitment on Marx's part to his teacher's philosophical and historical study of the evolution of property law within its concrete social context in preference to Savigny's emphasis on the facts of individual possession and disposal. So Marx's youthful crisis, though it touched all aspects of his intellectual and emotional life, first took the concrete form of a direct response to the prominent conflict between his two greatest teachers in Berlin, who were at that very time at the height of their dispute over the relation of persons to property.

The trajectory that carried Marx from teenage Romanticism to Kantian Idealism to Hegelianism was fairly typical of many young German intellectuals in the 1820s and 1830s, yet it must be emphasized that Marx came to Hegelianism when it was already in the process of dissolution. His reception of Hegel was influenced from the outset by critical Hegelians like Gans and his closest friends within the Doctors' Club, Rutenberg and Köppen. By the time Marx set to work earnestly assimilating Hegel's writings, the tension between the closed Hegelian system and the open-ended dialectical method had become a standard theme in the writings of prominent figures like Gans, Karl Ludwig Michelet, and Feuerbach; the controversy over Strauss's *Life of Jesus* was well under way; the split between left, right, and center Hegelianism had already been described by Strauss; and the defection of the right-wing Hegelians to Positive Philosophy had been duly noted by Strauss and Feuerbach. By 1839, when Marx began work on a dissertation on ancient Greek atomism, Cieszkowski had published his call for a practical realization of philosophy, Feuerbach had written his critique of Positive Philosophy and Hegel's speculative philosophy, and Bruno Bauer, who became Marx's teacher and friend in that year, had already begun to shift from orthodox Hegelianism to the philosophy of self-consciousness. A very active figure among the progressive Hegelians in Berlin until his departure in the summer of 1841, Marx would have been aware of all these currents within Hegelianism.

No specific post-Hegelian thinker exerted a singular influence upon Marx's dissertation, *The Difference Between the Democritean and Epicurean Philosophy of Nature;* but the doctoral treatise that he submitted to the University of Jena early in 1841 stood at the confluence of various streams of radical Hegelianism at the end of the 1830s. Thus, Marx's first Hegelian work already presupposed the need to break loose from the "fetters" of Hegelianism as a "particular system," and he was already committed to the conception of critical philosophy as a world-transforming "practical energy."[8] The dissertation on Democritus and Epicurus united this commitment to the radical Hegelians' attempt to transform philosophy into practice with a sophisticated and original philosophical intervention in the polemical struggles between the Young Hegelians and their reactionary philosophical opponents.

Indeed, although the dissertation treated ancient philosophy, it was fully animated by Marx's sense of the philosophical needs of the present. In common with other radical Hegelians at the end of the 1830s, Marx traced these needs to the perceived failure of Hegel's doctrine to meet its professed goals. Marx had been initially drawn to Hegel by the promise of a philosophical reconciliation between the ideal and the actual, subjectivity and objectivity, thought and being. In his 1837 letter to his father, Marx appeared to stand with moderate Hegelians who sought an accommodation between philosophy and existing reality. Whether Marx concealed from his father a more critical judgment of the relationship between the rational and the real cannot be guessed, but over the next three years, he arrived at the conclusion that Hegel had failed to achieve a genuine synthesis of thought and being in the present. Like the most radical Hegelians, Marx translated Hegel's vision of reconciliation into a goal to be attained in the future, and he

8 Marx, "Difference Between the Democritean and Epicurean Philosophy of Nature," *CW,* vol. 1, pp. 85–6.

thereby reconceived Hegel's retrospective orientation as a future-oriented philosophy of practice. The conviction that Hegel had failed to fulfill his philosophic goals, the effects of this failure upon the contemporary philosophical situation, and the prospects for a reconciliation of philosophy and reality in the future were the compelling concerns behind Marx's discussion of ancient Greek atomism.

Believing, like Cieszkowski and Feuerbach, that Hegel had attained a one-sided and abstract reconciliation of thought and being, Marx argued that as a consequence, "philosophy has sealed itself off to form a consummate, total world." In such an era, when a philosophy that has grown "total in itself" confronts a world that now appears divorced from spirit, thought turns toward the "subjective forms of individual consciousness in which it has life."[9] Marx contended that the separation of philosophy from the world in the wake of Hegel's philosophy had produced a split within philosophy itself between two bitterly opposed trends. On one side stood "the liberal party," the Young Hegelians, intent on liberating the "world from un-philosophy." On the other side was "Positive Philosophy," which perceived an inadequacy "immanent in philosophy" and sought to supplement philosophy's lack by returning to the "*non-concept, the moment of reality.*"[10] The liberal party attempted to turn outward from the concept to practice and the realization of the idea in the world; Positive Philosophy, and presumably the orthodox Hegelians who had fallen to the dark gravity of unmediated being, tried to move from a nonphilosophical ground to philosophy.

Sharply as Marx drew the line between the Young Hegelians and the Positive Philosophers, he argued that they both offered subjective forms of philosophy defined by the evident fact that "when the universal sun has gone down, the moth seeks the lamplight of the private individual."[11] This inner affinity between the Young Hegelians' philosophy of self-consciousness and the Positive Philosophy – or, better, between philosophy and unphilosophy in the aftermath of Hegel's total philosophy – explains Marx's interest in the subjective forms of Greek philosophy in the period after the great systems of Plato and Aristotle. In a short preface that Marx wrote for the dissertation in 1841, he identified the Epicureans as the "philosophers of self-consciousness." Although this clearly marked their association with the Young Hegelians, the dissertation was in fact largely concerned with the contrast between ancient and modern philosophies of self-consciousness. Whereas the ancient philosophy ultimately fell into fatal contradictions, Marx claimed to detect in

9 Marx, "Notebooks on Epicurean Philosophy," *CW,* vol. 1, p. 491.
10 "Difference," p. 86.    11 "Notebooks," p. 492.

the modern philosophy of self-consciousness a vital potential for development beyond the subjective form that thought had taken in the post-
Hegelian period. By tracing out the ancient contradictions of Epicurean
philosophy, Marx clearly meant to warn his own age of the perils of subjectivist philosophy.

Commentators have tended to overlook the critical dimension of Marx's
study of Epicurus. By contrast, Marx's apparent identification with the radical side of Epicurean atomism has received much attention and may be sum-
marized easily. Marx's presentation of Epicurus challenged a very old tradition of interpretation by insisting that Epicurus was not merely an epigone
of the atomist Democritus but had added a radical new element to Democritean physics. Whereas Democritus had imagined atoms as rigidly determined in their movement, Epicurus insisted on the possibility of undetermined motion, the "swerve" or "declination" that Marx made the keystone
of his discussion. In conceiving the possibility of undetermined motion,
Marx argued, Epicurus had found a way to overcome the "blind necessity"
and purely materialist physics of Democritus. Epicurus could thus ascribe to
atoms an "ideal" or spiritual side, a moment of "self-determination."[12] Marx
immediately emphasized that this abstract insight into atomic motion "*goes
through the whole Epicurean philosophy, in such a way, however, that, as goes without saying, the determination of its appearance depends on the domain in which it is
applied.*"[13] The crucial point of interest for Marx was that Epicurus's atomistic philosophy of nature provides an analogous theory of the emergence
of human self-consciousness because the assertion of self-determination
raises "man as man" above the blind dictates and uniformity of nature. In
turn, the autonomy of the atom suggests a theory of ethical freedom that is
revolutionary in its potential, because, by breaking the "*bonds of fate,*" the
Epicurean "swerve" implies that the atom contains "something in its breast
that can fight back and resist."[14] Finally, in Marx's positive assessment, the
freedom of atomic motion in Epicurus's theory dispensed with the need for
any theological explanation of being. Epicurus represented an advance in
philosophy because the self-sufficiency of the atomic principle freed the
atom not only from natural determination but also from the necessity of a
more primordial grounding in a First Cause or divine creator.[15] Epicurus
thereby liberated ontology and ethics from theology, a feat that made him
the "greatest representative of Greek enlightenment."[16] Marx recognized
an ancient ally of the Promethean struggle that the Young Hegelians had

12  "Difference," p. 52.      13  Ibid., p. 50.
14  Ibid., p. 49.      15  Ibid., p. 50.      16  Ibid., p. 73.

begun "against all heavenly and earthly gods who do not acknowledge human self-consciousness as the highest divinity."[17]

Despite Marx's acknowledgment of Epicurus's place in the pantheon of humanity's liberators, the dissertation critically exposed the limitations of Epicurean atomism and, by extension, of the subjective modes of thought that had taken shape in the aftermath of Hegel's total system. Sticking closely to the account found in Hegel's *History of Philosophy*, Marx argued that the essential feature of all Greek thinking was its subjective nature. The earliest period of Greek thought had identified knowledge directly with the characters of specific wisemen. Although later Greek thinking moved beyond the form of immediacy to the more universal philosophies of Plato and Aristotle, nonetheless, Marx wrote, the "positive interpretation of the Absolute is connected to the subjective character of Greek philosophy, with the definition of the wise man," because "these determinations in Plato and Aristotle are, as it were, presupposed, not developed out of immanent necessity."[18] Epicurus, the successor of the great Greek thinkers, epitomized this subjective orientation when he made the principle of the atom – abstract individuality – the "form of all existence whatsoever," whether one speaks of "self-consciousness," "the person," "the wise man," or "God."[19] However, Marx proceeded to argue that abstract individuality can maintain its "pure being-for-itself" only by "*abstracting from the being that confronts it.*" Consequently, for Epicurus, "the purpose of action is to be found in abstracting, swerving away from pain and confusion, in ataraxy [serenity]. . . ."[20] Therefore, Epicurean atomism must remain abstract, its conception of thought separated from being, its idea of freedom purely negative. Hence, Marx leveled what he considered to be a damaging judgment: "Abstract individuality is freedom from being, not freedom in being. It cannot shine in the light of being. This is an element in which this individuality loses its character and becomes material."[21]

Marx deepened this negative judgment of atomism when he turned his attention to Plutarch, the most prominent of Epicureanism's ancient critics. At the point where the "theologising intellect" of Plutarch confronted ancient philosophy, Marx discovered a close parallel to the theologizing philosophers who opposed Hegelianism in his own time. The copious notes on Plutarch found in the preparatory notebooks to Marx's dissertation have received little scholarly attention, but these materials actually offer important insights into what Marx considered the greatest temptation of subjective

17  Ibid., p. 30.    18  "Notebooks," p. 498.
19  Ibid., pp. 505–6.    20  "Difference," pp. 50–1.    21  Ibid., p. 62.

philosophy, namely the danger of sliding into irrationality and myth. Given that he regarded all post-Hegelian philosophy to be modes of subjective thought, the warning was not directed exclusively at the Schellingians and Speculative Theists. Indeed, Marx clearly believed that even progressive forms of subjective philosophy were exposed to this danger, because despite the fact that Epicurus rejected the gods, Marx actually detected an elective affinity between atomism and theism.

Here, it seems probable that Feuerbach had an influence upon Marx far earlier than has been recognized. Marx's dissertation contains numerous references to Feuerbach's analysis of the seventeenth-century atomist Gassendi found in his 1833 *History of Recent Philosophy*. In his chapter on Gassendi, Feuerbach had argued that atomism cannot provide a basis for a metaphysical system, because he could see no way to proceed from the quantitative enumeration of atoms to qualitative universal concepts. In Feuerbach's view, the atomic model effectively delimits reason to the narrow domain of the particular; but, significantly, far from thereby reducing human spirit to the single dimension of mechanism, the restriction of reason gives free rein to irrational belief outside the sphere of atomistic particularity. As Feuerbach summed up the paradoxical effect, "When God is driven from the Temple of Reason, from the open, free, clear and distinct world of thought into the secret recesses, the Old Ladies' Home, the *Asylum Ignorantiae* of the heart . . . – then, one becomes an intellectual atheist, in the open market-place of the understanding; but in the private backrooms of reason, one remains the most superstitious Christian, the most religious man in the world."[22] In short, Feuerbach, still an Idealist in 1833, saw an ever-present danger that reason would backslide into religion if it failed to derive from itself, from reason, a concept of unity between thought and being. Marx surely had Feuerbach's insights in mind when he belabored Gassendi for seeking to accommodate Epicurus to his "Catholic conscience."[23] Moreover, he applied the same analysis to Plutarch, who had attacked Epicurus from the side of piety for his denial of the gods and his rejection of personal immortality.

However, it would be easy to miss the vital point of Marx's argument, that the vigor of Plutarch's critique masked the inner connection between his "theologising intellect" and Epicurus. Marx wrote that although Epicurus's "abstract-individual self-consciousness" could shatter the theological illusions of mankind, it also blocked the path to "true and real science . . . inas-

22    Feuerbach quoted in Wartofsky, *Feuerbach*, p. 74.
23    "Difference," p. 29.

much as individuality does not rule within the nature of things themselves";
and when abstract individuality is raised to "an absolute principle, then the
door is opened wide to superstitious and unfree mysticism."[24] In his notebooks, Marx extended this Feuerbachian criticism to the Epicureans' pursuit of *ataraxy*, the serenity of the self. *Ataraxy* had required that the Epicureans deny any immanent rationality in being, because a rational – that
is, determinate – reality would constrain the abstract self-determination of
individuals. "Accident is known to be the dominating category with the Epicureans," noted Marx.

> A necessary consequence of this is that the idea is considered only as a *condi-
> tion;* condition is existence accidental in itself. . . . We find the same thing with
> the Pietists and Supernaturalists. The creation of the world, original sin, the re-
> demption, all this and all their godly determinations, such as paradise, etc., are
> not an eternal, timeless, immanent determination of the idea, but a condition.
> As Epicurus makes the ideality of his world, the void, into [the condition for]
> the creation of the world, so also the Supernaturalist gives embodiment to
> premiselessness, [namely] the idea of the world, in paradise.[25]

Like Feuerbach, Marx concluded that the separation of thought and being forms a secret connection between atomism and supernatural theism,
leading both to consign reality to irrationality, arbitrariness, and "premise-
lessness."

For Marx, Plutarch epitomized the theologizing impulse that lay in
atomism; and here, his criticism of Plutarch's defense of immortality unmistakably echoed the Hegelian critique of personalist theism that we first
encountered in Feuerbach's *Thoughts on Death and Immortality*. Hence, as
Feuerbach had attacked the Pietists and supernaturalists, so Marx charged
that Plutarch coveted the "eternity" of his "atomistic being" against its dissolution upon death and inevitable return into the "universal and eternal."[26] Like Feuerbach, Marx traced this back to "the naked empirical Ego,
the love of self, the oldest love,"[27] and he showed himself equally capable of
sharp sarcasm against the "philistines," those "good and clever men" whose
expectation of "the reward for life after life" represents "the pride of the
atom screwed up to the highest pitch."[28] There is no evidence that Marx
read Feuerbach's *Thoughts on Death and Immortality*. By 1839 or 1840, at any
rate, he would not have had to read that work in order to associate philosophical atomism with belief in personal immortality and both with egoism,

24  Ibid., pp. 72–3.    25  "Notebooks," p. 478.
26  Ibid., p. 455.    27  "Difference," p. 76.    28  "Notebooks," p. 456.

because that had become such a common theme among the Young Hegelians.

There is, however, a stronger reason to suppose that Marx had Feuerbach's 1838 "Critique of Positive Philosophy" before him as he worked through his critique of Plutarch, because we can see in Marx's complicated reasoning the same twofold move that we have already identified in Feuerbach's critique of the Positive Philosophers. It was this essay which introduced Feuerbach's argument that the Speculative Theist projects his own qualities, the predicates of his being, onto an illusory divine. Marx embraced this thesis when he noted at the end of his long discussion of Plutarch – the ancient analogue to the Speculative Theists – that "all philosophers have made the predicates themselves into subjects."[29] Marx was not far here from Feuerbach's own conclusion in 1838 and 1839 that all speculative philosophy embodies this theologizing impulse. But we have also emphasized that Feuerbach did not simply advocate the return of the subject and predicate – humanity and its qualities – to their rightful order, because the isolated personality that is projected onto the divine is itself a distortion of human essence. So, the second move that Feuerbach made was to criticize the process of hypostatization whereby human essence has been given a distorted representation in the form of the atomized, single person. Marx was equally unwilling to leave uncriticized the form of the subject and its predicates. Consequently, he identified not only the alienation of the "eternal" from the individual but also the hypostatization of that alienated essence: "[T]he individual shuts himself off from his eternal nature in his empirical nature; but is that not the same as to shut his eternal nature out of himself, to apprehend it in the form of persistent isolation in self, in the form of the empirical, and hence to consider it as an empirical god outside self?"[30]

A vast number of scholars have duly noted the crucial influence of Feuerbach's "transformative method" on Marx's important 1843 critique of Hegel's political philosophy. Few have recognized just how early this influence actually was, and still fewer have seen that the Feuerbachian critique involves not only exposure of the inversion of subject and predicate but also criticism of the process that reduced both the subject and the predicate to an atomistic form, a person or "empirical god."

In his notebooks, Marx attempted to link this process of hypostatization to a more general explanation of the relationship between philosophy and positive religion. He developed his thoughts in response to an 1837 book in which the theologian D.F.C. Baur had revisited the old Christian typology

29  Ibid., p. 458.    30  Ibid., p. 448.

of Plato's Socrates as the prefigurement of Christ. Marx easily dismissed this attempt to relate "personified philosophy" to "personified religion" and moved on to the question of why Plato had betrayed reason by providing "a positive, above all mythical, basis for what is cognised by philosophy."[31] Marx traced this betrayal back to the same hiatus between thought and being that he had identified in Epicurean atomism and the modern supernaturalists and pietists. Because Plato did not "find the objective force in his system itself, in the eternal power of the Idea," he could preserve the positive only by introducing mythical and allegorical constructs. In unfolding this interpretation of Plato's mythologizing ontology, Marx clearly had in mind its modern parallel in Schelling's retreat from Idealism into Christian myth:

> In expounding definite questions of morality, religion, or even natural philosophy, as in *Timaeus,* Plato sees that his negative interpretation of the Absolute is not sufficient; here it is not enough to sink everything in the one dark night in which, according to Hegel, all cows are black; at this point Plato has recourse to the positive interpretation of the Absolute, and its essential form, which has its basis in itself, is myth and allegory. Where the Absolute stands on one side, and limited positive reality on the other, and the positive must all the same be preserved, there this positive becomes the medium through which absolute light shines, the absolute light breaks up into a fabulous play of colours, and the finite, the positive, points to something other than itself, has in it a soul, to which this husk is an object of wonder; the whole world has become a world of myths. Every shape is a riddle. This has recurred in recent times, due to the operation of a similar law.[32]

In the "positive interpretation of the Absolute," Marx perceived the fountainhead of the "philosophy of transcendence." It represented to him the essential kinship of Platonic philosophy with "every positive religion, and primarily with the Christian religion, which is the consummate philosophy of transcendence."[33] This impulse toward irrational positivity, Marx maintained, was the deeper truth of the resemblance between Platonism and Christianity that Baur had discussed in his book *Das Christliche des Platonismus oder Sokrates und Christus.* In the absence of a conception of reason adequate to bridge the gap between thought and being, both Platonism and Christianity invested their principles in the transcendental sphere, thereby leaving immanent being unredeemed.

In his own time, Marx believed that Positive Philosophy had fallen to all

31 Ibid., pp. 494, 497.
32 Ibid., p. 497. See also "Difference," p. 103.
33 "Notebooks," p. 498.

the dangers that arise when thought severs itself from being but still searches for a "positive interpretation of the Absolute." By contrast, he contended that the "liberal party," the Young Hegelians, would develop beyond the present subjective form of philosophy and "realize" philosophy as the identity of thought and being. Unlike the Positive Philosophers, the Young Hegelians had not been led into myth and unreason, because the "party of the concept" recognized the truth of their age, that both subjectivity and the world are "spirit and both want to be acknowledged as such."[34] Confident of this truth, the Young Hegelians could endure the extreme separation of thought from being in their own age, and rather than seek accommodation with a world that remained hostile to the truths of reason, they could critically measure a recalcitrant reality against the sovereign standard of free self-consciousness. Clearly, this was a call for the transformation of philosophy into a revolutionary agent. Marx was not merely affirming Hegel's system; he was making it the principle of an actual new world; nor was he seeking "serenity," as if in emulation of the Epicurean Stoics whom he criticized.[35] In the terms of Marx's dissertation, serenity could be construed only as an end goal when philosophy had created a world in which it could once again be at home. How philosophy might achieve this was a question that Marx left vague, for, like Bruno Bauer's, his conception of practice went no further than the exercise of philosophical criticism itself.

Ultimately, however, Marx looked beyond the effects of philosophy's uncompromising campaign against reality to the workings of a dialectic that encompasses both thought and being. Only by presupposing the cunning of this dialectic could Marx summon the apocalyptic expectation of a sudden transition from the most extreme separation between philosophy and the world to their full reconciliation. This turn to dialectics complicated his relation to the philosophy of self-consciousness that otherwise was so clearly important to his thought at this stage. That is, even though the dialectic as Marx then conceived it has a spiritual essence, his descriptions of the operation of dialectic actually confront the subjective Idealism implied by Bauer's critical philosophy with a vitalistic naturalism reminiscent of the young Feuerbach:

34 "Difference," p. 86; and "Notebooks," p. 439.
35 Both Jerrold Seigel and Harold Mah argue that Marx was seeking *ataraxy* as a release or escape from the philosophical contradictions and tensions that plagued the situation of the radical German intellectual. See, in contrast, Auguste Cornu, *Karl Marx und Friedrich Engels. Leben und Werk. 1. Bd. 1818–1844* (Berlin, 1954), p. 178.

. . . dialectic is also the torrent which smashes the many and their bounds, which tears down the independent forms, sinking everything in the one sea of eternity. The myth of it is therefore death. Thus dialectic is death, but at the same time the vehicle of vitality, the efflorescence in the gardens of the spirit, the foaming in the bubbling goblet of the tiny seeds out of which the flower of the single flame of the spirit bursts forth.[36]

The implications of this view for the philosophy of self-consciousness become clear in another passage in which Marx praised the revolutionary practical implications of J. G. Fichte's "world-creating *ego*" but added pointedly that the ego "could not create any world."[37] This comment, made at a time when many Left Hegelians were turning to Fichte's subjective Idealism, reveals some skepticism about the potential of self-consciousness to remake the world through critique and self-assertion, even if the turgid mysticism with which Marx occasionally invoked a vitalist pantheism stands out as anomalous in a work dominated by a belief in the primacy of self-consciousness.

This anomaly may be attributed to the lingering influence of the same kind of youthful Romanticism that had led Feuerbach in 1830 to negate exclusive personhood by referring to the "bottomless abyss of nature."[38] Marx quickly abandoned this language as his conception of dialectic became more and more focused on human history. Nonetheless, his occasional invocations of dialectical pantheism in the dissertation and notebooks point meaningfully forward to his rejection of Bruno Bauer's critical philosophy. After 1842, Marx turned against Bauer and the Berlin *Freien* precisely because, in his view, their detachment from the world transformed their critical energies into self-indulgent posturing, frivolity, and, ultimately, futility. Marx, by contrast, adhered to the resolution he had made in 1837 to "seek the idea in reality," which by 1842 led him away from the metaphysical speculation of his dissertation toward the concrete analysis of politics and society. However, what remained constant in Marx's thought in the years after his dissertation was a desire to overcome the subjective forms of philosophical consciousness that dominated the post-Hegelian situation and to locate the operations of the dialectic in the objective world as well as in the critical self-consciousness. Moreover, as Marx turned to political and social issues, the connections between atomism and theism that he had first described in the dissertation were to persist in his approach to objects as diverse as the Prussian "Christian State" and the American liberal republic.

36 "Notebooks," p. 498.   37 Ibid., p. 494.
38 Feuerbach, *Thoughts on Death and Immortality*, p. 82.

From Atomism to Prussian Individualism:
Marx's Philosophical Journalism

Marx finished his dissertation early in 1841 and submitted it to the University of Jena. By July, he had joined Bruno Bauer in Bonn, where he hoped his friendship with the older philosopher would facilitate his own academic career. This proved to be a disastrous move for Marx, because shortly after his arrival, Bauer came under intense pressure from his conservative colleagues in the theology faculty to resign his post. Bauer's untenable situation convinced Marx that he had little hope of ever finding academic employment, and even before Eichhorn had Bauer dismissed in spring 1842, Marx had begun casting about for a new career in political journalism. By April 1842, Marx had begun to write his first article for the newly founded Rhenish liberal weekly, *Rheinische Zeitung;* by October, he was its editor. This change in activity coincided with his announced commitment to republicanism. As he told Arnold Ruge in March 1842, he was embarked upon a critique of Hegel's treatment of the domestic constitution: "The central point is the struggle against *constitutional monarchy* as a hybrid which from beginning to end contradicts and abolishes itself."[39] Marx's open avowal of republicanism has often been presented as yet another response to the political persecution of the Young Hegelians by the new reactionary regime of Friedrich Wilhelm IV. But it seems more probable that like Feuerbach, Ruge, or Bauer, Marx was not so much radicalized by the repressive politics of Friedrich Wilhelm IV as he was confirmed in his radicalism by the persecution of the government.

Richard Hunt has suggested that until roughly 1840 Marx shared the liberal constitutional monarchism of his father.[40] Contrary to Hunt, it seems unclear whether "constitutional monarchy" adequately describes the visions of a young philosopher who dreamed of fulfilling the philosophy of freedom in the real world and imagined his own age as the calm before a coming storm. The evidence from Marx's writings prior to 1841-2 is simply too thin to decide firmly on his views of the constitutional questions of the day. However, we have already seen how fraught were the debates about constitutional monarchy in the late 1830s, particularly among Hegelians dealing simultaneously with the internal collapse of their school and with external reactionary attacks. The line between upholding constitutional monarchy

39  Marx to Ruge, March 5 [1842], *CW*, vol. 1, pp. 382–3.
40  Richard N. Hunt, *The Political Ideas of Marx and Engels. I. Marxism and Totalitarian Democracy, 1818–1850* (Pittsburgh, 1974), p. 30.

as an ideal and enfranchizing the king as a "fellow citizen" within the community of spirit was thin indeed. Considering the apocalyptic tone of Marx's dissertation, his commitment to philosophy as practice, and his opposition to the metaphysical and theological consequences of Positive Philosophy, we can assume that Marx stood on the far left of Hegelians as the theologico-political debates about personal monarchic sovereignty and political participation played themselves out in the late 1830s. Marx arrived at openly declared republicanism at precisely the same time as many other left-leaning Hegelians like Arnold Ruge, Feuerbach, Förster, and Köppen. For all of them, open republicanism was the result of a complex process of radical-ization in which their involvements in philosophical, theological, and polit-ical debate were inextricable from their reactions to actual politics.

All of this suggests the need to read Marx's political journalism with a keen eye toward the context in which Hegelians like himself turned to re-publicanism. If Marx's critique of atomism and subjectivism in his disserta-tion amply reveals his engagement with the theological and philosophical debates about personalism, his political writings in 1842 reveal an equally deep reception of the political dimension of those debates. These political writings carried the critique of atomism from the metaphysical domain of the dissertation into the political and social situation of contemporary Prus-sia. Marx's articles on press censorship and the structure of estate repre-sentation, the central topics of his journalism in 1842, are so detailed and concrete that it is easy to overlook the profound impact of those theologico-political controversies upon his republican opposition to the Prussian monarchy. Indeed, Marx's impassioned pleas for a free press and broader political participation are unified by a sustained examination of the effects of the interlocking phenomena of transcendence and personification in Prussian society and politics. As befitted a thinker who continued to iden-tify *praxis* with Young Hegelian philosophic critique, Marx joined Ruge and Bauer's attacks on the foundations of the "Christian state." His contribution to the struggle against the "transcendental" Christian state and its ally "pos-itive religion" grew directly from the general link between "philosophies of transcendence" and "positive interpretations of the Absolute" that he had first described at the time of his dissertation.[41]

This was the central theme of four articles that Marx promised to send Ruge in April 1842. As he pointedly told Ruge, these articles on religious art, the Romantics, the Historical School of Law, and the *"Positivist Philosophers"*

---

41 See "Comments on the Latest Prussian Censorship Instruction," *CW*, vol. 1, p. 116; and Marx to Ruge, March 20 [1842], *CW*, vol. 1, p. 384.

were connected in content.[42] Of the four, only the essay on the Historical School survived to be published in the *Rheinische Zeitung.* The article shows that by 1842, the discomfort that Marx had felt in 1837 over Savigny's separation of historical fact from philosophical norm had mushroomed into a violent condemnation of the whole tendency of the Historical School. However, he chose to focus not on the current practitioners of the historical method but on their intellectual progenitor, Gustav Hugo. On the surface, the decision to attack Hugo instead of Savigny is curious. After all, by 1842, Hugo was nearing death and was no longer active. Donald Kelley has suggested that by centering on Hugo, Marx intended to disguise an attack on Savigny, who became the Prussian minister of Justice for the Reform of Laws in 1842,[43] but Marx's intention was not merely to launch an oblique campaign against Savigny.

Instead, Marx wrote that Hugo attracted his attention because he presented a pure species of legal positivism shorn of the "smokescreen of mysticism" behind which the later Positive Philosophers hid.[44] In contrast to these Christian legal theorists, Marx presented Hugo as the complete *skeptic* of the eighteenth century, whose denial of reason led him not merely to accept the positive but also to "prove that the *positive* is *irrational.*" His affirmation of all that is given "killed the *spirit* of the positive, in order to possess the purely positive as a residue and to feel comfortable in this *animal* state."[45] Significantly, as Marx turned in the essay's conclusion to Haller, Stahl, Leo, Savigny, and the other contemporary positive legal philosophers, he emphasized their move from positivity to transcendence: "If Hugo says that *marriage* and other *moral-legal* institutions are *irrational,* the *moderns* say that these institutions are indeed *not creations of human reason,* but are *representations* of a higher '*positive*' reason. Only *one* conclusion is voiced by *all* with equal crudity: *the right of arbitrary power.*"[46] Marx was here translating into political terms his earlier critique of Plato, when he had asserted that the "husk" of a world divorced from reason seeks its justification in something other than itself. Hence, where Hugo had merely defended the crude force of historically given facts, the modern Positive Philosophers attempted to legitimize these facts by embracing a transcendent political theology. Marx insisted, however, that in both Hugo and the modern positivists the irrational "animal law" of the created world is left in place.

42  Marx to Ruge, April 27 [1842], *CW,* vol. 1, p. 387.
43  Kelley, "Metaphysics of Law," p. 360.
44  Marx, "The Philosophical Manifesto of the Historical School of Law," *CW,* vol. 1, p. 209.
45  Ibid., p. 206.     46  Ibid., p. 209.

Much of Marx's writing in 1842 was directed to exploring the consequences of this "animal law." As he complained to Ruge, "the degradation of people to the level of animals has become for the government an article of faith and a principle. But this does not contradict religiosity, for the deification of animals is probably the most consistent form of religion."[47] The deified "animal" is man, but man in his unhuman form – that is to say, in his nonsocial, isolated condition. Here, Marx fully subscribed to the Young Hegelian sociopolitical critique of Christian personalism. Hence, he observed that the pious Prussian opponents of the freedom of the press and the deniers of the people's rationality "doubt mankind in general but canonise individuals. They draw a horrifying picture of human nature and at the same time demand that we should bow down before the holy image of certain privileged individuals."[48] However, Marx went much further even than Ruge in identifying incarnation and personalism as the keys to the concrete social and political structures of Prussia. So, he wrote, "the numerous champions of the Christian-knightly, modern feudal principle . . . want to regard freedom not as the natural gift of the universal sunlight of reason, but as the supernatural gift of a specially favorable constellation of the stars, because they regard freedom as merely an *individual property* of certain persons and social estates, [and] are in consequence compelled to include universal reason and universal freedom among the *bad ideas* and phantoms of '*logically constructed systems.*'"[49]

What struck Marx about Prussia's vestigial feudalism was not its lingering form of corporatist organicism but its bastard form of Christian individualism. The important feature of Prussian society was, therefore, not really its corporatist structure but its adoption of atomism as a principle of social or, more accurately, anti-social organization. In making this charge, Marx readily moved along a continuum between religion, politics, and social practices. "Needy, egoistic interest" dominates Prussia, he charged, from the pious "self-seeking which puts personal salvation above the salvation of all" to the "pressing need of private interests [which] is the architect of the political system based on *estates*."[50]

The full theologico-political weight of this Left Hegelian critique of personalism underlies Marx's first discussions of property. The apparent dominance of private interest in Prussian society led him to ask his readers, "Are

47  Marx to Ruge, March 20 [1842], p. 384.
48  "Debates on Freedom of the Press," p. 169.
49  Ibid., p. 151.
50  "On the Commissions of the Estates in Prussia," p. 303.

not most of your court cases and most of your civil laws concerned with property?"[51] Of course, Marx had in mind here mainly inherited landed property, but as he refined his views during 1842 and 1843, he treated it as paradigmatic of all forms of private property. For heritable landed property presented what he regarded as the essential feature of private property, though in the mystified form of primogeniture – that is, the essence of private property is its abstraction from the community as the presocial right of individuals.[52] Clearly, in an estate system dominated by large property owners, Marx's criticism was directed in the first instance against the aristocracy. He clearly believed, however, that the same egoistic, individualistic values pervaded other strata of Prussian society as well. An atomized society, he reasoned, based on the incarnation of particular rights in individuals, committed to the rights of "*private persons*" to the exclusion of the rights of mankind, reduced the people to a "*rabble of private individuals.*"[53]

So, even though Marx recognized vestiges of feudal corporatism in Prussian civil society, he chose instead to characterize Prussia by its extreme social fragmentation. Hence, in his judgment, the people formed a "crude, inorganic mass," while the "non-state spheres of life" were "unreal, mechanical, subordinated."[54] Moreover, when Marx discussed the "urban estate" in April 1842, he pointedly noted that it acted as "*bourgeois,*" not as "*citoyen.*"[55] It is important to emphasize that Marx's first reference to the conflict between the "bourgeois" and the "citizen" – the Rousseauian distinction that Hegel had consistently invoked in his discussions of civil society – emerged against a background in which the secular tension between private interest and public-spiritedness overlapped with the conflict between Christian atomism and immanent collective spirit.

Marx's idealist republicanism, like Feuerbach's and Ruge's, synthesized Rousseauian and Hegelian elements by identifying the general will with philosophical comprehension of this rational, collective spirit. Moreover, his republicanism had in common with theirs the fact that it was not exclusively or narrowly political. This was true even before Marx turned explicitly to the social question. His rigorous defense of immanence against transcendence and his monistic philosophy of spirit made the sharp distinction between politics and economics unintelligible. "Public spirit" in Marx's us-

51  "Leading Article in No. 179 of the *Kölnische Zeitung*," *CW*, vol. 1, p. 199.
52  "On the Commissions of the Estates in Prussia," p. 305.
53  "Debates on Freedom of the Press," p. 168.
54  "On the Commissions of the Estates in Prussia," pp. 296–7.
55  "Debates on Freedom of the Press," p. 169.

age was not reducible to democratic participation in the legislative and executive activities of the government. In distinction to the government, which fit this narrow definition of political action, Marx called the true state "the great organism."[56] This was obviously not meant to be a description of the atomized reality of Prussia; it was, rather, a description of what "social reason" discloses as the normative condition for human society. In a true state in which human self-consciousness could affirm the state as its own "achievement,"[57] the activity of spirit would be revealed equally in the construction of railways, the construction of (true) philosophy, and the political deliberations of the people.[58] Like Ruge's, Marx's ideal was a community of spirit that could neither acknowledge nor tolerate an "animal law" unredeemed by rational spirit.

That is to say, Marx's political journalism in 1842 rehearsed in Idealist terms the critique of the modern separation of state and civil society that was to emerge forcefully in his major works of the next year. Where the later critique started by assuming the primacy of human social life and then proceeded to attack the false autonomy of the state from society, the earlier attacked the separation of the spiritual ideal of the state from civil society, which in its atomized form stood under the sway of animal law – or, in other words, the competitive struggle of the state of nature. Hence, Marx insisted that the "Prussian state should not break off its real state life at a sphere which should be the conscious flowering of this state life."[59] "In a true state there is no landed property, no industry, no material thing, which as a crude element of this kind could make a bargain with the state," he wrote,

> in it there are only *spiritual forces,* and only in their state form of resurrection, in their political rebirth, are these natural forces entitled to a voice in the state. The state pervades the whole of nature with spiritual nerves, and at every point it must be apparent that what is dominant is not matter, but form, not nature without the state, but the nature of the state, not the *unfree object,* but the *free human being.*[60]

The spiritualization of civil society, the dissolution of separate, fixed, atomized differences into "the living movement of distinct functions, which are all inspired by one and the same life,"[61] was a crucial dimension of Marx's campaign against the transcendental personalism of the Christian state.

---

56 "Leading Article," p. 202.
57 "On the Commissions of the Estates in Prussia," p. 306.
58 See, for example, "Leading Article," p. 195.
59 "On the Commissions of the Estates in Prussia," p. 297.
60 Ibid., p. 306.     61 Ibid., p. 295

Marx's judgment radicalized the progressive Hegelians' earlier association of the Christian idea of the self and the atomized, egoistical form of modern society. Where those early insights had stemmed in large part from the confrontation of Hegelians with their positivist and personalist critics, Marx treated the connection between Christian personalism and egoism as the dominant reality of Prussian society. Consequently, in his journalism of 1842, he moved easily between Christian personalism and social egoism, condemning equally the theologico-philosophical and the sociopolitical "canonisation" of individuals.

In the course of that year, however, he also began to formulate a theory of ideology that regarded Christian personalism less as a cause of political and social egoism than as an ideological legitimation of private secular and material interests. Hence, in November, Marx proposed a fundamental shift in the target of radical critique when he insisted that "religion should be criticised in the framework of criticism of political conditions," instead of criticizing "political conditions . . . in the framework of religion. . . ; for religion in itself is without content, it owes its being not to heaven but to the earth, and with the abolition of distorted reality, of which it is the *theory*, it will collapse of itself."[62] The reduction of religion to an ideological reflection of reality had obvious consequences for Marx's evaluation of the whole Young Hegelian campaign against the theological tradition. Nonetheless, that campaign remained vital to Marx's thinking about state and society in 1842. Indeed, we can trace a line back from Marx to Gans, Cieszkowski, Hess, Heine, and Feuerbach, the critics of the 1830s who had already linked theological and social critique.

The true significance of these earlier critics for Marx's development has been virtually erased by our habit of thinking in terms of an archetypal confrontation between Marx and liberalism. However, as an examination of his journalism reveals, Marx did not arrive at his first criticisms of the anti-social effects of individualism through reflections on liberalism. Rather, he took aim at the constellation of individualizing tendencies that had come to predominate within the "Christian state." He addressed a specific theological, political, and social context in which egoistic individualism and authoritarianism were combined; their coexistence was suggested by Marx when he noted that "one can very conveniently be both liberal and reactionary if only one is always adroit enough to address oneself to the liberals of the recent past who know no other dilemma than that of Vidocq: either 'prisoner or gaoler.'"[63] As Marx turned his attention to the modern liberal state and society proper in 1843, the association of anti-social egoism and theological personalism continued to direct his thinking about individuals and society.

## Toward Feuerbach and Socialism

In mid-1842, Marx could criticize the "liberals of the recent past," while still identifying himself with the liberal movement of the present moment. Of course, we have already noted that like Ruge, Marx had gone beyond liberalism in his criticism of private life and the separation of state and society. His willingness to align himself with "liberalism" was an astute tactical move for the editor of a journal financed by businessmen in the historically liberal Rhineland. It shows the value that Marx placed on political alliances in the quest for greater political and social freedoms. Indeed, the uncompromising and tactless tone of the articles that the Berlin Young Hegelians submitted to the *Rheinische Zeitung* angered Marx as he attempted to tread the fine line between political opposition and tactical compromise. Beyond these strategic considerations, however, Marx had not yet adequately criticized the idea of a broad *Bewegungspartei* that had been the guiding organizational ideal of German progressive politics during the 1830s. Although Marx insufficiently distinguished between liberalism and his own radical republicanism, he was beginning to recognize the need to do so. Hence, in his 1842 article defending Left Hegelianism against the *Kölnische Zeitung,* he declared that "without parties there is no development, without demarcation there is no progress."[64] Marx was not alone in recognizing that the crude division of German politics into opposing parties of "movement" and "reaction" was no longer adequate to a complex reality. Earlier in 1842, Ruge had contended that the interests of the *Zeitgeist* were served neither by reactionaries who denied parties nor by an undifferentiated party of progress, and we remember that both Ruge and Edgar Bauer had begun openly to articulate the difference between liberalism and the Left Hegelians' democratic and social republicanism.

When Ruge's "Self-Critique of Liberalism" provoked Saxon and Prussian authorities to close both the *Deutsche Jahrbücher* and the *Rheinische Zeitung* early in 1843, Marx greeted the news with some relief, even though this action deprived him of his livelihood. As he wrote to Ruge, "It is a bad thing to have to perform menial duties even for the sake of freedom; to fight with

63  "Leading Article," p. 202.
64  Ibid., p. 202.

pinpricks, instead of with clubs. I have become tired of hypocrisy, stupidity, gross arbitrariness, and of our bowing and scraping, dodging, and hairsplitting over words. Consequently, the government has given me back my freedom."[65] Released from the compromises imposed on him by his editorial role, Marx resolved to pursue his critical work independently and rigorously. He agreed with Ruge that nothing further could be done in Germany under the present circumstances, and, almost immediately, he joined Ruge's plan to resurrect a Young Hegelian journal abroad. Ruge planned to move to Zürich, where the last articles intended for the *Deutsche Jahrbücher* had already been published as the *Anekdota*. He hoped to transform an already existing journal, the *Deutsche Bote aus der Schweiz*, into a new organ for radical Hegelianism. Marx intended to work for the journal there. This plan was shattered when alarming news reached Ruge in February that the Zürich authorities had closed down the *Deutsche Bote* and expelled its new editor, the socialist poet Georg Herwegh.[66] Undeterred, Ruge suggested to Marx that they consider Strassburg.

The idea of locating in a French city inspired Marx to reconceive the entire project, for he responded by suggesting to Ruge that they establish the new journal as a collaborative effort between French and German intellectuals in the interest of the emancipation of both peoples. Ruge's initial intention had been to continue his activities within the German cultural world. However, once Marx made his proposal, Ruge embraced it enthusiastically. Since the disillusioning response of Germany to the Revolution of 1830, the idea of a union of French and German principles had been the last refuge of German radicals driven to despair over the condition of their homeland. The ambition of such an alliance tapped into the long history of left-wing francophilism that had been revived by the Revolution of 1830 after lying dormant under the chill of reaction and German patriotism. Marx was also directly influenced by the latest incarnation of the dream of a union of national principles, Feuerbach's call for a union of French sensualist materialism and German Idealism. An infusion of French sensualism, Feuerbach hoped, would revolutionize the Germans by unifying the French "heart" and the German "head."[67]

Ruge and Marx soon abandoned Strassburg in favor of Paris, which they,

65  Marx to Ruge, January 25 [1843], *CW*, vol. 1, p. 397.
66  Under Herwegh's editorship, the *Bote* was to be transformed from a weekly into a monthly paper offering a broader spectrum of critical articles. As it turned out, only one issue was published after the imposition of censorship, the famous *Einundzwanzig Bogen aus der Schweiz* (Zürich und Winterthur, 1843).
67  Feuerbach, "Preliminary Theses on the Reform of Philosophy," p. 165.

along with virtually every other German progressive, regarded as the intellectual and political heart of Europe. Ruge reached Paris in the summer of
1843, but Marx delayed his departure from Germany until October. Marx's
experience as a journalist had convinced him that politics and society should
be the central objects of critique, but his abrupt shift from the esoteric concerns of his dissertation to the tumult of Rhenish and Prussian politics had
also convinced him that he was unprepared for such an undertaking. His
political journalism, while remarkably astute and trenchant, frequently proceeded from philosophic first principles, not from concrete knowledge of
history or political economy, and though he recognized this shortcoming,
the ambitious programs of study that Marx set himself in 1842 were thwarted
by the need to earn a living by his pen. Only after the closing of the *Rheinische Zeitung* was Marx able to plunge into an intense study of political economy, history, and political thought.

In June, Marx married Jenny von Westphalen, after their long engagement, and the couple retired for five months to the small town of Kreuz-
nach. In that rural retreat, Marx wrote the two major works of this transitional period, his "Critique of Hegel's Philosophy of Law" and "On the Jewish
Question." These two works settled a number of accounts, Marx's debt to
Hegel being prominent among them. Moreover, these writings announced
the most fateful development in Marx's intellectual career, his moral commitment to socialism. The remaining pages of this chapter will analyze these
two texts in detailed relation to the ideological context that was, as we shall
see, formative for the entire scope of Marx's work up to 1844. Although the
two texts were written at virtually the same time and their themes overlap
in many ways, the long essay on Hegel was conceived much earlier. For that,
as well as conceptual reasons, it will be treated apart from "On the Jewish
Question."

Before proceeding, something needs to be said about the two crucial influences that stamp these pivotal texts of 1843 – Feuerbach and French socialism. Scholars routinely date the Feuerbachian influence to Marx's reading of "Preliminary Theses to the Reform of Philosophy," arguing that until
late 1842 or early 1843, Bauer's philosophy of self-consciousness dominated
Marx's own radical Hegelianism.[68] Yet there is good reason not only to qualify Marx's allegiance to Bauer but also to regard Feuerbach's impact on
Marx as cumulative rather than sudden. We saw that even in his dissertation,

---

68  See, for example, Rosen, *Bruno Bauer and Karl Marx;* and L. Baronovitch, "Two Appendices to a Doctoral Dissertation: Some New Light on the Origin of Karl Marx's Dissociation from Bruno Bauer and the Young Hegelians," *Philosophical Forum* (1978), p. 229.

Marx regarded the philosophy of self-consciousness as a transitional stage on the path toward the full reconciliation of thought and being. This was a consistent conclusion given his general views of atomism, which were probably influenced by his reading of Feuerbach's *History of Recent Philosophy*. We also observed that Marx was likely impressed by Feuerbach's 1838 critique of Positive Philosophy, the text in which Feuerbach first articulated the premises of his transformative method. When *The Essence of Christianity* appeared, Marx quickly embraced Feuerbach's principle, though he told Ruge that he differed somewhat over the "conception" of the essence of religion.[69] The piece in which Marx worked out this difference is lost, but presumably Marx endorsed Feuerbach's theory of species-being while questioning his relatively positive view of the religious impulse. In rejecting the possibility of translating Christian love into love of humanity, Marx differed not only from Feuerbach but also from Ruge, whose Hegelian model of Protestant secularization easily adapted itself to Feuerbach's sanguine narrative of human essence regained. Significantly, however, even as Marx continued to hold Bauer's more vehement conviction that humanity's subjection to religious illusions is totally debasing, he accepted Feuerbach's explanation of religious feeling as alienated human species-being. And when Feuerbach elaborated on the unity of sensuous and spiritual elements in species-being in the "Preliminary Theses," Marx recognized a philosophical grounding for his own convictions about the social essence of human being. The cumulative effect of Feuerbach's vision of human emancipation finally led to Marx's qualitative, albeit temporary, conversion. Along with so many of his contemporaries, as Engels later recalled, Marx really did become a "Feuerbachean," though he did so in a more complex way than is generally supposed.[70]

Marx's growing interest in French socialism coincided with the general reorientation of the radical Hegelians toward French political and social thought that had begun in 1842. Bruno Bauer, having begun his retreat from Left Hegelianism, wryly observed in 1844 that just as the "German enlighteners were suddenly disappointed in their hopes of 1842, and in their predicament knew not what to do, news of the latest French systems came to them."[71] Bauer was referring to the effects of Lorenz von Stein's *Der Socialismus und Communismus des heutigen Frankreichs*. Knowledge of French so-

69  Marx to Ruge, March 20 [1842], *CW*, vol. 1, p. 386.
70  Engels, *Ludwig Feuerbach and the End of Classical German Philosophy* (Peking, 1976), p. 14.
71  Bruno Bauer, "Was ist jetzt Gegenstand der Kritik?" *Allgemeine Literatur-Zeitung*, 2, 8 (Juli 1844), p. 25.

cialism did not arrive as abruptly as Bauer had suggested, however, because the 1830s had witnessed a significant discussion of German social problems and new French social thought. Nor was the Left Hegelians' receptiveness to French socialism in the early 1840s merely an expression of their own ideological impasse. The pauperism crisis that had drawn commentary in the 1830s had steadily worsened, and by 1842, many German intellectuals were acutely aware of the plight of the poor. In this context, Stein's book, intended to warn Germans of the threat of impending social revolution, had the ironic effect of reviving German interest in the Saint-Simonians and Fourierists and popularizing the ideas of a younger generation of French socialists like Louis Blanc, Proudhon, Etienne Cabet, George Sand, Victor Considérant, and Pierre Leroux.

Although Marx had expressed frustration at the superficial socialist elements in the writings of Eduard Meyen, Rutenberg, and Edgar Bauer, his own interest in French socialist thought clearly strengthened during 1842. In Cologne, he was an occasional participant in the socialist reading circle organized by Moses Hess, who had become his friend and co-worker at the *Rheinische Zeitung*.[72] Only one year earlier, Hess had published the *Europäische Triarchie*, which had advanced an apocalyptic vision of social revolution ensuing from the union of Young Hegelian religious critique, French political activism, and English industrial materialism. Marx expressed reservations about existing communist theories when he wrote an article defending the *Rheinische Zeitung* against charges of advocating socialist ideas, but despite his guarded tone, he concluded the essay by insisting on the need for serious consideration of the leading French socialist writers.[73] That was certainly Marx's own intention in the latter half of 1842, though he began to study the French socialists closely only after he resigned his editorial duties.

By the summer of 1843, explicit socialist elements were evident in Marx's writings. Not only did he evoke humanity's shared "communist essence," but he also directly criticized private property, summoned the specter of class struggle, and advocated social revolution. Shlomo Avineri and Richard Hunt are both correct in arguing that Marx made a moral commitment to communism in that summer. They rightly emphasize that what is important to this question is the tone and general implications of his writings about state and society, not his specific or detailed knowledge of this or that communist

---

72  D. Gregory, "What Marx and Engels Knew of French Socialism," *Historical Reflections*, 10, no. 1 (Spring, 1983), p. 161.
73  "Communism and the Augsburg *Allgemeine Zeitung*," *CW*, vol. 1, p. 220.

theorist.[74] Their approach is superior to a reconstruction of Marx's readings in the hope of pinpointing the moment of his conversion, as if a moral
commitment must answer to an arbitrary standard of knowledge.[75] Nevertheless, it is still not adequate. Avineri persuasively counters the older belief
that in 1843 Marx was still a radical Jacobin-style democrat, but his challenge
could be applied to descriptions of Marx in 1842 as well, because his republicanism already envisioned the erasure of the division between society
and state.[76] Nor is it particularly convincing to suggest, as Hunt does, that
Marx arrived at his socialism in "solitary reflection."[77] Preceding chapters
have shown the subtle channels by which social themes had entered radical
German discourse in the 1830s. Virtually every major left-wing Hegelian of
or with whom the young Marx had knowledge or contact, from Heine and
Gans to Hess and Feuerbach, registered the impact of the convergence of
Hegelian and French socialist ideas. Without doubt, the original form of
that convergence, the meeting of Saint-Simonianism and Hegelianism, had
faded by 1840, and Marx could join others in lampooning "Father Enfantin." Such condescension aside, the social orientation that emerged from
that initial contact had become a part of the Hegelianism that the German
left-wing conjured with in the early 1840s. To insist on Marx's solitary path
to socialism neglects this entire setting. Far from representing a break from
the German and Left Hegelian context, Marx's turn to socialism, the crucial
turning point that was to define the rest of his intellectual career, was profoundly determined – even overdetermined – by that context.

### Marx *contra* Hegel

Scholarly accounts of the "Critique of Hegel's Philosophy of Law" have
tended to focus on Marx's translation of Feuerbach's critical "transformative method" from the domains of theology and speculative philosophy into
the "sphere of political philosophy."[78] Feuerbach had argued that Christianity conceals the true subject of religion, man, by making God an absolute
substance. In similar fashion, Marx now claimed that Hegel mystified the
true relationship between the state and civil society by making the state a

74  Shlomo Avineri, *The Social and Political Thought of Karl Marx* (Cambridge, 1968), pp. 33f;
    and Hunt, *The Political Ideas of Marx and Engels*, pp. 50, 74–5.
75  Hunt and Avineri's emphasis on moral commitment contrasts to Gregory, "What Marx and
    Engels Knew of French Socialism."
76  Avineri, *Social and Political Thought*, pp. 33–4.
77  Hunt, *The Political Ideas of Marx and Engels*, p. 52.
78  Avineri, *Social and Political Thought*, pp. 8–13.

logically prior embodiment of the Idea that then produces the life of civil society and family out of itself as determinations of its concept. This "logical, pantheistic mysticism," he charged, obscures the fact that "family and civil society are the premises, or foundations, of the state; they are the genuinely active elements, but in speculative philosophy things are inverted. When the idea is made the subject, however, the real subjects, namely civil society, family, 'circumstances, caprice, etc.,' become *unreal* objective elements of the idea with a changed significance."[79] If the secret of religion is man, then the secret of the state is society. So long as this is not recognized, Marx reasoned, humanity's genuine universal existence, its collective communal being, will be dissipated in the false universality of the political state. Marx's revolutionary "practice" at this time took as its starting point the Feuerbachian assumption that exposing the alienated essence of human species-being was tantamount to regaining it as the proper essence of humanity. For once humanity recognized its collective being as its own essence, how could it fail but to organize all aspects of its life, including the state, as expressions of that species-being?

The theme of transcendence and immanence, which had preoccupied Marx since his first attempts to philosophize in a Hegelian key, here finds a cogent application to the problem of the evolution of modern civil society and the state. In his new Feuerbachian formulation, Marx was able to argue that "Up till now the *political constitution* has been the *religious sphere*, the *religion* of national life, the heaven of its generality over against the *earthly existence* of its actuality."[80] Our discussion of the political and social dimensions of Feuerbach's critique of religious alienation enables us to challenge the suggestion that Marx's critique of Hegel represents a "translation" of Feuerbach's otherwise "unpolitical" philosophy. Having traced Feuerbach's concerns about Christianity's de-politicization of humanity and Christian society's fixation upon egoistical self-interest at the expense of the ethical community, as well as his critique of the separation of the Christian-bourgeois from the whole man of the true human society, we are in a position to recognize Marx's achievement in 1843 not as a "translation" of Feuerbach but as an *appropriation* and further *clarification* of the sociopolitical problematic posed by Feuerbach's work.

We will have occasion to elaborate on this presently, but another aspect of the familiar presentation of Marx's Feuerbachian critique of Hegel's political philosophy demands immediate scrutiny. For the conventional

79  Marx, "Contribution to the Critique of Hegel's Philosophy of Law," *CW*, vol. 3, p. 8.
80  Ibid., p. 31.

understanding of the "subject/predicate" inversion must again come into question. The image of the state as a political "heaven" possessing the "generality" denied to humanity in its fragmented, atomized "earthly existence" in civil society has made the nature of the inversion seem pretty clear. Emphasis on the displaced universality of humanity's social existence accords well with Marx's critical comments on Hegel's logical pantheism. However, Feuerbach's twofold treatment of the subject–predicate inversion must be recalled, as must Marx's early concern with the process by which universal human essence becomes hypostatized and personalized. Bearing this in mind, we see immediately that the theme of personification is present everywhere in Marx's treatment of Hegel's philosophy of the state. The many analyses of this famous text have, oddly, neglected this second dimension of the Feuerbachian transformative method. Without an appreciation of the background of theologico-political debate against which Marx wrote, his denunciation of personal monarchy might seem relatively unimportant compared with his analysis of the bureaucratic-administrative nature of the modern state. Properly read against this background, however, the problem of personification or hypostatization appears to be crucial to Marx's critique of Hegel and his understanding of the modern relationship of state and civil society.

Once the two elements in the transformative method – inversion of subject and predicate and exposure of the hypostatized form of both – are properly emphasized, several things come into clearer focus. For one thing, it is evident that Marx arrived at his critique of Hegel by following an already well-trodden path. That is, Marx's "Critique" attempted to de-legitimize Hegel by claiming an affinity between him and the personalist strains that appeared to corrupt the spirit of the age. Feuerbach had already made this charge in 1839, Ruge in 1841. Significantly, perhaps, Marx first announced his intention to criticize Hegel's treatment of the "domestic" constitution in early 1842, at the same time as he was busy with his essays on the Historical School, Positive Philosophy, Romanticism, and Christian art. Like Ruge, Marx's growing disgust with Prussian conditions, as well as his skepticism about speculative metaphysics *per se*, made him less and less interested in distinguishing Hegel from other metaphysical practitioners. Hegel's identification of his own philosophical vantage point with that of the Idea itself, his apparent acceptance of the incarnate God-Man, and his description of the personal monarch as the embodied subjectivity of the state all suggested to Marx Hegel's secret alliance with the very camp that had long reviled his pantheism. Moreover, with the reactionary new Prussian king aggressively championing the political theology of personalism, the most striking feature of Hegel's political philosophy was bound to be his apparent endorsement of personalism and not the painstaking mediations in which he embedded it.[81] These associations of Hegel with the Positive Philosophers may seem misguided, and they are best understood as an ironic outcome of the fraught polemics of the late 1830s and early 1840s. Whatever their actual heuristic value, and it is not my purpose to assess that, the association of Hegel and Christian personalism helped define the Left Hegelian revolt against Hegel.

Marx's "Contribution to the Critique of Hegel's Philosophy of Law" maps the theme of personification onto that of Hegel's logical pantheism. From Marx's general criticism of Hegel's mystifying inversion of subject and predicate, he proceeded to identify a series of incarnations whereby Hegel falsely personified collective attributes in empirical individuals. The most prominent of these, Marx wrote, is, of course, the monarch, whom Hegel treated as the "true 'God-man,' the *actual incarnation* of the Idea [of the state]." Marx traced this to Hegel's evident hostility toward democracy, but he also saw it as a product of methodological confusion. While he acknowledged that all conceptions of decision making depend on the analogy of personal choice, Marx contended that Hegel's elaborate argument for the necessity of the monarch "is so peculiar as to destroy all analogy and to put *magic* in the place of the 'nature of volition in general,'"[82] This "magic," this fantastic "one-person idea," led Hegel into mystifications because he failed to recognize the "general as being the actual nature of the actual-finite": "Hegel starts from the predicates of the general description instead of from the real *ens* (subject), and since, nevertheless, there has to be a bearer of these qualities, the mystical idea becomes this bearer."[83] The result, according to Marx, is that the

> general . . . appears everywhere as something specific, particular; and individuality, correspondingly, nowhere attains to its true generality. . . . [T]he natural bases of the state such as birth (in the case of the monarch) or private property (in primogeniture), which have not yet developed at all into genuine social actualisation, appear as the highest ideas directly personified. And it is self-evident. The correct method is stood on its head.[84]

Impelled by Feuerbach's philosophy, Marx believed that the correct method traces Hegel's "hypostatized abstractions" back to their genesis as

---

81  Marx commented to Ruge (March 1843, *CW*, vol. 3, p. 139) that Friedrich Wilhelm IV "is the sole political person. In one way or another, his personality determines the system." Comparing the new king with the old, he continued, "The King of Prussia has tried to alter the system by means of a theory which in this form his father really did not have."
82  "Critique of Hegel's Philosophy of Law," p. 34.
83  Ibid., pp. 23–4.    84  Ibid., p. 40.

attributes of species-being. In comparison to Feuerbach, however, Marx identified species-being more exclusively with social being. Feuerbach had, undoubtedly, also insisted on the collective, social nature of human being; but his parallel emphasis on physical nature also introduced an irreducible individual dimension that was at odds with the collectivizing impulse in the concept of species-being. The greater primacy that Marx assigned to the social and the historical probably reflects his readings in the French socialists. Of course, it also expressed a further radicalization of the tendency of the social pantheists of the 1830s to identify human social association as the negation of personalism.

Convinced that all human attributes are "*social products*,"[85] Marx's "Critique" set up a series of oppositions between personified abstractions and the true qualities of species-being: the "magic" of personal sovereignty versus the state as a "product of the self-conscious species"; the particular person versus the "the *actual idea* of personality as the embodiment of the species"; private property, which derives its structure from its analogy to sovereignty, versus "humanised" property; the abstract "person *quand même*" versus the concrete "social person."[86] Insofar as Marx makes Hegel the representative theorist of the "person *quand même*," we have an indication of the extent to which Hegel had become thoroughly confused with the Christian personalists. After all, it had been the ambition of the *Philosophy of Right* to move from "abstract personality" to a form of "concrete personality" grounded in the complex mediations of family, civil society, and the state. Even the modern division between the bourgeois and citizen appeared to Marx to be the result of the tension between incarnation and species. So, he charged, Hegel does not locate "political qualities" such as citizenship in the "individual who unfolds new attributes out of his social essence"; in a twofold mystification, Hegel attributed these qualities to the idea of the state and then fixed them as the qualities of specific persons.[87]

Marx's employment of the opposition between species-being and personification was truly Feuerbachian – not just in the general schema of immanence against transcendence, but in the details. It must be remembered that it was Feuerbach who noted in 1842 that Hegel's *Philosophy of Right* "fixed the separation of the essential qualities of man from man, thus deifying purely abstract qualities as independent beings."[88] And Feuerbach was equally willing to criticize all attempts to separate what he had called

85   Ibid., p. 105.    86   Ibid., pp. 105, 27, 98.
87   Ibid., p. 42; and see also p. 29.
88   Feuerbach, "Preliminary Theses," p. 171.

"public qualities" from man as man.[89] Following this lead, Marx came to view all such attempts, whether in thought or in political practice, as *theological* – that is, as dependent in form upon the abstraction and personification of attributes of human species-being.[90]

When Marx examined Hegel's treatment of the relationship between the state and civil society, his philosophic criticism of hypostatization and personification stood in the most intimate proximity to his perception of the fundamental developments of the modern state and society. Despite Marx's acute observations on the modern separation of civil society from the state, however, it must be emphasized that he, like Arnold Ruge, believed that the same form of personhood, the "person of civil law," prevails in both spheres. Hence, he wrote, "if the monarch is the abstract *person* who contains the *state within his own person*, this only means that the essence of the state is the abstract *private person*. Only in its flower does the state reveal its secret. The monarch is the one private person in whom the relation of private persons generally to the state is actualised."[91] Hegel's elevation of the abstract person to the essence of the state, in this view, helped to expose the true "morality of the modern state and of modern civil law," although he also erred, Marx thought, in passing "off the state which is based on such a morality for the actual idea of ethical life."[92]

Sharpening his insights of 1842, Marx contended that starting from the king and running through to the modest *Bürger,* the egoistic, self-centered private person had come to dominate society and state. Because private persons have no relation to the state except as isolated atoms, their self-interest, not their species-being, is the only source of unity. So, Marx wrote, "*Private property* is the general category, the general political bond."[93] In his treatment of Hegel's political philosophy as the theoretical articulation of this social arrangement, Marx triangulated sovereignty, private property, and abstract personality. If sovereignty exists as the private right of the monarch, then sovereignty is private property and private property is sovereign. Sovereignty and private property stand or fall together by virtue of the idea of transcendent personhood. This is why Marx called the Germans the "mystics of sovereign private property."[94] Conversely, "true democracy" and "humanised" property are both aspects of the idea of species-being.[95] In each of these associations, Marx preserved an exact opposition between transcendence and immanence.

89  Ibid., p. 171.
90  "Critique of Hegel's Philosophy of Law," p. 79.
91  Ibid., p. 40.    92  Ibid., p. 108.    93  Ibid., p. 109.
94  Ibid., p. 108.    95  Ibid., p. 98.

In arriving at these insights, Marx echoed the homologies that had run through the personality debate of the 1830s. The analogy between sovereign monarch and property owner was a mainstay of Christian positivist political theory; and in 1835, Feuerbach had framed his opposition to the egoism of both the sovereign and the property owner as a conflict between transcendence and immanence. Marx knew of Feuerbach's essay on Stahl by at least October 1843, when Feuerbach discussed it in a letter to him.[96] The *Hallische Jahrbücher*'s call for a sequel to the "epoch-making" 1835 essay makes it likely that he knew of the piece even earlier. At any rate, it is not necessary to claim the direct influence of Feuerbach's piece. On the other hand, it is very important to recognize that Marx's first substantial criticism of private property was deeply indebted to the association of Christian personalism and egoism that had become one of the structuring leitmotifs of Left Hegelianism. It was the sovereign person of the modern "Christian state," not the "sovereign individual"[97] of capitalism, that provoked Marx to his first sustained analysis of the role of private property in modern civil society.

Despite Marx's dependence on this ideological and rhetorical context, he made a crucial move that elevated him above the theoretical level of his contemporaries. It need hardly be mentioned again that Feuerbach's few explicit comments on politics and society can scarcely be compared to Marx's detailed commentary on political and social relations. But Marx also went beyond the most political of the Left Hegelians, Arnold Ruge, who deployed the array of sociopolitical associations entailed in the critique of Christian personalism. Ruge remained fettered by the parochial struggles of Prussian politics, whereas Marx broadened his Left Hegelian insights into the relationship between personalism and the Prussian state into a theory of the modern state as such. The key to this move was his belief that constitutional monarchy exposes the essence of the political state, for in the modern state as it has evolved in separation from humanity's concrete social life, all people must necessarily relate to the state as abstract beings:

> The *constitutional* monarch therefore expresses the idea of the constitutional state in its sharpest abstraction. He is on the one hand the *idea* of the state, the sanctified majesty of the state, and precisely as *this* person. At the same time he is *mere* imagination, as person and as monarch he has neither real power nor real activity. Here the separation of political and real, of formal and ma-

96  Feuerbach to Marx, 25 October 1843, *Briefwechsel*, vol. 2.
97  See Nicholas Abercrombie, et al., ed., *Sovereign Individuals of Capitalism* (London, 1986).

terial, of general and individual person, of human being and social person, is expressed in its supreme contradiction.[98]

It was a short step to apply the same analysis to the "republic as a merely particular form of state," because in it, too, "political man has his particular mode of being alongside unpolitical man, man as a private individual."[99] Marx could elide the old opposition between monarchy and republic and assert their essential identity as forms of the abstract political state: "Property, etc., in short, the entire content of law and the state, is the same in North America as in Prussia, with few modifications. The *republic* there is thus a mere state *form,* as is the monarchy here. The content of the state lies outside these constitutions."[100] In either case, Marx reasoned, sovereignty rests on an illusory notion of the political person. Granted that Marx acknowledged that political republicanism represents an advance over monarchy, it is surprising and disturbing that his studies of republicanism and the history of the United States, which he undertook in 1843, served only to *lessen* his interest in discriminating between these political systems. Before the brilliant vision of the socialized "true democracy," which would unite the "*formal* principle" and the "*material* principle" of the state, such discriminations seemed misleading, trivial, or even pernicious.

Marx's willingness to devalue the achievements of political modernity shows just how far he had moved from earlier critics of modern civil society, like his teacher Eduard Gans. The political theorist Jean Cohen has correctly identified a "curiously antimodern thrust" in Marx's "goal of de-differentiating state and society."[101] Marx's critique of Hegel's political philosophy fully articulated this goal, which remained the lifelong aspiration of Marx's theoretical and political struggle against bourgeois liberal capitalism. But from the preceding analysis, we are able to gain new appreciation of the transitional nature of Marx's "Critique of Hegel's Philosophy of Law." To repeat an earlier claim: Marx did not arrive at his criticism of the antisocial effects of individualism or the separation of the state and civil society through reflections on liberalism. The "Critique" was therefore a transitional text in Marx's evolution toward his later status as the great socialist opponent of liberalism. Conversely, Marx's essay "On the Jewish Question" completed the transfer of his analysis of Christian personalism from the monarchic to the postrevolutionary liberal state.

98   "Critique of Hegel's Philosophy of Law," p. 109.
99   Ibid., p. 30.   100   Ibid., p. 31.
101   J. L. Cohen, *Class and Civil Society. The Limits of Marxian Critical Theory* (Amherst, 1982), p. 35.

### From Theology to Liberalism and Back Again

"On the Jewish Question" was written immediately after Marx finished his "Critique of Hegel's Philosophy of Law," and it continued the inquiry into the conditions of the modern state and society begun in that work. Yet Marx's thinking was evolving quickly in the crucial year of 1843, and "The Jewish Question" represents a significant shift in the object of inquiry. Whereas the "Critique" extrapolated from the monarchic form of Christian personalism to the attributes of the "political state" as such, "The Jewish Question" dispensed with the former and focused almost exclusively on the postrevolutionary liberal state, the political republic. In doing so, the essay introduced an important new distinction between progressive and backward social orders that forever devalued the Prussian model in Marx's estimation. That is, he no longer insisted on the essential identity of Christian monarchy and political republicanism but relegated the former to the intransigently unmodern. Although Marx was to discuss Prussian society and politics in many subsequent essays, he never again believed that Prussia could yield general insights into the progressive social and political forms of modernity.

On what did Marx's division between progressive and backward political forms rest? The division had only passing relation to the question of productive forces or class relations, criteria that did not become important to Marx's thinking until he began his collaboration with Engels in 1844.[102] Rather, in "The Jewish Question," the central measure of political modernity is *secularization,* or, more precisely, the degree to which a state and a society have established a secular relationship to each other. This issue was at the heart of Marx's response to Bruno Bauer's attempt to resolve the problem of Jewish emancipation. Marx could fully endorse Bauer's insistence that the emancipation of Jews should be linked with the emancipation of humanity *as such* from religion. What he could not support was Bauer's belief that "the *political* abolition of religion" is "the abolition of religion as such" – that is, Bauer's equation of mere political emancipation from religion with "general human emancipation."[103] For in Marx's view, the political separation of private religion from the state, the liberal goal of a constitutional separation of church and state as it had been consummated in the United States, revealed the inadequacy of political emancipation itself. The political state emancipated the Jew and the Christian as citizens while re-

102   Hunt, *The Political Ideas of Marx and Engels,* p. 66. More generally, see Terrell Carver, *Marx and Engels. The Intellectual Relationship* (Sussex, 1983).
103   "On the Jewish Question," p. 149.

maining indifferent to their private beliefs; but this meant in truth that the state emancipated *itself* from religion while leaving the private person in the unfreedom of religious illusion.[104] As Marx famously declared, political emancipation is not human emancipation.

This observation in itself greatly distanced Marx from Bauer's liberalism, but he opened an entirely new direction when he urged the full secularization of the question of the relationship between religion and politics. Within the parochial context of the Christian state, which presupposed religion as its basis, the critic could only "continue to operate in the sphere of theology, however much we may operate *critically* within it." Only in regard to states that have grounded themselves on nonreligious foundations and adopted a *political,* that is indifferent, attitude toward religion can the critic find his proper object, the political state itself. This reasoning led Marx to a crucial demand for the full secularization of theological questions:

> If we find that even in the country of complete political emancipation [the United States], religion not only *exists,* but displays a *fresh and vigorous vitality,* that is proof that the existence of religion is not in contradiction to the perfection of the state. Since, however, the existence of religion is the existence of a defect, the source of this defect can only be sought in the *nature* of the state itself. We no longer regard religion as the *cause,* but only as the *manifestation* of secular narrowness. Therefore we explain the religious limitations of the free citizens by their secular limitations.[105]

The relation of the political state to religion thus became a symptom, not a cause, of the modern separation of civil society from the state, the private individual from his public *persona* as citizen, true universal (read *social*) human life from the illusory universality of the political state. This was the truly important "translation" that Marx performed on his Feuerbachian script. We have seen in detail that Marx did not have to convert Feuerbach's theological and metaphysical concerns into political and social terms. If he did perform an act of translation, it consisted in removing the critique of civil society and the state from the broader Left Hegelian campaign against Christianity and establishing sociopolitical critique as the object of an autonomous secular discourse of sociological and economic analysis.

Here, however, we need to proceed with considerable caution, for this was a questionable secularization indeed. Having called attention to the ideological nature of the religious question, one might reasonably expect Marx to trace theological issues back to their secular roots. That is what Marx

104  Ibid., p. 152.    105  Ibid., p. 151.

thought he was doing, but to have achieved that would have required the tools of secular analysis. Without question, those tools developed as Marx formulated the tenets of historical materialism and deepened his analysis of economic forces. But in 1843, Marx mistook an analogy for an analysis. That is, his treatment of the modern state depended on a brilliant extension of the structure of Left Hegelian politico-theological critique into the secular domain of society and politics. Through a curious alchemy, he recast a secular state of affairs, the separation of the modern state from civil society, as itself *theological*. "Man, even if he proclaims himself an atheist through the medium of the state, that is, if he proclaims the state to be atheist, still remains in the grip of religion, precisely because he acknowledges himself only by a roundabout route, only through an intermediary."[106] This is a compelling Feuerbachian metaphor, but in "The Jewish Question," where mere politics, the political republic, political emancipation, the "rights of man" are all condemned as "theological," the metaphor guides the analysis throughout. Indeed, metaphor becomes identity.

Hence, Marx made a telling revision in the discussion of the "Christian state" as it had developed in Bauer and Ruge's writings. "The perfect Christian state," Marx now claimed, "is not the so-called *Christian* state, which acknowledges Christianity as its basis, as the state religion, and therefore adopts an exclusive attitude towards the other religions. On the contrary, the perfect Christian state is the *atheistic* state, the *democratic* state, the state which relegates religion to a place among the other elements of civil society."[107] Paradoxically, it is the atheistic state that is the "political realisation of Christianity" because it consummates Christianity's separation of the particular man from the universality of humanity. Political democracy realizes Christianity's sovereign individualism in a way that personalist monarchy never could: "Political democracy is Christian since in it man, not merely one man, but every man, ranks as *sovereign*, as the highest being." In that the political citizen relates to the state only as an atomized being, he is "not yet a *real* species-being. That which is a creation of fantasy, a dream, a postulate of Christianity, i.e., the sovereignty of man – but man as an alien being different from the real man – becomes in democracy tangible reality, present existence, and secular principle."[108]

Likewise, Marx's descriptions of civil society are driven by the metaphoric identification of secular and theological phenomena. Indeed, his comments are nearly perfect distillations of the decade-long radical Hegelian objection to the social effects of Christian personalism. "Religion has become the

106  Ibid., p. 152.     107  Ibid., p. 156.     108  Ibid., p. 159.

spirit of *civil society*, of the sphere of egoism, of *bellum omnium contra omnes*. It is no longer the essence of *community*, but the essence of *difference*. It has become the expression of man's *separation* from his *community*, from himself and from other men."[109] Or again, he writes that

[t]he members of the political state are religious owing to the dualism between individual life and species-life, between the life of civil society and political life. They are religious because men treat the political life of the state, an area beyond their real individuality, as if it were their true life. They are religious insofar as religion here is the spirit of civil society, expressing the separation and remoteness of man from man.[110]

And finally, in a passage that epitomizes the entire discourse that we have traced in this book:

[it] is only in the *Christian* world that civil society attains perfection. Only under the dominance of Christianity, which makes *all* national, natural, moral, and theoretical conditions *extrinsic* to man, could civil society separate itself completely from the life of the state, sever all the species-ties of man, put egoism and selfish need in the place of these species-ties, and dissolve the human world into a world of atomistic individuals who are inimically opposed to one another.[111]

The contradictory basis of Marx's method should be clear. At the same time as he resolved to turn "theological questions into secular ones," he metaphorically converted secular phenomena into theology. His intention to explain religion as a manifestation of secular narrowness in fact exposed the "theological" structure of that secular base. So he concluded there can be no secularization within the terms of the political state. The true confrontation with theology must occur fully outside theology, on the ground of the modern separation of society from the state, individual from community, bourgeois from citizen, abstract person from concrete person. Thus, Marx conceived his first great work against liberalism as the last great act in the history of secularization. Secularizing zeal and hostility toward the intrusion of theology into human affairs lived on in his totalizing equation of social and political emancipation with human emancipation from all religious illusions.

Marx's struggle to *secularize* the *liberal* state completed a process that had been under way for over a decade – the Hegelian Left's growing identification of Christian personalism, particularly in its Protestant form, with liberal

---

individualism. It is tempting to say that the shape of Marx's thought in 1843 and thereafter was determined by this process, but intellectual context never determines. It only makes certain outcomes more likely than others. Allowing for the inventiveness of Marx's extraordinary intelligence, we have seen how profoundly this intellectual context acted upon him in the crucial years between his conversion to Hegelianism and his moral conversion to communism. By the summer of 1843, Marx had already taken two steps away from a direct engagement with Christian personalism. First, repeating a move already made by Feuerbach and Ruge, his critique of Hegel had transposed the issues of the campaign against personalism onto his erstwhile philosophical master. Second, "The Jewish Question" transferred those issues still further away from their original referent, by making them synonymous with the results of the modern political revolution.

Marx was by no means alone in shifting the center of gravity toward the critique of liberalism. Pietists, orthodox Protestants, Positive Philosophers, and Speculative Theists had become the objects of a Left Hegelian critique of egoistical and asocial individualism that we more readily associate with a leftist opposition to liberalism. In this association of personalism with asocial egoism, the difference between conservative theological and secular liberal ideas of personhood could easily disappear. Ruge had elided the crucial difference between these accounts of personhood in his 1843 critique of liberalism, when he identified liberal individualism with the theistic notion of the self. Edgar Bauer had branded liberalism a *theology* in his 1842 *Streit der Kritik*, a charge that Moses Hess echoed shortly afterward in his "Philosophy of the Deed." Marx followed a similar path. He fully embraced the Left Hegelian claim for the social ontology of the self, and he identified individual freedom and self-actualization with the individual's participation in humanity's collective social life.

Within a few years, Marx was to turn against the Feuerbachian version of this social ontology and reject the concept of species-being because of its ahistorical and essentialist elements. Nonetheless, he was among the true heirs of Feuerbach's humanism, and this was true not only in the sense that he, like Ruge, Engels, or Moses Hess, adopted Feuerbach's model of human essence. It was true also in the sense of his appropriation of Feuerbach's critique of the Christian conception of the self, a conception of the self that came to represent for Marx the very essence of heteronomy and alienation. "On the Jewish Question" marks the vital point in Marx's intellectual career when he extended the model of Christian personhood to all conceptions of personhood outside the one socialized idea of personality as collective human species-being. With the exception of social personality, the notion of

personhood threatened to become synonymous with heteronomy and alienation. The nonsocialized self, along with the social and political structures
that support it, came to appear as *theological* – that is, such a self derived its
substance from its metaphoric connection to the construction of divine personality that the radical Hegelians had condemned as anti-social and anti-
political. The hostility toward the isolated ego that had begun with Feuerbach's demand that the ego be "dethroned" culminated in Marx's demand
that the self be enfranchized to elect its full social being.

# CONCLUSION

The political theorist Kirstie McClure noted recently the "complicity between the sovereign subject and the sovereign state in modern political theory."[1] At one level, the Young Hegelians' struggle against the political theology of Restoration Germany seems to support her claim. After all, that contest in the 1830s and 1840s was ultimately a struggle over the complicity between concepts of the self and of sovereignty. On another level, however, this vital episode in the intellectual history of nineteenth-century Germany demonstrates just how complex that complicitous relationship has been. For the discourse of the "sovereign subject" is usually associated with what McClure describes as "the unitary self-present subject of modernity."[2] In its political form, this translates into the autonomous self of a modern "liberal" discourse that reached its German apogee in the political theory of Kant. Hence, in both the *impersonal* modern state and the *personal* self, "sovereignty" rests on the normative assumption of rational, autonomous, self-determining subjectivity. The political theology of the Restoration, by contrast, pursued the reactionary goal of reinvesting the state with *personal* power, thereby challenging the modern state's trajectory toward impersonal authority. The

1   McClure quoted in Elshtain, "Sovereign God, Sovereign State, Sovereign Self," p. 1375.
2   K. McClure, "On the Subject of Rights: Pluralism, Plurality and Political Identity," *Dimensions of Radical Democracy. Pluralism, Citizenship, Community*, ed. Chantal Mouffe (London, 1992), p. 115.

Restoration rebelled against the rationalist attempt to subordinate sovereignty to a normative order by insisting instead on the transcendence of a sovereign decision maker over any and all rational constraint.

Anti-modern, anti-liberal, and anti-rationalist as its goals were, however, the German Restoration also based its own construction of sovereignty upon a model of the "sovereign subject." Without question, the Restorationist concept of selfhood reversed the signs of the liberal idea. For rational autonomy, Restorationists substituted an autonomy born of the sinful separation of man from God; for a personhood based on the common possession of reason, they substituted a personhood based on an age-old image of the personal God. And the Restorationist and liberal concepts of sovereign selfhood, moreover, led to radically different theoretical constructions of the state, on the one hand, to authoritarianism, on the other, to a minimal state guaranteeing the rights and liberties of citizens. Yet despite these differences, liberal theory and Restorationist political theology both rest upon a strong claim about the ontological status of the person. Even though in one case the self is defined by reason, in the other by will, both assume that the reality of the self precedes the reality of society. This overlapping assumption has made "personalism" itself a highly flexible, ambiguous position, capable of supporting a reactionary authoritarian argument, as in Friedrich Julius Stahl's example, whereas in other historical contexts it has underpinned progressive arguments for civil liberties based on the inviolable dignity of all persons.

This overlap also complicated the Young Hegelian revolt against the dominant form of Christian personalism in Germany. For, as we have seen, the Hegelians' political critique targeted not only the despotic personalism of the sovereign monarch but also the apparent social and political effects of the Christian construction of the sovereign self. This latter aspect explains the paradoxical fact that the Young Hegelians directed a critique of egoistical and anti-social individualism against conservative Christian thinkers whose own anti-liberal credentials were unimpeachable. It was only subsequently, *after* the articulation of a radical critique of the social effects of Christian personalism, that the Left Hegelians launched a critique against liberalism itself, and their critical rejection of liberalism essentially involved grafting liberal individualism onto the stem of theologically based notions of the self. It was not only liberal and reactionary views of selfhood that they conflated and reviled, however. Feuerbach, Ruge, and Marx also came to associate Hegel with the coterie of orthodox Lutherans, Restorationists, and Positive Philosophers who had been his staunchest critics. Of course, they were not blind to the differences between Hegel and his conservative opponents, but the differences came to be outweighed by Hegel's perceived complicity in the discourse of Christian personalism.

This was a remarkable turn of affairs. For Hegel's philosophy of religion had long opposed the orthodox notion of the personality of God; and his political philosophy had made clear his strong opposition to both the neofeudalist ideology of Ludwig von Haller and all forms of personalist monarchical sovereignty. The transference of Feuerbach, Ruge, and Marx's critique of Christian Positivism and personalism to Hegel can be explained in part by the dynamic development of their critique itself. That is, their insights into the possible theological and political implications of Hegel's philosophy were sharpened through prior interactions with Schelling, orthodox Lutherans, and the Positive Philosophers. Furthermore, the Left Hegelians' critique of Hegel must also be explained in relation to the larger ideological and political context in the late 1830s and early 1840s. Of particular significance was the gradual accommodation of right-wing Hegelianism to the theistic discourse of Positive Philosophy and conservative political Romanticism. This was a process of accommodation stimulated both by the progressive clarification of the ideological ambiguities of Hegelianism itself and by the ascendancy of conservative forces in Prussian politics and culture. In the eyes of the Hegelian Left, the gravitation of many Hegelians toward those forces of reaction had the effect of blurring the distinction between Hegel and his erstwhile enemies. It was a process, therefore, that greatly contributed to the Young Hegelian revolt against Hegel himself.

In light of these conceptual elisions and slippages, it would clearly be mistaken to apply excessively firm political labels to the fluid period before 1848. Reactionaries were not strictly or exclusively organicist communitarians, nor was the leftist critique of "civil society," private property, and individualism directed solely against liberalism. The history of the debates over personalism demonstrates forcefully the power of context – ideological, social, and political – in shaping intellectual concerns and perceptions. That history cautions us against simplifying the "political" history of modern selfhood by reducing it to the fortunes of liberalism. The discourse of personalism reveals that other contending conceptions of the self were not simply historical anachronisms but stood right at the center of a development that we readily take as essential to the formation of political modernity. I refer to the archetypal clash between liberal individualism and socialist collectivism, a clash that was, as we saw, rehearsed and conditioned in the German context by the dispute between Hegelians and Christian personalists.

This conflict was waged within living memory of the French Revolution and under the immediate shadow of the Revolution of 1830. For the historian Leopold von Ranke, the July Days were a disheartening sign that the Restoration had been in vain. "The Revolution," he wrote, "which has often been pronounced at an end, seems never to be finished. It reappears in ever new and antagonistic forms."[3] The vehemence and the scope of a controversy over as esoteric a theme as "personality" are directly explained by the dilemma of democratic power, the permanent challenge of a permanently revolutionary age. For as Claude Lefort has observed, democracy's most basic feature is the radical "disincorporation" or, literally, the "disembodiment" of power. All earlier conceptions of power had demanded that power be invested inalienably in some *body,* some person or corporate assembly of persons; but democracy survives only so long as no one and everyone holds power. The center of democratic power is an "empty place." Democratic power may be contested – indeed, democracy depends on that contest – but it cannot be appropriated, nor can democratic power be represented. Even the "people," the democratic sovereign, eludes representation, embodiment, substantiality. In the institution of universal suffrage, writes Lefort, at "the very moment when popular sovereignty is assumed to manifest itself, when the people is assumed to actualize itself by expressing its will, . . . social interdependence breaks down and . . . the citizen is abstracted from all the networks in which his social life develops and becomes a mere statistic. Number replaces substance."[4]

The "empty place" of democratic power explains early-nineteenth-century intellectuals' intense preoccupation with the nature of sovereignty and the politicized problem of "incarnation." Against the indeterminacy of democracy and its subversion of the symbolic and real order of power and privilege, the personalist political theology of German conservatives was an attempt to "incorporate" power once again, to give it a body, substance, visibility, and representability. And this was not merely a throwback to medieval notions of kingship but also an anticipation of twentieth-century attempts, by right-wing theorists like Carl Schmitt, to embody a totalizing racialist "democracy" in the person of the dictator.

In combatting the political theology of Restoration, the Left Hegelians struggled to accept democracy's radical disincorporation of power. Yet in challenging the sovereign discourse of their day, in aiming to dethrone the self, the left-wing Hegelians faced the constant temptation to substitute one form of "embodiment" for another, to replace democracy's indeterminate

3  Ranke quoted in Stuke, *Philosophie der Tat,* p. 57.
4  Claude Lefort, "The Question of Democracy," *Democracy and Political Theory,* trans. David Macey (Cambridge, 1988), pp. 18–19.

and contestatory interactions with a more certain form of unity. For the Young Hegelians were quick to identify a human essence in which all humans share and to posit a vision of radical collectivization that would secure both – and it is important to emphasize both – the conditions for individual self-realization and the perfectibility of the species. The notion of a unitary subject, which they had attacked in Christian personalism, threatened constantly to reappear in the form of a hypostatized meta-person, "Man" as a collective essence. The Young Hegelians reinscribed personalism insofar as they conceived of humanity as a meta-subjective essence or species-being.

In dreaming of the full unification of humanity, the Young Hegelians were prey to a characteristic temptation of radical democratic theory. Following Rousseau, radical democrats in the late eighteenth and early nineteenth centuries constructed the image of the sovereign "people" as the exact opposite of the monarch. To the arbitrary unified will of the monarch was opposed the rational unified will of the people, to the natural personality of the monarch was opposed the moral personality of the people, to the private person of the monarch was opposed the "public person" formed, as Rousseau wrote, "by the union of individuals."[5] The radical democratic discourse of sovereignty neither fully escaped the structure of the monarchic discourse it sought to overthrow, nor did it fully resist the temptation to fill the "empty place" of democratic power. As Michel Foucault once remarked, "the representation of power has remained under the spell of monarchy. In political thought and analysis, we still have not cut off the head of the king."[6]

If the Left Hegelians revealed the difficulty of escaping the limits of a theory of power that searches for unitary embodiment, they also exposed the difficulty of breaking with the theologico-political terms against which they struggled. Claude Lefort has suggested that a wide range of early-nineteenth-century French political thinkers – from reactionary legitimists like De Maistre to the liberals Guizot and Tocqueville, the Saint-Simonians, Comtean positivists, and republican Romantics like Michelet – "all looked to the religious for the means to reconstitute a pole of unity which could ward off the threat of the break up of the social that arose out of the defeat of the Ancien Regime." Lefort's observation applies with equal force not only to the German Christian personalists but to their radical adversaries as well. For Heine,

---

5   Rousseau, "The Social Contract," *Social Contract. Essays by Locke, Hume and Rousseau* (Oxford, 1948), p. 257.
6   Foucault, *The History of Sexuality. An Introduction*, trans. Robert Hurley (New York, 1990), p. 89.

Hess, Cieszkowski, Ruge, and Feuerbach could not contemplate the possibility of democracy without reappropriating religion as a secular political faith. Hence, Left Hegelian "humanism" is conceived as exteriorized, demystified religion, but with its devotional core intact and ready to be self-consciously directed toward its true object, Man.

The status of the theological was a complex issue in the political debates of the early nineteenth century. Theology, Hans Blumenberg has cautioned, was not simply the underlying *substance* of political concepts, as Carl Schmitt had argued; rather, the controversy over personality reveals the category of the "theological" functioning complexly – as metaphor, parallel, analogy – in debates that groped for a transcendent presence to fill the empty place of democratic power. For the Young Hegelians, this impulse revealed itself in a double move – first, the negation of transcendence through the exposure of the anthropological secret of all mystifications, and second, the reinscription of the immanent community of men as itself a source of transcendence. The fact that the Left Hegelians lapsed into a quasi-religious language when they envisioned the politics of Humanity tied them to one of the most pervasive themes of early-nineteenth-century political theory, the intersection of politics and religion. Their language does not verify a Schmittian view of secularization, in which the political is *really* the theological; it diminishes neither the radical novelty of their critique of Christian culture, nor its status as the inaugural gesture of modern radical social theory. However, the theological remainder in the politics of Left Hegelian humanism does underscore the difficulties that a "secularizing" critique encounters once it begins to conjure with the panoply of religious analogies and metaphors that a Christian culture makes so omnipresently available.

The Left Hegelians were not oblivious to this difficulty, and their awareness helps to explain further shifts in Feuerbach's and Ruge's thinking in the years immediately before 1848. Feuerbach was deeply affected by Max Stirner's vigorous critique of his conception of species-being as a vestigial theological abstraction. Reluctant though he was to acknowledge the accuracy of Stirner's objections, Feuerbach moved away from the universalizing idea of humanity that had animated *The Essence of Christianity* in 1841 toward a greater emphasis on the sensuous, needful, individual human being. Ruge also grew troubled by some of the implications of Young Hegelian humanism, as well as by the communist position with which he had flirted during his collaboration with Marx on the *Deutsche-Französische Jahrbücher.* Impressed if not fully persuaded by Stirner's insistence on the "actual person," Ruge agonized over the "obliterating generality" of both socialism and

## CONCLUSION

Feuerbachian humanism.[7] He continued to hold his radical democratic views, which were to place him on the far Left at the Frankfurt Parliament in 1848, as well as his conviction that the "person" is not simply given but is a product of society. Yet he came to believe that the idea of the social construction of the person jeopardizes the basic rights and freedoms for which he had fought.[8] For the primacy of society threatens to undermine the reality of the person who is the bearer of rights and freedoms. In other words, an intelligible and emancipatory concept of rights and laws demands a subject of those rights and laws – a person who endorses them and bears them as his or hers. Ruge never succeeded in reconciling this new rights-based concern for personhood with his commitment to the actualization of civic and social personality; but the problem that made him retreat from communism in 1844 has dogged radical thought ever since.

And what of Marx? What of the radically secularizing thrust of his social critique? We have seen that the implicit sociopolitical dimension of the radical rejection of Christian personalism in the 1830s made it relatively easy for Marx to transfer the critique of Christian personhood to a more strictly secular criticism of civil society once the "critique of religion" was "completed," as he put it. As Marx and Engels developed their critique of political economy, they relegated Christianity more and more to an ideological function. They no longer regarded Christianity as both cause and symptom of an egoistical, de-politicized civil society, as had Rousseau, the young Hegel, Feuerbach, and Ruge. The critique of Christianity lost importance for Marx and Engels, not only because they believed religion had been dealt a killing blow by the Young Hegelians but also because they assigned far less causal importance to cultural phenomena in themselves. The older association of Christianity with civil society dropped away. In fact, as Derrida recently reminded us, Marx thought that "'Christianity has no history whatsoever,' no history of its own," that the forms of religion are, rather, subjected to the conditions of a "determined form of society" and "determined relations of exchange and industry."[9] No other radical emerging from the formative experience of the Hegelian School went so far in negating the substance and effects of religion.

Nonetheless, while Marx articulated a radical negation of Christianity, he remained tied to that negation. Indeed, Marx, too, reveals the dilemmas of

7   Ruge, "Unsre letzten zehn Jahre," p. 152.
8   See Ruge, "Freiheit und Recht," *Sämmtliche Werke*, vol. 6, pp. 352–8.
9   Derrida, *Specters of Marx. The State of the Debt, the Work of Mourning & the New International*, trans. Peggy Kamuf (New York, 1994), p. 122.

a radical critical project that founds itself upon religious analogy. This reliance on analogy, as we have observed, steered Marx's pivotal critique of political liberalism and the secular modern state. Years later, in *Capital*, we find Marx explaining commodity fetishism, that disguise of human social relations in the "fantastic form of a relation between things." "In order . . . to find an analogy," he writes, "we must take flight into the misty realm of religion. There the products of the human brain appear as autonomous figures endowed with a life of their own, which enter into relations both with each other and with the human race. So it is in the world of commodities with the products of men's hands."[10] The function of the analogy is clear, and it seems intended to establish a limited formal relation between otherwise disparate phenomena. Still, it is unclear at what point the analogy gives way to a substantial identity in the way in which the two phenomena are conceived and criticized. In drawing the analogy between liberalism and Christianity, or commodity fetishism and religion, Marx proceeded to criticize these secular phenomena as if they really did take the form prescribed to them by an analogy. Hence, as Derrida observes in relation to a different issue, for Marx, the "religious is not just one ideological phenomenon or phantomatic production among others. [It] gives to the production of . . . or the ideological phantasm its originary form or its paradigm of reference, its first 'analogy.'"[11]

This interplay between religious analogy and "ideological phenomenon" was nowhere as fateful as in Marx's critique of liberalism. Having identified Christian personhood with all forms of personality outside the one idea of social personality, Marx came to regard the nonsocialized self as *theological*, derived from the metaphor of divine personality, to be overcome through a radically secularizing critique. Ironically, from the standpoint of a radical social theory that would seek the "concrete individual" in the relations of society and production, the "self," in common with the Christianity in which it is implicated, has no "history."

The trajectory of the radical Left Hegelian critique of personality was toward the erasure of the category of personhood altogether or its displacement into a meta-personal universal identity. Marx followed this trajectory, even as he became more and more committed to the proletariat as the concrete locus of human species-being. The negation of the discourse of theistic personhood ceased to be the issue for Marx. What was at stake was the credibility of any conception of personhood outside that of the social individual. This

10  Marx, *Capital*, vol. I, trans. Ben Fowkes (New York, 1977), p. 165.
11  Derrida, *Specters of Marx*, p. 166.

quickly led Marx to indict the discourse of liberal democratic rights, with its core assumption that any meaningful conception of freedom must suppose some degree of tension or distinction between the individual and the society that shapes her or him. It need hardly be said that those liberal democratic rights have been vulnerable to ideological distortions in the course of their history or that Marxian critique continues to suggest ways to recognize and analyze such distortions. However, the main point is that, inadvertently and fatefully, in the quest for human emancipation from all external authority, in the search for the preconditions of the fullest individual self-realization, Marx left vacant the very *center* of the discourse of rights, the person as the bearer of rights and freedoms. With a single metaphoric leap, Marx traversed the ground separating theism and liberalism and dispensed with the focal concerns of contemporary juristic discourse. The dictum of his teacher, Eduard Gans, that "the person belongs to himself," a dictum that Gans had upheld even as he grappled with social inequity, could now be dismissed along with all the other illusory impediments to human emancipation. Having slipped from theistic personality to all forms of legal personality, Marx never returned again to the problem of the individual person except to deride it.

The vitally important debates of the 1830s and 1840s posed issues that have resurfaced as central concerns of the new discussion of civil society in the 1980s and 1990s. While some pundits have been content to associate civil society with triumphant liberal capitalism, democratic critical theorists have attempted to distinguish themselves from both Marxian and liberal capitalist views of society, state, and sovereignty. For these thinkers, the key to the new debate about civil society is the need to rethink both the sovereign state and the sovereign subject, to imagine what Jean Bethke Elshtain calls a "politics without strong sovereignty."[12] The politics of civil society, according to Andrew Arato and Jean Cohen, must involve a "self-limiting" process of democratization, a process that resists temptations to construct politics in terms of strong, monopolistic sovereign power, whether that is conceived as modern statism or as dreams of universal community, full transparency, total unification, or unitary identity. Similarly, evoking the ideal of "post-modern" pluralism, Chantal Mouffe writes that

> our understanding of radical democracy . . . postulates the very impossibility of a final realization of democracy. It affirms that the unresolvable tension between the principles of equality and liberty is the very condition for the preservation of the indeterminacy and undecidability which is constitutive of mod-

12  Elshtain, "Sovereign God, Sovereign State, Sovereign Self," p. 1376.

ern democracy. Moreover, it constitutes the principal guarantee against any attempt to realize a final closure that would result in the elimination of the political and the negation of democracy.[13]

Such a pluralism, in the words of Kirstie McClure, involves a critique of "unitary, monolithic or totalizing conceptions of the political domain," as well
as resistance to "constructions of political identity and subjectivity that take
state institutions as the principal sites, and state power as the primary object,
of political struggle."[14]

It would lead us too far afield to do any more than gesture toward this
dimension of the new discussion of politics and society. What must be emphasized here is that all of these current writers would agree that at its most
basic level, the new debate about civil society rests upon the question of the
self, as did the debate in the 1830s and 1840s. For the current discussion,
the really crucial move is to replace the notion of the sovereign subject with
a new appreciation for the manifold roles that help sustain and constitute
personal identity. Of course, for some, particularly those inspired by Nietzsche
and Heidegger, this recognition has led to a radical negation or decon-
struction of all received notions of the personal subject, individual identity, and agency, including those initiated by the Left Hegelian move toward the "species-subject" or the "class-subject" of Marxism. For others,
however, it has prompted an effort to reconceptualize the individual subject without effacing the "unresolvable tensions" that themselves provide
the terms and conditions for the articulation of identity in the social-po-
litical domain.[15]

Perhaps no one has expressed this new sensibility as powerfully and as
freed from party or jargon as Vaclav Havel. Ironically, at the end of this account of the Young Hegelians' emancipatory struggle against the sovereign
discourse of personal authority, we encounter Havel's summons "to the
globally crucial struggle against the momentum of impersonal power."
Against that momentum, Havel wrote in 1988 of "rehabilitating the personal experience of human beings as the initial measure of things, placing
morality above politics and responsibility above our desires, making human
community meaningful, returning content to human speaking, reconsti-
tuting, as the focus of all social activity, the autonomous, integral and dig-
nified human 'I.'" "I favor 'anti-political politics,'" Havel continued. "I favor politics as practical morality, as service to the truth, as essentially human

---

13  Chantal Mouffe, "Democratic Politics Today," *Dimensions of Radical Democracy*, p. 13.
14  McClure, "On the Subject of Rights," pp. 115, 120.
15  See, for example, the formulation in Ibid., pp. 123–4.

and humanly measured care for our fellow-humans."[16] Havel's own personalism is not to be understood as a restoration of "sovereign subjectivity," of isolated, atomized, egoistical selfhood, whether in the form of Christian personalism or of the liberal *homo economicus*. Instead, Havel, like many of the participants in the current discussion of civil society, has tried to follow a different direction by making visible the forcefield of private and public, social and civic associations within which freedoms are defended and extended, personal identities are formed, multiplied, and re-formed, and the indeterminacy and undecidability of modern democracy are affirmed and enacted.

It remains an open question whether a new model of interaction, multiplicity, and intersubjectivity can articulate an idea of porous and overlapping sovereignties that will be capable of replacing the strong sovereignty that was integral to past conceptions of power. It also remains unclear whether the theoretical challenge to strong sovereignty is simply following in the tail of global economic forces that have launched an infinitely stronger, and very different, challenge to the sovereign state and the sovereign subject. It remains, finally, uncertain whether current theorists can fundamentally rethink the complicities of sovereign subject and sovereign state when the very language of political thought keeps deferring Foucault's called-for conceptual "regicide," when our concepts keep pulling us back to identity, subjectivity, personalism, and sovereignty. But this, too, may be one of the unresolvable tensions to be affirmed, not denied, by a progressive and emancipatory politics that recognizes its own history and is chastened by it.

16 Vaclav Havel, "Anti-Political Politics," *Civil Society and the State*, ed. John Keane, pp. 392, 396–97.

# BIBLIOGRAPHY

## PRIMARY

### Journals and Newspapers

*Allgemeinen Literatur-Zeitung*, März, 1831.
*Blätter für literarische Unterhaltung*, 1837.
*Deutsche Jahrbücher für Wissenschaft und Kunst*, July 1841–Jan. 1843.
*Deutsche Vierteljahrsschrift*, 1844.
*Die Epigonen*, 1847.
*Die Evangelische Kirchenzeitung*, 1833–1838.
*Le Globe*, 1832.
*Hallische Jahrbücher für deutsche Wissenschaft und Kunst*, 1838–1841.
*Jahrbücher für wissenschaftliche Kritik*, 1827–1846.
*Kritische Zeitschrift für Rechtswissenschaft und Gesetzgebung des Auslandes*, 1832.
*Literarischer Zodiacus*, 1835.
*Raumers Historisches Taschenbuch*, 1834–1835.
*Tübinger Zeitschrift für Theologie*, 1832.
*Zeitschrift für Philosophie und Spekulative Theologie*, 1836–1839.

### Books

Anonymous. *Über den vierten Stand und die socialen Reformen.* Augsburg, 1844.
Barker, Ernest, ed. *Social Contract. Essays by Locke, Hume and Rousseau.* Oxford, 1948.

Bauer, Bruno. *Briefwechsel zwischen Bruno Bauer und Edgar Bauer während der Jahre 1839–1842 aus Bonn und Berlin.* Charlottenberg, 1844.

*Die evangelische Landeskirche Preussens und die Wissenschaft.* Leipzig, 1840.

*Feldzüge der reinen Kritik.* Ed. Hans-Martin Sass. Frankfurt, 1968.

*The Jewish Problem.* Trans. Helen Lederer. Cincinnati, 1958.

*Kritik der evangelischen Geschichte der Synoptiker.* Vols. 1–2. Leipzig: Otto Wigand, 1841.

Vol. 3: *Kritik der evangelischen Geschichte der Synoptiker und des Johannes.* Braunschweig, 1842.

*Die Religion des Alten Testamentes in der geschichtlichen Entwickelung ihrer Principien.* 2 vols. Berlin, 1838.

*The Trumpet of the Last Judgement Against Hegel the Atheist and Antichrist.* Trans. L. Stepelevich. Lewiston, N.Y., 1988.

Bauer, Edgar. *Die liberalen Bestrebungen in Deutschland. Volume I: Die Irrthümer der Ostpreußischen Opposition.* Zürich und Winterthur, 1843.

[Bauer, Edgar]. *Staat, Religion und Partei.* Leipzig, 1843.

Behler, Ernst, ed. *Philosophy of German Idealism.* New York, 1987.

Blanc, Louis. *Geschichte der zehn Jahre, 1830 bis 1840.* Trans. G. Fink. Leipzig, 1843.

Bodin, Jean. *On Sovereignty.* Trans. J. H. Franklin. Cambridge, 1992.

Börne, Ludwig. *Briefe aus Paris.* Wiesbaden, 1986.

*Schriften zur deutschen Literatur.* Ed. Walter Dietze. Leipzig, 1987.

Bretschneider, Karl Gottlieb. *Der Simonismus und das Christenthum. Oder: beurtheilende Darstellung der Simonistischen Religion, ihres Verhältnisses zur christlichen Kirche, und der Lage des Christenthums in unserer Zeit.* Leipzig, 1832.

[Buhl, Ludwig]. *Hegels Lehre vom Staat und seine Philosophie der Geschichte in ihren Hauptresultaten.* Berlin, 1837.

Carganico, L. A., and K. E. Schubarth. *Über Philosophie überhaupt und Hegels Encyclopädie der philosophischen Wissenschaften insbesondere.* Berlin, 1829.

[Carové, Friedrich Wilhelm]. *Hegel und Preußen. Principes mortales, res publica aeterna.* Frankfurt, 1841.

*Neorama,* 3 vols. Leipzig, 1838.

*Der Saint-Simonismus und die neuere französische Philosophie.* Leipzig, 1831.

Cieszkowski, August. *Du crédit et de la circulation.* Paris, 1839.

*Gott und Palingenesie.* Berlin, 1842.

*Prolegomena zur Historiosophie,* 2nd ed. Posen, 1908.

Echtermeyer, Theodor, and Arnold Ruge. *Der Protestantismus und die Romantik.* Ed. Norbert Ollers. Hildesheim, 1972.

Engels, Friedrich. *Ludwig Feuerbach and the End of Classical German Philosophy.* Peking, 1976.

Feuerbach, Friedrich. *Die Religion der Zukunft,* 2 vols. Zürich and Winterthur, 1843; Nürnberg, 1845.

Feuerbach, Ludwig. *Briefwechsel,* 4 vols. Ed. W. Schuffenhauer and E. Voigt. Berlin, 1984–8.

*The Essence of Christianity.* Trans. George Eliot. New York, 1957.

*The Fiery Brook: Selected Writings of Ludwig Feuerbach.* Trans. Zawar Hanfi. New York, 1972.

*Gesammelte Werke.* 18 vols. to date. Ed. Werner Schuffenhauer. Berlin, 1967– .

*Lectures on the Essence of Religion.* Trans. Ralph Manheim. New York, 1967– .

*Ludwig Feuerbach in seinem Briefwechsel und Nachlass.* 2 vols. Ed. Karl Grün. Leipzig, 1874.

*Principles of the Philosophy of the Future.* Trans. Manfred Vogel. Indianapolis, 1986.

*Sämtliche Werke.* 13 vols. Ed. W. Bolin and F. Jodl. Stuttgart, 1959–64.

*Thoughts on Death and Immortality, from the Papers of a Thinker, along with an Appendix of Theological-Satirical Epigrams, by One of His Friends.* Trans. James Massey. Berkeley, 1980.

*Werke in Sechs Bänden.* 6 vols. Ed. Erich Thies. Frankfurt, 1975.

*Das Wesen des Christenthums.* Leipzig, 1841.

Fichte, Immanuel Hermann. *Die Idee der Persönlichkeit und der individuellen Fortdauer.* Elberfeld, 1834.

*Sätze zur Vorschule der Theologie.* Stuttgart and Tübingen, 1826.

*Über Gegensatz, Wendepunkt und Ziel heutiger Philosophie. Erster kritischer Theil.* Heidelberg, 1832.

*Vermischte Schriften zur Philosophie, Theologie und Ethik.* 2 vols. Leipzig, 1969.

Fichte, J. G. *The Vocation of Man.* Trans. Peter Preuss. Indianapolis, 1987.

Fischer, K. Ph. *Die Freiheit des menschlichen Willens im Fortschritte ihrer Momente.* Tübingen, 1833.

Fried, Albert, and Ronald Sanders, eds. *Socialist Thought. A Documentary History.* New York, 1964.

Gans, Eduard. *Beiträge zur Revision der Preußischen Gesetzgebung* (Berlin, 1831).

*Eduard Gans (1797–1839): Hegelianer-Jude-Europaer.* Ed. Norbert Waszek. Frankfurt, 1991.

*Naturrecht und Universalgeschichte.* Ed. Manfred Riedel. Stuttgart, 1981.

*Philosophische Schriften.* Ed. Horst Schroder. Glashutten im Taunus, 1971.

*Rückblicke auf Personen und Zustände.* Berlin, 1836.

*Über die Grundlage des Besiztes.* Berlin, 1839.

*Vermischte Schriften, juristischen, historischen, staatswissenschaftlichen und ästhetischen Inhalts.* 2 vols. Berlin, 1834.

"Vorlesungen über die Geschichte der letzten fünfzig Jahre," *Raumers Historisches Taschenbuch,* 1834–5.

Gardiner, Patrick L., ed. *Nineteenth Century Philosophy.* New York, 1969.

Göschel, Karl Friedrich. *Beiträge zur spekulativen Philosophie von Gott und dem Menschen und von dem Gott-Menschen: Mit Rücksicht auf Dr. D.F. Strauss' Christologie.* Berlin, 1838.

*Von den Beweisen für die Unsterblichkeit der menschlichen Seele im Lichte der spekulativen Philosophie: Eine Ostergabe.* Berlin, 1835.

*Zerstreuten Blätter aus den Hand-und Hülfsacten eines Juristen,* 3 vols. Erfurt, 1832–42.

Gutzkow, Karl. *Beiträge zur Geschichte des neuesten Literatur.* Stuttgart, 1839.
    *Briefe eines Narren an eine Närrin.* Hamburg, 1832.
Halsted, John B., ed. *Romanticism.* New York, 1969.
Haym, Rudolf. *Hegel und seine Zeit.* Berlin, 1857.
Hegel, G.W.F. *Briefe von und an Hegel.* 3 vols. Ed. Johannes Hoffmeister. Hamburg, 1961.
    *Early Theological Writings.* Trans. T. M. Knox. Philadelphia, 1948.
    *Hegel: The Letters.* Trans. and ed. Clark Butler and Christiane Seiler. Bloomington, 1984.
    *Lectures on the History of Philosophy.* 3 vols. Trans. E. S. Haldane and F. H. Simson. Atlantic Highlands, 1983.
    *Lectures on the Philosophy of Religion.* 3 vols. Trans. E. B. Speirs and J. Burdon Sanderson. London, 1962.
    *Phenomenology of Spirit.* Trans. A. V. Miller. Oxford, 1977.
    *Philosophy of Hegel.* Ed. C. J. Friedrich. New York, 1953.
    *Philosophy of History.* Trans. J. Sibree. New York, 1956.
    *Philosophy of Right.* Trans. T. M. Knox. New York, 1967.
    *Science of Logic.* Trans. A. V. Miller. New York, 1976.
    *System of Ethical Life (1802/3) and First Philosophy of Spirit.* Trans. and ed. H. S. Harris and T. M. Knox. Albany, 1979.
    *Theologische Jugendschriften.* Ed. Hermann Nohl. Tübingen, 1907.
    *Vorlesungen über Rechtsphilosophie, 1818–1831.* 4 vols. Ed. K.-H. Ilting. Stuttgart-Bad Cannstatt, 1973.
    *Werke.* 20 vols. Ed. Eva Moldenhauer and Karl M. Michel. Frankfurt, 1969–71.
Heine, Heinrich. *Heinrich Heine. Sakularausgabe; Werke, Briefwechsel, Lebenszeugnisse.* 27 vols. Ed. Fritz H. Eisner. Berlin, 1970–86.
    *Historisch-kritische Gesamtausgabe der Werke.* Ed. Manfred Windfuhr. 15 vols. Hamburg, 1981.
    *Religion and Philosophy in Germany.* Trans. John Snodgrass. Albany, 1986.
    *The Romantic School and Other Essays.* Ed. Jost Hermand and R. C. Holub. New York, 1985.
    *Sämtliche Werke.* 10 vols. Ed. O. Walzel. Leipzig/Wien, 1911–15.
Hess, Moses. *Moses Hess. Sozialistische Aufsätze, 1841–1847.* Ed. Theodor Zlocisti. Berlin, 1921.
    *Philosophische und sozialistische Schriften 1837–1850. Eine Auswahl.* Ed. Wolfgang Mönke. Vaduz/Liechtenstein, 1980.
Hinrichs, H.F.W. *Die Religion im inneren Verhältnisse zur Wissenschaft: Nebst Darstellung und Beurtheilung der von Jacobi, Kant, Fichte und Schelling gemachten Versuche dieselbe wissenschaftlich zu erfassen, und nach ihrem Hauptinhalte zu entwickeln, mit einem Vorworte von G.W.F. Hegel.* Heidelberg, 1822; reprint, Brussels, 1970.
    *Politische Vorlesungen.* Halle, 1843.
Hobbes, Thomas. *Leviathan.* Ed. C. B. MacPherson. New York, 1985.
    *De Homine.* Trans. Charles T. Wood. Cambridge, 1991.
Iggers, G. G., trans. *The Doctrine of Saint-Simon: An Exposition. First Year, 1828–1829.* New York, 1958.

Jäsche, Gottlob Benjamin. *Der Pantheismus nach seinen verschiedenen Hauptformen, seinem Ursprung und Fortgange, seinem speculativen und praktischen Werth und Gehalt. Ein Beitrag zur Geschichte und Kritik dieser Lehre in alter und neuer Philosophie.* 3 vols. Berlin, 1826.

Jaeschke, Walter, ed. *Philosophie und Literatur im Vormärz. Der Streit um die Romantik (1820–1854),* 2 vols. Hamburg, 1995.

Jarcke, Carl Ernst. *Vermischte Schriften.* 4 vols. Munich, 1839–54.

Kahnis, K. A. *Dr. Ruge und Hegel.* Quedlinburg, 1838.

Kaiser, H. W. *Die Persönlichkeit des Eigenthums in Bezug auf den Socialismus und Communismus in heutigen Frankreich.* Bremen, 1843.

Kant, Immanuel. *Critique of Pure Reason.* Trans. Norman Kemp Smith. New York, 1965.

_____. *On History.* Ed. Lewis White Beck. Indianapolis, 1980.

Laube, Heinrich. *Ausgewählte Werke in zehn Bänden.* Ed. H. H. Houben. Leipzig, n.d.

Leo, Heinrich. *Die Hegelingen: Aktenstücke und Belege zu der s.g. Denunciation der ewigen Wahrheit.* Halle, 1838.

_____. *Studien und Skizzen zu einer Naturlehre des Staates.* Halle, 1833.

Lessing, G. E. *Lessing's Theological Writings.* Trans. Henry Chadwick. Stanford, 1956.

Lübbe, Hermann, ed. *Die Hegelsche Rechte.* Stuttgart-Bad Cannstatt, 1962.

Marx, Karl, and Friedrich Engels. *Collected Works.* Moscow, 1975– .

Michelet, C. L. *Anthropologie und Psychologie, oder die Philosophie des subjectiven Geistes.* Berlin, 1840.

_____. *Vorlesungen über die Persönlichkeit Gottes und Unsterblichkeit des Seele.* Berlin, 1841.

_____. *Wahrheit aus meinem Leben.* Berlin, 1884.

Mundt, Theodor. *Charaktere und Situationen.* Leipzig, 1837.

Oelckers, Theodor. *Die Bewegung des Socialismus und Communismus.* Leipzig, 1844.

Ogienski, Immanuel. *Hegel, Schubarth und die Idee der Persönlichkeit in ihrem Verhältnis zur preussischen Monarchie.* Trzemessno, 1840.

_____. *Die Idee der Person.* Breslau, 1853.

Pepperle, Inrid, and Heinz Pepperle, ed. *Die Hegelsche Linke.* Leipzig, 1985.

Richter, Friedrich. *Die Lehre von den letzten Dingen.* Vol. I: *Eine wissenschaftliche Kritik aus dem Standpunct der Religion unternommen.* Breslau, 1833.

_____. *Die neue Unsterblichkeitslehre: Gespräch einer Abendgesellschaft.* Breslau, 1833.

Rotteck, Carl von, and Carl Welcker, ed. *Staats-Lexicon oder Encyclopädie der Staatswissenschaften.* 1st ed. 15 vols. Altona, 1834–43.

Ruge, Arnold, ed. *Anekdota zur neuesten deutschen Philosophie und Publicistik.* Zürich, 1843.

_____. *Aus früherer Zeit.* 4 vols. Berlin, 1862–7.

_____. *Briefwechsel und Tägeblätter aus den Jahren 1825–1880.* 2 vols. Ed. P. Nerrlich. Berlin, 1886.

_____. *Gesammelte Schriften.* 10 vols. Mannheim, 1846.

_____. *Der Patriotismus.* Ed. Peter Wende. Frankfurt, 1968.

_____. *Polemische Briefe.* Mannheim, 1847.

_____. *Sämmtliche Werke.* 10 vols. Mannheim, 1848.

Schäfer, Rütger, ed. *Saint-Simonistische Texte. Abhandlungen von Saint-Simon, Bazard,*

*Blanqui, Buchez, Carnot, Comte, Enfantin, Leroux, Rodrigues, Thierry und Anderen in zeitgenössischen Übersetzungen.* 2 vols. Aalen, 1975.

Schelling, F.W.G. *Ideas for a Philosophy of Nature as Introduction to the Study of This Science.* Trans. E. E. Harris. Cambridge, 1988.

*The Ages of the World.* Trans. F. de Wolfe Bolman. New York, 1942.

*On the History of Modern Philosophy.* Trans. Andrew Bowie. New York, 1994.

*Sämmtliche Werke, 1833–1850.* 14 vols. Stuttgart and Augsburg, 1856–61.

Schiller, Friedrich. *On the Aesthetic Education of Man in a Series of Letters.* Trans. Reginald Snell. New York, 1990.

Scholz, H., ed. *Die Hauptschriften zum Pantheismus Streit zwischen Jacobi und Mendelssohn.* Berlin, 1916.

Schubarth, K. E. *Erklärung in Betreff der Recension des Hrn. Hegel.* Berlin, 1830.

Spinoza, Benedict de. *Ethics.* Trans. Andrew Boyle. London, 1989.

*A Theologico-Political Treatise.* Trans. R.H.M. Elwes. New York, 1951.

Stahl, Friedrich Julius. *Die Philosophie des Rechts.* Vol. 1: *Geschichte der Rechtsphilosophie.* Vol. 2: *Rechts- und Staatslehre auf der Grundlage Christlicher Weltanschauung.* Part I: *Die Allgemeinen Lehren und das Privatrecht.* Part II: *Die Staatslehre und die Principien des Staatsrechts.* Hildesheim, 1963.

Stepelevich, Lawrence, ed. *The Young Hegelians. An Anthology.* Cambridge, 1983.

Stirner, Max. *The Ego and Its Own.* Trans. David Leopold. Cambridge, 1995.

Strauss, David Friedrich. *Briefwechsel zwischen Strauss und Vischer.* Ed. Adolf Rapp. Stuttgart, 1952.

*Die christliche Glaubenslehre in ihrer geschichtlichen Entwicklung und im Kampfe mit der modernen Wissenschaft.* 2 vols. Tübingen, 1840–1.

*In Defense of My "Life of Jesus" Against the Hegelians.* Trans. Marilyn Chapin Massey. Hamden, 1984.

*The Life of Jesus.* Trans. George Eliot. Philadelphia, 1972.

*Streitschriften zur Vertheidigung meiner Schrift über das Leben Jesu und zur Charakteristik der gegenwärtigen Theologie.* Tübingen, 1837.

Streckfuß, Karl. *Über die Garantien der preußischen Zustände.* Halle, 1839.

Tappehorn, Friedrich. *Die vollkommene Association als Vermittler in der Einheit des Vernunftstaats und der Lehre Jesu. Ein Beitrag zur ruhigen Lösung aller großen Fragen dieser Zeit.* Augsburg, 1834.

Veit, Moritz. *Saint Simon und der Simonismus: Allgemeiner Völkerbund und ewiger Frieden.* Leipzig, 1834.

Weisse, Christian Hermann. *Grundzüge der Metaphysik.* Hamburg, 1835.

## SECONDARY

### Books

Abercrombie, Nicholas, et al., ed. *Sovereign Individuals of Capitalism.* London, 1986.

Abrams, M. H. *Natural Supernaturalism. Tradition and Revolution in Romantic Literature.* New York, 1971.

Adkins, Arthur. *From the Many to the One: A Study of Personality and Views of Human Nature in the Context of Ancient Greek Society, Values and Beliefs.* Ithaca, 1970.

Adler, E. R. *Der Staat als juristische und moralische Person.* Giessen, 1931.

Adorno, Theodor. *Stichwörte. Kritische Modelle 2.* Frankfurt, 1969.

Althaus, Horst. *Hegel und die heroischen Jahre der Philosophie.* Munich, 1992.

Amato, Joseph. *Mounier and Maritain: A French Catholic Understanding of the World.* University, Alabama, 1975.

Arnold, H. L., ed. *Heinrich Heine.* 2nd ed. Munich, 1971.

Avineri, Shlomo. *Hegel's Theory of the Modern State.* Cambridge, 1972.

*Moses Hess: Prophet of Communism and Zionism.* New York, 1985.

*The Social and Political Thought of Karl Marx.* Cambridge, 1968.

Ball, Terence. *Transforming Political Discourse: Political Theory and Critical Conceptual History.* New York, 1988.

Barclay, David, and E. D. Weitz, ed. *Between Reform and Revolution: Studies in the History of German Socialism and Communism from 1840–1990.* Oxford, 1998.

Barlow, Michel. *Le socialisme d'Emmanuel Mounier.* Toulouse, 1971.

Beck, Herman. *The Origins of the Authoritarian Welfare State in Prussia. Conservatives, Bureaucracy, and the Social Question, 1815–70.* Ann Arbor, 1995.

Beecher, Jonathan. *Charles Fourier. The Visionary and His World.* Berkeley, 1986.

Beiser, Frederick, ed. *The Cambridge Companion to Hegel.* Cambridge, 1993.

*Enlightenment, Revolution, and Romanticism. The Genesis of Modern German Political Thought, 1790–1800.* Cambridge, Mass., 1992.

*The Fate of Reason. German Philosophy from Kant to Fichte.* Cambridge, Mass., 1987.

Berdahl, Robert M. *The Politics of the Prussian Nobility. The Development of a Conservative Ideology, 1770–1848.* Princeton, 1988.

Berlin, Isaiah. *Against the Current.* New York, 1980.

Bigler, Robert M. *The Politics of German Protestantism. The Rise of the Protestant Church Elite in Prussia, 1815–1848.* Berkeley, 1972.

Blasius, Dirk. *Friedrich Wilhelm IV. 1795–1861: Psychopathologie und Geschichte.* Göttingen, 1992.

Blumenberg, Hans. *The Legitimacy of the Modern Age.* Trans. Robert M. Wallace. Cambridge, Mass., 1991.

Bobbio, Norberto. *Democracy and Dictatorship. The Nature and Limits of State Power.* Trans. Peter Kennealy. Cambridge, 1989.

Bode, H. W. Weise, ed. *Unzeit des Biedermeiers.* Leipzig, 1985.

Bowie, Andrew. *Schelling and Modern European Philosophy. An Introduction.* New York, 1993.

Boyle, Nicholas. *Goethe. The Poet and the Age. Vol. I. The Poetry of Desire.* Oxford, 1991.

Braun, Han-Jürg, et al., ed. *Ludwig Feuerbach und die Philosophie der Zukunft. Internationale Arbeitsgemeinschaft am ZiF der Universität Bielefeld, 1989.* Berlin, 1990.

Braun, Hans-Jürg, and Manfred Riedel, ed. *Natur und Geschichte: Karl Löwith zum 70. Geburtstag.* Stuttgart, 1967.

Brazill, William. *The Young Hegelians.* New Haven, 1970.

Briegelb, Klaus. *Opfer Heine? Versuche über Schriftzüge der Revolution.* Frankfurt, 1986.

Brown, R. F. *The Later Philosophy of Schelling: The Influence of Boehme on the Works of 1809–1815*. London, 1977.

Brunner, Otto, Werner Conze, and Reinhart Koselleck, ed. *Geschichtliche Grundbegriffe. Historisches Lexicon zur politisch-sozialen Sprache in Deutschland*. 7 vols. Stuttgart, 1972–90.

Bull, Malcolm, ed. *Apocalypse Theory and the Ends of the World*. Oxford, 1995.

Butler, E. M. *The Saint-Simonian Religion in Germany. A Study of the Young German Movement*. Cambridge, 1926.

*The Tyranny of Greece over Germany*. Cambridge, 1935.

Campbell, Joan. *Joy in Work, German Work. The National Debate, 1800–1945*. Princeton, 1989.

Carlisle, Robert. *The Proffered Crown. Saint-Simonianism and the Doctrine of Hope*. Baltimore, 1987.

Carver, Terrell. *Marx and Engels. The Intellectual Relationship*. Sussex, 1983.

Chadwick, Owen. *The Secularization of the European Mind in the Nineteenth Century*. Cambridge, 1990.

Chapin Massey, Marilyn. *Christ Unmasked. The Meaning of "The Life of Jesus" in German Politics*. Chapel Hill, 1983.

Chytry, Josef. *The Aesthetic State. A Quest in Modern German Thought*. Berkeley, 1989.

Claeys, Gregory. *Citizens and Saints. Politics and Anti-Politics in Early British Socialism*. New York, 1989.

Cohen, Jean L. *Class and Civil Society. The Limits of Marxian Critical Theory*. Amherst, 1982.

Colletti, Lucio. *From Rousseau to Lenin: Studies in Ideology and Society*. London, 1972. *Marxism and Hegel*. Trans. L. Garner. London, 1973.

Cornehl, Peter. *Die Zukunft der Versöhnung. Eschatologie und Emanzipation in der Aufklärung, bei Hegel und in der Hegelschen Schule*. Göttingen, 1971.

Cornu, Auguste. *Karl Marx und Friedrich Engels. Leben und Werk. 1. Bd. 1818–1844*. Berlin, 1954.

Dahlhaus, Carl. *Between Romanticism and Modernism. Four Studies in the Music of the Later Nineteenth Century*. Trans. Mary Whittall. Berkeley, 1980.

Derrida, Jacques. *Specters of Marx. The State of the Debt, the Work of Mourning & the New International*. Trans. Peggy Kamuf. New York, 1994.

Dickey, Laurence. *Hegel. Religion, Economics, and the Politics of Spirit, 1770–1807*. Cambridge, 1987.

Dufraisse, Roger, ed. *Revolution und Gegenrevolution, 1789–1830. Zur geistigen Auseinandersetzung in Frankreich und Deutschland*. Munich, 1991.

Dumont, Louis. *German Ideology: From France to Germany and Back*. Chicago, 1994.

Durkheim, Emile. *On Morality and Society. Selected Writings*. Ed. Robert Bellah. Chicago, 1973.

Eck, Else von. *Die Literaturkritik in den Hallischen und Deutschen Jahrbüchern (1838–1842)*. Berlin, 1925.

Ehret, Hermann. *Immanuel Hermann Fichte. Ein Denker gegen seine Zeit*. Stuttgart, 1986.

Epstein, Klaus. *The Genesis of German Conservatism*. Princeton, 1966.

Erdmann, J. E. *Die deutsche Philosophie seit Hegels Tode.* Stuttgart-Bad Cannstatt, 1964.
*A History of Philosophy.* 3 vols. Trans. W. S. Hough. London, 1890–2.

Eßbach, Wolfgang. *Die Junghegelianer. Soziologie einer Intellektuellengruppe.* Munich, 1988.

Evans, D. O. *Social Romanticism in France, 1830–1848.* Oxford, 1951.

Evans, R. J. *Proletarians and Politics. Socialism, Protest and the Working Class in Germany Before the First World War.* New York, 1990.

Fackenheim, Emil. *The Religious Dimension in Hegel's Thought.* Bloomington, 1967.

Forbes, Ian. *Marx and the New Individual.* London, 1990.

Förster, W., ed. *Klassische deutsche Philosophie in Berlin.* Berlin, 1988.

Foucault, Michel. *The History of Sexuality. An Introduction.* Trans. Robert Hurley. New York, 1990.

Frank, Manfred. *Der unendliche Mangel an Sein. Schellings Hegelkritik und die Anfänge der Marxschen Dialektik.* Frankfurt, 1975.

Frank, Manfred, and Anselm Haverkamp, ed. *Individualität.* Munich, 1988.

Füßl, Wilhelm. *Professor in der Politik: Friedrich Julius Stahl (1802–1861).* Munich, 1988.

Gamby, Erik. *Edgar Bauer. Junghegelianer, Publizist und Polizeiagent.* Trier, 1985.

Gebhardt, Jürgen. *Politik und Eschatologie: Studien zur Geschichte der Hegelschen Schule in den Jahren 1830–1840.* Munich, 1963.

Graf, F. W., and F. Wagner, ed. *Die Flucht in den Begriff. Materialien zu Hegels Religionsphilosophie.* Stuttgart, 1982.

Grimm, Dieter. *Recht und Staat der bürgerlichen Gesellschaft.* Frankfurt, 1987.

Grosser, Dieter. *Grundlagen und Struktur der Staatslehre Friedrich Julius Stahls.* Cologne, 1963.

Gurvitch, G. *La vocation actuelle de la Sociologie.* Paris, 1950.

Habermas, Jürgen. *The Philosophical Discourse of Modernity.* Trans. F. G. Lawrence. Cambridge, Mass., 1987.
*The Structural Transformation of the Public Sphere. An Inquiry into a Category of Bourgeois Society.* Trans. Thomas Burger. Cambridge, Mass., 1989.

Hamerow, Theodore S. *Restoration, Revolution, Reaction. Economics and Politics in Germany, 1815–1871.* Princeton, 1958.

Harris, H. S. *Hegel's Development: Toward the Sunlight (1770–1801).* Oxford, 1972.

Hartmann, Albert. *Der Spätidealismus und die hegelsche Dialektik.* Berlin, 1937.

Harvey, Van. *Feuerbach and the Interpretation of Religion.* Cambridge, 1995.

Hayek, Friedrich. *The Counter-Revolution of Science. Studies on the Abuse of Reason.* Glencoe, 1952.

Heidegger, Martin. *The Question Concerning Technology and Other Essays.* Trans. William Lovitt. New York, 1977.

Hellman, R. J. *Die Freien: The Young Hegelians of Berlin and the Religious Politics of 1840 Prussia.* Ph.D. Diss., Columbia University, 1976.

Hellmuth, Eckhart, ed. *The Transformation of Political Culture. England and Germany in the Late Eighteenth Century.* Oxford, 1990.

Himmelfarb, Gertrude. *The Idea of Poverty: England in the Early Industrial Age.* London, 1984.

Hinsley, F. H. *Sovereignty*. New York, 1966.

Hirschmann, A. O. *The Passions and the Interests. Political Arguments for Capitalism Before Its Triumph*. Princeton, 1977.

Honneth, Axel, et al., ed. *Philosophical Interventions in the Unfinished Project of Enlightenment*. Cambridge, Mass., 1992.

Hook, Sidney. *From Hegel to Marx*. Ann Arbor, 1962.

Huber, Ernst Rudolf. *Deutsche Verfassungsgeschichte seit 1789*. 3 vols. Stuttgart, 1960.

Hunt, Richard N. *The Political Ideas of Marx and Engels. I. Marxism and Totalitarian Democracy, 1818–1850*. Pittsburgh, 1974.

Iggers, Georg. *The Cult of Authority: The Political Philosophy of the Saint-Simonians*. The Hague, 1958.

Izenberg, Gerald N. *Impossible Individuality. Romanticism, Revolution, and the Origins of Modern Selfhood, 1787–1802*. Princeton, 1992.

Jacob, Margaret. *The Radical Enlightenment: Pantheists, Freemasons and Republicans*. London, 1981.

Jaeschke, Walter. *Reason in Religion: The Foundations of Hegel's Philosophy of Religion*. Trans. J. Michael Stewart and Peter C. Hodgson. Berkeley, 1990.

Jäger, Gertrud. *Schellings politische Anschauungen*. Berlin, 1940.

Jamme, Christoph, ed. *Die "Jahrbücher für wissenschaftliches Kritik." Hegels Berliner Gegenakademie*. Stuttgart, 1994.

Jantke, Carl, and Dietrich Hilger, ed. *Die Eigentumlosen. Der Deutsche Pauperismus und die Emanzipationskrise in Darstellungen und Deutungen der zeitgenössischen Literatur*. Freiburg and Munich, 1965.

Kamenka, Eugene. *The Philosophy of Ludwig Feuerbach*. London, 1970.

Kantorowicz, Ernst. *The King's Two Bodies. A Study in Medieval Political Theology*. Princeton, 1957.

Keane, John, ed. *Civil Society and the State. New European Perspectives*. London, 1988. *Democracy and Civil Society*. London, 1988.

Kelley, Donald. *History, Law and the Human Sciences. Medieval and Renaissance Perspectives*. London, 1984.
*The Human Measure. Social Thought in the Western Legal Tradition*. Cambridge, 1990.

Kelley, George Armstrong. *The Humane Comedy: Constant, Tocqueville and French Liberalism*. Cambridge, 1992.
*Idealism, Politics and History. Sources of Hegelian Thought*. Cambridge, 1969.

Kelly, Aileen. *Mikhail Bakunin. A Study in the Psychology and Politics of Utopianism*. New Haven, 1987.

Klenner, Hermann. *Deutsche Rechtsphilosophie im 19. Jahrhundert. Essays*. Berlin, 1991.

Kluckhohn, Paul. *Persönlichkeit und Gemeinschaft: Studien zur Staatsauffassung der deutschen Romantik*. Halle, 1925.

Knudsen, A. C. *The Philosophy of Personalism*. New York, 1927.

Koselleck, Reinhart. *Preussen zwischen Reform und Revolution. Allgemeines Landrecht, Verwaltung und soziale Bewegung von 1791 bis 1848*, 3rd ed. Munich, 1989.

Kroll, Frank-Lothar. *Friedrich Wilhelm IV. und das Staatsdenken der deutschen Romantik.* Berlin, 1990.

Krieger, Leonard. *The German Idea of Freedom. History of a Political Tradition from the Reformation to 1871.* Chicago, 1957.

Kühne, Walter. *Graf August Cieszkowski: Ein Schüler Hegels und des deutschen Geistes.* Leipzig, 1938.

LaCapra, Dominick. *Rethinking Intellectual History: Texts, Contexts, Language.* Cornell, 1983.

Lauer, Quentin. *A Reading of Hegel's Phenomenology of Spirit.* New York, 1982.

Leese, Kurt. *Philosophie und Theologie im Spätidealismus. Forschungen zur Auseinandersetzung von Christentum und idealistischer Philosophie im 19. Jahrhundert.* Berlin, 1929.

Lefort, Claude. *Democracy and Political Theory.* Trans. David Macey. Cambridge, 1988.

Levin, Michael. *Marx, Engels and Liberal Democracy.* London, 1989.

Lichtheim, George. *The Concept of Ideology and Other Essays.* New York, 1967.

Liebich, André. *Between Ideology and Utopia. The Politics and Philosophy of August Cieszkowski.* Boston, 1979.

Lobkowicz, Nicholas. *Theory and Practice. History of a Concept from Aristotle to Marx.* New York, 1967.

Loewenstein, Julius. *Hegels Staatsidee. Ihr Doppelgesicht und ihr Einfluss im 19. Jahrhundert.* Berlin, 1927.

Löwith, Karl. *From Hegel to Nietszche. The Revolution in Nineteenth-Century Thought.* Trans. David E. Green. New York, 1964.

Lübbe, Hermann, et al., ed. *Atheismus in der Diskussion. Kontroversen um Ludwig Feuerbach.* Grünwald, 1975.

Lukács, Georg. *Hegel's False and His Genuine Ontology.* Trans. David Fernbach. London, 1982.

Lukes, Steven, Michael Carrithers, and Steven Collins, ed. *The Category of the Person. Anthropology, Philosophy, History.* Cambridge, 1985.

MacPherson, C. B. *The Political Theory of Possessive Individualism. Hobbes to Locke.* Oxford, 1962.

Mah, Harold. *The End of Philosophy, The Origin of "Ideology." Karl Marx and the Crisis of the Young Hegelians.* Berkeley, 1987.

Malia, Martin. *Alexander Herzen and the Birth of Russian Socialism.* New York, 1961.

Manuel, Frank E. *The New World of Henri Saint-Simon.* Cambridge, Mass., 1956.
*The Prophets of Paris. Turgot, Condorcet, Saint-Simon, Fourier, Comte.* New York, 1962.
*Utopian Thought in the Western World.* Cambridge, Mass., 1979.

Marcuse, Herbert. *Reason and Revolution. Hegel and the Rise of Social Theory.* New York, 1941.

Marks, Ralph. *Die Entwicklung nationaler Geschichtsschreibung. Luden und seine Zeit.* Frankfurt, 1987.

Marquard, Odo, and Karlheinz Stierle, ed. *Identität.* Munich, 1979.

McLellan, David. *Marx Before Marxism.* London, 1970.

Mehring, Franz. *Geschichte der deutschen Sozialdemokratie,* 4 vols. Berlin, 1960.

McWilliam, Neil. *Dreams of Happiness: Social Art and the French Left, 1830–1850*. Princeton, 1993.

Meinecke, Friedrich. *Historism. The Rise of a New Historical Outlook*. Trans. J. E. Anderson. New York, 1972.

Mercier-Josa, Solange. *Théorie allemande et pratique française de la liberté. De la philosophie à la politique ou au socialisme?* Paris, 1993.

Merriam, C. E. *History of the Theory of Sovereignty Since Rousseau*. New York, 1900.

Mesmer-Strupp, Beatrix. *Arnold Ruges Plan einer Alliance intellectuelle zwischen Deutschen und Franzosen*. Bern, 1963.

Moore, James Willard. *Arnold Ruge: A Study in Democratic Caesarism*. Ph.D. Diss., University of California, Berkeley, 1977.

Moses, Claire. *French Feminism in the Nineteenth Century*. Albany, 1984.

Moses, Claire, and Leslie Wahl Rabine, ed. *Feminism, Socialism and French Romanticism*. Bloomington, 1994.

Mouffe, Chantal, ed. *Dimensions of Radical Democracy. Pluralism, Citizenship, Community*. London, 1992.

Nemoianu, Virgil. *The Taming of Romanticism. European Literature and the Age of Biedermeier*. Cambridge, Mass., 1984.

Neuhouser, Frederick. *Fichte's Theory of Subjectivity*. Cambridge, 1990.

Nipperdey, Thomas. *Deutsche Geschichte. 1800–1866. Bürgerwelt und starker Staat*, 6th ed. Munich, 1993.

　*Gesellschaft, Kultur, Theorie. Gesammelte Aufsätze zur neueren Geschichte*. Göttingen, 1976.

Oz-Salzberger, Fania. *Translating the Enlightenment: Scottish Civic Discourse in Eighteenth-Century Germany*. Oxford, 1995.

Ozment, Stephen. *The Age of Reform, 1250–1550. An Intellectual and Religious History of Late Medieval and Reformation Europe*. New Haven, 1980.

Pagden, A., ed. *The Languages of Political Theory in Early Modern Europe*. Cambridge, 1987.

Pelczynski, Z. A., ed. *The State and Civil Society: Studies in Hegel's Political Philosophy*. Cambridge, 1984.

Perrot, Michelle, ed. *A History of Private Life from the Fires of Revolution to the Great War*. Trans. Arthur Goldhammer. Cambridge, Mass., 1990.

Petermann, Thomas. *Der Saint-Simonismus in Deutschland. Bemerkungen zur Wirkungsgeschichte*. Frankfurt, 1983.

Philonenko, Alexis. *La jeunesse de Feuerbach. 1828–1841. Introduction à ses positions fondamentales*. 2 vols. Paris, 1990.

Pippin, Robert. *Hegel's Idealism. The Satisfactions of Self-Consciousness*. Cambridge, 1989.

Pocock, J.G.A. *The Machiavellian Moment. Florentine Political Thought and the Atlantic Republican Tradition*. Princeton, 1975.

Porter, Roy, and Mikulas Teich, ed. *The Enlightenment in National Context*. Cambridge, 1981.

Poynter, J. R. *Society and Pauperism: English Ideas on Poor Relief, 1795–1834.* London, 1969.

Prestige, G. L. *God in Patristic Thought.* London, 1981.

Radbruch, Gustav. *Paul Johann Anselm Feuerbach: Ein Juristenleben,* 2nd ed. Göttingen, 1957.

Rasmussen, David, ed. *Universalism vs. Communitarianism. Contemporary Debates in Ethics.* Cambridge, Mass., 1990.

Rawidowicz, S. *Ludwig Feuerbachs Philosophie. Ursprung und Schicksal.* Berlin, 1931.

Reardon, Bernard M.G. *Religion in the Age of Romanticism. Studies in Early Nineteenth Century Thought.* Cambridge, 1985.

Reeves, Marjorie, and Warwick Gould. *Joachim of Fiore and the Myth of the Eternal Evangel in the Nineteenth Century.* Oxford, 1987.

Reissner, H. G. *Eduard Gans. Ein Leben im Vormärz.* Tübingen, 1965.

Reitmeyer, Ursula. *Philosophie der Leiblichkeit. Ludwig Feuerbachs Entwurf einer Philosophie der Zukunft.* Frankfurt, 1988.

Riedel, Manfred. *Between Tradition and Revolution: The Hegelian Transformation of Political Philosophy.* Trans. Walter Wright. Cambridge, 1984.

Riedel, Manfred, ed. *Materialien zu Hegels Rechtsphilosophie.* Frankfurt, 1975.

Rihs, Charles. *L'école des jeunes hegeliens et les penseurs socialistes français.* Paris, 1978.

Ritter, Joachim. *Hegel and the French Revolution.* Trans. Richard Dien Winfield. Cambridge, Mass., 1982.

Rose, Margaret A. *Reading the Young Marx and Engels: Poetry, Parody, and the Censor.* London, 1978.

Rosen, Zwi. *Bruno Bauer and Karl Marx: The Influence of Bruno Bauer on Marx's Thought.* The Hague, 1977.

Rosenberg, Hans. *Bureaucracy, Aristocracy and Autocracy. The Prussian Experience, 1660–1815.* Cambridge, Mass., 1958.

*Politische Denkströmungen im deutschen Vormärz.* Göttingen, 1972.

Roth, Michael S., ed. *Rediscovering History. Culture, Politics, and the Psyche.* Stanford, 1994.

Sammons, J. L. *Heinrich Heine. A Modern Biography.* Princeton, 1979.

Samuel, Raphael, ed. *People's History and Socialist Theory.* London, 1981.

Sass, Hans-Martin. *Ludwig Feuerbach.* Hamburg, 1978.

Sass, H.-M., ed. *The Philosophical Forum,* vol. VIII, 2–4(1978). Special issue on the Left Hegelians.

*Untersuchungen zur Religionsphilosophie in der Hegelschule, 1830–1850.* Münster, 1963.

Schäfer, R. *Friedrich Buchholz – ein vergessener Vorläufer der Soziologie,* 2 vols. Göttingen, 1972.

Schieder, Theodor. *The State and Society in Our Times.* Trans. C.A.M. Sym. London, 1962.

Schilling, Heinz. *Civic Calvinism in Northwestern Germany and the Netherlands: Sixteenth to Nineteenth Centuries.* Kirksville, Mo., 1992.

Schmidt, Alfred. *Emanzipatorische Sinnlichkeit: Ludwig Feuerbachs anthropologischer Materialismus.* Munich, 1973.

Schmitt, Carl. *Political Theology. Four Chapters on the Concept of Sovereignty.* Trans. George Schwab. Cambridge, Mass., 1988.

Schnabel, Franz. *Deutsche Geschichte im neunzehnten Jahrhundert.* 4 vols. Freiburg, 1929–37.

Schott, Uwe. *Die Jugendentwicklung Ludwig Feuerbachs bis zum Fakultätswechsel 1825.* Göttingen, 1973.

Schuffenhauer, Werner. *Feuerbach und der junge Marx. Zur Entstehungsgeschichte der marxistischen Weltanschauung.* Berlin, 1965.

Schulz, Walter. *Die Vollendung des deutschen Idealismus in der Spätphilosophie Schellings.* Pfullingen, 1975.

Schürmann, Albert. *Friedrich Wilhelm Carové. Sein Werk als Beitrag zur Kritik an Staat und Kirche im frühliberalen Hegelianismus.* Bochum, 1971.

Seigel, Jerrold. *Marx's Fate. The Shape of a Life.* Princeton, 1978.

Sewell, William. *Work & Revolution in France: The Language of Labor from the Old Regime to 1848.* Cambridge, 1980.

Shanahan, W. O. *German Protestants Face the Social Question. Volume 1. The Conservative Phase, 1815–1871.* Notre Dame, 1954.

Shanks, Andrew. *Hegel's Political Theology.* Cambridge, 1991.

Sheehan, James. *German History 1770–1866.* Oxford, 1989.

Shklar, Judith. *Men and Citizens. A Study of Rousseau's Social Theory.* Cambridge, 1985.

Snow, Dale E. *Schelling and the End of Idealism.* Albany, N.Y., 1996.

Spiegel, Yorick. *Theologie der bürgerliche Gesellschaft: Sozialphilosophie und Glaubenslehre bei Friedrich Schleiermacher.* Munich, 1968.

Spitzer, Alan. *The French Generation of 1820.* Princeton, 1987.

Stedman Jones, Gareth. *Languages of Class. Studies in English Working Class History 1832–1982.* Cambridge, 1983.

Stuke, Horst. *Philosophie der Tat: Studien zur "Verwirklichung der Philosophie" bei den Junghegelianern und wahren Sozialisten.* Stuttgart, 1963.

Suhge, Walter. *Saint-Simonismus und junges Deutschland. Das Saint-Simonistische System in der deutschen Literatur der ersten Hälfte des 19. Jahrhunderts.* Berlin, 1935.

Talmon, J. L. *Origins of Totalitarian Democracy.* New York, 1969.

Taylor, Charles. *Hegel.* Cambridge, 1975.

   *Human Agency and Language.* Cambridge, 1985.

   *Sources of the Self. The Making of the Modern Identity.* Cambridge, Mass., 1989.

Thomas, Paul. *Alien Politics: Marxist State Theory Retrieved.* New York, 1994.

Toews, John E. *Hegelianism. The Path Toward Dialectical Humanism, 1805–1841.* Cambridge, 1980.

Tönnies, Ferdinand. *On Social Ideas and Ideologies.* Trans. E. G. Jacoby. New York, 1974.

Tribe, Keith. *Governing Economy: The Reformation of German Economic Discourse, 1750–1840.* Cambridge, 1988.

Walicki, Andrzej. *A History of Russian Thought. From the Enlightenment to Marxism.* Stanford, 1979.

Walter, Stephan. *Demokratisches Denken zwischen Hegel und Marx. Die politische Philoso-*

*phie Arnold Ruges. Eine Studie zur Geschichte der Demokratie in Deutschland.* Düsseldorf, 1995.

Wartofsky, Marx. *Feuerbach.* Cambridge, 1977.

Waszek, Norbert. *The Scottish Enlightenment and Hegel's Account of "Civil Society."* Boston, 1987.

Wehler, Hans-Ulrich. *The German Empire, 1871–1918.* Dover, 1985.

Wehler, H.-U., ed. *Moderne deutsche Sozialgeschichte.* Königstein, 1981.

*Sozialgeschichte Heute. Festschrift für Hans Rosenberg zum 70. Geburtstag.* Göttingen, 1974.

Weiss, Walter. *Enttäuschter Pantheismus. Zur Weltgestaltung der Dichtung in der Restaurationszeit.* Dornbirn, 1962.

Welch, Claude. *Protestant Thought in the Nineteenth Century, Volume 1, 1799–1870.* New Haven, 1972.

Wende, Peter. *Radikalismus im Vormärz. Untersuchungen zur politischen Theorie der frühen deutschen Demokratie.* Wiesbaden, 1975.

Wiegand, Christian. *Über Friedrich Julius Stahl (1801–1862): Recht, Staat, Kirche.* Munich, 1981.

Wilde, N. F. *H. Jacobi: A Study in the Origin of German Realism.* New York, 1966.

Yovel, Yirmiyahu. *Spinoza and Other Heretics. The Adventures of Immanence.* Princeton, 1989.

Zammito, John. *The Genesis of Kant's Critique of Judgment.* Chicago, 1992.

## Articles

Avineri, Shlomo. "Hegel Revisited." *Contemporary History,* III(1968), pp. 133–47.

Baronovitch, L. "Two Appendices to a Doctoral Dissertation: Some New Light on the Origin of Karl Marx's Dissociation from Bruno Bauer and the Young Hegelians." *Philosophical Forum,* vol. viii, nos. 2–4(1978), pp. 219–40.

Beyer, W. R. "Gans' Vorrede zur Hegelschen Rechtsphilosophie." *Archiv für Rechts- und Sozialphilosophie,* 45. Bd.(1959), pp. 257–73.

Blänkner, Reinhard. "'Der Absolutismus war ein Glück, der doch nicht zu den Absolutisten gehört.' Eduard Gans und die hegelianischen Ursprünge der Absolutismusforschung in Deutschland." *Historische Zeitschrift,* 256(1993), pp. 31–66.

Breckman, Warren. "Ludwig Feuerbach and the Political Theology of Restoration." *History of Political Thought,* vol. XIII, no. 3(Autumn, 1992), pp. 437–62.

Chapin Massey, Marilyn. "Censorship and the Language of Feuerbach's *Essence of Christianity* (1841)." *The Journal of Religion,* 65(1985), pp. 173–95.

Claeys, Gregory. "The Origins of the Rights of Labor: Republicanism, Commerce, and the Construction of Modern Social Theory in Britain, 1796–1805." *Journal of Modern History,* 66(June 1994), pp. 249–90.

Clark, Christopher. "The Wars of Liberation in Prussian Memory: Reflections on the Memorialization of War in Early Nineteenth-Century Germany." *Journal of Modern History,* 68, 3 (Sept. 1996), pp. 550–76.

Conze, Werner. "Staat und Gesellschaft in der Frührevolutionären Epoche Deutschlands." *Historische Zeitschrift*, 186(1958), pp. 1–34.

"Vom 'Pöbel' zum 'Proletariat.' Sozialgeschichtliche Voraussetzungen für den Sozialismus in Deutschland." *Vierteljahrsschrift für Sozial-und Wirtschaftsgeschichte*, (1954), pp. 333–64.

Crouter, Richard. "Hegel and Schleiermacher at Berlin: A Many-Sided Debate." *Journal of the American Academy of Religion*, 48 (March 1980), pp. 19–43.

"Schleiermacher and the Theology of Bourgeois Society: A Critique of the Critics." *The Journal of Religion*, 66(1986), pp. 302–23.

*Eastern Europe . . . Central Europe . . . Europe*, a special issue of *Daedalus*, vol. 119, no. 1 (Winter 1990).

Elshtain, Jean Bethke. "Sovereign God, Sovereign State, Sovereign Self." *Notre Dame Law Review*, vol. 66, 5(1991), pp. 1355–1384.

Fackenheim, Emil. "Schelling's Conception of Positive Philosophy." *Review of Metaphysics*, 1954, pp. 563–82.

"Schelling's Philosophy of Religion." *University of Toronto Quarterly*, XXII, no. 1 (Oct. 1952), pp. 1–17.

Gerrish, B. A. "The Secret Religion of Germany: Christian Piety and the Pantheism Controversy." *Journal of Religion*, 67(1987), pp. 437–55.

Hammen, O. J. "The Young Marx Reconsidered." *Journal of the History of Ideas*, 31 (Jan.–March 1970), pp. 109–20.

Hoover, Jeffrey. "The Origin of the Conflict between Hegel and Schleiermacher at Berlin." *Owl of Minerva*, 20, 1(Fall 1988), pp. 69–79.

Iggers, Georg. "Heine and the Saint-Simonians: A Re-Examination." *Comparative Literature*, X (Fall 1958), pp. 289–308.

Jaeschke, Walter. "Christianity and Secularity in Hegel's Concept of the State." *The Journal of Religion*, 61 (1981), pp. 127–45.

"Feuerbach redivivus." *Hegel-Studien*, 13(1978), pp. 199–237.

"Urmenschheit und Monarchie: Eine politische Christologie der Hegelschen Rechten." *Hegel-Studien*, 14(1979), pp. 73–107.

Kelley, Donald. "The Metaphysics of Law: An Essay on the Very Young Marx." *American Historical Review*, 83 (1978), pp. 350–67.

Kempski, Jürgen. "Über Bruno Bauer: Eine Studie zum Ausgang des Hegelianismus." *Archiv für Philosophie*, 11(1961–2), pp. 223–45.

Klenner, Hermann. "Zwei Savigny-Voten über Eduard Gans nebst Chronologie und Bibliographie." *Topos*, 1(1993), pp. 123–48.

La Vopa, A. J. "The Politics of Enlightenment: Friedrich Gedike and German Professional Ideology." *Journal of Modern History*, 62, 1(March 1990), pp. 34–56.

Lübbe, Hermann. "Die Politische Theorie der Hegelschen Rechten." *Archiv für Philosophie*, Bd. 10/3–4(1962), pp. 175–227.

Lukács, Georg. "Moses Hess and the Problem of the Idealist Dialectic." *Telos*, 10 (1971), pp. 23–35.

Lutz, Rolland. "The 'New Left' in Restoration Germany." *Journal of the History of Ideas*, 31(1970), pp. 235–52.

Mah, Harold. "The French Revolution and the Problem of German Modernity: Hegel, Heine and Marx." *New German Critique*, 50(1990), pp. 3–20.

Marquardt, F. D. "*Pauperismus* in Germany during the *Vormärz*." *Central European History*, 2(1969), pp. 77–88.

Massey, James. "Feuerbach and Religious Individualism." *Journal of Religion* (1976), pp. 366–81.

"The Hegelians, the Pietists, and the Nature of Religion." *Journal of Religion* (1978), pp. 108–29.

Mayer, Gustave. "Die Anfänge des politischen Radikalismus im vormärzlichen Preussen." *Zeitschrift für Politik*, 6(1913), pp. 1–113.

"Die Junghegelianer und der preussische Staat." *Historische Zeitschrift*, 121(1920), pp. 413–40.

Mombert, Paul. "Aus der Literatur über soziale Frage und über die Arbeiterbewegung in Deutschland in der ersten Hälfte des 19. Jahrhunderts." *Archiv für die Geschichte des Sozialismus und der Arbeiterbewegung*, IX (1921), pp. 169–236.

Nabrings, Arie. "Der Einfluss Hegels auf die Lehre vom Staat bei Stahl." *Der Staat*, 23 (1983), pp. 169–86.

Parkinson, G.H.R. "Hegel, Pantheism, and Spinoza." *Journal of the History of Ideas*, 3, 38(1977), pp. 449–59.

Picard, R. "Sur l'origine des mots *socialisme* et *socialiste*." *Revue socialiste*, li(1910), pp. 379–90.

Pickering, Mary. "New Evidence of the Link Between Comte and German Philosophy." *Journal of the History of Ideas*, L, 3(July–Sept., 1989), pp. 443–63.

Sass, Hans-Martin. "Bruno Bauer's Idee der 'Rheinische Zeitung.'" *Zeitschrift für Religions-und Geistesgeschichte*, 19(1967), pp. 321–32.

"The Concept of Revolution in Marx's Dissertation (The Non-Hegelian Origin of Karl Marx's Early Concept of Dialectics)." *Philosophical Forum*, viii, 2–4(1978), pp. 241–55.

Schmidt, James. "A *Paideia* for the '*Bürger als Bourgeois*': The Concept of 'Civil Society' in Hegel's Political Thought." *History of Political Thought*, II, 3 (Winter, 1981), pp. 471–93.

"The Question of Enlightenment: Kant, Mendelssohn and the Mittwochsgesellschaft." *Journal of the History of Ideas* (April–June 1989), pp. 269–91.

Seigel, Jerrold. "The Human Subject as a Language-Effect," *History of European Ideas*, 18, 4(1994), pp. 481–95.

Spies, Andre. "Towards a Prosopography of Young Hegelians." *German Studies Review*, XIX, 2(May 1996), pp. 321–39.

Strauß, Herbert. "Zur sozial-und ideengeschichtlichen Einordnung Arnold Ruges." *Schweitzer Beiträge zur allgemeine Geschichte*, 12 (1954), pp. 162–73.

Teeple, G. "The Doctoral Dissertation of Karl Marx." *History of Political Thought*, xi, 1(Spring 1990), pp. 81–118.

Toews, John E. "The Immanent Genesis and Transcendental Goal of Law: Savigny, Stahl, and the Ideology of the Christian German State." *The Americal Journal of Comparative Law*, XXXVII, 1(Winter, 1989), pp. 139–69.

Treichgraeber, R. "Hegel on Property and Poverty." *Journal of the History of Ideas*, 38(1977), pp. 47–64.

Trendelenberg, Adolf. "A Contribution to the History of the Word Person." *Monist*, 20(1910), pp. 336–63.

Waszek, Norbert. "Eduard Gans on Poverty: Between Hegel and Saint-Simon." *Owl of Minerva*, 18, 2(Spring 1987), pp. 167–78.

Wundt, Max. "Die Philosophie in der Zeit des Biedermeiers." *Deutsche Vierteljahrsschrift*, XIII, i (1935), pp. 118–48.

# INDEX

LaVergne, TN USA
28 January 2010

171461LV00002B/73/P